The Robertses of Northern New England

Thomas A. Jacobsen

HERITAGE BOOKS
2023

HERITAGE BOOKS
AN IMPRINT OF HERITAGE BOOKS, INC.

Books, CDs, and more—Worldwide

For our listing of thousands of titles see our website at
www.HeritageBooks.com

Published 2023 by
HERITAGE BOOKS, INC.
Publishing Division
5810 Ruatan Street
Berwyn Heights, Md. 20740

Copyright © 1995 Thomas A. Jacobsen

Map on page 20 by Nick Ackermann

Illustrations on pages 16, 24, 28, 46, 142, 180, 224, 228, 356, and 394: Dover Pictorial Archives Series

All rights reserved. No part of this book may be reproduced or transmitted in any form or by any means, electronic or mechanical, including photocopying, recording or by any information storage and retrieval system without written permission from the author, except for the inclusion of brief quotations in a review.

International Standard Book Numbers
Paperbound: 978-0-7884-0242-5
Clothbound: 978-0-7884-6051-7

Dedicated to the memory of my Roberts grandparents

TABLE OF CONTENTS

	Page
Preface	vii
Introduction	1
Descendants of Thomas & Rebecca Roberts:	
First Generation	21
Second Generation	25
Third Generation	29
Fourth Generation	35
Fifth Generation	47
Sixth Generation	69
Seventh Generation	103
Eighth Generation	143
Ninth Generation	181
Tenth Generation	209
Eleventh Generation	219
Descendants of George & Mary Roberts:	
First Generation	221
Second Generation	225
Third Generation	229
Fourth Generation	237
Fifth Generation	249
Sixth Generation	265
Seventh Generation	297
Eighth Generation	327
Ninth Generation	357
Tenth Generation	375
Eleventh Generation	389
Twelfth Generation	393
Bibliography	395
Photographs	399
Index	413

PREFACE

This book would never have made it to publication without the encouragement, assistance, and critical eye of a number of individuals involved in genealogical research and particularly in digging for the roots of the Robertses of Northern New England.
The seeds of this book were a number of separate submissions during 1984, 1985, and 1986 (particulary Volume 4, Nos. 1 & 3) by various correspondents to the Roberts Register, edited by Maxine Roberts. But for the existence of that little quarterly (now defunct) the researchers from various branches of these families would never have made contact with one another.
One of the submissions was by Frances Jones, who had been researching the Roberts family for decades. She was extremely helpful in sharing her voluminous notes, pointing out sources, digging for new clues, and rigorously challenging the various interpretations that took shape during our several years of correspondence. It was during this correspondence that I decided it was time that someone set the record straight on the earliest generations of these families. There were so many false leads, unfounded conjectures that had been accepted as truth, and just plain errors that seemed to take on a life of their own.
Eventually, several other Roberts researchers joined in the correspondence. Isabel Coburn submitted valuable original documentation and lent her critical eye to the proceedings. Mary Arnott was conducting important investigations on the scene in Maine and New Hampshire, and I met with her in Concord at the state archives, where we unearthed several documents that had slipped by earlier researchers. Neither Isabel nor Mary is completely satisfied with some of the documentation (or lack thereof) on their particular Roberts lines; and they are still digging for further substantiation.
Bobbi Bryant provided some noteworthy documentation on the Revolutionary War record of the patriarch of the Vermont branch. She also generously shared her copy of the voluminous records of Vermont Robertses compiled by the late Blanche (Judd) Roberts and notes she had previously compiled with the aid of Jane Verret.
The late Elizabeth Hilton kindly provided copies of some very critical correspondence from her Roberts ancestor and graciously invited me to the annual Roberts reunion in Sangerville, Maine, where I met Ervin Roberts, who later submitted a great deal of material on the Maine side of the family, some of which

had been written up by his in-law, Edward Cafferty.

A number of other Roberts researchers submitted new information or generously shared their own research notes. Among them were David Dewsnap, Helen Dotts, Clayton H. Roberts, Esther Wyatt, Barbara Baylis, and John Bayard Peri. Karen Hanson Messer submitted many quality photographs of her branch, along with voluminous records.

It is safe to say that almost any genealogical research project would take three or four times longer if it were not for the Family History Center library of the Latter Day Saints Church. Their collection of records on microfilm is so extensive, so well catalogued, and so accessible through their branch library system, that it almost makes on-site research unnecessary. I made extensive use of their main library in Salt Lake City and the Oakland, California branch.

I received a great deal of assistance from the librarians at the New Hampshire Historical Society, the New England Historic Genealogical Society, and the Maine Historical Society. The clerks at the New Hampshire Division of Records Management and Archives patiently pulled I don't know how many dozens of files. In addition I was able to get very prompt mail service from several county offices, particulary the Rockingham County (N.H.) offices of the Register of Probate and the Register of Deeds. Closer to home, the Sutro Library in San Francisco provided a number of important books, census films, and periodicals.

Credit should also be given to Roberts researchers of the past, whose published works have provided a solid foundation for my own research. The works of these individuals, most notably Henry Hardon, John Scales, Amorena (Roberts) Grant, Elizabeth Hilton, Alonzo Quint, and Blanche (Judd) Roberts, are discussed in the bibliography.

Acknowledgements would not be complete without mentioning various family members who have encouraged me along the way: my great aunt Theresa Avis Roberts, my mother Myrtle (Roberts) Jacobsen, my father Andrew B. Jacobsen, who oversaw the preparation of the photographs, my cousins Fern (Roberts) Williams and Helen (Roberts) BeVier and my daughters Sara and Hilary. Last, but not least, I must recognize the patience of my wife, Deborah, who, on our three trips to New England, graciously allowed me an occasional research time out from shopping the factory outlet stores and chasing the elusive color changes of the fall foliage.

Corte Madera, California　　　　　　　September 1994

INTRODUCTION

Historical Background: The 1600's

In 1614 Captain John Smith, of Virginia fame, made his first voyage to the area that was later to be named New England. Among his crew members was a Thomas Roberts.[*] In 1616 the *Garland*, commanded by Sir Richard Hawkins, the president of the Plymouth Company, docked at Monhegan Island, off the coast of what is now Maine. Hawkins records that he found there a fishing vessel out of London, the *Nachen*, whose crew of twenty men included a Thomas Roberts.[+] Whether these citations refer to the Thomas Roberts who a decade later became one of the founding fathers of New Hampshire cannot be determined.

We do know, however, that fishing boats, mostly from England, had been plying the waters off New England for decades before any adventurers attempted to form a permanent settlement there. It took weeks to make the trip out and back from England to the New England coast, and yet, it was well worth the time, because of the abundance of cod and salmon. Usually the fishermen stayed several months, time to establish temporary stations on land to dry and cure the fish for the long voyage back to England. In fact there is some evidence to suggest that Monhegan Island and nearby Pemaquid were more than temporary stations, but were in fact tiny, yet permanent fishing settlements, dating from 1610, or earlier.

1620 is, of course, a date that is etched in the collective consciousness of the American people. In that year the Pilgrims, blown off their course for Virginia and fearing that the fragile *Mayflower* could go no further, set foot on Plymouth Rock. Despite the brutal conditions afforded these first settlers and the frightful

---

[*] Noyes, Sybil, Libby, Charles T., & Davis, Walter G. *Genealogical Dictionary of Maine and New Hampshire*. Baltimore: Genealogical Publishing Company, 1983 (originally published in five parts, Portland, Maine, 1928-1939), p. 2.

[+] Spencer, Wilbur D. *Pioneers on Maine Rivers*. Baltimore: Genealogical Publishing Company, 1973 (originally privately published Portland, Maine, 1930), p. 17.

loss of life the first couple of winters, Captain John Smith wrote glowingly in 1622 about the possibilities of establishing major settlements in New England. By claiming this rocky, desolate real estate, England could more easily keep the valuable offshore fisheries out of the hands of the other European powers, he argued.

1620 was a momentous year in another respect. Sir Fernando Gorges convinced his friend and patron, King James I, to grant all of the land in America between the 40th and 48th parallels to the old Plymouth Company, now reorganized as the Council of New England. This grant encompased everything between approximately present-day Philadelphia and central Newfoundland. On April 19, 1622, the Council of New England in turn granted all of the land between the Merrimack and Kennebeck Rivers to Gorges and John Mason, another crony of James I, the secretary of the Council and one-time governor of Newfoundland. This grant-within-a-grant covered everything between what is now northern Massachusetts and central Maine.[*]

Efforts to colonize the grant to Gorges and Mason began as early as 1623, with the dispatch of a small group of men to set up permanent fishing stations on the Piscataqua River (along what is now the border of Maine and New Hampshire). The leader of these men was David Thomson, an officer of the Council. Near the same time or within a handful of years, came the Hilton brothers, Edward and William, and Thomas Roberts, all three members of the Fishmongers Guild of London. The few records that exist for these early years are sketchy at best, but it seems clear that, by 1628 at the latest, the Hiltons and Roberts were permanently settled on what is now Dover Point, a peninsula between the Piscataqua River and Great Bay, considered by many to be the first permanent settlement in what is now New Hampshire.[+]

In 1629 Mason and Gorges divided their American colony, with Mason taking the portion to the south of the Piscataqua (including Dover Point) and Gorges the portion to the north. This division was ultimately ratified as the boundary between the present states

---

[*] Clark, Charles E. *The Eastern Frontier: Settlement of Northern New England*. Hanover and London: The University Press of New England, 1983, pp. 14-7.

[+] Scales, John. *History of Dover, New Hampshire*. Dover, N.H.: Privately published, 1923, pp. 5-22 & 34-9.

of New Hampshire and Maine. Mason soon busied himself in sending more men and establishing below Dover Point a village called Strawberry Bank in what became the town of Portsmouth.*

Thomas Roberts and his associates the Hilton Brothers soon found themselves in something of a power struggle with Mason's agents, now intent on confirming Mason's sovereignty over Dover. Fortunately, for the settlers, Mason, who never did set foot on his American property, died in England in 1635. Mason's widow, who was also heir and executor of her husband's estate, gave up effective control of the American properties within a few years, although Mason's other heirs carried the fight for legal title over the New Hampshire property into the 1700's.[+]

In 1638, about the time the Masons had lost effective control, a breakaway faction of Puritans from Boston moved north into what became New Hampshire and founded the town of Exeter, on a patent acquired by purchase from the local Indians. There were no Robertses among this group, although many later generations of Robertses, through maternal lines, could claim descent from one or more of the founders of Exeter.[#]

Meanwhile, in Dover, Thomas Roberts was elected President of the Court of Dover in 1639/40, and he and his neighbors began the serious business of divying up the property under their jurisdiction. Roberts himself was granted Dover lot number one, consisting of twenty acres, in 1642.** At about the same time Dover and the three other small nearby settlements came under the political jurisdiction of Massachusetts. This development was acceptable to both sides. For Dover and its neighboring settlements it meant additional men and resources available in case of Indian or foreign attack. Massachusetts authority also provided a cover for the defacto take-over of Mason's estate. For the Massachusetts Bay

---

  * Clark, pp. 17-18.
  [+] Clark, p. 53.
  [#] Bell, Charles H. *History of Exeter, New Hampshire*. Bowie, Maryland: Heritage Books, Inc. (originally published Boston: J.E. Farwell & Co., 1888), 1979, pp. 3-12.
  ** Noyes, Libby, & Davis, p. 589; Scales, John, ed. *Historical Memoranda Concerning Persons and Places in Old Dover, N.H. Collected by Rev. Dr. Alonzo Quint.* . . Bowie, Maryland: Heritage Books, Inc. (originally privately published Dover, N.H., 1900), 1983, p. 350.

Colony it fit perfectly into its plans to control all of New England.*

The decade of the 1640's was one of political turmoil in Great Britain, and the repercussions were felt directly in New England. James I's son, Charles I, succeeded to the throne in 1625. His reign was marred with constant conflict with parliament and religious dissenters, and, finally, open civil war. When Charles I was beheaded in 1649 it looked as if the Stuart monarchy were ended. The downfall of the Stuarts was greeted with cheer in New Hampshire, for the obvious reason that the Mason family's claims were only enforcable with the backing of the King. The colonists in neighboring Massachusetts were also pleased by the developments in England, but more so because their allies in the dissenter movement were now in control than because of any concerns they had about the territorial claims of the Stuart cronies.

In 1650 what was to become New Hampshire consisted of these four very small towns: Portsmouth, Dover, Exeter, and Hampton, the latter of which was settled beginning in 1638 with settlers moving north from Massachusetts. There was also a tiny settlement offshore, on the Isle of Shoals, which was generally considered part of New Hampshire. Up until the royal province of New Hampshire was established by the restored Stuart monarchy in 1680, the four towns were more or less governed by the Massachusetts Bay Colony.⁺

New Hampshire served pretty much as a frontier buffer area between the Indians and French to the north and the more settled towns of Massachusetts to the south. The difficulty of life in these early years cannot be overemphasized. Before permanent shelter could be built, settlers froze to death in the harsh winters. Others starved while waiting for the first crops to come in. Infant mortality was frightfully high. With almost all travel by water, boating accidents and drownings were all too frequent. Indians were a constant threat, and many of these early pioneers were either killed or carried off to Canada.

From the perspective of the 17th century, these folk were living on the far outer frontier fringes of English civilization; and those back in the mother country had at best only a passing interest in

---

    * Clark, p. 54.
    ⁺ Towle, Laird C. & Brown, Ann N. *New Hampshire Genealogical Research Guide*. Bowie, Maryland: Heritage Books, Inc., 1983, p. 3.

what was happening in the New England economy or in the personal lives of the people "out there". While traders and some of the leading citizens of the colonies did make the lengthy and dangerous trip to England on occasion, for the vast majority of these early settlers, the trek to the New World was strictly one-way. The earliest settlers eked out a living in one of two ways, fishing or cutting trees for lumber, timber, and staves. Throughout the four towns of what became New Hampshire, cutting trees and milling lumber became major industries by the mid-1600's. There were about 20 mills on the Piscataqua and its tributaries and neighboring rivers coursing through Dover and Exeter.

Agriculture was difficult owing to the rocky soil and the thick cover of trees. The growing season was also very short. Despite all of these hazards, agriculture by necessity became at least a part-time avocation for almost all of the families. They grew feed for their small number of farm animals and a few fruits and vegetables for themselves. Fortunately, there were fish and wild game in abundance and wild nuts and berries to gather. For things which could not be grown, gathered or caught, there were traders who came by. Barter was the common method of exchange.[*]

The First Robertses

Thomas Roberts, as previously mentioned, filled a key roll in the early history of New Hampshire. He had two sons, John and Thomas, who were leading citizens of Dover and who bore large families; and he left many descendants, through his married daughters, as well. But there were also other Robertses in early New Hampshire.

George Roberts of Exeter first appears in the public record in connection with producing pipe staves in 1674. He had but one child who lived to adulthood, but that one child left six married sons, three married daughters, and dozens of grandchildren.

Joseph Roberts was sent to Portsmouth by Mason in 1632. It is not clear if he became a permanent resident of New Hampshire, nor is it clear if he was the same Joseph Roberts who drowned there in

---

[*] Clark, pp. 63-9.

1664. He left no record of descendants or even of a marriage.*
William Roberts first appears in the public record of Dover for being fined for "mending the stocks" in 1643. He was killed by the Indians in 1675. William had daughters (known to us only because of subsequent legal action over the disposition of his estate) of record but left only one (apparently unmarried) son described as a "simple youth".+

In the four towns of what was to become New Hampshire, there were at most three hundred to four hundred households (or nuclear families) in the mid-1600's. Given the prevalence of the surname Roberts in the American population, one would expect to find one, or perhaps at most two, distinct and separate families named Roberts in so small a population. So, it is more likely than not that there was some familial connection among these four early Roberts pioneers.# Unfortunately, due to the passage of time and the paucity of surviving written records, today there seems to be no evidence of what these relationships might have been.

In 1689/90 there were but seven Roberts households in New Hampshire, six of the Thomas clan, in and around Dover, and the family of George Roberts in Exeter.**

---

* Hotten, John C., ed. *The Original Lists of Persons of Quality. . . who Went from Great Britain to the American Plantations 1600-1700. . .* Baltimore: Genealogical Publishing Company, 1962 (originally privately published New York, 1880 and London, 1874), p. 150; Noyes, Libby & Davis, p. 589.

+ Stackpole, Everett S. & Thompson, Lucien. *History of the Town of Durham, New Hampshire. . .* Durham: Privately published, no date (c. 1900), Vol. II, pp. 318-9.

In 1790 approximately one out of every 550 families in the U.S. was named Roberts. Amazingly, in 1980, the incidence of Robertses in the U.S. population had changed only slightly, to about one out of every 600 families. Projecting back to New England of the mid-1600's, one might guess that there should have been, on average, about one Roberts family out of every 300-400 families. See Smith, Elsdon C. *American Surnames.* Baltimore: Genealogical Publishing Company, 1986, pp. 298-301.

** Massachusetts Archives, Book 35, p. 229, cited in "Petition of New Hampshire Settlers", *New England Historical and Genealogical Register*, Vol. VIII, no. 3 (1854), pp. 233-5. Holbrook, Jay M. *New Hampshire Residents 1633-1699.* Oxford, Mass.: Holbrook Research Institute, 1979, p. i.

Robertses into the 1700's

At the dawn of the 18th century demographic and geographic change in New Hampshire accelerated, almost imperceptibly at first and then much more rapidly as the colonial period drew to a close. In the first third of the 1700's the frontier edge of settlement bulged slightly, but 90% of the inhabitants still lived within 25 miles of the Atlantic Ocean. The big change in this period of time was a steady increase in the founding population, due mostly to stabilizing living conditions and the resulting drop in infant mortality and the death rate in general. As the four parent towns grew in population, they split and re-split, forming a dozen or more new towns. In addition a fresh layer of frontier towns sprang up to the west and north of the original four.

The land, never being very rich to begin with, now was being divided and subdivided among sons, and then grandsons. Virgin 300-acre grants from the 1600's were now "supporting" five or ten households. Often the oldest son had the largest and best of the family property, with some of the younger sons just renting or subsisting on a few acres. In order to support their families men usually carried on a trade, such as weaving or shoemaking, in addition to small scale farming and husbandry. By the 1730's most of the timber in the settled areas had been cut, and enterprising groups of men ventured into the wilds to locate new sources of wood.

In 1732 there were now at least seventeen Roberts households in New Hampshire. Fourteen or so of the Thomas clan were living in Dover or in the neighboring towns of Durham (Madbury), Rochester, and Somersworth. George's son John and two grandsons headed up households in Exeter.[*] By the 1740's a third Roberts family group shows up in New Hampshire, in Hampton Falls.[+]

---

[*] Holbrook, Jay M. *New Hampshire 1732 Census*. Oxford, Mass.: Holbrook Research Institute, 1981. This is a reconstruction of "heads of household", based on local tax lists and tells nothing about ancestry. The breakdown between descendants of the various Roberts families is my own estimate, based on the research forming the body of this book.

[+] Brown, Warren. *History of the Town of Hampton Falls, New Hampshire*. Manchester, N.H.: John B. Clarke Co., 1900, vol. 1, pp. 139 & 457 & vol. 2, p. 113.

They were apparently from among the descendants of Robert Roberts of Ipswich, Massachusetts, who were numerous in the northeastern part of that state, and in Maine, as well. Over the next generation the population increased even more, and the burden on the land began to reach the breaking point. But it wasn't until the early 1760's and the end of the French and Indian War that the frontier of New Hampshire literally disappeared under foot as the march of settlement pushed over and through that state and into Vermont and the interior of Maine. With relief from the ever-present threat of Indian attack, the younger sons and the grandsons and their young families poured into the interior and the north of the state to lay their claim to their own little piece of land. These locals were joined by similiarly-minded pioneers from the southern New England states of Massachusetts, Rhode Island, and Connecticut. As the promise of land spread, an influx of Irish immigrants began.

The population of New Hampshire reached about 40,000 in 1760, as compared to but 4,000 in 1690. And between 1760 and 1776 New Hampshire was the fastest growing colony in the Americas.[*] By 1776 there were over forty Roberts households in New Hampshire, probably close to twenty-five of the Thomas clan, six of the George clan, and three of the Robert Roberts descendants. And there were additional Robertses newly settled in the southwestern corner of the state, probably migrants from Connecticut. Some of these were likely descendants of Giles Roberts, an early settler of Scarborough, Maine.[+] By this time perhaps a fourth of George Roberts' descendants were in Maine or Vermont.

---

[*] Clark, pp. 336 & 354.
[+] Nichols, Joann H. *Descendants of Giles Roberts of Scarborough, Maine.* Baltimore: Gateway Press, 1994. Holbrook, Jay M. *New Hampshire 1776 Census.* Oxford, Mass.: Holbrook Research Institute, 1976, p. 123. This is a compilation from the Association Tests of 1776. Unfortunately, a number of major towns such as Dover are not included, either because they never held or recorded such a test or the documents have been lost. For these towns I have reconstructed the estimates from data from the text of this book.

Robertses in the Revolution

Robertses played a leading role in the Revolutionary War effort in the colonies of New Hampshire, Massachusetts (Maine), and Vermont.

George Roberts of Somerworth, New Hampshire, served as an officer, along with John Paul Jones, on the *Ranger* and the *Bon Homme Richard.* The story of his exploits has been chronicled in the *Granite Monthly* (Vol. 33, p. 91).

The town of Somersworth must have been, indeed, a hotbed of independence fervor. No less than eleven other Robertses from that town served in this noble endeavor: John Roberts, Joshua Roberts, Ichabod Roberts, James Roberts, Love Roberts, Timothy Roberts, Joseph Roberts, Paul Roberts, Nathan Roberts, Simon Roberts, and Benjamin Roberts.

The Roberts boys of Windham, Maine were among the first contingents of irregular militia (the legendary "embattled farmers") who rallied at Bunker Hill: Jonathan Roberts, Joseph Roberts and Joseph Roberts, Jr.

Eliphalet Roberts of Strafford, Vermont, while in the service of the infant nation, was forced to "turn-coat". Months later, when he returned home, he was exonerated by his neighbors, but was unjustly tarred with the label of "tory" by later generations.

Other Robertses whose Revolutionary War record is documented are Edmund Roberts of Portsmouth, New Hampshire, and Joseph Roberts of Meredith, New Hampshire. Many of the Robertses in the Dover vicinity were Quakers and thus were excused from service.

Not too many women are known to have taken up arms in the war effort. But one that has come to our attention is Tabitha Roberts of Buckfield, Maine. Left alone to guard the family farm, it is said that she pitchforked a British soldier who was rustling their last cow.* Often forgotten is that while most of the young men were off on service for months on end, the womenfolk performed double duty, tending the farm animals, harvesting the crops, and overseeing all of the operations of large rural households.

---

* Since women were not allowed to serve in regular military units, it is almost impossible to verify legends such as this one. See page 256.

Robertses in the New Nation

The 1790 Census for New Hampshire shows sixty-five households with the surname of Roberts. Of these, approximately forty were descendants of Thomas and Rebecca of Dover (mostly in Dover, Rochester and Somersworth), ten were descendants of George and Mary of Exeter (only two in Brentwood, the remainder in Salisbury, Andover, and Raymond), and the remainder were unrelated to these two families.* By this date almost one-half of George's descendants were in Maine or Vermont, where a very small percentage of Thomas' descendants could also be found.

During the 1800's the descendants of the Robertses of early New Hampshire migrated west in greater and greater numbers, particularly to the midwestern states of Minnesota, Iowa, and Illinois and the far western state of California. By the late 1900's, descendants could be found throughout the United States. By 1820 the Roberts name had all but disappeared from the Exeter/Brentwood area. In the Dover area the name carried forward into the late 1900's, although the numbers of Robertses there (as a percentage of the local population) aren't nearly what they were two hundred years ago. While today there are relatively few Roberts-surnamed descendants left in New Hampshire, the descendants there who now bear other surnames undoubtedly number in the tens of thousands.

Most of the early Robertses were farmers who also practiced a craft on the side, such as shoemaking or weaving. Others were mariners and lumbermen. Into the 1800's an increasing number of Robertses took up teaching, law and medicine. For those who grew up after the Civil War, both men and women, a remarkable number graduated from college and went on to pursue careers in business and engineering, as well as the traditional professions.

Politics seems to have been in the blood of these Robertses, starting with Thomas Roberts in 1640. So many of them served as town selectmen or other local officials that it would be impossible to name them here. Quite a few served in their state legislatures, among whom were Tobias and Joshua Roberts of Strafford, New

---

* U.S. Dept. of Commerce & Labor, Bureau of the Census. *Heads of Families at the First Census of the United States. Taken in the Year 1790. New Hampshire.* Washington, D.C.: U.S. Government Printing Office, 1907.

SOUTHWESTERN MAINE 1800's TO PRESENT

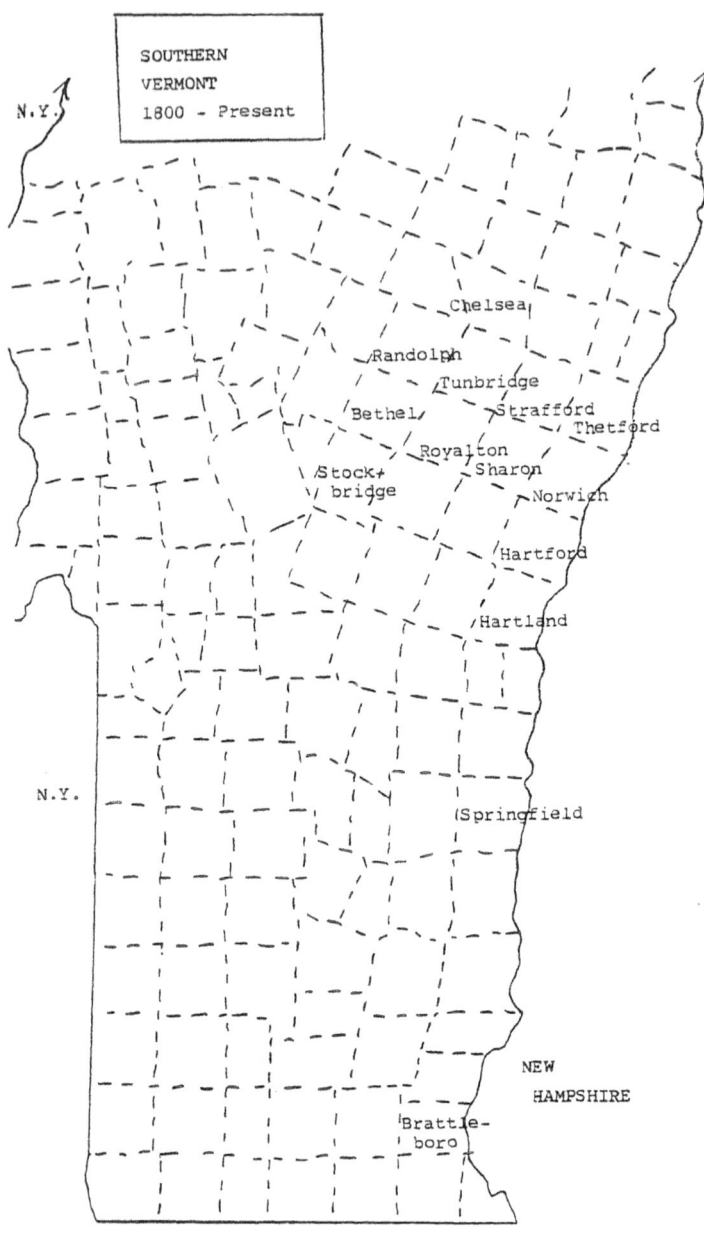

Hampshire, James Wakefield Roberts of Lyman, Maine, Jeremiah Roberts of Farmington, New Hampshire, Stephen William Roberts of Dover, George Belknap Roberts of Rochester, New Hampshire, Hiram Rollins Roberts and Joseph Doe Roberts of Rollinsford, New Hampshire, James Arthur Roberts of Buffalo, New York, Winslow Roberts and Barnabus Myrick Roberts of Brooks, Maine, Cassius Clay Roberts of Stockton, Maine, and Otis Jackson Roberts of Dexter, Maine.

Many Robertses were active in the abolitionist movement, especially in Maine, and were prominent among the founders of the Free Soil Party, and later the Republican Party there.

Robertses in the Civil War

In this the bloodiest war in our history, the name Roberts is all too prominent. No less than forty-three of the men in this book served with distinction in the struggle to preserve the union. Of these forty-three, fourteen never returned, having paid the ultimate price for their country, their comrades, and their families.

One little town in Eastern Maine marshalled no less than fifteen Robertses to the Union cause. Certainly we should recognize this extraordinary outpouring of patriotism by listing first the fifteen Roberts men of Brooks, Maine:

Frank Roberts (died)	Benjamin Roberts
Charles Justin Roberts	Jay Roberts (died)
Samuel Gilman Roberts	Manter A. Roberts (died)
Laurens Roberts (died)	Levi Roberts
Albert Roberts	Thomas Loring Roberts
Rufus Roberts	Oscar Roberts
Winslow Roberts	Alfred Roberts (died)
Ezra Roberts	

Other Robertses in this book who served with distinction in the Civil War were:

Freeman Myrick Roberts
John H. Roberts
Orpheus Roberts (died)
Charles Wentworth Roberts
Lloyd Roberts
Franklin Kimball Roberts
Cassius Clay Roberts
James Arthur Roberts
John P. Roberts
Seth Roberts, Jr. (died)
Albert Augustus Roberts
George Roberts (died)
Watson Clifford Roberts
Leavitt Sylvester Roberts
Joseph Hall Roberts (died)
Jonathan M. Roberts (died)
John S. Roberts (died)
Daniel West Roberts
John H. Roberts (died)
Franklin B. Roberts
Isaac H. Roberts
Amos B. Roberts
Orsino Roberts
Otis Oakes Roberts
Oliver Ayer Roberts
George B. Roberts (died)
Benjamin T. Roberts (died)
George Henry Roberts

The Roberts Name

It is tempting to conclude that all persons of a specific surname must be related, and, that if one could but only trace back far enough, one could find the relationship. Anyone with an understanding of the origins of surnames, however, would appreciate the fact that a common name like Roberts would have had hundreds of different and independent points of origination.

The name Roberts had its origin, of course, as a patronymic for someone whose father was named Robert. The construction Roberts, as opposed to Robertson, is peculiarly Welsh, but that fact doesn't necessarily mean that these Robertses of early New Hampshire were from Wales. By 1600 there were Roberts families established in virtually every shire of England and Wales, although it would appear that the name was most commonly found in Wales and western England.

In early documents, Thomas' family consistently favored the modern spelling of Roberts, while George's family's name often appears in various records as "Robards", or some variation. But this fact really doesn't tell us anything about their relatedness or lack thereof. It was very common to find in the 1600's and 1700's people within the same household spelling their common last name in different ways. It also has to be remembered that most early records were written down by clerks and other officials, who more often than not decided for themselves how a name should be spelled.

Organization of this Book

This book has been organized in accordance with a traditional genealogical format as established by the New England Historic Genealogical Society. Children within a family group are numbered in lower case roman numerals, in the order of their birth or, where birthdates are unknown, in the probable order of birth. Those male children who are known to have had children are carried forward into the succeeding generation. Each one is assigned a unique, consecutive arabic numeral for ease of reference backward to the father's generation and forward to the son's generation.

The object of this book has been to trace all of the known Roberts-surnamed descendants of Thomas and Rebecca Roberts and George and Mary Roberts down to as close to the present time as possible. This volume does not attempt to trace down lines of the many thousands of descendants with surnames other than Roberts. Some of the non-Roberts surnamed descendants can be found in other sources, such as the Hardon manuscript or the books by Grant or Hilton (refer to bibliography at end). In some cases, mostly in the earlier generations, a close reading of the footnotes will alert the reader to an existing genealogy for the families of various Roberts spouses. Where it is known that a female Roberts offspring had descendants, the author has generally attempted to indicated the number of known children she had, as well as the name of her spouse(s).

For each Roberts-surnamed ancestor who is known to have left descendants the author of this book has attempted, where possible, to present more than just the bare facts of date of birth, name of spouse, date of death, and where buried. Especially in the early generations, he has tried to emphasize what might be of historical interest or what might give some insight into the person's interests and accomplishments. Regrettably, this type of information does not always survive. Mundane references to records such as taxpayer lists or property transfers have not always been included, except perhaps where they might be critical to establishing someone's age, economic standing or geographic location at some particular time.

About Genealogical Research

Genealogy is the study of ancestries. It attempts to answer the questions of who were our forebearers, what were their names, where did they live, what did they do, and what were they like. Few of us have first hand knowledge of any ancestors before our own grandparents. So, to go back in a family tree, it becomes necessary to find documents, records of births, deaths, marriages, inheritances and bequests, and property ownership. Finding these records is not always easy. It involves tracking down the location of obscure, often unpublished, records that are scattered among hundreds of libraries, archives, family associations, and historical societies. There are some indexes and catalogs available, but even these are difficult and time consuming to ferret out.

If there is one iron rule in genealogy, it is that you will never locate all of the records you would like to have, in order to establish the facts of a relationship. This is especially true for events before 1900. Some genealogically significant events in the past (a birth, a marriage, a death, etc.) were never recorded to begin with. Other events were recorded but have been lost in various disasters or have been simply misplaced. In some cases the record may exist somewhere, but it does not appear on an index; it may have been misfiled or misread. If enough records can be found, the relationships and life story of an ancestor can be pieced together, even if some vital facts about the individual cannot be recovered.

It is never a case of the facts or the records speaking for themselves. Often the genealogist has to fit the available scraps of isolated facts together in such a way that the result is the simplest possible reconstruction of past relationships without leaving out any significant piece of data. Sometimes you are lucky enough to follow on the work of another genealogist who has already done some of the reconstruction. In those cases it is incumbent on the genealogist to scrutinize the sources used, to re-examine the data, and to reconcile any discrepancies with his own research. In many cases a judgment call has to be made, and if there is disclosure of the potential ambiguity and the conclusions drawn, this is legitimate.

Nothing is ever "proven" in genealogy. Unless the genealogist himself is at the conception and birth of an individual, how can he assert that this person was the offspring of that couple? A more appropriate standard than "proof" would be "preponderance of the evidence". And here it is not a matter of the number of sources, but the quality of sources. Genealogical writings are notorious for perpetuating errors. Usually, the genealogist does not have the funds or the time to turn every library upside down and then to insure that his work is thoroughly edited and proofread.*

Especially in the generations after the first four, the author of this book has relied on material supplied by other Roberts descendants, sometimes from unique records, such as family bibles. Unfortunately, for a volume of this magnitude, it would not be humanly possible in one life time to re-check every date or other fact submitted by all of the other researchers. There are undoubtedly errors of fact and judgment. If brought to the author's attention, they will be corrected in any subsequent editions.

---

* For a good discussion of these issues, see Stevenson, Noel C. *Genealogical Evidence*. Laguna Hills, California: Aegean Park Press, 1989, especially pp. 181-3.

SOUTHEASTERN NEW HAMPSHIRE AREA TODAY

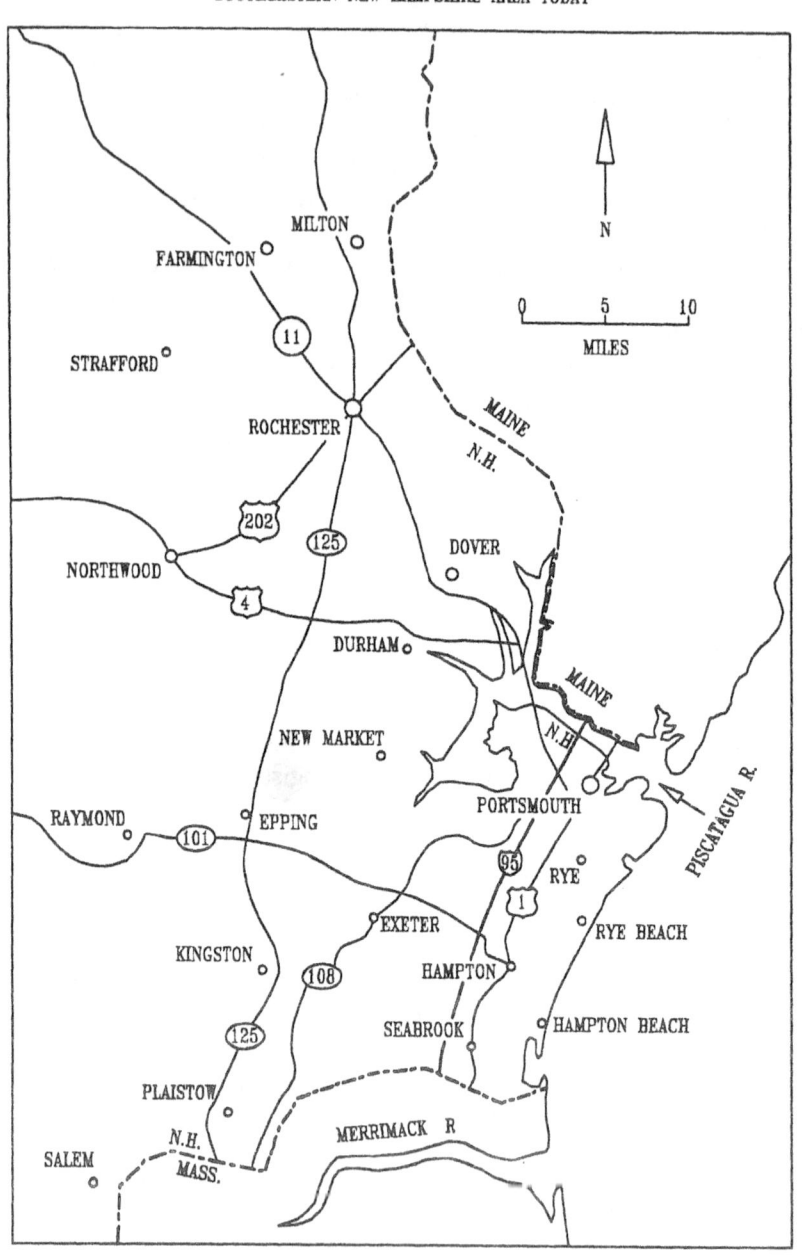

FIRST GENERATION

1. **Thomas Roberts**, one of the founding fathers of New Hampshire, was born in England about 1600 and died in Dover, New Hampshire between September 27, 1673 (date of will) and June 30, 1674 (date proved). He was buried in the northeast corner of the old burying ground, on Dover Neck, where several subsequent generations of Robertses also lie. In the early 1900's a monument was erected that marks the approximate spot of burial.[*]

There are two theories about the parentage of Thomas. One has it that Thomas was apprenticed to a fishmonger of London (Edward Hilton?), as "son of a John Roberts, of Woolaston, Co. Worcestershire, (England) 29 April, 1622."[*+] Another, less likely, theory suggests that he was the son of Sir Thomas and Frances (James) Roberts of Glassenbury (Park), Kent.[#]

He and his wife Rebecca were apparently married in the mid to late 1620's. Tradition says that she was a sister of Edward Hilton, however there does not seem to any evidence in the matter. Rebecca apparently died before Thomas.

Thomas was a member of the Fishmongers' Company of London and was sent, along with another member, Edward Hilton, to New England to set up a fishing station under the auspices of the Council

---

[*] Metcalf, Henry H., ed. *Probate Records of the Province of New Hampshire.* (N.H. State Papers Series) Bristol, N.H.: State of New Hampshire, c. 1910, Vol. 30, p. 145; Quint, Alonzo H., "Genealogical Items Relating to the Early Settlers of Dover, N.H.", *New England Historical and Genealogical Register*, Vol. 7, No. 3 (October 1853), p. 356 & Vol. 8, No. 1 (January 1854), pp. 63-4; Scales, John. *History of Dover, N. H.*, pp. 302-4.

[+] Scales, *History of Dover, N.H.*, p. 302. Scales quotes the Rev. Dr. Everett S. Stackpole, who learned this information on "excellent authority". There were several Woolastons (various spellings) in England at the time. A recent perusal of the L.D.S. International Genealogical Index (I.G.I.) does show there was a Roberts clan in and around Woolaston, Glocestershire, in the 1600's, but with no specific entry that connects to Thomas of Dover. There doesn't seem to be much, if any, Roberts presence in Woolaston, Worcestershire.

[#] MacKenzie, George N. *Colonial Families of the United States...* Baltimore: Seaforth Press, 1914, Vol. 2, pp. 619 et seq. However, there is no evidence in MacKenzie (or in any other source, for that matter) that connects Thomas of Dover to this family.

DESCENDANTS OF THOMAS & REBECCA ROBERTS

of New England, which had been granted most of Northern New England by King James I. Hilton established a small village on what is now Dover Neck as early as 1623; however, whether Roberts was a permanent resident from that early date is not proven by what little documentation exists. It is clear, however, that he was there on a permanent basis from 1628, if not earlier. In any event, Thomas Roberts was indeed among the first handful of permanent residents of the land that now constitutes the present state of New Hampshire.[*]

Thomas Roberts was selected "President of the Court" of the Bristol Company, the proprietory owners of Dover and neighboring Portsmouth, in 1639/40. He was one of 41 settlers who signed the Dover Combination October 22, 1640, the oldest document of any government in what is now New Hampshire. Thomas was granted 20 acres of land in Dover, designated lot #1, in 1642, and later a further 30 acres. This latter property, along with "half his marsh at the mouth of Winnicott River on its west side at the bottom of Great Bay" was given to his two sons Thomas and John in 1670. In 1671 he gave half of his remaining property to his daughter and son-in-law, Sarah and Richard Rich, with the balance to them at his death.[+]

Part of this land on Dover Neck was inhabited by Roberts descendants into the 1930's, if not later.[#]

Thomas Roberts was one of the few residents who were consistently referenced as "Mr." in a number of surviving early tax lists for Dover, and he regularly paid the highest amount of tax in town. In 1661 he was fined by the town of Dover for missing meetings for thirteen days and ordered to forfeit one cow, and in the next year, he publicly rebuked his sons, constables of Dover, for their harsh treatment of the local Quakers. There is no evidence that he was a Quaker himself, but it may be inferred from the

---

[*] Scales, *History of Dover, N.H.*, pp. 5-22, 34-9, & 302-3; Noyes, Libby & Davis, p. 589.

[+] Scales, John, ed., *Historical Memoranda Concerning Persons and Places in Old Dover, N.H., Collected by Rev. Dr. Alonzo Hall Quint*... Bowie, Maryland: Heritage Books Inc., 1983 (originally published Dover, N.H., 1900), pp. 18-21, 350, 408 & 412.

[#] Scales, *History of Dover, N.H.*, p. 80.

SECOND GENERATION

record that he was more tolerant in his views than most of the other leaders of Puritan New England.*

We learn of the first six children below from his will, so it is quite possible there were others who predeceased.⁺ Children:

2.   i. John, b. 1628 or 1629.
3.   ii. Thomas, b. 1633-6.
      iii. Hester, m. John Martyn. Seven children.
      iv. Anna, m.(1) James Philbrick, (2) William Marston. Seven children.
      v. Elizabeth, m. Benjamin Heard. Six children.
      vi. Sarah, m. Richard Rich. Six children.
      vii. (?) Joseph. A Joseph Roberts received a Dover town bounty in 1665 for killing wolves. No Joseph is named in Thomas's will, so perhaps he predeceased, leaving no children.#

---

  * Scales, *Historical Memoranda*. . ., pp. 38, 171-2 & 349-65.
  ⁺ Quint, *N.E.H.G.R.*, Vol. 8, No. 1, pp. 63-4.
  # This Joseph Roberts apparently was not the same Joseph Roberts who drowned off Portsmouth in the prior year. Scales, *Historical Memoranda*. . ., p. 71, and Noyes, Libby & Davis, p. 589.

SECOND GENERATION

2. John Roberts (Thomas[1]), son of Thomas and Rebecca Roberts, was born, apparently in what is now Dover, New Hampshire, in 1628 or 1629 (making him one of the first children born there), and died there January 21, 1694/5 of dropsy.

He married Abigail Nutter, the daughter of Hatevil and (Anne?) Nutter of Dover.

John was a prominent citizen of early Dover, serving as a selectman for six years in the 1660's and 1670's, as the surveyor of highways in 1661 and 1668, and a sergeant (later lieutenant) of the militia. In his role as constable, along with his brother Thomas, he was charged by Massachusetts Bay authorities with ridding the colony of Quakers. In one well-recorded incident in 1662 the two brothers literally dragged two proselytizing Quaker women through the winter snow and threw them into a canoe.[*]

In 1680 Charles II decided to set off New Hampshire as a separate royal province. To that end he appointed several local leaders to establish a new government. As one of these leaders, John Roberts was named Marshall of the Province. He resigned his office, however, shortly after the grandson of John Mason appeared on the scene to begin exercising his inherited rights as the landlord of all of New Hampshire. As it turned out, the younger Mason was successfully opposed by the new government at every turn, but it is easy to see why John, a prominent landholder in Dover, would be reluctant to be put in a position of possibly having to enforce Mason's claims.[+]

The Glorious Revolution of 1689 in England, which resulted in William of Orange succeeding James II as monarch, reverberated throughout New England, and for a time there was no government in the colonies. John Roberts was among six prominent Dover

---
[*] Noyes, Libby & Davis, pp. 516 & 589; Scales, *Historical Memoranda*. . ., pp. 3, 65,70, 114-5, 132, 140-2, 148, 171-2, 374-6, & 379; Hardon, Henry W. "Roberts Family" (unpublished manuscript at the New Hampshire Historical Society), Vol. I, pp. 8-10; Scales, *History of Dover, N.H.*, pp. 128-133.

[+] Belknap, Jeremy. *The History of New Hampshire*. Bowie, Maryland: Heritage Books, Inc.(a facsimile reprint of the 1831 edition of the original), 1992, pp. 91-4.

citizens who convened a convention with like-minded citizens of Portsmouth and Exeter. It was the recommendation of this convention that New Hampshire be reunited under the government of Massachusetts.*

John made numerous gifts of property to his children and grandchildren, most notably land in what became Kittery, Maine (the "fowling marsh") to son John, April 20, 1680 and land on the west side of Great Bay to sons Joseph, Hatevil & Thomas, on November 29, 1694.⁺ He was in all probability a literate man, as his signature on many early documents would attest. Children:

4.   i.   John.
5.   ii.   Thomas.
6.   iii.   Hatevil, b. 1661.
7.   iv.   Joseph.
         v.   Abigail, m. (1) 11/8/1671, John Hall, Jr., (2) 10/24/1698, Thomas Downes. Six children.
         vi.   Mary, m. Timothy Robinson. Seven children.
         vii.   Sarah, m. Zachariah Field. Seven children.

3. Thomas Roberts (Thomas¹), son of Thomas and Rebecca Roberts, was born in Dover, New Hampshire, between 1633 and 1636 and died there some time after 1705.

He married Mary Leighton, the daughter of Thomas and (Joanna?) Leighton of Dover.

Thomas was constable of Dover during the Quaker incident (see

---
    * Belknap, pp. 120-3.
    ⁺ N.H. Deeds, Book 29, p. 222 and York Co. Deeds, Book 3, p. 70, as cited in Underhill, Lora A.W. *Descendants of Edward Small of New England.* . . Boston & New York: Houghton Mifflin Company, 1934, pp. 1120 & 1122-4.

SECOND GENERATION

John No. 2.) and a selectman of Dover in 1670 and 1671, as well as a sergeant of the militia.[*]

In 1683 a newly-appointed governor, backing various prior royal rulings in favor of the Mason heirs, began ordering New Hampshire landholders to begin paying rent to Robert Mason. Thomas Roberts was one of three prominent residents and "large landowners" summoned to appear before the governor and ordered to arrive at some sort of settlement with Mason. The three engaged Mason in a rancorous session, refused to recognize his title or to pay rent, and demanded instead that the matter be brought directly before the King. (Very few of the resident landholders in New Hampshire acceded to Mason's demands. After many years of political manuevering, litigation, appeals, petitions, and changes in government in both England and New England, the resident landholders ultimately prevailed and obtained clear title to the lands they had worked and fought over for more than one hundred years.)[+] Children:

      i. Thomas, m. Sarah Canney; d. 1755. No children.

8.   ii. Nathaniel.

9.   iii. John.

      iv. Joanna, m. 3/24/1689/90, Thomas Potts. 2 ch.

      v. Mary, m. Thomas Young; d. 1745. Eight children.

      vi. Lydia, m. first cousin Hatevil (No. 6) Roberts.

      vii. Sarah, m. 6/8/1704, Howard Henderson. 3 ch.

---

[*] Noyes, Libby & Davis, pp. 324, 427, 564 & 589; Scales, *Historical Memoranda...*, pp. 3 & 218-9; Dover Historical Society. *Vital Records of Dover, New Hampshire 1686-1850*. Bowie, Maryland: Heritage Books, Inc., 1986 (originally published as *Collections of the Dover, N.H. Historical Society*. Dover, N.H.: Scales & Quimby, 1894), pp. 129-31; Hardon, p. 15.

[+] Belknap, pp. 100-1.

DESCENDANTS OF THOMAS & REBECCA ROBERTS

THIRD GENERATION

4. John Roberts (John², Thomas¹), son of John and Abigail (Nutter) Roberts, was born in Dover, New Hampshire about 1645-1650 and died near there before August 6, 1691. His wife's name was Mary, but that is all that is known about her. This John is apparently the John Roberts Jr. who received a Dover town bounty for killing wolves in 1665. John received land on Harrod's Cove in Great Bay in exchange for a marsh at Welchman's Cove in 1664. In 1680 he received from his father property in nearby Kittery, Maine, known as the "fowling marsh". Subsequent conveyances of part ownerships in this latter property would indicate that John had but three children who survived him.* Children:

10.   i. John.
11.   ii. William.
         iii. Mary; living unm. in Somersworth, N.H. in 1736.
         iv. (?) Joseph, b.c. 1683. A Joseph Roberts was captured by the Indians in a raid between 1689 and 1691. He was taken to Canada, where his marriage record to Marie-Madeleine Demers indicate parents were John and Anne (Austin?) Roberts. Two daughters were from this union.⁺

5. Thomas Roberts (John², Thomas¹), son of John and Abigail (Nutter) Roberts, was born in Dover, New Hampshire, about 1655-60 and died there or near there about 1735. He married, as his second wife, in 1711 or 1712, the Widow Elizabeth (Tucker) Hopley. She was the widow of Robert Hopley and the daughter of John and Ursula Tucker. She was born about 1670. Thomas was a selectman of Dover in 1706-1709 and again in 1720 and held other town offices as well. In various town records he is referred to as "Sergeant" Thomas Roberts. He received land from his father in 1694 and in turn conveyed land to his son Love in 1707 and his homestead to his son Benjamin in 1734. His son Benjamin was an

---

   * Noyes, Libby & Davis, p. 589; Hardon, p. 22; Scales, *Historical Memoranda...*,p. 376; Quint, p. 71.
   ⁺ Notes of John Bayard Peri.

DESCENDANTS OF THOMAS & REBECCA ROBERTS

offspring of his second marriage, and it would appear that the other three children were of the first marriage.* Children:

12.   i.   Love, b.c. 1685.

        ii.   Lydia.

13.   iii.   Timothy, b.c. 1695.

14.   iv.   Benjamin, b.c. 1712.

6. Hatevil Roberts (John², Thomas¹), son of John and Abigail (Nutter) Roberts, was born in Dover, New Hampshire, in 1661 and died in 1724 or 1725. He married his first cousin Lydia Roberts, the daughter of Thomas (No. 3) and Mary (Leighton) Roberts of Dover. Hatevil, who was known as Lieutenant, served as constable of Dover in 1694 and 1695 and as grand juror in 1697 and 1700. This family lived in the part of Dover which became the town of Somersworth in 1754 and Rollinsford in 1849.⁺ Children:

15.   i.   Samuel, b. 12/12/1686.

       ii.   Abigail, b. 7/29/1689; m. Daniel Goodwin, 12/30/1708. Eight children.

16.   iii.   Joshua, b. 10/11/1698.

      iv.   Mary, b. 7/20/1701, m. 4/7/1720, James Heard. Five children.

       v.   Benjamin, b. 1691-2; d. 10/13/1708.

      vi.   Hatevil.

7. Joseph Roberts (John², Thomas¹), son of John and Abigail (Nutter) Roberts, was born in Dover, New Hampshire, about 1660 and died there before 1742. He married, firstly, Elizabeth Jones,

---

    * Scales, *Historical Memoranda.* . ., pp. 160-1, 195, 236, & 253; Hardon, Vol. I, p. 23.

    ⁺ Noyes, Libby & Davis, p. 589; *Dover N.H. Historical Society, Collections of,* Vol. I, p. 30; "Journal of Rev. John Pike", *New Hampshire Genealogical Record,* Vol. III, No. 4 (April 1906), p. 152; Hardon, Vol. I, p. 24.

THIRD GENERATION

the daughter of Stephen and (Elizabeth Field?) Jones. She was born in New Hampshire in 1672 or 1673 and died after 1757. The children below are by Elizabeth. Purportedly, Joseph married, secondly, Abigail -----. (Was she the Mrs. Abigail Roberts who died in Durham, New Hampshire, April 21, 1823, age 104?) Joseph held a number of offices in Dover, including assessor in 1708, "viewer of fences" in 1709, surveyor of highways in 1706 and 1707, selectman in 1721/2. And he was a lieutenant in the militia. In 1726 Joseph and Elizabeth conveyed land to their son Joseph in Cocheco (Dover) and in 1734 sold land in Somersworth and Rochester to their son Ebenezer.* Children:

17.	i.	Joseph, b. 10/27/1692.
18.	ii.	John, b. 12/6/1694.
	iii.	Elizabeth, b. 3/13/1697, m. (1) Philip Hubbard, (2) John Gage. Eight children.
	iv.	Abigail, b. 7/16/1701.
19.	v.	Stephen, b. 8/20/1704.
20.	vi.	Ebenezer, b. 2/24/1705/6.
21.	vii.	Benjamin, b. 9/20/1709.
22.	viii.	Samuel, b. 4/11/1712.
	ix.	Lydia, b. 4/11/1712; m. Samuel Ham. 9 children.
	x.	Mary, b. 3/13/1716; m. Samuel Wingate.

8. **Nathaniel Roberts** (Thomas[2], Thomas[1]), son of Thomas and Mary (Leighton) Roberts, was born in Dover, New Hampshire, about 1670 and died there in 1752 or 1753. He married Elizabeth Mason, April 11, 1706. She was named in her husband's will dated March 3, 1745/6. Nathaniel was chosen constable of Dover in

---

* Noyes, Libby & Davis, pp. 388 & 589; Dover Historical Society, p. 14; Scales, *Historical Memoranda. . .*, pp. 161-2, 236, & 255; Dewsnap notes; Hardon, Vol. I, pp. 27-40; N.H. Deeds, Book 16, p. 142 & Book 26, p. 14, as cited in Underhill, p. 1120; Stackpole and Thompson, Vol. I, p. 396.

DESCENDANTS OF THOMAS & REBECCA ROBERTS

1712.* Children:

 i. Paul, b. 2/18/1706/7; d. unm. c. 1739.

 ii. Miriam, b. 1/4/1708/9; m. Benjamin Davis, 1/5/1726/7. One child.

 iii. Thomas, b. 7/23/1710; m. Abigail Jones; d. 1761. No children.

23. iv. Nathaniel, b. 4/22/1713.

24. v. Aaron, b. 4/16/1716.

25. vi. Moses, b. 6/22/1718.

 vii. Elizabeth, b. 2/3/1722/3.

 viii. Abigail.

 ix. Isaac.

9. **John Roberts** (Thomas^2, Thomas^1), son of Thomas and Mary (Leighton) Roberts, was born in the part of Dover, which became Somersworth and later Rollinsford, about 1675-80 and died there in 1756. His tombstone can be found in Rollinsford, where there is a monument erected in 1891 stating that the "Roberts family settled here in 1702." He married, firstly, at Dover, in October 1704, Deborah Church, the daughter of John and Sarah Church. She was born at Dover, August 15, 1683 and died before May 17, 1720, at which date John married, secondly, Frances Emery, daughter of James and Margaret (Hitchcock) Emery. Frances was born in Kittery, Maine, December 17, 1694. John is referred to as a weaver in two early deeds.⁺ Children:

---

 * Scales, *Historical Memoranda*. . ., pp. 92, 104 & 196; Dover Historical Society, pp. 24-5 & 131; Hardon, Vol. I, pp. 41-2 & 84.

 ⁺ Dover Historical Society, pp. 11, 25 & 35; Quint, pp. 63-4; Rockingham County Deeds, Vol. 35, pp. 155-6; Hardon, Vol. I, pp. 43-4; Goss, Mrs. Charles C. *Colonial Gravestone Inscriptions in the State of New Hampshire.* Dover, N.H.: National Society of Colonial Dames of America in N.H., 1942, p. 120; Wentworth, John. *The Wentworth Genealogy.* . . . Chicago: Privately published, 1870, Vol. I, pp. 144-5 & 155-6.

THIRD GENERATION

- i. Joanna, b. 10/20/1705; m. Samuel Wentworth, 8/29/1725; d. 7/4/1780. Five children.
- ii. Sarah, b. 2/18/1708/9; bapt. 2/14/1739 by Rev. Cushing "in private, being sick"; m. Ebenezer Wentworth; d. 2/10/1770. Nine children.
- iii. Mary, b. 7/20/1711.
- iv. Phebe, b. 9/20/1716; m. Ebenezer Tuttle.
- 26. v. Ebenezer, b. 2/5/1721/2.
- vi. Deborah(twin), b. 1/15/1725/6; m. (1) Thomas Miller, (2) Phineas Ricker. Five children.
- 27. vii. Alexander(twin), b. 1/15/1725/6.

FOURTH GENERATION

10. John Roberts (John[3], John[2], Thomas[1]), son of John and Mary Roberts was born in the Dover/Kittery area about 1675-1685. He married Mary Jose, in Portsmouth, in 1712. John was a mastmaker or a mastliner in Dover, Portsmouth, and finally Falmouth (later Portland), Maine, where he sold property in the 1740's.* Child:

    i. John, b.c. 1719, m. Mehitable Bangs, 5/2/1752; d. 11/27/1752, leaving a childless widow.

11. William Roberts (John[3], John[2], Thomas[1]), son of John and Mary Roberts, was born in the Dover/Kittery area about 1675-85, and died some time in 1713. He was apparently married twice, once to an Elizabeth and once to an Abigail. After William's death, Abigail married, Nathaniel Perkins, probably his second wife, March 15, 1715. The first two children below were by Elizabeth.⁺ Children:

    i. William, b. 6/30/1701.

28. ii. George, b. 3/30/1704.

    iii. Sarah, m. Robert Morrill, 5/29/1729.

12. Love Roberts (Thomas[3], John[2], Thomas[1]), son of Thomas Roberts, was born in or near Dover, New Hampshire, about 1685 and died in Somersworth, New Hampshire in 1755. He married Elizabeth Drew, the daughter of John and Sarah (Field) Drew. She was born in Dover and was living at the time of her husband's death. In 1707 Love received land from his father near Salmon Falls River and in 1727 obtained thirteen acres of land in Berwick, Maine. Love is referred to by the title "gentleman" in his will. He left real estate in Somersworth, Berwick, and Rochester, New Hampshire, to his two sons Love and Francis. He also owned a "negro man Phil", whose "use and improvement" was bequeathed to his wife for her natural life.# Children:

---

    * Underhill, vol. I, pp. 1126-8; Noyes, Libby & Davis, p. 589; "Portsmouth Marriages", *N.H.G.R.*, Vol. V, No. 1 (Jan. 1908), p. 41.

    ⁺ Underhill, vol. I, pp. 1130-4; Hardon, Vol.I, p. 51.

    # Hardon, Vol. I, p. 52; Dover Historical Society, p. 29; Hammond,

DESCENDANTS OF THOMAS & REBECCA ROBERTS

        i.   Hannah, b. 5/10/1713; d. unm.
29.   ii. Love, b. 4/21/1721.
30.   iii. Francis, b. 6/12/1723.

13. Timothy Roberts (Thomas^3, John^2, Thomas^1), son of Thomas Roberts, was born in or near Dover, New Hampshire, about 1695, and died in Rochester, New Hampshire, December 31, 1774. He married about 1728 Anna Waldron, the daughter of John and Mary (Ham) Waldron. Anna was born at Dover in 1703 and died in Rochester in 1783. Timothy, known as Captain, is considered to be the first settler of the town of Rochester, which was separated off from Dover in 1722. He was a tanner and an innkeeper, and referred to as "gentleman". He made gifts of land to his sons at various times.* Children:

31.   i.   John.
32.   ii. Thomas.
33.   iii. Timothy, bapt. 5/11/1740.
        iv. Sarah, bapt. 7/1742; m. Daniel Garland; d. 1827. Ten children.
        v. Mary, bapt. 4/28/1745.
34.   vi. Moses, bapt. 2/9/1755.

14. Benjamin Roberts (Thomas^3, John^2, Thomas^1), son of Thomas and Elizabeth (Tucker) Roberts, was born in or near Dover, New Hampshire, about 1712 and died some time after 1773. He married Mary Furbush of Kittery, Maine, the daughter of Daniel and Dorothy (Pray) Furbush, October 15, 1743. She met an unfortunate death on May 23, 1759, from the effects of her husband hitting her on the head with an eighteen-ounce stone four days

---

ed. *Probate Records of N.H.*, Vol. 6, pp. 223-4.

   * Hardon, Vol. I, pp. 53-4; McDuffee, Franklin. *History of the Town of Rochester, N.H. from 1722 to 1890*. Manchester, N.H.: Privately published, 1892, pp. 584 & 587-9; Notes of Deborah Wilson.

FOURTH GENERATION

earlier. Benjamin was convicted of a crime in connection with the death of his wife, and he was charged twenty-two shillings and six pence for "instruments of branding", apparently used to mete out his punishment. In 1762 he was presented for sentencing for having failed to attend church for three months.* Children:

    i. Moses.

    ii. Daniel.

    iii. Benjamin (?).

15. Samuel Roberts (Hatevil³, John², Thomas¹), son of Hatevil and Lydia (Roberts) Roberts, was born in Dover, New Hampshire, December 12, 1686, and died in New Hampshire in 1751. He married at Berwick, Maine, on September 20, 1716, Sarah Lord, the daughter of Nathan and Martha (Tozer) Lord. Sarah was born in Berwick, March 28, 1696, and was living when her husband died. Samuel and Sarah "owned the covenant" at the First Church in Berwick, May 7, 1721, and their first two children were baptized there that day. Samuel's will indicates that Hatevil was the eldest child. Samuel is referred to as Lieutenant Roberts in early records. This couple is said to have had five sons and four daughters in all.⁺ Children:

35.	i.	Hatevil, b. 7/16/1717.
36.	ii.	Benjamin, b. 9/1/1719.
	iii.	Lydia, b. 5/16/1721.
37.	iv.	Samuel, b. 5/7/1723.
	v.	Sarah, b. 10/18/1726; m. (1) John Philpot, (2) Moses Stevens. Six children.

---

    * Hardon, Vol. I, pp. 58-9; Baylis, Barbara Roberts. "Is Daniel Roberts of Lebanon, Maine the Son of Benjamin⁴ Roberts?", *New Hampshire Genealogical Record* (New), Vol. 11, No. 1 (January-April 1994), pp. 20-4. The answer seems to be yes.

    ⁺ Hardon, Vol. I, pp. 59-60; Noyes, Libby & Davis, p. 444; Dover Historical Society, p. 32 (some of the birthdates are off; Hardon appears to have corrected.); Scales, *Historical Memoranda. . .*, p. 93.

DESCENDANTS OF THOMAS & REBECCA ROBERTS

38.   vi.   Nathan.

16. Joshua Roberts (Hatevil[3], John[2], Thomas[1]), son of Hatevil and Lydia (Roberts) Roberts, was born in Dover, New Hampshire, October 11, 1698, and died, apparently in Somersworth, New Hampshire, December 29, 1771. He married Sarah Wallingford, the daughter of John and Mary (Tuttle) Wallingford. She was born in Bradford, Massachusetts, December 29, 1693; and she survived her husband. Joshua had lands in the "new township at the head of Rochester", which he sold shortly before he died. He was among those who signed a petition to set off Somersworth in 1729 and is listed among the "Somersworth Army" (the local militia) in 1746. The children listed below were all born in Somersworth.* Children:

   i.   Hannah, b. 1735; m. -----Foss.

   ii. Elizabeth (Betsey), b. 4/18/1737; m. 2nd cousin James Rollins (No. 45) Roberts.

39.   iii. Thomas, b. 11/1/1740.

   iv. Lydia, b. 7/31/1743; m. John Knight.

40.   v.   Joshua, b. 7/13/1746.

   vi. Mary, b. 1748; m. John Roberts (probably a relative). Three ch: Hatevil, Samuel & Olive.

17. Joseph Roberts (Joseph[3], John[2], Thomas[1]), a joiner, son of Joseph and Elizabeth (Jones) Roberts, was born in Dover, or vicinity, October 27, 1692, and died there in 1761. He married, firstly, Elizabeth Ham, the daughter of John and Elizabeth (Knight) Ham, and, secondly, Joanna -----.⁺ Children:

   i.   Ephraim, b. 3/23/1727; d. unm. 1748.

41.   ii. Joseph, b. 2/7/1729.

---

   * Hardon, Vol. I, pp. 61-2; Scales, *Historical Memoranda. . .*, pp. 61-3; Dover Historical Society, p. 30; "The Diary of Master Joseph Tate of Somersworth, N.H.", *N.E.H.G.R.*, Vol. LXXIV (1920), p. 39.
   ⁺ Hardon, Vol. I, pp. 65-9.

FOURTH GENERATION

   iii. Eliza, b. 4/21/1731; m. -----Evans.

   iv. Mary, b. 10/8/1733; m. John Gage. Two children.

   v. Abigail, b. 2/18/1736; m. Joshua Wingate, 1757; d. 8/22/1813. Five children.

   vi. Lydia, b. 10/22/1738; m. Isaac Hill; d. 9/17/1769.

18. John Roberts (Joseph[3], John[2], Thomas[1]), son of Joseph and Elizabeth (Jones) Roberts, was born in Dover, New Hampshire, December 6, 1694, and died in Madbury, New Hampshire, January 22, 1771. His remains lie in a cemetery in Madbury on the south side of Cherry Lane.

He married Sarah (Buzzell) Williams, the daughter of John and Sarah Buzzell and the widow of -----Williams. She was born in Dover, November 28, 1698, and died in Madbury, December 9, 1770. Her grave stone lies next to her husband's. John received a gift of 72 acres of land in Dover from his father Joseph. Here John and Sarah farmed for many years, on property which became part of Madbury, when that town was set off from Dover in 1755. He also owned 40 acres of land in Barrington, which went to his son Samuel by his will. His son John and his widow Sarah received the farm in Madbury; and two daughters, Elizabeth and Sarah, each received fifty pounds "old tenor" money. Sarah's son by a prior marriage, Joseph, also known as Ensign Joseph, took on the name Roberts. He married Elizabeth ----- and they had several children baptized in Dover between 1760 and 1772: Abigail, Elizabeth, Joseph, Mary and James.* Children:

   i. Samuel, bapt. 3/21/1736.

   ii. Elizabeth, bapt. 3/21/1736; m. -----Davis.

   iii. Sarah, bapt. 2/14/1739; m. -----Buzzell.

---

   * Hardon, Vol. I, pp. 70-1; Dover Historical Society, pp. 142,145, & 150; Rockingham Co. Deeds Vol 51, pp. 307-8 & Vol 15, pp. 229-30; Stackpole & Thompson, pp. 26 & 196-7;Hammond, Otis G., ed. *Probate Records of. . .N. H.* Vol. 7, pp. 403-5; Dover Historical Society, pp. 142 & 150.

DESCENDANTS OF THOMAS & REBECCA ROBERTS

    iv. Mary, bapt. 8/24/1740.

    v. John, bapt. 5/22/1743; m. Jane (Meserve?).

19. Stephen Roberts (Joseph[3], John[2], Thomas[1]), son of Joseph and Elizabeth (Jones) Roberts, was born in Dover, New Hampshire, August 20, 1704, and died there in 1757 or 1758. He married Keziah Lamos, who was living at the time of his death.keeping a tavern, operating a ferry and owning a tannery, Stephen was a prominent businessman on Dover Point. He did not make a will, but an inventory of his estate shows a value of 8,029.6 pounds, a sizable sum for that period of history.* Children:

    i. Sarah, b. 1/19/1737; m. Nathaniel Austin, 5/12/1757; d. 2/18/1817. Two children.

    ii. Abigail, b. 1/1/1745; m. Nathaniel Lamos, 5/1/1766; d. 7/27/1829. Six children.

42.   iii. Joseph, b. 6/26/1747.

    iv. Keziah, m. Jonathan Dow, 11/4/1760.

    v. Elizabeth, m. James Neal, 11/26/1761.

    vi. Hannah, m. Elijah Austin, 12/30/1762; d. 4/23/1812. Eight children.

43.   vii. John. b. 7/20/1751.

    viii. Lydia, b. 1752; m. James Neal, 10/31/1772. 4 ch.

    ix. Thomas, b. 2/20/1757.

    x. Stephen.

20. Ebenezer Roberts (Joseph[3], John[2], Thomas[1]), son of Joseph and Elizabeth (Jones) Roberts, was born in Dover, New Hampshire, February 24, 1705/6, and died, in Somersworth, New Hampshire, in 1754 or 1755. In 1733 he married Mary Rollins, the

---

* Quint, pp 63-4; Scales, *Historical Memoranda...*, p. 93; Hammond, ed. *Probate Records*, Vol 5, p. 286; Hardon, Vol. I, pp. 72-8.

FOURTH GENERATION

daughter of Jeremiah and Elizabeth (Ham) Rollins. She was born in what became Rollinsford, New Hampshire, January 23, 1714, and died after 1793. Ebenezer is described as an artisan. This family lived in Somersworth, not far from the village of South Berwick, Maine. Most of the children were born in Maine, in Berwick, Alfred Gore, Lyman, or Waterborough.* Children:

	i.	Moses.
44.	ii.	Aaron, b. 1735 (?).
45.	iii.	James Rollins, b. 4/24/1737.
46.	iv.	John, b. 1741.
47.	v.	Ebenezer, b.c. 1745.
48.	vi.	Ichabod, b. 9/17/1748.
	vii.	Samuel.
	viii.	Jeremiah, b. 11/17/1753; apparently d. aged 94.
	ix.	William, bapt. 12/15/1754.
	x.	a daughter, who died a young woman.

21. **Benjamin Roberts** (Joseph[3], John[2], Thomas[1]), son of Joseph and Elizabeth (Jones) Roberts, was born in Dover, New Hampshire, September 20, 1709, and died there November 10, 1784. He married Mary Heard, the daughter of Nathaniel and Margaret (Warren) Heard. Benjamin owned land in Somersworth and Dover, the latter of which he conveyed to his sons Samuel and Stephen shortly before he died. The children below were born in Dover.⁺ Children:

i. Samuel, b.c. 1730(?); m. Mary Estes; apparently no children.

---

* Hardon, Vol. I, pp. 79-80; Little, George T. *Genealogical and Family History of the State of Maine*. New York: Lewis Historical Publishing Company, 1909, Vol. III, pp. 1634-5.
⁺ Hardon, Vol. I, pp. 81-2 & 159.

DESCENDANTS OF THOMAS & REBECCA ROBERTS

    ii.   Stephen.

    iii. Benjamin, b. 1735(?).

    iv. Heard (?), b. 1741.

    v.   Sarah, m. Caleb Estes. Three children.

22. Samuel Roberts (Joseph^3, John^2, Thomas^1), son of Joseph and Elizabeth (Jones) Roberts, was born in Dover, New Hampshire, April 11, 1712. He married firstly Abigail Perkins and, secondly, Sarah (Lord?). Sarah Roberts, widow of Samuel, conveyed on September 22, 1806, to Edmund Roberts of Portsmouth, merchant, and Sarah Roberts, a single woman, her dower rights in the estate of Samuel Roberts.* Children:

49.   i.   Edmund, b. 9/1/1744.

       ii. Sarah, b. 4/4/1747; m. Joshua Pray. Four children.

       iii. Josiah.

23. Nathaniel Roberts (Nathaniel^3, Thomas^2, Thomas^1), son of Nathaniel and Elizabeth (Mason) Roberts, was born in Dover, New Hampshire, April 22, 1713. He married ----- Thompson. Nathaniel lived in Somersworth and Berwick, Maine. He was lost at sea.$^+$ Children:

       i.   Isaac, b. 1745; m. 11/22/1770, Abigail Rollins (or Rawlings); d. at sea 10/1782, apparently no ch.

50.   ii. David.

51.   iii. Nathaniel.

      iv. Elizabeth.

52.   v.   George, b. 8/21/1755.

24. Aaron Roberts (Nathaniel^3, Thomas^2, Thomas^1), son of

---

   * Hardon, Vol. I, p. 83.

   $^+$ Hardon, Vol. I, pp. 85 & 160; Dover Historical Society, pp. 171 & 191.

FOURTH GENERATION

Nathaniel and Elizabeth (Mason) Roberts, was born in Dover, New Hampshire, April 16, 1716, and died there January 10, 1797. He married Sarah Tibbetts, who died November 8, 1785. Sarah was the daughter of John and Mary Tibbetts of Dover. The first eight children below are named in Aaron's will, which provided that his land was to go to his son Aaron.* Children:

	i.	Aaron, d. unm. 1803.
	ii.	John, b. 5/19/1758.
53.	iii.	Silas, b. 1761 (or 1764?).
54.	iv.	Daniel, b. 6/12/1772.
	v.	Elizabeth, m. Isaac Varney. Four children.
	vi.	Abigail, b. 2/19/1779; m. Jonathan Bickford, 2/19/1799. Lived in Wolfeboro, NH.
	vii.	Sarah, m. Elijah Varney, 11/25/1779(?).
	viii.	Hannah, m. (1) Francis Footman, (2) Otis Tuttle, 12/15/1810.
	ix.	Tamsen, m. Thomas Varney, 6/21/1786. Eight ch.

25. Moses Roberts (Nathaniel³, Thomas², Thomas¹), son of Nathaniel and Elizabeth (Mason) Roberts, was born in Dover, New Hampshire, June 22, 1718, and died April 13, 1807. He married, firstly, Elizabeth Whitehouse, the daughter of Thomas and Rachel Whitehouse, and, secondly, Abigail (Varney) Hanson, the daughter of John and Sarah (Robinson) Varney and the widow of Silas Hanson, January 10, 1798. Elizabeth was born November 1, 1725 and died in April of 1792. Abigail was born in 1725 and died

---

* Hardon, Vol. I, pp. 86-92; Jarvis, May (Tibbetts). "Henry Tibbetts of Dover, N.H. and Some of His Descendants", *N.E.H.G.R.*, Vol. XCVIII(1944), pp. 217-8.

September 25, 1807. The children below were by Elizabeth. This family was active in the Friends meeting in Dover.* Children:

    i. Anna, b. 6/3/1749; m. Joshua Varney, 11/30/1768; d. 8/24/1823. Eleven children.

    ii. Mary, b. 3/17/1751; unm. in June 1832.

55.   iii. Thomas, b. 2/20/1757.

56.   iv. James, b. 8/17/1760.

    v. Hannah, b. 12/12/1763; d. unm. 11/26/1786.

57.   vi. Moses, b. 8/25/1766.

    vii. Elizabeth, b. 8/28/1770; m. Stephen Roberts of Dover; d. 11/30/1831.

58.   viii. Ephraim, b. 3/27/1772.

26. Ebenezer Roberts (John^3, Thomas^2, Thomas^1), son of John and Frances (Emery) Roberts, was born in Dover, New Hampshire, February 15, 1721/2 and died in Somersworth, New Hampshire, April 4, 1804, and is buried in the Rollinsford Cemetery. He married Sarah Miller, who was born in Dover in 1721 (or 1731?) and died in Somersworth, May 9, 1799, and is also buried in the Rollinsford Cemetery. Sarah was the daughter of Dr. Thomas Miller of Somersworth. Described as a yeoman, Ebenezer had a homestead in the part of Dover which became Somersworth, which he bequeathed to his son John, in his will dated 1787. The following children were born in Somersworth.⁺
Children:

    i. Joanna, b. 1758 (or 1761?); d. unm. 4/3/1847.

    ii. Deborah, b. 5/10/1762; m. Daniel Plumer; d. 12/4/1846.

---

   * Hardon, Vol. I, pp. 93-5; Scales, *Historical Memoranda*...; "Dover Monthly Meeting Records", *New Hampshire Genealogical Record*, Vol. III, No. 2, p 36.

   ⁺ Hardon, Vol. I, pp. 96-7; Goss, p. 120.

FOURTH GENERATION

        iii. Lydia, b. 4/1767; d. unm. 3/2/1798.

59.   iv. John, b. 8/5/1770.

27. Alexander Roberts (John[3], Thomas[2], Thomas[1]), son of John and Frances (Emery) Roberts, was born in Dover, New Hampshire, February 15, 1725/6. He married Rebecca Garland, the daughter of Ebenezer and Abigail (Powell) Garland. This family lived in the part of Dover which became Somersworth, where the following children were born.* Children:

        i. George, b. 5/8/1752; d. 3/8/1778.

60.   ii. John, b. 10/4/1754.

61.   iii. James, b. 11/5/1757.

62.   iv. Thomas, b. 3/22/1760.

        v. Alexander, b. 6/1/1765; d. Somersworth, 1815, a carpenter, apparently unm.

63.   vi. Ebenezer, b. 9/1767.

        vii. Joshua, b. 3/17/1770.

        viii. Abigail, b. 3/7/1772.

---

* Hardon, Vol. I, p. 98.

FIFTH GENERATION

28. George Roberts (William[4], John[3], John[2], Thomas[1]), son of William and Elizabeth Roberts, was born in Kittery, Maine, March 30, 1704. He married Catherine Skillings, the daughter of Samuel Skillings, about February, 1730. George and Catherine moved to the Falmouth (now Portland), Maine area, where they "acknowledged the covenant" in the First Church of Falmouth, July 1, 1731. They owned property and made a number of deeds there from 1734 to 1762. George and Catherine were deceased by 1781, when some of their property was sold by their children.[*] Children:

	i.	Rhoda, bapt. 8/1731.
64.	ii.	William, bapt. 9/19/1733.
	iii.	Elizabeth, b. 3/5/1736; m. Richard Crockett, 11/14/1755.
65.	iv.	George Copson, b. 6/1/1738.
66.	v.	Joseph.
	vi.	Benjamin, b.c. 1741.
	vii.	Joshua, b.c. 1742.
	viii.	Lydia, m. Thomas Millett, 12/18/1766.

29. Love Roberts (Love[4], Thomas[3], John[2], Thomas[1]), son of Love and Elizabeth (Drew) Roberts, was born in or near Dover, New Hampshire, April 21, 1721, and died in 1780, as a result of injuries suffered during a barn raising. He married, firstly, Mary Roberts, at Portsmouth, New Hampshire, December 9, 1741, and, secondly, widow Anna (Stillings) Pray. Except for the last two, the children below were Love and Mary's. Love sold his home in Somersworth, New Hampshire, in 1775 and removed his family to Lyman, Maine.[+] Children:

67.	i.	Jedediah, b. 1745.
	ii.	Elizabeth, b. 1747; m. 5/20/1777, Mark Tate.

---

[*] Underhill, vol. I, pp. 1134-43.
[+] Hardon, Vol. I, pp. 99-103.

    iii. Joanna, b. 1749; m. 3/3/1768, Daniel Straw. 7 ch.

    iv. Hannah, m. 7/21/1774, Reuben Downs. 9 ch.

    v. Mary, b. 1757; m. 8/1777, David Hanson.

    vi. Alice, m. 2/16/1781, Jonathan Hanson.

68. vii. Moses.

69. viii. Love, b.c. 1764 (or 1756?).

    ix. Anna, b. 11/23/1764.

70. x. Peter, b. 7/1/1766.

30. Francis Roberts (Love^4, Thomas^3, John^2, Thomas^1), son of Love and Elizabeth (Drew) Roberts, was born in or near Dover, New Hampshire, June 12, 1723, and died in Somersworth, New Hampshire in 1758. He married Sarah Carr, in Newbury, Massachusetts, September 19, 1745. Sarah was the daughter of John and Elizabeth Carr. She was born, apparently in Newbury, February 4, 1721/2. Francis did not leave a will, and his estate was valued at over 5000 pounds (a fairly large amount for that era). After Francis died, Sarah married, as his second wife, Charles Baker of Rollinsford, New Hampshire.* Children:

    i. Elizabeth (Betty), b. 9/25/1746;m. John Ham. 7 ch.

    ii. Sarah, b. 6/2/1750.

71. iii. Francis, b. 4/14/1753.

    iv. John Carr, b. 12/23/1754, a joiner in Somersworth and a Revolutionary War veteran; d. 1787.

    v. Mary (Molly), b. 12/4/1756; m. Jonathan Palmer, 1771.

31. John Roberts (Timothy^4, Thomas^3, John^2, Thomas^1), son

---

* Hardon, Vol. I, pp. 104-6; Hammond, ed., *N.H. State Papers· Probate Records*, vol. 6, p. 307; *Vital Records of Newbury, MA*, Vol. II, p. 421.

FIFTH GENERATION

of Timothy and Anna (Waldron) Roberts, was born in or near Dover, New Hampshire, about 1735 and died near there in 1772 or 1773. He married Susanna Burnham, who was born at Durham, New Hampshire, January 17, 1740/1 and died August 3, 1815. Susanna was the daughter of Nathaniel and Mehitable (Colbath) Burnham. After John died Susanna married Wentworth Hayes of Rochester and Farmington, New Hampshire, March 13, 1777. John pursued a career as an inn-keeper and merchant in Rochester and Somersworth, New Hampshire. The following children were born in Somersworth.* Children:

72. i. Timothy, b. 8/3/1759.

   ii. John, b. 12/19/1761; d. 1/22/1764.

73. iii. Joseph, b. 12/29/1762.

   iv. Susanna, b. 11/7/1764; d. 11/10/1764.

   v. Relief, b. 6/22/1767; m. 6/8/1788, Daniel Horn.

32. Thomas Roberts (Timothy^4, Thomas^3, John^2, Thomas^1), son of Timothy and Anna (Waldron) Roberts, was born in or near Dover, New Hampshire, probably about 1737 and died in Rochester, New Hampshire, in 1798. His wife (or wives), whose name(s) has escaped recordation, apparently died before Thomas made his will in 1798. The three youngest daughters were under age at the time of Thomas' death, and Moses Roberts, Joshua Allen, and Wentworth Cook, all of Rochester, were named as guardians. Thomas is variously described as a colonel, gentleman, husbandman, and tax collector.⁺ Children:

74. i. John, b. 5/21/1772.

   ii. Anna, b. 1774; m. 4/23/1795, Enoch Tibbetts; d. 8/25/1828.

  iii. Mary, b. 9/18/1779; m. 1/26/1802, Daniel Currier.

---

   * Hardon, Vol. I, p. 107; Hurd, D. Hamilton. *History of Rockingham and Strafford Counties, N.H.* . . Philadelphia: J.W. Lewis & Co., 1882, p. 634.
   ⁺ Hardon, Vol. I, pp. 109-12.

DESCENDANTS OF THOMAS & REBECCA ROBERTS

    iv. Mehitable, m. 4/15/1801, Joshua Place.

    v. Sarah.

33. Timothy Roberts (Timothy[4], Thomas[3], John[2], Thomas[1]), a yeoman and "gentleman", son of Timothy and Anna (Waldron) Roberts, was baptized in Rochester, New Hampshire, May 11, 1740, and died there in 1787. He married Sarah Furber, July 16, 1761. Born at Newington, New Hampshire, March 1, 1744/5, she was the daughter of Nehemiah and Mary (Hart) Furber. Sarah died in Rochester, October 31, 1823. The children below were born in Rochester.* Children:

    i. John, bapt. 10/3/1779.

    ii. Margaret, bapt. 10/3/1779.

    iii. Mary, bapt. 10/3/1779.

    iv. Abigail, bapt. 10/3/1779.

    v. Rebecca Forst, bapt. 10/3/1779.

    vi. Sarah.

75. vii. Thomas(?), b. 1785.

34. Moses Roberts (Timothy[4], Thomas[3], John[2], Thomas[1]), son of Timothy and Anna (Waldron) Roberts, was baptized in Rochester, New Hampshire, February 9, 1755, and died some time after 1814. He married Elizabeth Wingate, the daughter of Samuel and Sarah (Titcomb) Wingate. Moses is described variously as a captain, yeoman, trader, and "gentleman". The children below were born in Rochester.⁺ Children:

    i. Elizabeth, bapt. 4/28/1781.

76. ii. Ezra, b. 1774.

    iii. Susanna, bapt. 4/28/1781; m. 10/27/1803, William Warren. Five children.

---

    * Hardon, Vol. I, p 113.
    ⁺ Hardon, Vol. I, pp. 114-5.

FIFTH GENERATION

    iv. Moses, bapt. 6/23/1782.

    v. Sarah, bapt. 4/10/1785.

35. Hatevil Roberts (Samuel[4], Hatevil[3], John[2], Thomas[1]), son of Samuel and Sarah (Lord) Roberts was born in or near Dover, New Hampshire, July 16, 1717. He married, firstly, Mary Roberts, who married, as her second husband, Job Clements of Somersworth, New Hampshire. The following children were born in Somersworth.* Children:

    i. Samuel, b. 4/12/1751.

    ii. Olive, b. 12/29/1752; m. 12/28/1775, Benjamin Philpot.

36. Benjamin Roberts (Samuel[4], Hatevil[3], John[2], Thomas[1]), son of Samuel and Sarah (Lord) Roberts, was born in Berwick, Maine, September 1, 1719, and died apparently in 1763. His wife's name was Deborah, who died after 1778. Apparently, after Benjamin died, she married Aaron Stackpole.⁺ Children:

    i. Abigail, m. Daniel Crocker Deacon, 3/30/1762, Chebogue, NS.

    ii. Joanna, m. John Spinney, 11/19/1759.

    iii. Mary, m. Ezra Churchill, 5/6/1779.

    iv. Anna, m. Nathaniel Ricker, 4/8/1782.

77.   v. Benjamin.

    vi. Daniel, b.c. 1757; d. 4/14/1850.

    vii. Samuel, b. 9/17/1763.

37. Samuel Roberts (Samuel[4], Hatevil[3], John[2], Thomas[1]), son of Samuel and Sarah (Lord) Roberts, was born in or near Dover, New Hampshire, May 7, 1723. He married Judith Randall. The

---

  * Hardon, Vol. I, p. 116.
  ⁺ Hardon, Vol. I, p. 117; Notes of Clayton H. Roberts.

following children were born in Somersworth, New Hampshire.*
Children:

    i. Ruth, b. 6/3/1754.

    ii. Sarah, b. 9/14/1755.

    iii. Hannah, b.c. 1756.

    iv. Samuel, b.c. 1758; m. 4/13/1775, Sarah Wentworth. They lived in Somerworth and Waterboro, ME. There were ch., names unknown.

78.   v. Paul, b. 11/19/1760.

    vi. Lydia, b. 1/1765.

    vii. Judith, b. 6/7/1767; m. 4/23/1792, Simeon Brock.

    viii. Deborah, b. 1/15/1770; d.c. 1857, unm.

79.   ix. Moses, b. 7/8/1777.

80.   x. Aaron, b.c. 1780.

38. Nathan Roberts (Samuel[4], Hatevil[3], John[2], Thomas[1]), son of Samuel and Sarah (Lord) Roberts, was born in or near Dover, New Hampshire, probably about 1730, and died near there before 1794. He married Olive Mason, the daughter of John and Esther (Weymouth?) Mason. Olive was born in Dover and died near there September 16, 1771. The following children were born in Somersworth.⁺ Children:

    i. Esther, b. 8/7/1754; m. 1/2/1776, Enoch Ricker. One child.

81.   ii. Hatevil, b. 12/28/1755.

---

  * Hardon, Vol. I, pp. 118-9 & Vol. II, p. 38; Wentworth, Vol. I, p. 150.
  ⁺ Hardon, Vol. I, pp. 120-3.

FIFTH GENERATION

	iii.	John, b. 1/26/1757; d. unm. 9/21/1845. A soldier in the Revolutionary War and master-at-arms on the *Ranger*. Hiram R. Roberts was granted guardianship 12/5/1843.
82.	iv.	Nathan, b. 12/26/1758.
83.	v.	Simon, b. 7/14/1760.
84.	vi.	Benjamin, b. 12/20/1761.
85.	vii.	Daniel, b. 2/15/1765.
	viii.	Eunice, b. 2/17/1767; m. 1788 Tobias Stackpole; d. 12/2/1849. Eight children.
	ix.	Joseph, b. 1/7/1769; living in 1794.

39. Thomas Roberts (Joshua^4, Hatevil^3, John^2, Thomas^1), son of Joshua and Sarah (Wallingford) Roberts, was born in Somersworth, New Hampshire, November 1, 1740, and died there July 17, 1769. He married Elizabeth Fall, the daughter of John and Lydia Fall. Elizabeth was baptized in Berwick, Maine, July 15, 1739. After Thomas died she married, secondly, William Jones of Berwick, Maine, October 25, 1773. The following children were born in Somersworth.* Children:

	i.	Mary, b. 12/1766.
86.	ii.	Jonathan, b. 11/16/1767.

40. Joshua Roberts (Joshua^4, Hatevil^3, John^2, Thomas^1), son of Joshua and Sarah (Wallingford) Roberts, was born in Somerworth, New Hampshire, July 13, 1746, and died in Brunswick, Maine, March 19, 1822. He married, firstly, Joanna Wentworth, the daughter of Mark and Elizabeth (Wentworth) Wentworth, December 8, 1766. Joanna was born in August of 1750 and died in 1785. Joshua married, secondly, the widow Elizabeth (Hughes) Nicols. Joshua was a captain in the Revolution. He entered service in 1777 as a first lieutenant in Capt. James Libbey's

---

* Hardon, Vol. I, p. 124.

Company, Col. Stephen Evans' Regiment. The first seven children below were Joanna's, born in Somersworth; the last three were either Joanna's or Elizabeth's, born in Brunswick.* Children:

	i.	Elizabeth, b. 4/25/1768; m. Moses Stevens; d. 4/14/1814.
	ii.	Sarah, b. 12/26/1770;m. Benjamin Wentworth.1 ch.
87.	iii.	Thomas, b. 9/14/1773.
	iv.	Mary, b. 1/8/1775; d. 8/19/1775.
	v.	a son, b. 1/12/1776.
	vi.	Joanna, b. 10/14/1777; m. James Tuttle; d. 9/27/1849. Seven children.
88.	vii.	Mark, b. 1/12/1779.
89.	viii.	Joshua, b. 4/7/1778 (or 1780?).
90.	ix.	Tobias, b. 3/18/1781 (or 3/21/1782?).
	x.	Mary, b. 4/7/1783; m. George (No. 126) Roberts; d. 1/14/1858.

41. Joseph Roberts (Joseph[4], Joseph[3], John[2], Thomas[1]), son of Joseph and Elizabeth (Ham) Roberts, was born in Dover, New Hampshire, February 7, 1729, and died some time after 1796. He married Elizabeth Pike, July 5, 1755, the daughter of Rev. James and Sarah (Gilman) Pike. Elizabeth was born at Somersworth, New Hampshire, February 1, 1738, and died February 2, 1810. Elizabeth was admitted to the First Church in Dover May 10, 1769. Joseph and his wife "Betty" conveyed all of their interest in the Indigo Hill Farm in Dover, and removed to Alton, New Hampshire, where the last four of their children were born. The first nine named below were born in Dover.+ Children:

---

* Hardon, Vol. I, pp. 125-8; Wentworth, Vol. I, pp. 286-7. The sources disagree over the maternity and birth dates of the last three children. If Joanna died in 1785, it seems probable that all of the children were hers.

+ Hardon, Vol. I, pp. 137-8.

FIFTH GENERATION

- 91. i. Ephraim, b. 7/14/1756.
- ii. Sarah, b. 3/14/1758; d. in infancy.
- iii. Abigail, b. 12/14/1759.
- iv. Sarah, b. 11/10/1761; prob. d. young.
- 92. v. Joseph, b. 1/10/1763.
- vi. a daughter, b. & d. 8/1764.
- vii. Elizabeth, b. 7/27/1765.
- 93. viii. James, b. 8/12/1768.
- ix. Mary, b. 8/1/1770.
- x. Daniel(twin), b. 9/10/1773.
- xi. Lydia(twin), b. 9/10/1773; d. in infancy.
- xii. Lydia, b. 12/16/1774; m. Joseph Knight. 2 ch.
- xiii. a son, apparently d. in infancy.

42. Joseph Roberts (Stephen[4], Joseph[3], John[2], Thomas[1]), son of Stephen and Keziah (Lamos) Roberts, was born in Dover, New Hampshire, June 26, 1747, and died there June 26, 1813. He married, firstly, November 24, 1773, Elizabeth Hanson, the daughter of Thomas and Hannah (Sawyer) Hanson. Elizabeth was born in Dover, May 26, 1756. Joseph married, secondly, December 8, 1784, Anna Hanson, the daughter of Maul and Ann (Austin) Hanson. Anna was born in Dover, August 3, 1764 and died there (or near there) January 12, 1832. All but the first child below were by Anna, and all of the children were born in Dover. This family was associated with the Friends meeting in Dover.* Children:

- i. Sarah, b. 4/11/1775; m. Benjamin Canney; d. 2/10/1846.
- ii. Anna, b. 11/28/1786; d. 1/27/1863.

---

* Hardon, Vol. I, pp. 141-2.

94. iii. Nicholas Hanson, b. 4/23/1789.
95. iv. Hanson, b. 1/29/1793.
    v. Peavey, b. 10/16/1795; d. 8/3/1796.
    vi. Lydia, b. 12/16/1796; d. 11/15/1798.
96. vii. Joseph, b. 5/25/1799.
    viii. Elizabeth N., b. 4/24/1804; m. 5/30/1827, Elijah Jenkins; d. 1/14/1831. One child.

43. John Roberts (Stephen^4, Joseph^3, John^2, Thomas^1), son of Stephen and Keziah (Lamos) Roberts, was born in Dover, New Hampshire, July 20, 1751, and died, apparently in North Berwick, Maine, August 20, 1817. He married, firstly, September 27, 1775, Lois Hanson, the daughter of Thomas and Hannah (Sawyer) Hanson. Lois was born in Dover, April 11, 1758. John married, secondly, January 23, 1799, Phebe Heard, the daughter of Thomas and Mary (Wentworth) Heard. Phebe was born at Berwick, Maine, August 4, 1769, and died September 16, 1848. The first twelve children below are by Lois and the last eight by Phebe. This family was associated with the Friends meeting in Dover.* Children:

97. i. Stephen, b. 12/6/1775.
    ii. Thomas, b. 8/28/1777; m. 7/17/1802, Elizabeth Quint; d. 9/3/1831.
    iii. Hannah, b. 6/19/1779; m. 6/2/1805, John Hanscom.
    iv. Joseph, b. 2/8/1781; d. by drowning, unm. 1/26/1803.
    v. John, b. 12/10/1782; m. (1) 2/22/1807, Mary Quint, (2) Julia Ann Cook.
98. vi. James, b. 11/2/1784.

* Hardon, Vol. I, pp. 140 & 148-53.

FIFTH GENERATION

	vii.	a child, b. 11/5/1786; d. 11/21/1786.
99.	viii.	Temple, b. 6/1/1788.
	ix.	Lydia, b. 3/21/1790; m. Samuel Quint.
	x.	Elijah, b. 11/2/1792; m. Mary Hanson, 10/23/1813.
	xi.	Lois, b. 1/6/1795; m. Joel Towle of Dexter, ME.
	xii.	Sarah, b. 6/3/1797; m. Mark Rollins of Vassalboro, ME.
	xiii.	Keziah, b. 11/27/1799; m. Braddock Weeks of Brunswick, ME.
100.	xiv.	David Sands, b. 1/1/1801.
101.	xv.	Nicholas Hanson, b. 3/1/1802.
	xvi.	Joseph, b. 6/15/1804.
102.	xvii.	William, b. 2/1/1806.
103.	xviii.	Oliver Heard, b. 9/20/1807.
	xix.	Mary, b. 7/2/1809; m. William Chase.
104.	xx.	Stephen, b. 9/26/1813.

44. Aaron Roberts (Ebenezer[4], Joseph[3], John[2], Thomas[1]), son of Ebenezer and Mary (Rollins) Roberts, was born about 1735 in Dover or Somersworth, New Hampshire, and died, apparently, in Berwick, Maine, January 1, 1818. He married May 5, 1768, Mary Hanson. She died in Berwick, January 29, 1819. This family was in Berwick by 1778, when Mary was admitted to the Second Church. Aaron was admitted in 1782.* Children:

	i.	Mary, b. 1769; m. 1806, Millet Hamilton.
105.	ii.	Aaron, b. 6/18/1771.

---

* Hardon, Vol. I, pp. 143-4; Dover Historical Society, pp. 170 & 193.

iii. Moses, b. 1773.

iv. Bathsheba, b. 1775; m. 1804 Oliver W. Norton.

v. William, b. 1777(?).

45. James Rollins Roberts (Ebenezer[4], Joseph[3], John[2], Thomas[1]), son of Ebenezer and Mary (Rollins) Roberts, was born in Dover or Somersworth, New Hampshire, April 24, 1737, and died in Somersworth, December 26, 1833. He is buried in the Rollinsford Cemetery. He married, about 1755, his second cousin, Elizabeth Roberts, the daughter of Joshua (No. 16) and Sarah (Wallingford) Roberts. She died August 27, 1831, age 94, and is buried in the Rollinsford Cemetery. James apparently married, secondly, Martha -----, who died in May of 1841, age 83. Martha is also buried in the Rollinsford Cemetery. James was a housewright in Somersworth. In 1823 he conveyed by gift to his grandnephew William H. Roberts land at the lower end of Cocheco Point in Dover. This transfer would suggest that James's son Joseph had departed the area by then and that his other son Moses had no living issue.[*] Children:

106.   i. Joseph, b.c. 1758.

ii. Moses, b. 12/23/1760; m. Mercy Warren; d. 8/26/1826. Both buried in Rollinsford Cemetery.

iii. Elizabeth, d. unm.

46. John Roberts (Ebenezer[4], Joseph[3], John[2], Thomas[1]), son of Ebenezer and Mary (Rollins) Roberts, was born in Somersworth, New Hampshire, in 1741 and died in Berwick, Maine, where he is buried, in 1819. He married in Berwick, December 13, 1768, Elizabeth Hodsdon, the daughter of John and Elizabeth (Wingate) Hodsdon. Elizabeth was born in Berwick, in 1740, and died and was buried there in 1825. John was a tailor in Somersworth, where he owned land, conveyed in 1817 to his son Stephen.[+] Children:

---

[*] Hardon, Vol. I, p. 146; Goss, p. 120.
[+] Hardon, Vol. I, p. 147.

FIFTH GENERATION

107.   i. Reuben, b. 1/7/1770.
108. ii. John (?), b. 12/11/1771.
109. iii. Stephen, b. 7/21/1775.
       iv. Molly, b. 2/1/1782.

47.   Ebenezer Roberts, Jr. (Ebenezer[4], Joseph[3], John[2], Thomas[1]), son of Ebenezer and Mary (Rollins) Roberts, was born in Somersworth, New Hampshire, about 1745, and died, apparently in Maine, some time after 1812. He married his second cousin once removed, Rachel Philpot, March 12, 1771. She was the daughter of John and Sarah (Roberts) Philpot and granddaughter of Samuel (No. 15) Roberts. Ebenezer Jr., a joiner, moved in 1773 to Waterboro, Maine; and in 1790 this family was in Sanford (from which Alfred was later set off). The census for that year reported a family of two males and three females, so there were daughters not reported below. In 1809 Ebenezer was declared incompetent, and his son James was appointed his guardian. In 1812 he was declared sane.* Child:

   i. James, b.c. 1775.

48.   Ichabod Roberts (Ebenezer[4], Joseph[3], John[2], Thomas[1]), son of Ebenezer and Mary (Rollins) Roberts, was born in Somersworth, New Hampshire, September 17, 1748, and died in Waterboro, Maine, December 24, 1833. He married in Somersworth on December 21, 1772, Susanna Roberts, the daughter of Joseph and Joanna (Goodwin) Roberts. Susanna was born in Somersworth, May 7, 1750. Ichabod was a veteran of the Revolution. By 1790 this family was in Waterboro, Maine.⁺ Children:

         i. Job, b. 1/19/1774, m. Jane-----. May have had a son Samuel K., b. 1812.
110.   ii. Jeremiah, b. 5/17/1775.

---

   * Hardon, Vol. I, p. 145.
   ⁺ Hardon, Vol. I, pp. 154-7; Little, p. 1634.

59

      iii. Mary.

      iv. Andrew.

      v. Susanna.

      vi. Joanna.

      vii. Rachel.

49. Edmund Roberts (Samuel^4, Joseph^3, John^2, Thomas^1), son of Samuel Roberts, was born, apparently in Somersworth, New Hampshire, September 1, 1744, and died November 19, 1787, in Portsmouth, New Hampshire. He married Sarah Griffith, the daughter of David and Sarah (Bowles) Griffith. After Edmund died Sarah married Moses Woodward of Portsmouth, September 2, 1789. Edmund was a master mariner and was a lieutenant aboard the *Hampden* in the Revolutionary War.* Children:

      i. Sarah, b. 8/7/1780.

111. ii. Edmund H., b. 6/29/1784.

50. David Roberts (Nathaniel^4, Nathaniel^3, Thomas^2, Thomas^1), son of Nathaniel and -----(Thompson) Roberts, was born in New Hampshire, some time in the 1740's. He married Elizabeth Pinkham at Dover, New Hampshire, January 13, 1762. She was the daughter of John and Phebe (Tibbetts) Pinkham. This family lived in Farmington, New Hampshire.⁺ Child:

      i. Hannah, b. 2/27/1787; m. first cousin once removed Ephraim (No. 58) Roberts, 2/4/1813; d. 3/21/1839.

51. Nathaniel Roberts (Nathaniel^4, Nathaniel^3, Thomas^2, Thomas^1), son of Nathaniel and -----(Thompson) Roberts, was born in or near Somerworth, New Hampshire, in the 1740's or early 1750's and died, apparently in Berwick, Maine, some time before 1797. His wife's name was Mary; but that is all that is known

---

    * Hardon, Vol. I, p. 158.
    ⁺ Hardon, Vol. I, p. 163.

FIFTH GENERATION

about her.* Children:

112.   i.   David, b. 1760(?).

       ii. Thomas (?).

52. George Roberts (Nathaniel⁴, Nathaniel³, Thomas², Thomas¹), son of Nathaniel and -----(Thompson) Roberts, was born in Dover or Somersworth, New Hampshire, August 21, 1755, and died May 12, 1829. He marrried, in Dover, January 17, 1782, Elizabeth Horn, the daughter of John and Mary Horn. Elizabeth was born in Dover, August 31, 1762, and died there (or near there) April 3, 1856. George was a mariner and blacksmith and gained fame as a sailor on the *Ranger* and the *Bon Homme Richard* during the Revolutionary War. (See the *Granite Monthly*, Vol. 33, p. 91).⁺ Children:

       i.   Elizabeth, b. 1783; d. unm.

113.   ii. John, b. 2/4/1788.

       iii. George.

53. Silas Roberts (Aaron⁴, Nathaniel³, Thomas², Thomas¹), a cordwainer, son of Aaron and Sarah (Tibbetts) Roberts, was born in New Hampshire in 1761 (or 1764?) and died there December 8, 1851, apparently at Tuftonboro. He married Sarah Beck, who was born in 1769 and died April 10, 1855. The children below were born in Tuftonboro.# Children:

       i.   Gideon, b. 1/28/1792; m. 2/22/1816, Abigail Eastman.

       ii. Ebenezer, b. 2/14/1794; m. Hannah -----. Lived in Alton.

       iii. Andrew, b. 3/9/1796.

       iv. George, b. 3/28/1798.

       v.   Aahalo, b. 4/10/1800.

---

* Hardon, Vol. I, p. 162.
⁺ Hardon, Vol. I, pp. 161 & 164.
Hardon, Vol. I, pp. 165-6.

vi. Sarah, b. 6/1/1802.

vii. Moses, b. 4/10/1804. Lived in Alton.

viii. Patty, b. 5/7/1806; m. 12/2/1829, David James.

ix. Mary Ann, b. 4/15/1808.

x. Samuel B., b. 2/5/1810; d. 1/20/1901.

xi. Francis Jane, b. 5/22/1813; m. 9/19/1841, John Stevens. Three children.

xii. L.F., b. 7/8/1817.

54. Daniel Roberts (Aaron^4, Nathaniel^3, Thomas^2, Thomas^1), a tailor, son of Aaron and Sarah (Tibbets) Roberts, was born in or near Dover, New Hampshire, June 12, 1772 and died thereabouts September 12, 1866. He married Hannah Gage, the daughter of Moses and Mary (Baich) Gage. Hannah was born in Dover, November 23, 1779, and died November 17, 1840. The following children were born in Dover.* Children:

114. i. Aaron, b. 5/27/1797.

115. ii. Alonzo, b. 10/11(or 31?)/1799.

iii. Mary, b. 4/17/1807.

55. Thomas Roberts (Moses^4, Nathaniel^3, Thomas^2, Thomas^1), son of Moses and Elizabeth (Whitehouse) Roberts, was born in or near Dover, New Hampshire, February 20, 1757, and died thereabouts, June 25, 1822. He married his third cousin once removed Hannah Lamos, the daughter of Nathaniel and Abigail (Roberts) Lamos and granddaughter of Stephen (No. 19) Roberts. The following children were born in Dover.⁺ Children:

116. i. James, b. 1/11/1790.

---

* Hardon, Vol. I, p. 167.
⁺ Hardon, Vol. I, pp. 175-6 & Vol. II, p. 136.

FIFTH GENERATION

      ii. Elizabeth, b. 3/29/1791; m. her fourth cousin Nicholas Hanson (No. 94) Roberts, 2/1/1813; d. 12/16/1863.

     iii. Walter, b. 8/12/1792; d. 2/18/1796.

117.   iv. Jeremiah, b. 1/14/1795.

      v. Abigail, b. 10/18/1798; m. 4/14/1825, Philip Tibbetts; d. 12/10/1872, Muscatine, Iowa. 2 ch.

     vi. (?) George K., m. Almira Pinkham. One son George Alvin Roberts, b. 6/21/1844.

56. James Roberts (Moses^4, Nathaniel^3, Thomas^2, Thomas^1), a farmer, son of Moses and Elizabeth (Whitehouse) Roberts, was born in or near Dover, New Hampshire, August 17, 1760, and died, apparently in Farmington, New Hampshire, November 17, 1849. He married March 5, 1788, Eunice Varney, the daughter of Stephen and Deliverance (Lamos) Varney. Eunice was born in Dover, December 4, 1765, and died April 23, 1836. The following children were born in Farmington.* Children:

      i. Hannah, b. 1/23/1789; m. 3/2/1809, James Bean. 11 ch.

118. ii. Thomas, b. 10/22/1790.

119. iii. Jeremiah, b. 2/14/1793.

120. iv. Moses, b. 3/11/1795.

121. v. Stephen, b. 5/29(or 25?)/1797.

     vi. Eunice, b. 8/6/1799; m. 1/4/1821, Jonathan Wingate; d. 7/11/1839. Eight children.

122. vii. Jesse, b. 5/13/1802.

     viii. Joel, b. 4/8/1805; d. unm. 10/29/1880. He was a brick maker in Rochester, NH.

123. ix. Walter, b. 5/4/1808.

---

* Hardon, Vol. I, pp. 168-173.

x. Eliza, b. 1/31/1812; m. 4/18/1839, John Beede; d. 12/6/1852. Eight ch.

57. Moses Roberts (Moses[4], Nathaniel[3], Thomas[2], Thomas[1]), son of Moses and Elizabeth (Whitehouse) Roberts, was born in or near Dover, New Hampshire, August 25, 1766, and died in Rochester, New Hampshire, July 26, 1839, and is buried in the Wingate Burying Grounds there. He married September 24, 1794, Alice Tibbetts, the daughter of Ezekiel and Ruth (Tibbets) Tibbetts. Alice was born in Rochester, August 22, 1774, and died in Bridgewater, New Hampshire, May 26, 1860. This family were members of the Society of Friends.* Children:

124.	i.	Ezekiel, b. 4/9/1796.
	ii.	Anna, b. 1/28/1798; m. James Rankin.
	iii.	Elizabeth, b. 12/26/1799; m. 9/21/1817, John Fifield.
125.	iv.	Moses, b. 1/28/1802.
	v.	Ruth, b. 4/21/1804; d. 8/13/1807.
	vi.	Mary L., b. 9/1/1806; m. 1841, William Hammond.
	vii.	Hannah, b. 8/6/1809; m. 3/10/1833, Lewis Tibbetts; d. 3/17/1879.
	viii.	Ruth Tibbetts, b. 4/15/1812; m. 2/22/1832, Frederick G. Downs of Lebanon, Me.
	ix.	Lucy M., b. 10/18/1814; m. 2/13/1840, Joshua Heard.
	x.	James H., b. 10/29/1819; d. 3/3/1823.

58. Ephraim Roberts (Moses[4], Nathaniel[3], Thomas[2], Thomas[1]), son of Moses and Elizabeth (Whitehouse) Roberts, was

---

* Hardon, Vol. 1, pp. 179-83; Jarvis, *N.E.H.G.R.*, Vol. XCIX, p. 111; Goss, p. 118.

FIFTH GENERATION

born in or near Dover, New Hampshire, March 27, 1772, and died, apparently at Farmington, New Hampshire, September 25, 1857. He married at Rochester, New Hampshire, February 4, 1813, his first cousin once removed Hannah Roberts, the daughter of David (No. 50) and Elizabeth (Langley) Roberts. Ephraim served as selectman of Farmington in 1808, 1822, and 1824-6. He was declared incompetent in 1857, shortly before his death.* Children:

  i. Amasa, b. 3/2/1812; m. Juliette W. Perkins; d.s.p. 5/8/1877. He was a graduate of Dartmouth, a lawyer in Dover, and registrar of probates there.

  ii. Emily, b. 12/26/1815; m. George Leighton; d. 12/15/1855. Five children.

  iii. Andietta L., b. 10/11/1820; m. 3/23/1842, David L. Drew; d.s.p.v. 2/28/1843.

59. John Roberts (Ebenezer[4], John[3], Thomas[2], Thomas[1]), son of Ebenezer and Sarah (Miller) Roberts, was born in Somersworth, New Hampshire, August 5, 1770 and died in Berwick, Maine (or possibly Rollinsford, New Hampshire), August 12, 1834. He married his third cousin twice removed Elizabeth Hall, the daughter of William and Sarah (Roberts) Hall. Elizabeth was born in North Berwick, Maine, February 16, 1791, and died November 30, 1831.+ Child:

  i. Ebenezer, b. 11/23/1824; d. unm. 5/18/1899. A farmer in Rollinsford.

60. John Roberts (Alexander[4], John[3], Thomas[2], Thomas[1]), son of Alexander and Rebecca (Garland) Roberts, was born in Somersworth, New Hampshire, October 4, 1754 and died there (or near there) July 20, 1837. His wife's name was Hannah. It is thought that her maiden name was either Brown or Roberts.# Children:

---

  * Hardon, Vol. I, pp. 184-5. Elizabeth Langley may have been a second wife of David. Alternatively, Hardon was in error; and Hannah's mother was Elizabeth (Pinkham) Roberts.
  + Hardon, Vol. I, p. 97.
  # Hardon, Vol. I, p. 186.

i. a daughter, b. 1779.

126.   ii. George, b. 1782.

iii. (?) Thomas, b. 1785(?).

61. James Roberts (Alexander[4], John[3], Thomas[2], Thomas[1]), son of Alexander and Rebecca (Garland) Roberts, was born in Somersworth, New Hampshire, November 5, 1757, and died in or near there, May 5, 1806. He married August 18, 1779, Martha Goodwin, who was born in Somersworth, February 10, 1761, and died May 1, 1844. James was a joiner and a veteran of the Revolutionary War.* Children:

    i. George, b. 5/11/1780; d. 5/19/1786.

    ii. Dorcas, b. 12/14/1782; m. Jonathan Moulton. 1 ch.

    iii. Sabra, b. 4/1/1785; d.unm. 6/23/1845.

    iv. Ruth, b. 9/13/1787; m. Benjamin Hawks, Windham, ME

    v. Lydia, b. 4/19/1790; d. 10/11/1790.

    vi. Abigail, b. 9/20/1791; m. Silas Leighton.

    vii. Huldah, b. 6/26/1794; m. 2/12/1814, James H. Horn of Milton, NH.

    viii. Louisa, m. Webster Miller.

    ix. Clifford, b. 1798(?).

    x. Lydia G., b. 1800(?); m. 11/13/1828, Benjamin G. Twombly. One child.

    xi. Martha, b. 1802(?), m. George Hale of Westbrook, ME.

    xii. Granville C., of Westbrook, ME.

62. Thomas Roberts (Alexander[4], John[3], Thomas[2], Thomas[1]), a tailor, son of Alexander and Rebecca (Garland) Roberts, was born in Somersworth, New Hampshire, March 22, 1760 and died there,

---

* Hardon, Vol. I, pp. 187-92.

FIFTH GENERATION

December 7, 1810. He married, January 28, 1790, Elizabeth Garvin, the daughter of James and Sarah (Hobbs) Garvin. Elizabeth was born in Somersworth, May 3, 1772, and died there, November 30, 1831. The following children were born in Somersworth.*
Children:

    i. Elizabeth, b. 12/30/1790; m. 5/14/1818(?), Dudley Roberts, the son of Heard and Mary (Watson) Roberts; d. 12/1831. Two children.

    ii. Sarah, b. 9/23/1792; d. 8/23/1813.

    iii. Edward, b. 8/17/1794; d. 12/21/1795.

    iv. Clarissa, b. 10/22/1796; m. Jonathan Place; d. 10/22/1818. One child.

127.   v. George W., b. 9/23/1798.

    vi. Alexander, b. 8/4/1800; d. 5/28/1825 of consumption.

    vii. Lydia, b. 5/6/1802.

    viii. Joshua Thomas, b. 3/6/1804; d. 3/7/1804.

    ix. Rebecca, b. 4/27/1805; m. 1/5/1832, William P. Barker of Kennebunk, ME.

    x. Thomas Joshua, b. 6/11/1807; m. 10/15(or 14?)/1832, Dorothy J. Wentworth; d. 2/18/1834. One child died in infancy.

    xi. Edward, b. 7/21/1809; d. 3/1/1812.

63. Ebenezer Roberts (Alexander[4], John[3], Thomas[2], Thomas[1]), son of Alexander and Rebecca (Garland) Roberts, was born in Somersworth, New Hampshire, in September of 1767 and died in 1823, apparently in Wolfeboro, New Hampshire. He married November 28, 1799, Sarah Roberts, the daughter of Colonel James and Martha (Woodsum) Roberts. Sarah was born in

---

* Hardon, Vol. I, pp. 193-5; Wentworth, Vol I, p. 513.

DESCENDANTS OF THOMAS & REBECCA ROBERTS

Berwick, Maine. The following children were born in Wolfeboro.*
Children:

	i.	Sarah, b. 10/18/1806; m. Daniel Deland.
	ii.	Robert, b. 4/20/1808, m. Elizabeth Shepard.
	iii.	Hannah, b. 6/18/1810; m. Daniel Shepard.
	iv.	James, b. 1/20/1813, m. Louisa Roberts.
	v.	Elizabeth, b. 1815(?); m. 7/2/1835, Michael Tibbetts of Berwick, ME. Two children.
	vi.	John, b. 12/10/1818; m. Emily Marden.
128.	vii.	Joshua, b.c. 1820.

---

* Hardon, Vol. I, pp. 196-8 & Vol. II, pp. 147-9.

SIXTH GENERATION

64. William Roberts (George⁵, William⁴, John³, John², Thomas¹), son of George and Catherine (Skillings) Roberts, was baptized in Falmouth, Maine, September 19, 1733. His wife's name was Molly. Nothing else is known about this family, other than that they lived in Sidney, Maine, and had the following children.*
Children:

    i. Mary, b. 1/29/1763.

    ii. William, b. 3/29/1765.

    iii. Sarah, b. 8/30/1767.

    iv. Temperance, b. 7/13/1770.

    v. Samuel, b. 12/27/1777.

    vi. Joanna, b. 8/30/1779.

65. George Copson Roberts (George⁵, William⁴, John³, John², Thomas¹), son of George and Catherine (Skillings) Roberts, was born in Falmouth, Maine, June 1, 1738, and died in Cape Elizabeth, Maine, August 28, 1824. He married October 20, 1759, Deborah York, daughter of Samuel and Joanna (Skillings) York, of Cape Elizabeth. This family lived for many years at Long Creek, in Cape Elizabeth. George was a veteran of the Penobscot campaign, during the French and Indian War.⁺ Children:

    i. Deborah, m. Nathaniel Skillings, 4/28/1796.

    ii. Richard.

    iii. George, m. Susan Woodbury, 12/16/1805.

66. Joseph Roberts (George⁵, William⁴, John³, John², Thomas¹), son of George and Catherine (Skillings) Roberts, was born in Falmouth, Maine, between 1739 and 1745. He married Ruth White, probably the daughter of William and Christina (Simonton) White, April 12, 1767, in St. Paul's Episcopal Church in Falmouth. Ruth died May 12, 1784, aged 40. Joseph served in

---

    * Underhill, vol. I, p. 1140; I.G.I.
    ⁺ Underhill, vol. I, p. 1141.

the French and Indian War.* Children:

129.   i. John, b. 10/26/1769.

130.   ii. George, b. 3/1/1773.

      iii. Polly, bapt. 10/31/1780; m. Henry McKenney, 10/2/1803.

      iv. Priscilla, b. 5/1784; m. James Slater, 9/23/1804; d. 5/26/1806. One child.

67. Jedediah Roberts (Love^5, Love^4, Thomas^3, John^2, Thomas^1), son of Love and Mary (Roberts) Roberts, was born in Somerworth, Maine, in 1745. He married Eunice Pray. The following children were born in Somersworth. Apparently, this family also lived in Shapleigh, Maine.⁺ Children:

      i. Mary, b. 3/28/1766.

      ii. Dorothy, b. 11/6/1768; m. Benjamin Estes of Berwick, ME, 2/24/1791(?).

      iii. Alice, b. 11/7(or 9?)/1770.

      iv. Hannah, b. 12/30/1772; m. 6/17/1807, Joseph Quint of Topsham & Sanford, ME. Two ch.

      v. Eunice, b. 11/26/1774.

131.   vi. Jedediah, b. 11/19/1776.

68. Moses Roberts (Love^5, Love^4, Thomas^3, John^2, Thomas^1), son of Love and Mary (Roberts) Roberts, was born, apparently in Somersworth, New Hampshire. He and wife (name unknown) lived in Kennebunk and Wiscasset, Maine.# Children:

      i. Moses, a farmer; m. Melinda -----.

      ii. James, a farmer; m. Hannah -----.

69. Love Roberts (Love^5, Love^4, Thomas^3, John^2, Thomas^1),

---

   * Underhill, vol. I, pp. 1143-65.
   ⁺ Hardon, Vol. II, pp. 1-2.
   # Hardon, Vol. II, p. 13.

SIXTH GENERATION

son of Love and Mary (Roberts) Roberts, was born in Somersworth, New Hampshire in 1756 (or about 1764?), and died at Lebanon, Maine, November 14, 1840. He married, firstly, (Elizabeth Brown?), and, secondly, Anna (Cook) Libby, the widow of Samuel Libby, January 6, 1820, in Shapleigh, Maine. Love married, thirdly, Elizabeth Hershom, the daughter of Benjamin and Dorcas (Ricker) Hershom, in Lebanon, Maine, November 14, 1833. Love was a veteran of the Revolution. In 1783 he bought land in Shapleigh, and in 1809 and 1814 he sold land and part ownership in a mill at Milton, New Hampshire.* Children:

	i.	Elizabeth, b. 8/17/1779; m. Timothy Wentworth 9/21/1800. Eight children.
132.	ii.	James, b. 9/9(or 7?)/1782.
133.	iii.	Love, b. 4/8/1784(or 1785?).
134.	iv.	Paul, b. 4/17/1786.
	v.	Sarah, b. 9/25/1787; m. John Kimball, 7/10/1810; d. 9/4/1819. Four children.
	vi.	Mary ("Polly"), b. 7/23/1789; m. 11/10/1808, Daniel Fox. Three children.
135.	vii.	Ezekiel, b. 4/8/1791.
	viii.	Hannah, b. 4/15/1795; m. 1/28/1818, Wentworth Lowd; d. 8/26/1849. Nine children.
	ix.	Martha, b. 6/6/1797; m. 1/4/1816, James Jones.
	x.	Charles, b. 11/11/1799.
	xi.	Clarissa, b. 1800.
	xii.	Nancy, b. 7/2/1804.

70. Peter Roberts (Love^5, Love^4, Thomas^3, John^2, Thomas^1), son of Love and Anna (Stillings) Roberts, was born, apparently in Somersworth, New Hampshire, July 1, 1766. He married Abigail

---

* Hardon, Vol. II, pp. 3-12.

Wakefield in 1787. She was born in Maine, August 27, 1770, and died there June 12, 1852. In 1790 this family was of Coxhall (Lyman), Maine, where the following children were born.* Children:

- 136. i. James Wakefield, b. 9/7/1788
-       ii. Anna.
-       iii. Amos.
- 137. iv. Joseph Dennett, b. 8/29/1796.
- 138. v. John, b. 1800.
-       vi. Ivory, b. 6/21/1802, m. Nancy C. Fall.
- 139. vii. Nahum, b. 4/16/1804.
-       viii. Sarah.
- 140. ix. Dimon, b. 1/1/1810.

71. Francis Roberts (Francis[5], Love[4], Thomas[3], John[2], Thomas[1]), a joiner, son of Francis and Sarah (Carr) Roberts, was born in Somerworth, New Hampshire, April 14, 1753. He married Jane Lovering.⁺ Children:

- i. Richard Smith, a mason in Boston, MA.
- ii. Jane, m. 4th cousin Reuben (No. 154) Roberts.

72. Timothy Roberts (John[5], Timothy[4], Thomas[3], John[2], Thomas[1]), son of John and Susanna (Burnham) Roberts, was born in Somerworth, New Hampshire, August 3, 1759, and died August 3, 1835. He married his stepsister Elizabeth Hayes, November 28, 1782. The daughter of Wentworth and Mary (Main) Hayes, Elizabeth was born in Rochester, New Hampshire, July 24, 1757. Timothy was an officer in the Revolutionary War, and also was a sailor. The following children were born in Milton, New Hampshire.# Children:

---

* Hardon, Vol. II, pp. 14-5 & Vol. III, pp. 53, 78, 83 & 92.
⁺ Hardon, Vol. II, pp. 16 & 153.
Hardon, Vol. II, pp. 17-20.

SIXTH GENERATION

141. i.   James, b. 12/24/1783.
142. ii. John, b. 2/4/1788.
      iii. Elizabeth, b. 5/31/1790; m. 10/17/1816, Charles Corson of Lebanon, NH. Eight children.
      iv. Mary Main, b. 1/20/1791(?), m. 1811, David Jones of Lebanon, NH; d. 5/16/1868, Union, NH. Ten ch.
143. v.   Wentworth.
      vi. Hezekiah, d. unm.
144. vii. Amos Main, b. 5/6/1801.

73. Joseph Roberts (John^5, Timothy^4, Thomas^3, John^2, Thomas^1), son of John and Susanna (Burnham) Roberts, was born in Somersworth, New Hampshire, December 29, 1762, and died there, January 15, 1841. He married Elizabeth Dame, the daughter of Joseph Dame, July 29, 1784. She was born in Rochester, New Hampshire, in 1763, and died in Somersworth, April 15, 1841. Their homestead was at the turn of the road between Rochester and Farmington, near Rattlesnake Brook. (It was destroyed in a fire in 1933.) Joseph was a captain in the Revolution and a marine on the *Ranger*.* Children:

145. i.   Jonathan Dame, b. 1785.
      ii. Elizabeth, b. 1788; m. 12/14/1809, Joseph Jones; d. 5/4/1870. Six children.
146. iii. John, b. 1789.
      iv. Tamsen, m. 3/12/1826, Jeremiah Jones. One child.
      v.   Susan H., m. 3/18/1816, Joseph Hammons.
147. vi. Joseph, b. 5/29/1797.

---

* Hardon, Vol. II, pp. 21-31 & Vol. III, p. 127.

DESCENDANTS OF THOMAS & REBECCA ROBERTS

148.   vii.   Nathaniel Burnham, b. 8/4/1799.

          viii.   Tryphena Burnham, b. 4/8/1802; m. 5/22/1825, Joseph C. Wentworth of Milton, NH; d. 7/17/1882. Six children.

149.   ix.   Jeremiah, b. 11/28/1804.

          x.   James Madison, b. 7/3/1808; d. 3/14/1892. Will dated 1886 names only niece Julia M. Smith.

74. John Roberts (Thomas^5, Timothy^4, Thomas^3, John^2, Thomas^1), son of Thomas Roberts, was born in or near Rochester, New Hampshire, May 21, 1772, and died thereabouts, June 3, 1847. He married Abigail Jones, October 4, 1792, the daughter of Joseph and Lydia Jones. Abigail was born in Farmington, New Hampshire, in 1769, and died thereabouts August 18, 1848. John owned land in Rochester, where the following children were born. He is described in various deeds as a farmer and gentleman.* Children:

          i.   Sarah, m. 1/30/1820, Benjamin Plummer.

          ii.   Rebecca, b.c. 1802; d. unm.

          iii.   Anna W., b.c. 1804; m. 3/1/1824, Daniel Rogers.

150.   iv.   John Love, b. 8/18/1805.

          v.   Lydia M., b.c. 1808; m. 12/15/1829, Joseph Dame.

          vi.   Abigail Corson, b. 1810; m. 4/17/1831, James W. Downs; d. 12/24/1886. One child.

75. Thomas Roberts (Timothy^5, Timothy^4, Thomas^3, John^2, Thomas^1), a farmer, son of Timothy and Sarah (Furber) Roberts, was born in Rochester, New Hampshire, in 1785, and died some time after 1860. He married Mehitable Jones, January 19, 1809. The following children were born in Rochester.⁺ Children:

---

     * Hardon, Vol. II, pp. 33-5.
     ⁺ Hardon, Vol. II, p. 36 & Vol. III, pp. 135-6.

SIXTH GENERATION

       i. Anna W., b. 1810; m. 1833, Jewett Wrisley; d. 10/24/1882. No children.

151.   ii. William Jones, b. 3/2/1812.

152.   iii. Levi F., b. 11/2/1829.

76. Ezra Roberts (Moses[5], Timothy[4], Thomas[3], John[2], Thomas[1]), son of Moses and Elizabeth (Wingate) Roberts, was born in Rochester, New Hampshire, in 1774, was baptized there April 28, 1781, and died there March 1, 1854. He married Mary Willey, December 20, 1798. She was born at New Durham, New Hampshire, November 18, 1781, and died in Rochester, September 3, 1845.* Child:

       i. Mary G., b. 7/3/1807; d. unm. 1/29/1894.

77. Benjamin Roberts (Benjamin[5], Samuel[4], Hatevil[3], John[2], Thomas[1]), son of Benjamin and Deborah Roberts, was born about 1754 and died March 21, 1824. He married Didamia Nickerson, March 21, 1775. She was the daughter of Elisha and Desire Nickerson and was born March 15, 1756 and died June 16, 1849.⁺ Children:

       i. Benjamin, b. 12/3/1776.

       ii. Eunice, b. 1/2/1779.

       iii. Mercy, b. 7/21/1781.

       iv. Deidamia, b. 7/3/1784.

       v. Elizabeth, b. 10/21/1786.

       vi. Rhoda, b. 7/9/1789.

       vii. Susannah, b. 3/9/1793.

153.   viii. Joseph D., b. 8/21/1795.

78. Paul Roberts (Samuel[5], Samuel[4], Hatevil[3], John[2], Thomas[1]), son of Samuel and Judith (Randall) Roberts, was born November

---

* Hardon, Vol. I, p. 114.
⁺ Clayton H. Roberts notes.

19, 1760, in Somersworth, New Hampshire, and died in 1840, apparently in Maine. He married Elizabeth Floyd. Paul served in the Revolutionary War and was present at the execution of the infamous spy Major Andre. After the War he removed to Maine, where he lived in Lebanon, Acton, and Newfield.* Child:

    154.   i. Reuben.

79. Moses Roberts (Samuel[5], Samuel[4], Hatevil[3], John[2], Thomas[1]), son of Samuel and Judith (Randall) Roberts, was born in Somersworth, New Hampshire, July 8, 1777. He married Nancy Butler, October 26, 1800. She was the daughter of Charles and Sarah (Cross) Butler. This family lived in the part of Somersworth which became Rollinsford in 1849.+ Children:

    i.   Sophia, b. 7/9/1801; d. unm. 11/18/1887.

    ii.   Nancy(?).

80. Aaron Roberts (Samuel[5], Samuel[4], Hatevil[3], John[2], Thomas[1]), son of Samuel and Judith (Randall) Roberts, was born in Somersworth, New Hampshire, about 1780, and died there in 1837. He married Sarah Nock, in 1798. She was born in Berwick, Maine, and died some time after her husband. This family lived in the part of Somersworth which became Rollinsford in 1849. The following children were born there.# Children:

    i.   Mary Jane, b. 3/17/1800; m. Oliver Ricker of Brooklyn, NY; d. 8/1885. At least one child.

    ii.   Elias, m. Sarah -----; lived in Brooklyn, NY.

    iii.   Samuel, m. Ann Reeves. Merchant in NY City.

    iv.   Paul, m. 11/16/1840, Judith Welch. Lived in New York City, Buffalo & Tonawanda, NY.

    v.   Zaccheus. A merchant in St. Louis, MO.

---

* Hardon, Vol. II, p. 39.
+ Hardon, Vol. II, p. 40.
# Hardon, Vol. II, pp. 41-5 & Vol. III, pp. 155-7.

SIXTH GENERATION

155.   vi.   Aaron, b. 9/23/1817.

   vii. Ruth, m. 2/8/1832, Robert Guptill. Two children.

   viii. Judith, m. Charles Wormwood. Two children.

   ix. Susan, b. 2/17/1815; m. John A. Guptill of Chelsea, MA; d. 6/17/1857. Six children.

81. Hatevil Roberts (Nathan^5, Samuel^4, Hatevil^3, John^2, Thomas^1), son of Nathan and Olive (Mason) Roberts, was born in Somersworth, New Hampshire, December 28, 1755. His wife Mehitable died in Berwick, Maine, December 16, 1810.* Child:

   i. Elizabeth, m. 1805, Ebenezer Pray.

82. Nathan Roberts (Nathan^5, Samuel^4, Hatevil^3, John^2, Thomas^1), son of Nathan and Olive (Mason) Roberts, was born in Somersworth, New Hampshire, December 26, 1758, and died there March 2, 1835. He married Hannah W. Plummer, in Somersworth, March 17, 1786. Nathan was a veteran of the Revolutionary War. In 1826 he was declared incompetent, and John Wentworth was appointed his guardian, October 17, 1826. The following children were born in Somersworth.⁺ Children:

   i. Judith, b. 1786; m. -----Hutchins of Berwick, ME.

   ii. George, b. 1788; d. 1830.

   iii. John G., b. 1792 or 1793; d. 1873.

83. Simon Roberts (Nathan^5, Samuel^4, Hatevil^3, John^2, Thomas^1), son of Nathan and Olive (Mason) Roberts, was born in Somersworth, New Hampshire, July 14, 1760, and died October 5, 1832, in Maine. The name of his wife is not known. Simon served in the Revolution, was a sailor on the *Hampden*, and was present when the infamous spy Major Andre was executed. Later he moved to Maine, and was in Acton and Berwick.# Children:

---

 * Hardon, Vol. II, p. 46.
 ⁺ Hardon, Vol. II, p. 47 & Vol. III, pp. 116-7.
 # Hardon, Vol. II, p. 48.

DESCENDANTS OF THOMAS & REBECCA ROBERTS

        i.   James.

        ii. Hiram.

        iii. Elizabeth.

156. iv. Simon.

84. Benjamin Roberts (Nathan[5], Samuel[4], Hatevil[3], John[2], Thomas[1]), son of Nathan and Olive (Mason) Roberts, was born in Somersworth, New Hampshire, December 20, 1761, and died, apparently in Rochester, New Hampshire, April 3, 1830. On November 7, 1785, he married Sarah Stevens, who was born in 1757. Benjamin was a veteran of the Revolution, but was unable to claim a pension for his service, apparently due to the fact he owned too much property. This family owned land in Rochester and Farmington.[*] Children:

157. i.   Caleb, b. 1798.

        ii. Mary, b. 1810; prob. d. unm.

        iii. Elizabeth, b. 1817; m. Richard Garland.

85. Daniel Roberts (Nathan[5], Samuel[4], Hatevil[3], John[2], Thomas[1]), son of Nathan and Olive (Mason) Roberts, was born in Somersworth, New Hampshire, February 15, 1765, and died apparently in Rollinsford, New Hampshire, October 20, 1840. He married Susan Hobbs, who was born in Somersworth (later Rollinsford), where the following child was also born.[+] Child:

        i. Rebecca Hobbs, b. 7/12/1793; m. 12/25/1824, John Garvin; d. 5/13/1893. Six children.

86. Jonathan Roberts (Thomas[5], Joshua[4], Hatevil[3], John[2], Thomas[1]), son of Thomas and Elizabeth (Fall) Roberts, was born in Somersworth, New Hampshire, November 16, 1767, and died, apparently in Barnstead, New Hampshire, October 24, 1823. He married Elizabeth Foss, January 14, 1789, in Barrington, New Hampshire. She was the daughter of Joshua and Abigail (Locke)

---

[*] Hardon, Vol. II, p. 49.
[+] Hardon, Vol. II, pp. 50-1.

SIXTH GENERATION

Foss. Elizabeth was born in Barrington, January 22, 1768, and died August 24, 1855. Jonathan was a blacksmith and town officer of Barrington, where he moved after selling land in Somersworth inherited from his grandfather Joshua Roberts. He and wife Elizabeth sold all of their land in Barrington and bought a homestead in Barnstead in 1806. The first eight children below were born in Barrington, the balance in Barnstead.* Children:

158.   i. Joshua, b. 7/2/1789.

        ii. Thomas, b. 4/23/1791.

        iii. David, b. 4/19/1793.

        iv. Mary J., b. 2/28/1795; m. 1816, Nathaniel Wilson.

        v. William, b. 3/31/1797; d. 9/30/1813.

        vi. Daniel, b. 7/12/1799. Went west.

        vii. Elizabeth Fall, b. 3/19/1802; m. Caleb Pickering; d. 10/12/1890. At least two children.

        viii. Asa, b. 3/1/1805; d. 2/12/1806.

        ix. Jonathan, b. 4/9/1807; d. 7/2/1816.

159.   x. Tobias, b. 7/11/1809.

160.   xi. George Seward, b. 10/8/1811.

161.   xii. William, b. 7/2(or 1?)/1814.

87. Thomas Roberts (Joshua^5, Joshua^4, Hatevil^3, John^2, Thomas^1), a mariner, son of Joshua and Joanna (Wentworth) Roberts, was born in Somersworth, New Hampshire, September 14, 1773, and died at sea, of smallpox. He married Lydia Plummer.⁺ Children:

---

* Hardon, Vol. II, pp. 52-5.
⁺ Hardon, Vol. II, p. 57; Wentworth, Vol. I, pp. 286-7.

DESCENDANTS OF THOMAS & REBECCA ROBERTS

    i. Joanna, b. 5/30/1796; m. Hubbard Goldsmith of Ossipee, NH.

    ii. Abigail, b. 8/29/1798; m. John S. Wentworth.

88. Mark Roberts (Joshua^5, Joshua^4, Hatevil^3, John^2, Thomas^1), son of Joshua and Joanna (Wentworth) Roberts, was born in Somersworth, New Hampshire, January 12, 1779, and died May 12, 1852. He married Sarah Thompson, who died November 30, 1840. Mark was a veteran of the War of 1812.* Children:

    i. Benjamin Thompson, b. 9/29/1804.

    ii. Joanna, b. 12/3/1806; m. Samuel Wise.

    iii. Mary Adaline, b. 12/23/1808; m. Joseph Nash.

    iv. Rhoda, b. 2/21/1811; m. Howard Small.

    v. Isaac, b. 12/26/1815.

    vi. Emeline, b. 4/1/1818; m. John Robinson; d. 8/5/1856.

    vii. Hannah, b. 3/5/1822; m. Morris Crisp.

89. Joshua Roberts (Joshua^5, Joshua^4, Hatevil^3, John^2, Thomas^1), son of Joshua and Elizabeth (Hughes) Roberts or Joanna (Wentworth) Roberts, was born in Brunswick, Maine, April 7, 1778 (or 1780?), and died August 21, 1822. He married Sarah (or Sally) Powers, who was born October 8, 1787, and died January 28, 1859.⁺ Children:

    i. Thomas, b. 11/22/1805; d. 3/31/1835.

    ii. Milton, b. 2/13/1807; d. 2/16/1840.

    iii. Sarah, b. 3/3/1809; m. Addison Saunders; d. 2/16/1852.

    iv. a daughter, b. 5/29/1811; m. Joseph Howard.

---

* Hardon, Vol. II, pp. 60-4; Wentworth, Vol. I, pp. 286-7.
⁺ Hardon, Vol. II, pp. 65-9; Wentworth, Vol. I, pp. 286-7.

SIXTH GENERATION

    v.   John, b. 5/1813; d. 4/17/1817.

    vi. Elizabeth, b. 6/7/1815; m. Asa Howard; d. 5/18/1861.

    vii. Leonora, b. 5/14/1817; m. Zenas W. Bartlett.

    viii. James, b. 7/16/1820.

    ix. Joanna, b. 9/26/1822; m. Hall B. Willis.

90. Tobias Roberts (Joshua^5, Joshua^4, Hatevil^3, John^2, Thomas^1), son of Joshua and Elizabeth (Hughes) Roberts or Joanna (Wentworth) Roberts, was born in Brunswick, Maine, March 18, 1781 (or March 21, 1782?), and died, apparently in Strafford, New Hampshire, January 12, 1833. He married July 5, 1807, Lydia Yeaton, who was born September 14, 1789, and died March 12, 1854. Tobias was a blacksmith and a member of the state legislature in 1824-7. In his will he gave his real estate to his son Joshua.* Children:

         i.   Joanna W., b. 3/13/1811; m. William T. Blake, 11/6/1836; d. 8/28/1850.

         ii. Marcia (or Mercy?), b. 2/24/1813; m. David Hayes, 11/6/1836; d. 6/11/1861. No children.

162.   iii. Joshua, b. 4/21/1815.

         iv. Mary Jane, b. 7/18/1817; m. Joseph Hayes, 6/5/1840; d. 8/28/1842. No children.

163.   v.   Tobias Westerly, b. 8/16/1820.

164.   vi. John Yeaton, b. 10/20/1826.

         vii. Samuel H., b. 1830; d. 3/26/1854.

91. Ephraim Roberts (Joseph^5, Joseph^4, Joseph^3, John^2, Thomas^1), son of Joseph and Elizabeth (Pike) Roberts, was born in Dover, New Hampshire, July 14, 1756, and died June 17, 1835. He married Sarah Willey, November 30, 1788. She was born in

---

* Hardon, Vol. II, pp. 70-1; Wentworth, Vol. I, pp. 286-7.

DESCENDANTS OF THOMAS & REBECCA ROBERTS

Durham, New Hampshire, February 1, 1761, and died February 22, 1842. Ephraim's house in New Durham Gore (now Alton), New Hampshire, was built in 1794. The property was in the possession of Ella S. (Trask) Roberts, widow of Sewell E. Roberts, in 1930. The following children were all born in Alton.* Children:

    i. James Pike, b. 10/2/1790; d. 12/18/1829. Lived in Acton, ME.

    ii. Samuel, b. 2/13/1792.

    iii. Sarah B., b. 11/18/1794; m. Ephraim Langley; d. 4/16/1883. Two children.

    iv. Joseph, b. 6/29/1797; m. Susan Langley; d. 5/27/1865. No children.

    v. John, b. 9/9/1799.

    vi. Hannah L., b. 12/23/1802.

    vii. Joseph March, b. 11/18/1814.

92. Joseph Roberts (Joseph^5, Joseph^4, Joseph^3, John^2, Thomas^1), son of Joseph and Elizabeth (Pike) Roberts, was born in Dover, New Hampshire, January 10, 1763, and died August 15, 1833. He married Anna Trevett, who was born in 1762 and died July 18, 1826. Joseph was a farmer in Alton, New Hampshire. He is referred to as a "gentleman" and was commissioned a lieutenant in the militia, January 20, 1789.⁺ Children:

165.   i. Richard, b. 4/4/1788.

    ii. Joseph, b. 2/1/1790; d. 8/24/1791.

    iii. Nancy, b. 2/12/1792; m. (1) 12/25/1817, Joseph Sawyer, (2) 11/6/1832, Timothy Pendergast.

    iv. Hannah S., b. 7/8/1796; m. Solomon Hayes, 9/29/1833; d. 5/13/1862. No children.

---

* Hardon, Vol. II, pp. 72-3 & Vol. IV, p. 25.
⁺ Hardon, Vol. II, pp. 74-6.

SIXTH GENERATION

    v. Mary (Polly), b. 10/23/1798; m. Jonathan McDuffee, 3/18/1824. Two children.

    vi. Martha T., b. 3/25/1801; m. William C. Crockett, 5/14/1833; d. 11/5/1865. No children.

    vii. Joseph, b. 8/26/1804; d. 10/4/1804.

93. James Roberts (Joseph^5, Joseph^4, Joseph^3, John^2, Thomas^1), son of Joseph and Elizabeth (Pike) Roberts, was born in Dover, New Hampshire, August 12, 1768, and died some time after 1834. He married Mary Leighton, November 10, 1791, at New Durham, New Hampshire. This family lived in Alton, where the following children were born, and Farmington, New Hampshire.* Children:

166.   i. Nathaniel, b. 12/8/1792.

    ii. Stephen, b. 10/14/1795; d. 5/8/1798.

    iii. Abigail, b. 3/27/1801(?); d. 1/20/1804.

    iv. Moses, b. 5/8/1801.

    v. Jonathan, b. 7/20/1804; d. 6/20/1805.

    vi. Mary, b. 4/14/1809.

    vii. William Wingate, b. 12/26/1815. A farmer in Rochester, NH.

94. Nicholas Hanson Roberts (Joseph^5, Stephen^4, Joseph^3, John^2, Thomas^1), son of Joseph and Anna (Hanson) Roberts, was born in Dover, New Hampshire, April 23, 1789, and died December 15, 1857. He married a fourth cousin, Elizabeth Roberts, December 1, 1813. She was the daughter of Thomas (No. 55) and Hannah (Lamos) Roberts. Nicholas was in the Alms House in Dover in 1850. The children below were all born in Dover. This family attended the Quaker Dover Monthly Meeting, but were later

---

* Hardon, Vol. II, pp. 77-8.

disowned by that group.⁺ Children:

    i. Charlotte G., b. 9/9/1814.

    ii. Joseph (twin), b. 9/10/1818; d. 9/17/1831.

    iii. Thomas (twin), b. 9/10/1818.

    iv. Walter, b. 10/17/1823; d. 11/29/1824.

    v. Hannah E., b. 10/25/1825; d. 3/13/1826.

    vi. George K., b. 4/27/1827; d. 9/10/1830.

    vii. Francis A., b. 10/25/1831; d. 9/23/1855.

95. Hanson Roberts (Joseph^5, Stephen^4, Joseph^3, John^2, Thomas^1), a farmer, son of Joseph and Anna (Hanson) Roberts, was born in Dover, New Hampshire, January 29, 1793, and died there August 27, 1870. He married Lydia Henderson, the daughter of Thomas Henderson, February 5, 1814. She was born in Dover, November 13, 1792, and died August 24, 1870. The following children were born in Dover. This family attended the Quaker Dover Monthly Meeting. Hanson was disowned for "marrying out", but apparently Lydia became a Quaker, and the family was reinstated.⁺ Children:

    i. Charles W., b. 1/29/1815.

    ii. Eliza Ann, b. 12/12/1816; m. 4/5/1855, Andrew Tetherly; d. 11/26/1885. Two children.

167.   iii. John, b. 2/12/1819.

    iv. Samuel H., b. 4/30/1821; d. unm. 2/16/1880.

168.   v. Oliver L., b. 7/8/1823.

169.   vi. Thomas H., b. 7/20/1825.

---

    * Hardon, Vol. II, p. 114; "Dover Monthly Meeting Records", *N.H.G.R.*, Vol. VI, No. 2, p. 83.
    ⁺ Hardon, Vol. II, pp. 115-6; "Dover Monthly Meeting Records", *N.H.G.R.*, Vol. VI, No. 2, p. 126.

SIXTH GENERATION

        vii. Andrew J., b. 9/5/1827; d. 8/7/1840.

        viii. Stephen N., b. 12/28/1829. A street commissioner in San Francisco, CA.

170.   ix. Howard Millet, b. 8/15/1832.

        x. Mary C., b. 2/3/1841; m. James Jackson.

        xi. Esther.

96. Joseph Roberts (Joseph^5, Stephen^4, Joseph^3, John^2, Thomas^1), son of Joseph and Anna (Hanson) Roberts, was born in Dover, New Hampshire, May 25, 1799, and died there October 4, 1867. He married Maria Henderson, who was born in Dover in 1812. The following child was born in Dover.* Child:

        i. Mary E., b. 1846.

97. Stephen Roberts (John^5, Stephen^4, Joseph^3, John^2, Thomas^1), a farmer, son of John and Lois (Hanson) Roberts, was born in New Hampshire, December 6, 1775, and died August 11, 1813, by drowning. He married in Berwick, Maine, June 3, 1800, Lydia Ricker, the daughter of David and Lydia (Noble) Ricker. She was born in Berwick, in 1792. The following children were born in North Berwick, Maine.⁺ Children:

171.   i. Daniel, b. 9/6/1800.

172.   ii. John, b. 8/14/1802.

        iii. Lydia, m. 3/26/1838, David F. Boynton. 6 ch.

        iv. Lois, m. Robert Renfrew. Three children.

        v. Thomas, d. unm. A lawyer in Groton.

173.   vi. Stephen, b. 6/26/1806(?).

        vii. Sarah, b. 5/25/1808; m. 6/24/1830, Matthew Renfrew. Two children.

---

* Hardon, Vol. II, p. 119.
⁺ Hardon, Vol. II, pp. 88-94.

DESCENDANTS OF THOMAS & REBECCA ROBERTS

98. James Roberts (John⁵, Stephen⁴, Joseph³, John², Thomas¹), son of John and Lois (Hanson) Roberts, was born November 2, 1784, and died August 1, 1862. He married, firstly, Susan M. Clark, in Alfred, Maine, October 2, 1808, and secondly, Margaret Brown. The child below is by Susan. James was a soldier in the War of 1812 and lived in Waterboro, Maine.* Child:

    i. John B., b. 4/28/1822; d. 7/7/1904, Wolfeboro, NH. A farmer in Tamworth, NH.

99. Temple Roberts (John⁵, Stephen⁴, Joseph³, John², Thomas¹), son of John and Lois (Hanson) Roberts, was born June 1, 1788, and died November 4, 1861. He married Rebecca Wilson, who was born in Danvers, Massachusetts, October 16, 1792, and died March 19, 1870. The first two children below were born in Danvers, the remainder in Salem, New Hampshire.⁺ Children:

174.	i.	James.
175.	ii.	Stephen, b. 2/2/1815.
	iii.	Eliza, b. 6/1817; m. William K. Morrison, 6/17/1847; d. 2/15/1895.
	iv.	Susanna, b. 3/29/1823.
176.	v.	John Clendenin, b. 4/11/1830.
177.	vi.	George, b. 3/24/1836.

100. David Sands Roberts (John⁵, Stephen⁴, Joseph³, John², Thomas¹), son of John and Phebe (Heard) Roberts, was born January 1, 1801, and died January 31, 1871. He married Abigail Hall, the daughter of Silas and Sarah (Clement) Hall, July 5, 1827, at Berwick, Maine. Abigail was born in Berwick, July 7, 1800, and died there December 14, 1871. David was a carder in South Berwick, Maine. The following children were born in North Berwick.# Children:

---

    * Hardon, Vol. II, p. 97.
    ⁺ Hardon, Vol. II, pp. 98-9.
    # Hardon, Vol. II, pp. 101-2.

SIXTH GENERATION

    i. Sarah Hall, b. 3/9/1831; m. Joseph W. Ham, 1851; d. 8/22/1905. Seven children.

    ii. Mary Hall, b. 2/1833; m. Charles Greenleaf, 1856; d. 3/24/1863. Two children.

    iii. Joseph Hall, b. 7/1837; d. unm. 5/9/1863, Camp Chantilly, VA. He was a sergeant in the 27th Me. Vol. Infantry.

101. Nicholas Hanson Roberts (John[5], Stephen[4], Joseph[3], John[2], Thomas[1]), a farmer, son of John and Phebe (Heard) Roberts, was born March 1, 1802, and died September 12, 1879. He married his first cousin Dorothy Heard, December 29, 1832, the daughter of Thomas and Hannah (Stillings) Heard. She was born August 12, 1801 and died May 17, 1872. Their first child was born in Albion, Maine, the next two in Augusta, Maine, and the others in Acton, Maine.* Children:

178.   i. Thomas Heard, b. 12/20/1833.

    ii. Mary, b. 3/31/1836; d. 4/15/1836.

    iii. Mary A., b. 10/4/1837; m. Franklin G. Furlong, 12/25/1882; d. 2/22/1900. No children.

    iv. Hannah, b. 8/27/1837(?); d. 2/22/1900.

    v. Auguste Phebe, b. 11/15/1845; m. Edwin Fernald; d. 7/6/1907. Three children.

    vi. Anna Dorothy, b. 5/25/1846; m. 6/15/18--, Oliver C. Titcomb; d. 6/15/1900. Two children.

102. William Roberts (John[5], Stephen[4], Joseph[3], John[2], Thomas[1]), son of John and Phebe (Heard) Roberts, was born February 1, 1806, and died December 7, 1888. He married Lucy E., who was born in Maine in 1805 and died February 8, 1882. This family lived in Berwick, Maine, Haverhill, Massachusetts, North Berwick, Maine, and Wakefield, New Hampshire. The first

---

* Hardon, Vol. II, pp. 105-10.

DESCENDANTS OF THOMAS & REBECCA ROBERTS

three children below were born in North Berwick, Maine, the remainder in Massachusetts.* Children:

    i. Stephen, b. 1835.

    ii. Abigail, b. 1836; m. John W. Roberts, 7/4/1855; d. 1856, North Berwick, ME. One child d.in infancy.

    iii. William J., b. 1841.

    iv. Sarah E., b. 1843; m. 9/5/1862, Lyman W. Lord; d. 2/5/1870.

    v. Mary E., b. 1845; m. Lyman W. Long.

103. Oliver Heard Roberts (John^5, Stephen^4, Joseph^3, John^2, Thomas^1), son of John and Phebe (Heard) Roberts, was born September 20, 1807, and died October 17, 1876. He married Julia Ann Ayer, the daughter of George Washington and Priscilla (Hobbs) Ayer, October 20, 1831. She was born in Wenham, Massachusetts, February 4, 1810, and died February 17, 1890. Oliver was a merchant in Haverhill, Massachusetts, where the following children were born.⁺ Children:

    i. Julia Priscilla, b. 8/13/1832; m. Alvin M. Whittier, 3/14/1855. Three children.

    ii. Phebe Ann, b. 2/25/1834; m. David Atkinson, 4/4/1860. Four children.

    iii. Mary Jackson, b. 6/15/1836; d. 9/11/1839.

179. iv. Oliver Ayer, b. 3/17/1838.

    v. Joseph Warren, b. 7/11/1840; d. 11/19/1840.

    vi. Joseph Warren, b. 12/11/1843.

    vii. Mary Ella, b. 10/31/1848; d. 9/11/1849.

104. Stephen Roberts (John^5, Stephen^4, Joseph^3, John^2, Thomas^1), son of John and Phebe (Heard) Roberts, was born

---

    * Hardon, Vol. II, pp. 109-10.
    ⁺ Hardon, Vol. II, pp. 111-2.

SIXTH GENERATION

September 26, 1813, and died February 6, 1876. He married Nancy Griffin, in Haverhill, Massachusetts. They had five children, but only one lived beyond infancy. This Stephen was named for his older half-brother Stephen (No. 97), who tragically drowned a few weeks before his birth.* Child:

    i. Mary H., m. Leonard B. Hatch.

105. Aaron Roberts (Aaron^5, Ebenezer^4, Joseph^3, John^2, Thomas^1), son of Aaron and Mary (Hanson) Roberts, was born in or near Berwick, Maine, June 18, 1771 (or June 25, 1779?). He married August 22, 1801, Mary Knight. The following children were born in Berwick.⁺ Children:

	i.	Sarah, b. 5/11/1802; d. 2/9/1819.
180.	ii.	Benjamin, b. 9/28/1804.
	iii.	Mary, b. 6/22/1805; d. 5/28/1826.
	iv.	Lydia, b. 6/25/1807.
	v.	Olive, b. 8/20/1809; m. 9/20/1829, Levi Quint.
181.	vi.	Aaron H., b. 4/6/1812.
	vii.	Moses, b. 7/30/1814; m. 9/27/1838, Lydia Stacy; d. 4/10/1852. No children.
	viii.	Hiram Norton, b. 4/5/1818; d. 4/25/1821.
	ix.	Elizabeth, b. 4/11/1819.

106. Joseph Roberts (James^5, Ebenezer^4, Joseph^3, John^2, Thomas^1), son of James Rollins and Elizabeth (Roberts) Roberts, was born in Somersworth, New Hampshire, in or about 1758. He married Mercy Hobbs, who was born in or about 1763 and died November 12, 1856. The children below were born in Lyman,

---

    * Hardon, Vol. II, p. 113.

    ⁺ Hardon, Vol. I, p. 144 & Vol. II, pp. 80-1. This may need some additional work, given a discrepancy in birthdates and the fact that Hardon shows the 4th generation as John in one place and Ebenezer in the other.

DESCENDANTS OF THOMAS & REBECCA ROBERTS

Maine.* Children:

182. i. Isaac, b. 1779.
183. ii. James H., b. 8/23/1789.

107. Reuben Roberts (John^5, Ebenezer^4, Joseph^3, John^2, Thomas^1), son of John and Elizabeth (Hodsdon) Roberts, was born in New Hampshire, January 7, 1770. He was a farmer in Lyman, Maine. Nothing else is known about him aside from the name of one son below.$^+$ Child:

184. i. James H., b. 1816.

108. John Roberts (John^5, Ebenezer^4, Joseph^3, John^2, Thomas^1), apparently the son of John and Elizabeth (Hodsdon) Roberts, was born in Somersworth, New Hampshire, December 11, 1771. He married Joanna Hutchins. John was a tailor and lived variously in Rochester, Farmington, and New Durham, New Hampshire, the latter being the birthplace of the child below.$^#$ Child:

  i. John.

109. Stephen Roberts (John^5, Ebenezer^4, Joseph^3, John^2, Thomas^1), son of John and Elizabeth (Hodsdon) Roberts, was born in New Hampshire, July 21, 1775, and died there January 30, 1821. He married Deborah Wentworth, July 4, 1803. She was the daughter of Bartholomew and Ruth (Hall) Wentworth, and was born in Somersworth, New Hampshire, November 18, 1779 and died near there April 25, 1862. This family lived in the part of Somersworth that became Rollinsford, where the children listed below were born.** Children:

  i. Susanna, b. 4/19/1804; m. Samuel Garvin. 1 ch.
185. ii. Hiram Rollins, b. 5/16/1806.

---

  * Hardon, Vol. II, p. 121.
  + Hardon, Vol. II, p. 82.
  # Hardon, Vol. II, p. 122 & Vol. I, p. 147. See Hardon for a discussion of the parentage of this John.
  ** Hardon, Vol. II, p. 79; Wentworth, Vol. I, p. 519.

SIXTH GENERATION

186.   iii. William Hall, b. 7/1/1808.

       iv. Hall, b. 11/7/1813; m. Jane Curtis, 1851; d. 10/13/1862. He was a bank president in Concord, NH. No children.

       v. Stephen, d. infancy.

110. Jeremiah Roberts (Ichabod[5], Ebenezer[4], Joseph[3], John[2], Thomas[1]), a farmer, son of Ichabod and Susanna (Roberts) Roberts, was born May 17, 1775. He married, January 18, 1799, Elizabeth Lord, the daughter of John and Charity (Curtis) Lord. She was born in Kennebunkport, Maine, June 25, 1780, and died May 1, 1850. The following children were born in Waterboro, Maine.*
Children:

       i. Eliza.

187.   ii. Ichabod, b. 1803.

       iii. Phebe, b. 1805; m. Samuel Davis(?).

       iv. Mary.

       v. John.

       vi. Charity.

188.   vii. Jeremiah, b. 4/22/1817.

111. Edmund H. Roberts (Edmund[5], Samuel[4], Joseph[3], John[2], Thomas[1]), son of Edmund and Sarah (Griffith) Roberts, was born in Portsmouth, New Hampshire, June 29, 1784, and died in Macao, China, in 1836. He married, in 1808, Catherine Whipple Langdon, the daughter of Woodbury and Sarah (Sherburn) Langdon. Edmund was a prominent merchant and mariner of Portsmouth. He died while serving as a special agent of the U.S. government in the Orient. He did not leave a will, and the administration of his estate was quite involved. Because of the discovery of a very old, but large debt, the estate ended up insolvent, and the eight daughters

---

* Hardon, Vol. II, pp. 129-32.

DESCENDANTS OF THOMAS & REBECCA ROBERTS

received nothing.* Children:

 i. Catherine W., m. Andrew Peabody of Portsmouth.

 ii. Caroline Whipple, m.(?) Rev. Andrew P. Peabody of Harvard College.

 iii. Sarah, m. 9/20/1858, Dr. James Boyle, of New York, NY.

 iv. Harriet Langdon, m. Amasa J. Parker, Albany, NY.

 v. Marianna Langdon, m. Charles Perry of Delhi, NY.

 vi. Caroline Eustis, m. Robert Parker of Delhi, NY.

 vii. Ann Henry Langdon, m. Truman H. Wheeler, Delhi.

 viii. Frances Lear, m. Calvin H. Bell of Delhi, NY.

112. David Roberts (Nathaniel^5, Nathaniel^4, Nathaniel^3, Thomas^2, Thomas^1), son of Nathaniel and Mary Roberts, was born in New Hampshire, about 1760, and died in or near Farmington, New Hampshire, February 13, 1839. He married, firstly, Elizabeth Langley, and, secondly, Hannah Meader, October 27, 1796, the daughter of Benjamin and Patience (Hanson) Meader. Hannah was born in Dover, New Hampshire, April 27, 1763. The following children were born in Farmington, the first four by Elizabeth and the remainder by Hannah. David was a farmer and served as Selectman of Farmington, 1799-1803.⁺ Children:

189. i. Isaac, b. 10/23/1781.

 ii. Edmund, of Springfield, IL.

 iii. Hannah, b. 2/27/1787; m. Ephraim Roberts, 2/4/1813.

---

 * Hardon, Vol. II, p. 140; Seaver, J. Montgomery. *Roberts Family Records*. Philadelphia, PA: American Historical-Genealogical Society, no date, pp. 19-20; Rockingham County Probate Court, docket no. 13281. The probate file mentions only Sarah Roberts, unmarried, and Catherine W. Peabody, wife of Andrew Peabody. The others are from Seaver.

 ⁺ Hardon, Vol. II, p. 146.

SIXTH GENERATION

190.   iv. David, b. 1789.
191.   v. Hanson, b. 12(or 10?)/23/1797.
      vi. Susan, b. 1799; d. unm. 1/13/1882.
      vii. Elizabeth, b. 5/2/1799; m. 9/21/1817, Thomas (No. 118) Roberts; d. 10/5/1871.
192.   viii. Jedediah, b. 4/25/1801.

113. John Roberts (George^5, Nathaniel^4, Nathaniel^3, Thomas^2, Thomas^1), a farmer, son of George and Elizabeth (Horn) Roberts, was born in Middleton, New Hampshire, February 4, 1788, and died March 3, 1876. He married, firstly, November 26, 1808, Mary Davis, who was born in Middleton, November 25, 1790, and died May 1, 1837. John married secondly Lydia D. York, who was born May 22, 1800, and died November 1, 1869. The following children, all by the first wife, were born in Middleton.* Children:

      i. Mary Horn, b. 1/24/1808; d. 7/30/1831.
193.   ii. Ira, b. 3/4/1810.
      iii. Elizabeth March, b. 12/2/1813; m. Charles Y. Meserve, 7/10/1836; d. 1900. Two children.
      iv. Sarah Pottle, b. 11/18/1816; d. 4/13/1818.
194.   v. George Belknap, b. 12/9/1819.
195.   vi. John Davis, b. 5/4/1822.
      vii. Sophia Davis, b. 9/21/1825; m. Ira F. Twombly; d. 6/7/1866. Five children.
      viii. Charles Henry, b. 9/20/1828; m. (1) 5/27/1855, Charlotte (Davis) Roberts, (2) 7/30/1887, Eliza Jane Day; d. 4/8/1913. No children.

114. Aaron Roberts (Daniel^5, Aaron^4, Nathaniel^3, Thomas^2, Thomas^1), a merchant, son of Daniel and Hannah (Gage) Roberts,

---

* Hardon, Vol. II, pp. 141-3.

DESCENDANTS OF THOMAS & REBECCA ROBERTS

was born in Dover, New Hampshire, May 27, 1797, and died January 15, 1874. His grave, along with his wives and some of his children, lies in the North Wolfeboro Cemetery. He married, firstly, in Wolfeboro, New Hampshire, August 28, 1823, Mary Bickford, who was born in 1801 and died September 26, 1835, and, secondly, April 18, 1837, his fourth cousin once removed, Maria A. Gage, the daughter of Moses and Dorothy (Dearborn) Gage. Maria was born in Wakefield, New Hampshire, in 1807, and died December 14, 1875. The first three children below are by Mary, the remainder by Maria.* Children:

  i. an infant, d. 9/1826.

  ii. an infant, d. 1/1828.

  iii. Susan A., m. Charles F. Blake, 1/27/1857. 2 ch.

  iv. Abigail, b. 1829.

196. v. Alonzo, b. 5/7/1830.

  vi. Porter D., b. 1831; m. 9/21/1862, Ellen Melissa Copp. No children. A merchant in Lacon & Chicago, IL.

  vii. Caroline C., b. 1833; m. Frederick Gage.

  viii. Mary B.G., b. 1835; d. 6/9/1853.

  ix. Aaron J., b. 1/1/1845; d. 3/2/1845.

115. Alonzo Roberts (Daniel[5], Aaron[4], Nathaniel[3], Thomas[2], Thomas[1]), a farmer and brickmaker, son of Daniel and Hannah (Gage) Roberts, was born in Dover, New Hampshire, October 11 (or 31?), 1799, and died there January 4, 1881. He married May 19, 1825, Mary Torr, the daughter of Vincent and Sarah (Torr) Torr. Mary was born in Durham, New Hampshire, May 17, 1807, and died in Strafford County, New Hampshire, August 10, 1892. The

---

  * Hardon, Vol. II, pp. 168-9; Fipphen, John. *Cemetery Inscriptions Wolfeboro, New Hampshire*. Bowie, Maryland: Heritage Books, Inc., 1993, pp. 176-7.

SIXTH GENERATION

following children were born in Dover.* Children:

    i. Hannah Augusta, b. 5/28/1826; m. 2/13/1848, Aaron Pinkham; d. 3/15/1878. One child.

197. ii. Andrew Torr, b. 2/2/1828.

198. iii. Aaron, b. 5/30/1829.

199. iv. Daniel William, b. 3/29/1833.

    v. Mary Ellen, b. 12/24/1834; m. 1/21/1858, Andrew J. Hough; d. 7/2/1924. Two children.

    vi. Eliza T., b. 8/14/1836; m. (1) 3/1861, John T. Hanson, (2) Charles M. Murphy. Two children.

    vii. Sarah Torr, b. 7/10/1838; m. Howard Millet (No. 170). Roberts; d. 5/29/1923.

    viii. Alonzo, b. 1/20/1840; d. unm. 5/15/1865.

    ix. William Estes, b. 3/16/1842; m. (1) 12/8/1865, Rosetta M. Chesley, (2) Hannah Rand. No ch. A liveryman in Sioux City, IA.

    x. Frances Augusta, b. 4/22/1847; d. 10/7/1865.

    xi. George W., b. 8/6/1850; d. 9/12/1863.

116. James Roberts (Thomas⁵, Moses⁴, Nathaniel³, Thomas², Thomas¹), son of Thomas and Hannah (Lamos) Roberts, was born in Dover, New Hampshire, January 11, 1790, and died April 29, 1837. He married Hannah Heard, July 31, 1831. Their one child was born in Dover. James "disowned" the Quaker faith.⁺ Child:

    i. George K., b. 8/18/1832; d. unm. 3/3/1851.

117. Jeremiah Roberts (Thomas⁵, Moses⁴, Nathaniel³, Thomas², Thomas¹), son of Thomas and Hannah (Lamos) Roberts, was born in Dover, New Hampshire, January 14, 1795, and died July 14, 1848. He married, March 1, 1839, Hannah F. Beede, the

---

* Hardon, Vol. II, p. 170-3.
⁺ Hardon, Vol. I, pp. 175-6.

daughter of Moses and Miriam (Peaslee) Beede. Hannah was born in Poplin, New Hampshire, February 9, 1801, and died in Sandwich, New Hampshire, March 3, 1890. Their only child was born in Dover.* Child:

  i. Abigail Ellen, b. 11/2/1839; m. 12/11/1861, Daniel Beede.

118. Thomas Roberts (James^5, Moses^4, Nathaniel^3, Thomas^2, Thomas^1), a blacksmith, son of James and Eunice (Varney) Roberts, was born in Farmington, New Hampshire, October 22, 1790, and died July 30, 1869. He married September 21, 1817, Elizabeth Roberts, a second cousin once removed, the daughter of David (No. 112) and Hannah (Meader) Roberts. Elizabeth was born in Farmington, May 2, 1799, and died October 5, 1871. The children below were born in New Durham, New Hampshire. This family attended the Quaker Dover Monthly Meeting.⁺ Children:

	i.	Hannah, b. 12/24/1817.
200.	ii.	Stephen, b. 7/27/1820.
	iii.	Clarissa, b. 3/12/1824; d. 12/1/1847.
	iv.	Elizabeth Jane, b. 3/14/1826; m. Nathan C. Page.
	v.	George, b. 3/11/1828; d. unm. 2/7/1861.
	vi.	Levi, b. 11/25/1830. Went to Iowa.
	vii.	Susan Lamb, b. 2/8/1834; m. Charles Clarence (No. 273) Roberts, in Minnesota.
201.	viii.	Thomas Elwood, b. 11/8/1836.
	ix.	Mary Abby, b. 1/7/1846.

119. Jeremiah Roberts (James^5, Moses^4, Nathaniel^3, Thomas^2, Thomas^1), a farmer and blacksmith, son of James and Eunice (Varney) Roberts, was born in Farmington, New Hampshire,

---

 * Hardon, Vol. II, p. 134.
 ⁺ Hardon, Vol. II, p. 135 & 174-6; "Dover Monthly Meeting Records", *N.H.G.R.*, Vol. VI, No. 2, p. 121.

SIXTH GENERATION

February 14, 1793, and died in Muscatine, Iowa, February 23, 1872. He married in Rochester, New Hampshire, October 1, 1818, Love Wingate, the daughter of John and Susanna (Canney) Wingate. Love was born in Sandwich, New Hampshire, in 1800, and died in Muscatine, in September of 1867. The following children were born in Sandwich, except for the last one, who was born in Dover, New Hampshire. This family sold its property in Sandwich, June 7, 1839, and it was apparently soon thereafter that they went west to Iowa. They attended the Quaker Dover Monthly Meeting.* Children:

202. i. Charles White, b. 3/1/1822.
203. ii. John Meder, b. 11/19/1824.
 iii. Susanna Canney, b. 2/17/1831; m. George Jones.
 iv. Elizabeth Meder, b. 8/22/1836; m. 6/1860, John B. Hanson; d. 11/21/1906. Four children.
204. v. Daniel W., b. 1/19/1842.

120. Moses Roberts (James^5, Moses^4, Nathaniel^3, Thomas^2, Thomas^1), son of James and Eunice (Varney) Roberts, was born in Farmington, New Hampshire, March 11, 1795, and died, apparently in or near there, April 5, 1880. He married in Rochester, New Hampshire, September 30, 1824, Sarah Place, the daughter of Jonathan and Lydia Place. Sarah was born in Rochester, New Hampshire, September 2, 1794, and died December 30, 1869. The following children were born in Farmington. This family attended the Quaker Dover Monthly Meeting.+ Children:

 i. Eunice V., b. 8/18/1826; d. 3/29/1856.
 ii. Cyrus P., b. 8/31/1828; d. 11/22/1910.
 iii. John, b. 1/10/1831; d. 9/1/1832.

---

 * Hardon, Vol. II, pp. 177-80; "Dover Monthly Meeting Records", *N.H.G.R.*, Vol VI, No. 2, p. 84.
 + Hardon, Vol. II, p. 137; "Dover Monthly Meeting Records", *N.H.G.R.*, Vol. VI, No. 2, p. 89.

DESCENDANTS OF THOMAS & REBECCA ROBERTS

    iv.   James, b. 9/20/1834; d. 9/26/1909.

121. Stephen Roberts (James[5], Moses[4], Nathaniel[3], Thomas[2], Thomas[1]), son of James and Eunice (Varney) Roberts, a blacksmith, was born in Farmington, New Hampshire, May 25(or 29?), 1797, and died in Dover, New Hampshire, June 17, 1890. He married Love Canney, October 7, 1824. Born in New Durham, New Hampshire, March 14, 1806, Love was the daughter of John and Ann (Meader) Canney. Love died in 1893. They were members of the Society of Friends and built a home on Garrison Hill in Dover. The following children were born in Rochester, New Hampshire.[*] Children:

    i.   Elvira, b. 3/21/1826; d. 4/15/1826.

    ii.   Almira, b. 4/28/1829; d. unm. 3/5/1921.

    iii.   Anna A., b. 1827; m. John Meader. Six children.

    iv.   Achsa R., b. 1833; m. Joseph Hanson; d. 1883. One child.

205.   v.   Amos K., b. 12/19/1835.

122. Jesse Roberts (James[5], Moses[4], Nathaniel[3], Thomas[2], Thomas[1]), a farmer, son of James and Eunice (Varney) Roberts, was born in Farmington, New Hampshire, May 13, 1802, and died July 27, 1884. He married, firstly, November 28, 1833, at Sandwich, New Hampshire, Sarah Beede, the daughter of Jonathan and Anna Beede. Sarah was born in Sandwich, February 14, 1796, and died in Rochester, New Hampshire, October 4, 1863. Jesse married, secondly, Martha Austin. The children below, born in Middleton, New Hampshire, are by Sarah. This family attended the Quaker Dover Monthly Meeting.[+] Children:

---

    [*] Hardon, Vol. II, pp. 181-2; "Dover Monthly Meeting Records", *N.H.G.R.*, Vol. VI, No. 2, p. 122; Wilson, Mark C. *The Second Hundred and Fifty Years*. Privately published, 1952, pp. 10 ff.

    [+] Hardon, Vol. II, p. 138; "Dover Monthly Meeting Records", *N.H.G.R.*, Vol. VI, No. 2, p. 123.

SIXTH GENERATION

    i. Anne Maria, b. 3/24/1835; m. 7/30/1857, Thomas Evans. Two children.

    ii. Ruth Elma, b. 1/25/1838; d. 11/24/1838.

    iii. Edward E., b. 1841.

123. Walter Roberts (James[5], Moses[4], Nathaniel[3], Thomas[2], Thomas[1]), son of James and Eunice (Varney) Roberts, was born in Farmington, New Hampshire, May 4, 1808. He married in New Durham, New Hampshire, Mary Elkins, October 3, 1838. The daughter of John and Mary Elkins, she died in Rochester, New Hampshire, January 16, 1889. Walter was a shoemaker in New Durham and Dover, New Hampshire. This family attended the Quaker Dover Monthly Meeting.* Children:

    i. Mary Eliza, b. 8/15/1839; m. George Evans. 5 ch.

    ii. Olney T., b. 2/2/1841.

    iii. Lewis, b. 12/14/1842.

    iv. Olive Ann, b. 6/16/1844; m. Charles L'Oiseau of Des Moines, IA.

    v. Ann, b. 1846.

    vi. Eunice Elma, b. 6/6/1847; m. William Spear of IA.

    vii. James W., b. 5/1/1849; d. 7/15/1861.

124. Ezekiel Roberts (Moses[5], Moses[4], Nathaniel[3], Thomas[2], Thomas[1]), a farmer, son of Moses and Alice (Tibbetts) Roberts, was born in Rochester, New Hampshire, April 9, 1796, and died, apparently in Alfred, Maine, August 6, 1865. He married in Alfred, December 30, 1818, Sabra White, the daughter of Deacon Samuel White. Sabra was born in Alfred, in 1797, and died in Maine, May 3, 1873. Their first child was born in Alton, Maine (or N.H.?), the

---

* Hardon, Vol. II, pp. 139 & 183-5; "Dover Monthly Meeting Records", *N.H.G.R.*, Vol VI, No. 2, p. 181.

DESCENDANTS OF THOMAS & REBECCA ROBERTS

second in Acton, Maine, and the remainder in Alfred.* Children:

    i. Charles, b. 1822; m. Ellen J. Bickford, 1849; d. 1/24/1868.

    ii. Bradford, b. 1824; d. 7/16/1855.

    iii. Franklin W., b. 1829.

    iv. Andrew L., b. 1829.

    v. Mary Jane, b. 1835.

    vi. Elizabeth Ann, b. 1839.

125. Moses Roberts (Moses^5, Moses^4, Nathaniel^3, Thomas^2, Thomas^1), son of Moses and Alice (Tibbetts) Roberts, was born in Rochester, New Hampshire, January 28, 1802. He married, firstly, March 15, 1828, Sophia Nute, the daughter of Jotham and Sarah (Twombly) Nute. Sophia was born in Milton, New Hampshire, March 16, 1809, and died April 5, 1840. Moses married, secondly, in Brooklyn, New York, May 2, 1841, Eliza Hodgdon.⁺ Children:

    i. James H., b. 1828.

    ii. Sarah E., b. 1833.

    iii. George A., b. 1835.

    iv. Moses N., b. 1837.

    v. Israel N., b. 1839.

    vi. Levi M. N., b. 1841.

    vii. Ezekiel L., b. 1843.

    viii. Edward P., b. 1844.

    ix. Nancy E., b. 1847.

    x. Frederick D., b. 1849.

---

    * Hardon, Vol. II, p. 188 & Vol. IV, pp. 66 & 144. See Ezekiel No. 135. It is not clear which Ezekiel married Sabra White and had six children.
    ⁺ Hardon, Vol. II, pp. 189-90.

SIXTH GENERATION

126. George Roberts (John[5], Alexander[4], John[3], Thomas[2], Thomas[1]), son of John and Hannah (Roberts?) Roberts, was born in New Hampshire in 1782. He married his fourth cousin, Mary Roberts, the daughter of Joshua (No. 40) and Joanna (Wentworth) Roberts. Mary was born April 7, 1783 and died January 14, 1858.*
Children:

    i. Edmund.

    ii. Joshua, b. 1809.

    iii. Noah, b. 1809.

    iv. Joanna, b. 11/5/1811;m. 11/20/1831,Ezekiel Ricker.

206.   v. George, b. 1819.

127. George W. Roberts (Thomas[5], Alexander[4], John[3], Thomas[2], Thomas[1]), a farmer in Rollinsford, New Hampshire, son of Thomas and Elizabeth (Garvin) Roberts, was born in Somersworth, New Hampshire, September 23, 1798, and died in New Hampshire, June 22, 1886. He married, firstly, May 6, 1829, Sarah Woodhouse, the daughter of James and Sarah Woodhouse. Sarah was born October 29, 1805 and died September 17, 1842. George married, secondly, Susan Woodhouse, the sister of his deceased wife Sarah, November 19, 1843. Susan was born in Thornton, New Hampshire, February 15, 1814 and died December 3, 1852. Thirdly, George married, November 6, 1853, Esther Blaisdell, the daughter of Enoch and Mary Blaisdell. Esther was born in Lebanon, New Hampshire, February 7, 1812, and died September 17, 1889. The children below, by the first wife, were born in Rochester.⁺ Children:

    i. Lydia Emily, b. 3/6/1830; d. 9/17/1838.

207.   ii. Alexander, b. 1832.

    iii. Mary, b. 9/23/1834; d. 9/9/1836.

---

* Hardon, Vol. II, p. 191; Wentworth, Vol. I, pp. 286-7.
⁺ Hardon, Vol. III, p. 1.

208.   iv. George Thomas, b. 11/9/1836.
       v. Mary Emily, b. 10/24/1838; d. 3/25/1853.
       vi. Charles Carroll, b. 8/30/1840; d. unm., IA farmer.

128. Joshua Roberts (Ebenezer[5], Alexander[4], John[3], Thomas[2], Thomas[1]), son of Ebenezer and Sarah (Roberts) Roberts, was born in Wolfeboro, New Hampshire, about 1820. Nothing else is known about this family, except the name of the one child below.* Child:

   i. Martha Ann, m. James Horn.

---

* Hardon, Vol. III, p. 8.

SEVENTH GENERATION

129. John Roberts (Joseph[6], George[5], William[4], John[3], John[2], Thomas[1]), son of Joseph and Ruth (White) Roberts, was born in Falmouth, Maine, October 26, 1769. He married in Portland, Maine, April 21, 1799, Mary Snow, the daughter of Samuel and Mary (Deane) Snow. She was born in Brunswick, Maine, February 5, 1768, and died in Portland, Maine, July 12, 1849, many years after John's death. She has been described as a "little woman" and went by the nickname "Polly". John was a caulker of vessels in Portland. He and Mary built a house on Mountfort Street (#10) in Portland, where they lived most of their lives, and where the following children were born.* Children:

 i. Mary A., b. 12/12/1802; d. 12/23/1802.

 ii. Mary Ann, b. 5/6/1804; m. Osgood Noyes, 6/7/1824. Four children.

 iii. Catherine, b. 1/7/1806; m. Moses N. Carr, 5/10/1828. Five children.

 iv. Franklin, b. 12/27/1808.

 v. Francis, b. 7/18/1810; d. 12/4/1828.

 vi. George, b. 9/12/1814; d. 8/3/1834.

130. George Roberts (Joseph[6], George[5], William[4], John[3], John[2], Thomas[1]), a mariner, son of Joseph and Ruth (White) Roberts, was born in Falmouth, Maine, March 1, 1773. He was lost at sea, January 23, 1815. George married in Portland, Maine, October 25, 1797, Hannah Davis, the daughter of Samuel and Hannah (Dyer) Davis, of Falmouth. Hannah was born in Falmouth, November 10, 1774, and died in Portland, August 4, 1855. She was described as a "dainty little woman", who regularly attended the Methodist church in Portland. George and Hannah owned property on Mountfort Street (#12) in Portland. During the War of 1812 George was serving as ship's carpenter aboard the *Dash*, when it went down during a gale. The following children were born in

---

* Underhill, Vol. I, pp. 1157-1164.

DESCENDANTS OF THOMAS & REBECCA ROBERTS

Portland.* Children:

209.   i. Reuben Davis, b. 11/4/1798.

      ii. Mary Caroline, b. 2/26/1801; d. unm. 4/16/1848.

210. iii. Benjamin, b. 8/2/1803.

131. Jedediah Roberts (Jedediah[6], Love[5], Love[4], Thomas[3], John[2], Thomas[1]), son of Jedediah and Eunice (Pray) Roberts, was born in Somersworth, New Hampshire, November 19, 1776, and died in Brighton, Massachusetts, May 20, 1860. He married in Shapleigh, Maine, March 13, 1803, Elizabeth Goodwin, the daughter of Jeremiah and Mary (Remick) Goodwin. Elizabeth was born in Kittery, Maine, December 24, 1781, and died, apparently in Acton, Maine, in 1828. Jedediah and Elizabeth owned a farm in Acton, on the New Hampshire border. There they ran a grist and sawmill on the Salmon Falls River. The following children were born in Acton.⁺ Children:

    i. Mary, m. Moses Hanson. One child.

   ii. Clarissa, b. 5/1806; m. Ezekiel Merrow; d. 7/8/1849.

  iii. Elizabeth L., m. 4/11/1839, James L. Brock.

  iv. Eunice, b. 1823; m. 8/6/1842, John Horn. Three ch.

   v. Hannah Quint, b. 8/12/1825; m. 12/12/1849, Abner J. Nutter; d. 9/28/1916, West Roxbury, MA.

  vi. Sarah, m. Nathan Saunders.

132. James Roberts (Love[6], Love[5], Love[4], Thomas[3], John[2], Thomas[1]), son of Love and (Elizabeth Brown?) Roberts, was born in Maine, September 7 (or 9?), 1782, and died, apparently in Maine, August 30, 1852. He married, firstly, July 14, 1800, Hannah Smith, who was born in Shapleigh (now Acton), Maine, March 15, 1780, and died March 15, 1834. James married, secondly, September 15, 1835, Hepsibah Thompson, the daughter of Daniel and Olive

---

* Underhill, Vol. I, pp. 1171-1187.
⁺ Hardon, Vol. III, pp. 9-14.

SEVENTH GENERATION

Thompson. Hepsibah was born in Shapleigh (now Acton), June 15, 1802, and died January 28, 1858. The children below are by Hannah, except for the last one, Millet Wentworth.[*] Children:

    i. Eliza, m. William Downing.

    ii. Sarah, b. 12/9/1804; d. unm. 12/10/1825.

    iii. Pamela, b. 9/28/1805; m. 8/8/1824, George Horn.

    iv. Azuba, m. 2/4/1833, Edward Knox.

    v. Elizabeth B., m. Aaron Downs.

    vi. Martha, b. 5/5/1810; d. unm. 5/5/1829.

    vii. Hannah Smith, b. 12/22/1812; m. 11/8/1843, Beza Ramsey.

    viii. George Washington, b. 1/1/1815; m. (1) 12/31/1846, Mehitable F. Ricker, (2) Mary J. Farnum; d. 10/18/1900. No children.

    ix. Abigail W., m. 5/14/1843, Joseph B. Jones. 6 ch.

    x. Mary, m. -----Morgan.

    xi. Elizabeth, b. 8/15/1821; d. 2/15/1824.

211.   xii. Millet Wentworth, b. 6/29/1837.

133. Love Roberts (Love[6], Love[5], Love[4], Thomas[3], John[2], Thomas[1]), son of Love and (Elizabeth Brown?) Roberts, was born in Maine, April 8, 1784 (or 1785?), and died, apparently in Maine, July 27, 1827. He married, firstly, May 28, 1810, Sarah True, the daughter of John and Sarah (West) True. Sarah was born in Litchfield, Maine, February 9, 1792, and died February 13, 1822. Love married, secondly, March 15, 1824, Mary Phillips, who was born August 29, 1798, and died November 13, 1846. Love was an innkeeper in Wayne, Maine, and an officer in the War of 1812. The following children of Love and Sarah were born in Wayne.[+]

---

[*] Hardon, Vol. III, pp. 15-24.
[+] Hardon, Vol. III, pp. 28-34.

DESCENDANTS OF THOMAS & REBECCA ROBERTS

Children:

	i.	Mary Ann, b. 3/22/1811; m. 6/2/1831, Uriah Virgin, of New Orleans, LA.
	ii.	Elmira Haskell, b. 9/10/1812; m. Ephraim Sturtevant; d. 9/17/1865. Three children.
212.	iii.	Loring True, b. 9/24/1814.
	iv.	Julia True, b. 2/9/1817; d. 12/17/1833.
213.	v.	William Harrison, b. 11/8/1819.
214.	vi.	Charles Ellery Fordyce, b. 2/27/1826.

134. Paul Roberts (Love^6, Love^5, Love^4, Thomas^3, John^2, Thomas^1), an artisan, son of Love and (Elizabeth Brown?) Roberts, was born in Maine, April 17, 1786. He married his cousin Anna Roberts, November 1, 1814, in Shapleigh, Maine, where the following children were born.* Children:

   i. Elizabeth J., b. 1/1825; d. unm. 10/6/1853.

   ii. Abigail C., b.c. 1830; m. 6/11/1853, Wentworth Lowd; d. 1853(?). No children.

   iii. Martha H., b. 1833.

135. Ezekiel Roberts (Love^6, Love^5, Love^4, Thomas^3, John^2, Thomas^1), a farmer, son of Love and (Elizabeth Brown?) Roberts, was born in Maine, April 8, 1791, and died, apparently in Alfred, Maine, August 6, 1865. He married in Alfred, January 30, 1818, Sabra White, the daughter of Deacon Samuel White. Sabra was born in Alfred, in 1797, and died May 3, 1873. The first child below was born in Alton, New Hampshire, the second in Acton, Maine, and the remainder in Alfred.† Children:

   i. Charles, b. 1822; m. Ellen J. Bickford, 5/19/1849; d. 1/24/1868. A stage-driver in Alfred.

---

* Hardon, Vol. III, p. 50.

† Hardon, Vol. III, pp. 51-2. See Ezekiel No. 124. It is not clear which Ezekiel married Sabra White and had six children.

SEVENTH GENERATION

    ii.   Bradford, b. 1824; d. 7/16/1855.

    iii. Franklin White, b. 1829. A stage-driver.

    iv. Andrew L., b. 1829. Lived in New York, NY.

    v.   Mary Jane, b. 1835.

    vi. Elizabeth Ann, b. 1839.

136. James Wakefield Roberts (Peter^6, Love^5, Love^4, Thomas^3, John^2, Thomas^1), son of Peter and Abigail (Wakefield) Roberts, was born in Lyman, Maine, September 7, 1788, and died, apparently in Maine, March 21, 1881. He married, firstly, July 14, 1811, Martha Hill, the daughter of Charles and Abigail Hill. Martha was born in 1792. James married, secondly, May 10, 1855, in Alfred, Maine, Paulina (Hasty) Conant, who was born in 1809 and died March 8, 1893. James owned and farmed land inherited from his grandfather. He served as a county commissioner and was a member of the state legislature. During the War of 1812 he was a lieutenant, and eventually achieved the rank of captain. The following children were born in Lyman.* Children:

	i.	Abigail Hill, b. 12/11/1812; d. unm.
215.	ii.	Horace, b. 8/5/1815.
216.	iii.	Jacob Waterhouse, b. 6/24/1818.(?)
217.	iv.	Charles Hill, b. 11/27/1818.(?)
	v.	Amos.
218.	vi.	James Wakefield, b. 6/12/1825.
219.	vii.	Peter Stillings, b. 10/21/1827.
	viii.	Dimon A., b. 5/21/1830.
220.	ix.	Benjamin Dudley, b. 12/18/1839.

137. Joseph Dennett Roberts (Peter^6, Love^5, Love^4, Thomas^3, John^2, Thomas^1), son of Peter and Abigail (Wakefield) Roberts, was

---

* Hardon, Vol. III, pp. 53-71.

DESCENDANTS OF THOMAS & REBECCA ROBERTS

born in Lyman, Maine, August 29, 1796, and died there (or near there), September 5, 1879. He married March 28, 1829, Rhoda Fall, the daughter of Stephen and Elizabeth (Gerrish?) Fall. Rhoda was born July 17, 1797, and died February 18, 1886. Joseph farmed a homestead in Lyman, which was in the possession of Winnefred (Emerson) Roberts, in 1930. The following children were born in Lyman.* Children:

		i.	Porter Sands, b. 6/1/1830; d. unm. 4/1917. A wholesale grocer in Somerville, MA.
221.		ii.	Alonzo, b. 2/21/1832.
		iii.	Elizabeth J., b. 9/30/1823; d. 8/26/1824.
		iv.	Elizabeth J., b. 11/4/1838; d. 11/22/1839.

138. John Roberts (Peter[6], Love[5], Love[4], Thomas[3], John[2], Thomas[1]), a farmer, son of Peter and Abigail (Wakefield) Roberts, was born in Lyman, Maine, in 1800. He married Abigail A. Conant, who was born in Shapleigh, Maine, in 1801, and died in Maine in 1884. The following children were born in Lyman.+ Children:

		i.	Emily, b. 1827; d. unm.
		ii.	Elizabeth T., b. 1829; m. -----Emmons.
		iii.	Jane b. 1839; m. -----Osgood.
		iv.	Anna, b. 1840; d. unm.
222.		v.	George Henry, b. 1842.
223.		vi.	Luke.
		vii.	John.

139. Nahum Roberts (Peter[6], Love[5], Love[4], Thomas[3], John[2], Thomas[1]), a farmer, son of Peter and Abigail (Wakefield) Roberts, was born in Lyman, Maine, April 16, 1804, and died, apparently in

---

    * Hardon, Vol. III, pp. 72-3.
    + Hardon, Vol. III, pp. 78-82.

SEVENTH GENERATION

Alfred, Maine, December 14, 1859. He married November 15, 1828, Sarah B. Hemmenway, who was born in Lyman, May 23, 1806, and died January 25, 1884. The following children were born in Alfred.* Children:

   i. Mary Charlotte, b. 12/23/1829; m. 11/6/1850, Franklin O. Reed; d. 11/12/1883. Five children.

224. ii. John H., b. 10/8/1831.

225. iii. Philander, b. 11/3/1833.

   iv. Bion, b. 10/20/1835; m. Maria Hill; d. 1/16/1909. No children.

   v. Abigail H., b. 11/15/1837; m. Franklin O. Reed; d. 1/12/1890. No children.

226. vi. William Henry Harrison, b. 11/2/1840.

227. vii. Luke Hemmenway, b. 8/6/1843.

228. viii. Albert F.(twin), b. 12/12/1845.

   ix. Sarah Olivia (twin), b. 12/12/1845; m. 12/25/1867, James Roberts, of Waterboro, ME.; d. 4/9/1895. One child, Melvin Albert Roberts (b. 6/18/1869, d. unm. 9/21/1898, Spanish American War.).

229. x. Nahum Frank, b. 2/5/1849.

140. Dimon Roberts (Peter^6, Love^5, Love^4, Thomas^3, John^2, Thomas^1), a farmer, son of Peter and Abigail (Wakefield) Roberts, was born in Lyman, Maine, January 1, 1810, and died there or near there, May 2, 1881. He married April 19, 1832, Martha Hemmenway, the daughter of Jonathan and Sarah Hemmenway. Martha was born in Lyman, December 12, 1812, and died March 13, 1891. The following children were born in Lyman.⁺ Children:

---

 * Hardon, Vol. III, pp. 83-9.
 ⁺ Hardon, Vol. III, pp. 92-9.

DESCENDANTS OF THOMAS & REBECCA ROBERTS

      i. Sarah, b. 4/26/1835; m. 9/30/1860, Alexander Mann; d. 7/29/1901.

      ii. Mary Hemmenway, b. 7/17/1837; m. 7/25/1862, Jacob Smith; d. 3/4/1901. Four children.

      iii. John Stillings, b. 6/16/1839; d. unm. 8/19/1864. A mechanic in Somerville, MA, killed in the battle of Wendel Railroad, VA, while serving in the 39th Mass. Vol. Inf.

      iv. Dimon, b. 4/25/1844; m. 4/9/1870, Martha Jane Merrill; d. 6/1914. No children.

230.   v. Willie Crosby, b. 1/29/1853.

      vi. Emma Louise, b. 1/3/1857; m. 11/30/1882, Charles T. Merrill. Three children.

141. James Roberts (Timothy[6], John[5], Timothy[4], Thomas[3], John[2], Thomas[1]), son of Timothy and Elizabeth (Hayes) Roberts, was born in Milton, New Hampshire, December 24, 1783, and died there of drowning, July 6, 1839. He married July 2, 1804, Mercy Wentworth, the daughter of John and Rebecca (Horn) Wentworth. Mercy was born in Milton, in 1784, and died September 10, 1845. James was a trader and served as a town officer in Milton, where the following children were born.* Children:

      i. Rebecca Horn, b. 12/12/1804; d. 11/30/1825.

      ii. Susanna, b. 12/4/1806; d. 1/30/1832.

231.   iii. John Weston (twin), b. 3/27/1810.

232.   iv. James Cutts (twin), b. 3/27/1810.

233.   v. Owen Swain, b. 4/4/1813.

234.   vi. Beard Page, b. 6/26/1815.

---

* Hardon, Vol. III, pp. 100-6; Wentworth, Vol. I, p. 523.

SEVENTH GENERATION

vii. Betsey Hayes, b. 11/16/1818; m. 5/22/1842, Daniel Wentworth; d. 7/28/1840. Two children.

viii. Mary Ann Adams, b. 3/4/1822; m. 11/28/1841, Daniel W. Dame. One child.

ix. (?) Hezekiah Wentworth.

142. John Roberts (Timothy⁶, John⁵, Timothy⁴, Thomas³, John², Thomas¹), son of Timothy and Elizabeth (Hayes) Roberts, was born in Milton, New Hampshire, February 4, 1788, and died in Covington, Kentucky, December 25, 1833. He married June 14, 1819, Mary Ann Adams, the daughter of Abijah and Lucy (Coolidge) Adams. Mary Ann was born September 4, 1794, and died November 19, 1822. John was a merchant in Boston, Massachusetts, where the following children were born.* Children:

235. i. Davis Ballard, b. 12/21/1820.

ii. Mary Anne, b. 9/1/1822; m. 9/15/1839, Maturin M. Ballou; d. 1/1918. One child.

143. Wentworth Roberts (Timothy⁶, John⁵, Timothy⁴, Thomas³, John², Thomas¹), son of Timothy and Elizabeth (Hayes) Roberts, was born in Milton, New Hampshire, in the 1790's. He was of New Durham, New Hampshire and Bangor, Maine. He married Caroline Holt, who was born in 1829 and died March 1, 1861.⁺ Children:

i. Mary Ella.

ii. Ella I.(twin), b. 8/31/1853; d. 8/18/1854.

iii. Caroline May (twin), b. 8/31/1853; d. 5/4/1869.

144. Amos Main Roberts (Timothy⁶, John⁵, Timothy⁴, Thomas³, John², Thomas¹), son of Timothy and Elizabeth (Hayes) Roberts, was born in Milton, New Hampshire, May 6, 1801, and died in Boston, Massachusetts, March 16, 1879. He married, July 26, 1827, Charlotte Barker Rich, the daughter of Dr. Hosea and

---

* Hardon, Vol. III, pp. 107-8.
⁺ Hardon, Vol. III, p. 111.

Frances (Goodale) Rich. Charlotte was born in Bangor, Maine, May 24, 1808, and died September 9, 1882. Amos was a lumber merchant and the president of Eastern Bank. He lived at various times in Oldtown, Orono and Bangor, Maine, the latter of which is the birthplace of the following children.* Children:

236. i. Charles Wentworth, b. 10/22/1828.

  ii. Frances Elizabeth, b. 2/25/1838; m. 9/23/1857, John A. Peters; d. 1/20/1916.

  iii. Annie Charlotte, b. 5/20/1842; m. 12/21/1864, Noah G. Higgins; d. 2/23/1905. No children.

145. Jonathan Dame Roberts (Joseph^6, John^5, Timothy^4, Thomas^3, John^2, Thomas^1), son of Joseph and Elizabeth (Dame) Roberts, was born in Rochester, New Hampshire, in 1785, was baptized September 18, 1791, and died in or near Farmington, New Hampshire, September 10, 1874. He married, firstly, in Rochester, November 10, 1806, Lydia Jones, who was born in 1781 and died April 26, 1851. Jonathan married, secondly, November 9, 1851, Deborah (Fernald) Towle, the daughter of William and Elizabeth (Johnson) Fernald, and the widow of Philip Towle. Deborah was born in Farmington, January 19, 1809, and died July 30, 1894. Jonathan was elected selectman of Farmington, and served from 1823 to 1831. He was a Quaker, but was disowned in 1811.⁺ Children:

  i. Mary E.P., b. 5/13/1807; m. -----Jones.

237. ii. Joseph J., b. 10/28/1810.

238. iii. David S., b. 4/6/1813.

  iv. John Comley, b. 5/14/1816; d. 5/22/1840, Gilmanton, NH. A student of theology.

  v. (?) Eliza, m. -----Bean, of Lawrence, MA.

146. John Roberts (Joseph^6, John^5, Timothy^4, Thomas^3, John^2,

---

* Hardon, Vol. III, pp. 112-4.
⁺ Hardon, Vol. III, pp. 115-8.

SEVENTH GENERATION

Thomas¹), a farmer, son of Joseph and Elizabeth (Dame) Roberts, was born in Rochester, New Hampshire, in 1789, baptized September 18, 1791, and died in or near Farmington, New Hampshire, November 26, 1847. He married, January 19, 1815, Sarah Abigail Wingate, the daughter of William and Deborah (Buzzell) Wingate. Sarah Abigail was born in Farmington, August 19, 1791. She was living when John died, and was appointed guardian of sons George E. and Henry L. The following children were born in Farmington.* Children:

  i. William Wingate, b. 1/6/1816; d. 8/16/1837. A student at Dartmouth College.

  ii. Horatio Gates, b. 3/5/1819; d. 11/2/1847. No ch.

  iii. John Franklin, b. 10/31/1820; m.(1) 1844, Lydia A.M. Jones, (2) 6/6/1849, Charlotte Davis; d. 2/16/1854. No children. A shoe manufacturer in Farmington.

  iv. Charles Bartlett, b. 5/21/1822; d. 8/20/1846, Camargo, Mexico, while in the Mexican War.

239. v. Joseph Augustus, b. 9/23/1826.

240. vi. George Edwin, b. 4/5/1829.

241. vii. Henry Laurens, b. 10/18/1831.

147. Joseph Roberts (Joseph⁶, John⁵, Timothy⁴, Thomas³, John², Thomas¹), a carpenter, son of Joseph and Elizabeth (Dame) Roberts, was born in Rochester, New Hampshire, May 29, 1797, and died in or near there August 25, 1886. He married, firstly, April 15, 1827, Priscilla Edgerly, the daughter of Josiah and Mary (Tash) Edgerly. Priscilla was born in New Durham, New Hampshire, July 31, 1802, and died June 2, 1840. Joseph married, secondly, October 24, 1841, Sarah Edgerly, the sister of his deceased first wife. Sarah was born in Farmington, New Hampshire, November 1, 1813, and died September 11, 1884. The first two children below were by Priscilla and the remainder by

---

* Hardon, Vol. III, pp. 119-22.

DESCENDANTS OF THOMAS & REBECCA ROBERTS

Sarah. All were born in Rochester.* Children:
    i. Charles Wesley, b. 7/4/1829; d. unm. 8/16/1852.
    ii. Henry Burns, b. 3/10/1831; d. 12/29/1849.
    iii. Priscilla Arabella, b. 9/5/1842; d. unm.(?).
    iv. Joseph Arthur, b. 5/5/1844; d. unm. 7/30/1911. A carpenter in Rochester, a.k.a. Arthur J.
    v. Ida E., b. 10/27/1850; m. 6/1883,Charles S. Brock.

148. Nathaniel Burnham Roberts (Joseph^6, John^5, Timothy^4, Thomas^3, John^2, Thomas^1), son of Joseph and Elizabeth (Dame) Roberts, was born in Rochester, New Hampshire, August 4, 1799, and died in Farmington or Milton, New Hampshire, June 14, 1886. He married, firstly, June 29, 1823, Leah Hayes, the daughter of Ichabod and Deborah (French) Hayes. Leah was born in Farmington, March 16, 1800, and died November 22, 1825. Nathaniel married, secondly, June 3, 1827, Abigail D. Young, and, thirdly, April 26, 1843, Nancy (Waldron) Thurston, the widow of John Thurston. Nancy was born in Farmington, in 1808, and died in October of 1876. Nathaniel was a blacksmith in Farmington and Milton. His house and contents were destroyed in the "Great Fire of 1867". The only child below is by his third wife.⁺ Child:
    i. Leah Helen, b. 9/10/1848; m. 9/16/1866, John M. Berry; d. 7/1/1921, Malden, MA.

149. Jeremiah Roberts (Joseph^6, John^5, Timothy^4, Thomas^3, John^2, Thomas^1), son of Joseph and Elizabeth (Dame) Roberts, was born in Rochester, New Hampshire, November 28, 1804, and died there or near there, March 9, 1892. He married May 14, 1828, Clarissa Harlowe Edgerly, the daughter of Josiah and Mary (Tash) Edgerly. Clarissa was born in New Durham, New Hampshire, August 17, 1806, and died January 5, 1875. Jeremiah was a farmer and a general in the state militia. He also served as a member of the state legislature. His farm in Farmington was still known as the

---

    * Hardon, Vol. III, pp. 125-6.
    ⁺ Hardon, Vol. III, pp. 132-4.

SEVENTH GENERATION

"General Roberts Place" as late as the 1930's. The following children were born there.* Children:

    i. Emily Ann Gates, b. 2/1/1834; m. 4/8/1858, Edward F. Jones; d. 3/9/1918. Two children.

    ii. Julia Ann Maria, b. 9/15/1835; m. 4/10/1861, Lucius F. Smith; d. 1/31/1932. One child.

    iii. Jeremiah Bartlett, b. 3/12/1840; m. Sarah E. Willey; d. 7/1/1894. A machinist in Farmington. One son died at birth.

    iv. Clara Helen, b. 7/18/1842; m. 12/11/1880, Clarence Huntoon; d. 2/12/1892. One child.

    v. Charles Wesley, b. 7/7/1856; m. (1) Caroline E. Cloutman, (2) 10/1/1895, Alice (Nute) Fernald; d. 2/15/1931, Ware MA. A shoe cutter. He had one son by first marriage.

150. John Love Roberts (John[6], Thomas[5], Timothy[4], Thomas[3], John[2], Thomas[1]), a farmer, son of John and Abigail (Jones) Roberts, was born in Rochester, New Hampshire, August 18, 1805, and died there or near there, January 18, 1880. He married November 26, 1829, Rebecca Pinkham Horn, the daughter of Noah and Sarah (Wentworth) Horn. Rebecca was born in Farmington, New Hampshire, February 20, 1807, and died May 27, 1888. The children below were born in West Lebanon, Maine.⁺ Children:

242.   i. Noah Horn, b. 10/11/1831.

    ii. John Harrison, b. 7/30/1840; d. unm. 8/13/1863, Concord, NH. A student at Bowdoin College and a soldier in the Civil War (15th N.H. Vol. Inf.).

243.   iii. Henry Kirkwood, b. 10/3/1845.

244.   iv. Herman Winfield, b. 5/5/1847.

151. William Jones Roberts (Thomas[6], Timothy[5], Timothy[4],

---

* Hardon, Vol. III, pp. 127-9.
⁺ Hardon, Vol. III, pp. 137-42.

Thomas³, John², Thomas¹), a farmer, son of Thomas and Mehitable (Jones) Roberts, was born in Rochester, New Hampshire, March 2, 1812, and died February 27, 1900. He married, firstly, in 1834, Susan Ann Hayes, the daughter of Ezra and Rachel Hayes. Susan Ann was born in Rochester, January 25, 1815, and died March 20, 1875. William married, secondly, Ellen Hyde, who was born in Ossipee, New Hampshire, in 1834. The following children were born in Rochester, the first by the first wife and the remainder by the second.* Children:

        i. Sarah Ann Maria, b. 1842; d. 8/26/1843.

245.   ii. Thomas Herbert, b. 9/10/1852.

        iii. Julia A., b. 1854; m. 1872, Otis K. Perkins of Peabody, MA.

        iv. Sarah E., b. 1856.

        v. Grace Darling, b. 6/29/1858; m. 8/31/1879, Frank Calef; d. 2/3/1905. Six children.

        vi. John Jones, b. 2/8/1860; a carpenter, living unmarried in Louisville, KY in 1930.

152. Levi F. Roberts (Thomas⁶, Timothy⁵, Timothy⁴, Thomas³, John², Thomas¹), son of Thomas and Mehitable (Jones) Roberts, was born in Rochester, New Hampshire, November 2, 1829, and died July 7, 1885. He married Rachel M. Harriman, September 8, 1854. The daughter of David L. and Hannah (Goodwin) Harriman, Rachel was born in Conway, New Hampshire, January 30, 1831 and died January 2, 1911. Levi was an innkeeper in Epping, New Hampshire. The following children were born in Somersworth, New Hampshire.⁺ Children:

        i. Mark L., b. 10/1858; d. 11/9/1891.

        ii. Martha Ann, b. 9/16/1862; m. 4/18/1900, Edgar J. Ham; d. 8/15/1913. No children.

---

    * Hardon, Vol. III, pp. 135 & 144-6.
    ⁺ Hardon, Vol. III, pp. 136 & 149.

SEVENTH GENERATION

153. Joseph D. Roberts (Benjamin⁶, Benjamin⁵, Samuel⁴, Hatevil³, John², Thomas¹), son of Benjamin and Didamia (Nickerson) Roberts, was born August 21, 1795, and died September 2, 1853, apparently in Nova Scotia. He married Mercy Chandler, who was born February 5, 1798.* Children:

- i. Sarah, b. 9/12/1819.
- ii. Mathew, b. 11/24/1820.
- iii. Ephraim, b. 2/9/1823.
- iv. James A., b. 3/24/1825.
- v. Deidamia Anne, b. 11/22/1826.
- 246. vi. Joseph, b. 3/5/1829.
- vii. Mercy, b. 1/14/1831.
- viii. Hiram, b. 11/20/1832; m. Martha -----; d. 3/3/1910, Argyle, Yarmouth, NS.
- ix. Mary Ellen, b. 1/24/1835.
- x. David, b. 2/4/1837.
- xi. Lavinia, b. 1/15/1839.
- xii. Albert, b. 10/11/1840.

154. Reuben Roberts (Paul⁶, Samuel⁵, Samuel⁴, Hatevil³, John², Thomas¹), a mariner, son of Paul and Elizabeth (Floyd) Roberts, was born in Maine, about 1785. He married his fourth cousin Jane Roberts, the daughter of Francis (No. 71) and Jane (Lovering) Roberts. The following child was born in Newfield, Maine.⁺ Child:

247. i. Reuben, b. 8/7/1807.

155. Aaron Roberts (Aaron⁶, Samuel⁵, Samuel⁴, Hatevil³, John², Thomas¹), a farmer, son of Aaron and Sarah (Nock) Roberts,

---

* Clayton H. Roberts notes.
⁺ Hardon, Vol. III, pp. 158-62.

was born in Rollinsford, New Hampshire, September 23, 1817, and died in Providence, Rhode Island, January 27, 1897. He married Elizabeth Fernald, the daughter of Tristram and Judith (Brock) Fernald. Elizabeth was born in Waterboro, Maine, January 15, 1820, and died September 18, 1913. The following children were born in Rollinsford.* Children:

    i. Tristram Fernald, b. 10/8/1840; d. in infancy.

    ii. Martha Jane, b. 6/7/1844; m. 4/10/1870, Joel A. Cobb of Salem, MA; d. 9/21/1908. Two children.

    iii. Sarah Elizabeth, b. 7/4/1846; d. in infancy.

    iv. Susan Ellen, b. 1847; m. 3/30/1870, Albert E. Emerson. One child. Res. La Junta, CA in 1930.

248.   v. Simeon Brock, b. 1/18/1850.

    vi. Sarah Elizabeth, b. 11/30/1852; m. 8/11/1874, Walter S. McIntire. 6 children. Res. Boston 1930.

    vii. Mary Adeline, b. 1/14/1855; m. (1) 5/13/1882, John E. Sias, (2) 11/12/1919, William C. McKay. Four children. Living in Wilmar(?), CA in 1933.

    viii. Emma Francis, b. 3/27/1857; d. 9/23/1876.

156. Simon Roberts (Simon[6], Nathan[5], Samuel[4], Hatevil[3], John[2], Thomas[1]), son of Simon Roberts, was born in Maine, about 1789, and died there October 5, 1832. He married Agnes Woodbury, in Shapleigh, Maine, December 28, 1825. This family lived in Acton, Maine.⁺ Child:

    i. James, of Benton, ME.

157. Caleb Roberts (Benjamin[6], Nathan[5], Samuel[4], Hatevil[3], John[2], Thomas[1]), son of Benjamin and Sarah (Stevens) Roberts, was born in New Hampshire, in 1798, and died there April 9, 1844. He married March 5, 1826, Rhoda Horn, the daughter of Paul and

---

   * Hardon, Vol. III, pp. 158-165.
   ⁺ Hardon, Vol. III, p. 168.

SEVENTH GENERATION

Elizabeth (Pierce) Horn. She was born in Farmington, New Hampshire, October 19, 1798, and died August 6, 1887. The following children were born in Rochester.* Children:

249.   i. Samuel E., b. 1826.

250.   ii. Benjamin, b. 7/5/1827

     iii. Elizabeth, d. unm.

158. Joshua Roberts (Jonathan[6], Thomas[5], Joshua[4], Hatevil[3], John[2], Thomas[1]), son of Jonathan and Elizabeth (Foss) Roberts, was born in Barrington, New Hampshire, July 2, 1789. Except for the fact he had the following children, nothing else is known about him.⁺ Children:

  i. Moses, b. 10/15/1816.

  ii. Elizabeth, b. 3/20/1818.

  iii. Jonathan Ely, b. 12/10/1819.

  iv. William, b. 6/22/1821.

  v. Rufus K., b. 6/9/1823.

  vi. a son, b. 2/25/1825.

  vii. Joshua F., b. 3/28/1830.

159. Tobias Roberts (Jonathan[6], Thomas[5], Joshua[4], Hatevil[3], John[2], Thomas[1]), son of Jonathan and Elizabeth (Foss) Roberts, was born in Barnstead, New Hampshire, July 11, 1809, and apparently killed "in the West, 1868-1870." He married, firstly, July 24, 1842, Mary Adeline Cogswell, the daughter of the Rev. Frederic and Hannah Rogers (Peavey) Cogswell. Mary Adeline was born in Gilmanton, New Hampshire, July 16, 1818, and died November 2, 1849. Tobias married, secondly, January 9, 1851, Judith Frances Upham Cogswell, the sister of his deceased first wife. Judith was born in Gilmanton, February 14, 1834, and died August 20, 1875. Tobias was a machinist in Barnstead and Northwood, New

---

* Hardon, Vol. III, pp. 169-72.
⁺ Hardon, Vol. IV, p. 1.

Hampshire. This family moved to Cuba in 1848, and later to the U.S. West. The first two children, born in Barnstead, were by the first wife. The third child, also by the first wife, was born in Cuba. The fourth child, the only one with the second wife, was born in Northwood.* Children:

    i. Laura Frances Cogswell, b. 5/8/1845; m. 11/27/1862, Wentworth B. Hobbs of West Ossipee, NH; d. 3/27/1913.

    ii. Cynthia Allen, b. 5/17/1847; m. 3/13/1873, Melville A. Lynch of Boston, MA; d. 1/23/1918. No children.

    iii. Mary Adeline, b. 10/5/1849; m. 9/11/1872, Charles H. Ferguson of Dorchester, MA;d. 4/20/1931. 1 ch.

251.   iv. Ernest Upham, b. 10/29/1855.

160. George Seward Roberts (Jonathan[6], Thomas[5], Joshua[4], Hatevil[3], John[2], Thomas[1]), son of Jonathan and Elizabeth (Foss) Roberts, was born in Barnstead, New Hampshire, October 8, 1811, and died there or near there, September 27, 1897. He married September 20, 1837, Eliza Ann Bunker, who was born June 28, 1814, and died June 17, 1884. The following children were born in Barnstead.⁺ Children:

    i. Sarah Elizabeth, b. 6/27/1840; d. 8/24/1855.

252.   ii. Edwin Jonathan, b. 7/5/1842.

253.   iii. George Franklin, b. 3/25/1848.

254.   iv. Everett Lemuel, b. 8/8/1851.

161. William Roberts (Jonathan[6], Thomas[5], Joshua[4], Hatevil[3], John[2], Thomas[1]), a farmer, son of Jonathan and Elizabeth (Foss) Roberts, was born in Barnstead, New Hampshire, July 1 (or 2?), 1814, and died there or near there, June 27, 1882. He married,

---

* Hardon, Vol. IV, pp. 2-4.
⁺ Hardon, Vol. IV, pp. 6-8.

SEVENTH GENERATION

February 21, 1853, Mary Pickering, who was born in Barnstead, where the following child was also born.* Child:
    i. Charles, b. 1855; m. 11/30/1877, Ella A. Nutter; d. 5/6/1897. A farmer in Pittsfield, MA.

162. Joshua Roberts (Tobias⁶, Joshua⁵, Joshua⁴, Hatevil³, John², Thomas¹), son of Tobias and Lydia (Yeaton) Roberts, was born in Strafford, New Hampshire, April 21, 1815, and died there or near there, in March 1882. He married August 22, 1836, a cousin, Sarah Scruton, the daughter of William and Mary (Yeaton) Scruton. Sarah was born in Strafford, May 2, 1815, and died April 16, 1880. Joshua was a blacksmith and served as Selectman of Strafford and as a member of the state legislature. The following children were born in Strafford.⁺ Children:

    i. Mercy Adeline, b. 8/9/1837; m. 3/22/1866, Samuel S. Hale; d. 6/3/1925. Seven children.

255.   ii. Tobias, b. 11/30/1839.

    iii. Charles Edwin, b. 8/25/1841; d. 4/15/1859.

    iv. John Wesley, b. 5/23/1850; m. Jerusha A. Pease; d. 5/24/1887. A teacher in New Hampton.

    v. Mary Jane, b. 1853; m. 12/22/1878, Slorim Swain. Living in 1930.

    vi. Ella.

163. Tobias Westerly Roberts (Tobias⁶, Joshua⁵, Joshua⁴, Hatevil³, John², Thomas¹), son of Tobias and Lydia (Yeaton) Roberts, was born in Strafford, New Hampshire, August 16, 1820. He married, firstly, November 17, 1842, Mary Frances Smith, and, secondly, in 1846, Sarah Hammond, the daughter of Joseph and Sarah (Frost) Hammond. Sarah was born in Eliot, Maine, in 1826. Tobias was a manufacturer in Somersworth, and Lawrence, Massachusetts. The following child was by his first wife.# Child:

---

    * Hardon, Vol. IV, p. 12.
    ⁺ Hardon, Vol. III, pp. 3-7 & Vol. IV, pp. 15-8.
    # Hardon, Vol. IV, p. 23.

DESCENDANTS OF THOMAS & REBECCA ROBERTS

    i. Helen F., b. 1845.

164. John Yeaton Roberts (Tobias⁶, Joshua⁵, Joshua⁴, Hatevil³, John², Thomas¹), a manufacturer, son of Tobias and Lydia (Yeaton) Roberts, was born in Strafford, New Hampshire, October 20, 1826, and died in Providence, Rhode Island, May 22, 1864. He married August 29, 1849, Tamsen Mehitable Hayes, the daughter of Asa Brewster and Mehitable (Hayes) Hayes. Tamsen was born in Farmington, New Hampshire, in 1832, and died in Strafford, February 1, 1870. The following child was born in Providence.*
Child:

    i. John Herbert, b. 4/17/1860; m. 7/10/1889, Ethelyn H. Cargill. Living in Providence in 1930.

165. Richard Roberts (Joseph⁶, Joseph⁵, Joseph⁴, Joseph³, John², Thomas¹), son of Joseph and Anna (Trevett) Roberts, was born in Alton, New Hampshire, April 4, 1788, and died there or near there May 19, 1866. He married October 31, 1813, Hannah Willey, who was born in New Durham, New Hampshire, July 8, 1791, and died September 7, 1877. Richard was a farmer in Alton. In 1930 the farm was in the possession of Mrs. Ella S. Roberts, the widow of his grandson Sewell Edson Roberts. Richard was a captain in the militia, served in the War of 1812, and was also a deacon in the local church. The following children were born in New Durham.⁺ Children:

    i. Harriet, b. 4/20/1812; m. 2/2/1837, Nathaniel Willey; d. 4/14/1861. Two children.

    ii. Lydia S, b. 5/2/1814; m. 11/28/1833, Benjamin Evans; d. 1877(?). Six children. Went to MN.

    iii. Joseph, b. 7/27/1816; d. (drowning) 12/10/1831.

    iv. Clarissa, b. 5/14/1819; d. unm. 12/1/1840.

    v. a son (twin), b. 2/21/1822; d. 2/23/1822.

---

    * Hardon, Vol. IV, p. 24.
    ⁺ Hardon, Vol. IV, pp. 26-31.

SEVENTH GENERATION

256.	vi.	Sewall Trevett (twin), b. 2/21/1822.
257.	vii.	Samuel Woodbury, b. 1/8/1825.
	viii.	Orrin, b. 1827; d. (drowning) 7/20/1837.
258.	ix.	Richard, b. 5/12/1830.

166. Nathaniel Roberts (James⁶, Joseph⁵, Joseph⁴, Joseph³, John², Thomas¹), son of James and Mary (Leighton) Roberts, was born in Alton, New Hampshire, December 8, 1792. He married, firstly, December 31, 1814, Sarah Wentworth, the daughter of Paul and Deborah (Naylor) Wentworth. Sarah was born in Acton, Maine. Nathaniel married, secondly, in 1848, Love (Baker) Allard, who was born in Alton, in 1804. Nathaniel was superintendent of the County Farm. The following child, born in Alton, is by the first wife Sarah.* Child:

259.	i.	Allen, b. 1817.

167. John Roberts (Hanson⁶, Joseph⁵, Stephen⁴, Joseph³, John², Thomas¹), son of Hanson and Lydia (Henderson) Roberts, was born in Dover, New Hampshire, February 12, 1819, and died August 20, 1891. He married in Boston, Massachusetts, September 29, 1844, Mary Jane Banks, who was born in Nottingham, New Hampshire, September 3, 1818, and died March 26, 1880. The following children were born in Chelsea, Massachusetts.⁺ Children:

	i.	John F., b. 3/9/1845; d. 3/29/1861.
	ii.	Mary, b. 1847; d. 10/14/1847.
260.	iii.	Charles Samuel, b. 10/3/1859.

168. Oliver L. Roberts (Hanson⁶, Joseph⁵, Stephen⁴, Joseph³, John², Thomas¹), son of Hanson and Lydia (Henderson) Roberts, was born in Dover, New Hampshire, July 8, 1823, and died in 1885, apparently in Dover. He married Myrtilla A. Jackson, who was born in Abbott, Maine, in 1826 and died in Dover, June 14,

---

* Hardon, Vol. IV, p. 34.
⁺ Hardon, Vol. II, p. 83 & Vol. IV, p. 80.

1886. Oliver and his family lived in Boston at one time.* Children:

261.   i. Charles Andrew, b. 12/23/1857.

    ii. Elizabeth U.

169. Thomas H. Roberts (Hanson[6], Joseph[5], Stephen[4], Joseph[3], John[2], Thomas[1]), son of Hanson and Lydia (Henderson) Roberts, was born in Dover, New Hampshire, July 20, 1825, and died June 21, 1900 in Dover. He married Anstis H. -----, who was born April 12, 1832 and died September 22, 1887. Thomas was a tailor in Boston.[+] Child:

    i. Maria A., d. 12/16/1867, Boston.

170. Howard Millet Roberts (Hanson[6], Joseph[5], Stephen[4], Joseph[3], John[2], Thomas[1]), son of Hanson and Lydia (Henderson) Roberts, was born in Dover, New Hampshire, August 15, 1832, and died July 28, 1917. He married, April 25, 1858, his fifth cousin, Sarah Torr Roberts, the daughter of Alonzo (No. 115) and Mary (Torr) Roberts. Sarah was born July 10, 1838, and died May 29, 1923. The following children were born in Dover. Howard was a farmer and a brick maker in Dover.[#] Children:

    i. Fred Howard, b. 3/7/1859; d. unm. 10/7/1928. A farmer in Dover.

    ii. Stephen William, b. 2/7/1872; d. unm. 7/26/1930 "of drink". Member of the NH state legis. 1923-4.

171. Daniel Roberts (Stephen[6], John[5], Stephen[4], Joseph[3], John[2], Thomas[1]), son of Stephen and Lydia (Ricker) Roberts, was born in North Berwick, Maine, September 6, 1800, and died December 21, 1884. He married Lucy Frost, who was born July 28, 1803, and died July 23, 1899.** Children:

    i. Jane, m. 6/7/1853, Alexander Nelson.

    ii. Lois, m. Robert Gibson.

---

    * Hardon, Vol. II, p. 84 & Vol IV, pp. 81-3.
    + Hardon, Vol. II, p. 116.
    # Hardon, Vol. II, p. 116.
    ** Hardon, Vol. IV, pp. 42-6.

SEVENTH GENERATION

    iii. Lydia Maria, b. 2/1857; m. 10/26/1880, Andrew Buchanan; d. 11/1878.

    iv. George, of Los Angeles, CA.

    v. Hugh Wellington, of Los Angeles, CA.

172. John Roberts (Stephen^6, John^5, Stephen^4, Joseph^3, John^2, Thomas^1), son of Stephen and Lydia (Ricker) Roberts, was born in North Berwick, Maine, August 14, 1802, and died, apparently in Groton, Vermont, May 28, 1890. He married December 4, 1828, Charlotte Rhodes, the daughter of Oliver and Martha (Pratt) Rhodes. Charlotte was born in Groton, November 19, 1806, and died July 1, 1859. John was a farmer and town officer in Groton.* Children:

    i. Emily, b. 10/5/1829; m. 1/3/1847, John W. Plummer; d. March 15, 1915. This family went to farm in Washington, IA.

    ii. (?).

262.   iii. Jackson, b. 5/9/1836.

    iv. Daniel, b. 4/5/1838; m. 1877, Martha Noyes. Went to mine in French Corral, CA. Appar. no ch.

    v. John Homan, b. 12/25/1843; m. (1) Sarah Powers, (2) Martha Noyes; d. 10/28/1923. Went to farm in San Diego, CA. No children.

    vi. Thomas Gilmore, b. 10/18/1850; m. (1) 10/12/1884, Nettie A. Wagner, (2) 6/2/1904, Josephine (McKenzie) Keister, (3) 6/26/1912, Laura Josephine Winkler; d. 4/24/1922, Davenport, IA. No children. He was a homeopathic physician and graduate of and lecturer at Herring Medical School in Chicago.

173. Stephen Roberts (Stephen^6, John^5, Stephen^4, Joseph^3,

---

* Hardon, Vol. IV, pp. 50-4.

DESCENDANTS OF THOMAS & REBECCA ROBERTS

John[2], Thomas[1]), son of Stephen and Lydia (Ricker) Roberts, was born in North Berwick, Maine, June 26, 1806(?). He married Olive Hodgdon. Nothing else is known about this family, apart from the fact they had the following children.* Children:

    i. Lydia, m. Asa Harriman; d. 1868, Craftsbury, VT. One child.

    ii. Mary Ann, m.(1) Herman Fitz, (2) -----Sawyer. Lived in Iowa and South Dakota.

    iii. Sarah, m. Noble Kinney of Albany, VT. 3 ch.

    iv. Thomas J., of Willimantic, CT.

    v. Chastine H., b. 6/26/1846; m. Asa M. Harriman. Two children.

    vi. John, a jeweler, of Marshalltown, IA.

174. James Roberts (Temple[6], John[5], Stephen[4], Joseph[3], John[2], Thomas[1]), son of Temple and Rebecca (Wilson) Roberts, was born in Danvers, Massachusetts, about 1810. His wife's name was Lucy, but that is all that is known about her, except that she and James had the following children in Salem, New Hampshire.⁺ Children:

    i. Susan P., b. 6/20/1830; d. unm.

    ii. Isaac H., b. 7/15/1836. Served in the 14th and/or the First NH Vol. Infantry in the Civil War.

    iii. Orsino, b. 6/25/1839. Served in the 9th NH Vol. Infantry in the Civil War. Lived in Salem, NH.

175. Stephen Roberts (Temple[6], John[5], Stephen[4], Joseph[3], John[2], Thomas[1]), son of Temple and Rebecca (Wilson) Roberts, was born in Danvers, Massachusetts, February 2, 1815. His wife's name was Mary, but that is all that is known about this family except that Stephen and Mary had the following children, the first two of which were born in Salem, New Hampshire, and the remainder in

---

    * Hardon, Vol. IV, pp. 63-5.
    ⁺ Hardon, Vol. IV, p. 67.

SEVENTH GENERATION

Somersworth, New Hampshire.* Children:
- i. Walter Jackson, b. 8/16/1843.
- ii. Eliza Plummer, b. 11/6/1844.
- iii. Mary Ann Gray, b. 7/7/1846.
- iv. May Elizabeth, b. 7/31/1848.

176. John Clendenin Roberts (Temple[6], John[5], Stephen[4], Joseph[3], John[2], Thomas[1]), a farmer, son of Temple and Rebecca (Wilson) Roberts, was born in Salem, New Hampshire, April 11, 1830, and died there or near there, January 22, 1891. He married March 12, 1869, Evelyn A. Hysler, who was born in Warren, Maine. The following children were born in Salem.⁺ Children:
- i. Frederick M., b. 1/21/1870; m. (1) ?, (2) 3/31/1923, Linnie E. (Smith) Hill. A shoemaker in Nashua, NH. They were living in 1930.
- ii. Frank M., b. 11/28/1877; m. 10/28/1903, Harriet Robie. A farmer in Salem. Living in 1930.

177. George Roberts (Temple[6], John[5], Stephen[4], Joseph[3], John[2], Thomas[1]), a shoemaker, son of Temple and Rebecca (Wilson) Roberts, was born in Salem, New Hampshire, March 24, 1836, and died there or near there, December 3, 1913. He married, firstly, Mary -----, and secondly, Mary E. Estes, who was born in Fairfield, Maine. Nothing else is known about this family, other than the following children, who were born in Salem, the first four by the first Mary and the fifth by the second Mary.# Children:
- i. a child, b. 1/23/1868.
- ii. William V., b. 9/18/1870.
- iii. Rufus T., b. 11/22/1876.
- iv. Clara A., b. 3/26/1878.

---

* Hardon, Vol. IV, pp. 68-9.
⁺ Hardon, Vol. IV, p. 70.
Hardon, Vol. IV, pp. 71-2.

v. Edwin, b. 12/10/1884; d. 12/12/1884.

178. Thomas Heard Roberts (Nicholas[6], John[5], Stephen[4], Joseph[3], John[2], Thomas[1]), son of Nicholas Hanson and Dorothy (Heard) Roberts, was born in Albion, Maine, December 20, 1833, and died March 29, 1916. He married November 24, 1866, Eliza Jane Hilton, the daughter of Andrew and Eliza Ann (Paul) Hilton. Eliza was born in Acton, Maine, February 28, 1841, and died October 1, 1927. Thomas was a farmer in Acton, Maine. The following children were born in Milton or Milton Mills, New Hampshire.[*] Children:

        i. Dora Etta, b. 4/22/1872. Living unmarried, a dietician at Bates College in 1930.

263.   ii. John Hilton, b. 3/9/1875.

179. Oliver Ayer Roberts (Oliver[6], John[5], Stephen[4], Joseph[3], John[2], Thomas[1]), son of Oliver Heard and Julia Ann (Ayer) Roberts, was born in Haverhill, Massachusetts, March 17, 1838, and died, apparently in Ohio, some time after 1922. He married at Yellow Springs, Ohio, March 17, 1864, Emily Wilbor Botsford, the daughter of Josiah L. and Lucy Anne (Brewster) Botsford. Emily was born in Huron, Ohio, May 21, 1840. Oliver studied divinity at Antioch College, and then worked as a teacher and minister in Melrose, Massachusetts. At the outbreak of the Civil War he enlisted in the 50th Massachusetts Volunteer Infantry, and later moved to Ohio, where he enlisted in the 110th Ohio Volunteer Infantry. After the War he authored a book entitled the *History of the Ancient and Honorable Artillery*.[+] Children:

        i. Oliver Brewster, b. 3/5/1869, Le Grand, Iowa; d. unm. 11/9/1926. A graduate of Harvard (1890) and a teacher in Southboro, MA.

264.   ii. Stephen Herbert, b. 11/7/1874.

180. Benjamin Roberts (Aaron[6], Aaron[5], Ebenezer[4], Joseph[3], John[2], Thomas[1]), a farmer, son of Aaron and Mary (Knight)

---

[*] Hardon, Vol. IV, p. 74.
[+] Hardon, Vol. IV, pp. 78-9.

SEVENTH GENERATION

Roberts, was born in Berwick, Maine, September 28, 1804. He married in Berwick, February 22, 1849, Lois Stone. Nothing else is known about this family, and there may well have been additional children.* Child:

    i. Sarah, b. 1850.

181. Aaron H. Roberts (Aaron⁶, Aaron⁵, Ebenezer⁴, Joseph³, John², Thomas¹), son of Aaron and Mary (Knight) Roberts, was born in Berwick, Maine, April 6, 1812, and died there, or near there, in 1853. He married Jane Stone, who was born in 1813.⁺ Children:

    i. Mary A., b. 1842.

    ii. Oliver, b. 1844.

    iii. Laura F., b. 1848.

182. Isaac Roberts (Joseph⁶, James⁵, Ebenezer⁴, Joseph³, John², Thomas¹), a farmer, son of Joseph and Mercy (Hobbs) Roberts, was born in Lyman, Maine, in 1779, and died some time between 1860 and 1870, apparently in Lyman or thereabouts. He married, firstly, in Alfred, Maine, January 24, 1811, Lois Whitten (or Whittier), and secondly, Ruth -----, who was born in 1787 and died between 1860 and 1870. The following children were born in Lyman.# Children:

    i. Charles, b. 1816. A farmer in Lyman.

    ii. Louisa, b. 1818; living unm. in 1870.

    iii. Sarah L., b. 1820; living unm. in 1870.

    iv. Julia A., b. 1824.

183. James H. Roberts (Joseph⁶, James⁵, Ebenezer⁴, Joseph³, John², Thomas¹), son of Joseph and Mercy (Hobbs) Roberts, was born in Lyman, Maine, August 23, 1789, and died some time after 1840. He married Olive -----, who was born in 1793. The

---

    * Hardon, Vol. IV, p. 86.
    ⁺ Hardon, Vol. IV, p. 87.
    # Hardon, Vol. IV, p. 84.

following children were born in Lyman.* Children:

    i. Joseph B., b. 1831; m. Cordelia -----; d. 8/4/1873. No children.

    ii. Alma, m. 10/28/1838, Jeremiah (No. 188) Roberts, her second cousin once removed; d. Buffalo, NY, 11/22/1897.

    iii. Ellen E., m. ----- Bedell.

184. James H. Roberts (Reuben^6, John^5, Ebenezer^4, Joseph^3, John^2, Thomas^1), a farmer, son of Reuben Roberts, was born in Maine in 1816. He married Rachel -----, who was born in Maine in 1814.⁺ Children:

    i. Walter J., b. 1846.

    ii. Emma J., b. 1849.

    iii. Alonzo F., b. 1851; m. (1) Alfred, ME, 5/17/1890, Elizabeth M. Marshall, (2) 10/30/1912, Harriet Sander. This family lived in Lyman, ME.

    iv. Sarah, b. 1851.

    v. Lillie Martha, b. 1855.

185. Hiram Rollins Roberts (Stephen^6, John^5, Ebenezer^4, Joseph^3, John^2, Thomas^1), son of Stephen and Deborah (Wentworth) Roberts, was born in Somersworth (now Rollinsford), New Hampshire, May 16, 1806, and died there May 30, 1876. He married November 7, 1830, in Dover, New Hampshire, Ruth Ham, the daughter of John and Mercy (Wentworth) Ham. Ruth was born in Dover, November 23, 1808, and died February 5, 1901.

Hiram's father died when he was fourteen and he became the sole support of his widowed mother. He managed the family farm, which was the original homestead of his great-grandfather, Ebenezer Roberts, and became one of the organizers of the Strafford Agricultural Society. He also attended the academy at South

---

    * Hardon, Vol. IV, p. 85.
    ⁺ Hardon, Vol. IV, p. 88.

SEVENTH GENERATION

Berwick, Maine, and taught school. First holding the office of town selectman, Hiram represented the town of Somersworth in the state legislature in 1837. In 1839 he was appointed as a justice of the Court of Common Pleas, and in 1852, probate judge. In 1875 he was nominated as the Democratic Party candidate for governor of New Hampshire, but lost by some 200 votes.

Hiram also had a career in finance, having been one of the incorporators of and president of both the Salmon Falls Bank and the Rollinsford Savings Bank. For over forty years he was a member of the Baptist Church in South Berwick and served for most of that time as superintendent of the Sunday school. The following children were born in Somersworth (now Rollinsford).*
Children:

    i. John Ham, b. 10/27/1831; d. unm. 7/26/1889.

    ii. Stephen, b. 2/25/1834; d. unm. 10/2/1854.

    iii. Elizabeth, b. 11/25/1836; d. 8/12/1842.

    iv. Edward H., b. 6/11/1839; d. unm. 11/11/1859.

265. v. Walter Scott, b. 1/21/1842.

266. vi. Hall, b. 3/7/1844.

    vii. Susan Jane, b. 3/13/1847; m. 12/1/1875, Samuel H. Rollins; d. 10/25/1925. No children.

267. viii. Joseph Doe, b. 11/12/1848.

268. ix. Francis Wayland, b. 12/16/1851.

186. William Hall Roberts (Stephen^6, John^5, Ebenezer^4, Joseph^3, John^2, Thomas^1), son of Stephen and Deborah (Wentworth) Roberts, was born in Somersworth (now Rollinsford), New Hampshire, July 1, 1808, and died there, or near there, May 11, 1859. He married September 7, 1831, his second cousin, Clarissa

---

  * Hardon, Vol. IV, pp. 89-93; Hurd, D. Hamilton. *History of Rockingham & Strafford Counties, New Hampshire...* Philadelphia: J.W. Lewis, 1882, p. 674.

DESCENDANTS OF THOMAS & REBECCA ROBERTS

Hall, the daughter of Philip and Joanna (Nason) Hall. She was born in North Berwick, Maine, March 3, 1813, and died September 26, 1899. William was a farmer and the first president of the Rollinsford State Bank and the Rollinsford Savings Bank. The following children were born in Somersworth (now Rollinsford).*
Children:

269.
   i. Moses, b. 6/7/1832.

   ii. Mercy Hall, b. 8/3/1835; d. unm. 5/31/1924.

   iii. Elizabeth Aville, b. 12/31/1836; m. Samuel Tolman of Chicago, in 1860; d. 4/22/1926. 2 ch.

   iv. George Hall, b. 2/28/1839; d. 1/7/1840.

   v. Harriet Augusta, b. 12/28/1841; m. 7/2/1873, William S. Walker, Chicago; d. 1/24/1923. 2 ch.

187. Ichabod Roberts (Jeremiah[6], Ichabod[5], Ebenezer[4], Joseph[3], John[2], Thomas[1]), a farmer, son of Jeremiah and Elizabeth (Lord) Roberts, was born in Waterboro, Maine, in 1803. He married Elizabeth S. Smith, the daughter of Daniel and Elizabeth Smith. Elizabeth was born in Somersworth, New Hampshire, in 1806 and died April 9, 1881. The following children were born in Waterboro.⁺ Children:

   i. Silas S., b. 1831.

   ii. Helen A., b. 1833.

   iii. Elizabeth J., b. 1838; m. 6/6/1867, Henry A. Hubbard.

   iv. Milton S., b. 1840.

   v. Marcia Ann, b. 11/26/1844; d. unm. 1/2/1926, Dover.

188. Jeremiah Roberts (Jeremiah[6], Ichabod[5], Ebenezer[4], Joseph[3], John[2], Thomas[1]), a farmer, son of Jeremiah and Elizabeth

---

* Hardon, Vol. IV, pp. 100-1.
⁺ Hardon, Vol. IV, p. 106.

SEVENTH GENERATION

(Lord) Roberts, was born in Waterboro, Maine, April 22, 1817 and died in Buffalo, New York, May 8, 1890. He married, October 28, 1838, his second cousin once removed, Alma Roberts, the daughter of James H. (No. 183) and Olive Roberts. The following children were born in Waterboro.* Children:

270. i.   Franklin Kimball, b. 1840.

271. ii. James Arthur, b. 3/8/1847.

189. Isaac Roberts (David[6], Nathaniel[5], Nathaniel[4], Nathaniel[3], Thomas[2], Thomas[1]), a saddler, son of David and Elizabeth (Langley) Roberts, was born in Farmington, New Hampshire, October 23, 1781. He married, February 24, 1804, Elsie Pinkham. The following children were born in Farmington.⁺ Children:

i.   Elizabeth, b. 5/19/1805.

ii.   Samuel, b. 10/31/1806.

iii. Nancy, b. 9/29/1808.

iv.   Hannah, b. 9/16/1810.

v.   Sarah, b. 12/12/1812.

vi.   John W., b. 7/22/1815; d. 4/17/1834.

vii. Mary, b. 6/15/1818.

viii. Martha, b. 9/13/1820.

190. David Roberts (David[6], Nathaniel[5], Nathaniel[4], Nathaniel[3], Thomas[2], Thomas[1]), son of David and Elizabeth (Langley) Roberts, was born in Farmington, New Hampshire, in 1789, and died April 5, 1864. He married February 11, 1819, Elizabeth Canney, the daughter of John and Anna Canney. Elizabeth was born in 1800. David was a farmer in Farmington and New Durham, New Hampshire.# Children:

---

* Hardon, Vol. IV, pp. 106-7; Little, Vol. III, p. 1635.
⁺ Hardon, Vol. IV, p. 13.
Hardon, Vol. IV, p. 14.

i. Anna, b. 8/19/1824; d. 8/31/1826.

ii. Jonas, b. 10/23/1828.

iii. Procinda, b. 1/10/1831.

191. Hanson Roberts (David[6], Nathaniel[5], Nathaniel[4], Nathaniel[3], Thomas[2], Thomas[1]), son of David and Hannah (Meader) Roberts, was born in Farmington, New Hampshire, October 23 (or December 23?), 1797, and died there, or near there, August 26, 1869. He married Eleanor Cooper Kimball, the daughter of Ephraim and Hannah (Emerson) Kimball. Eleanor was born in Rochester, New Hampshire, March 31, 1801, and died September 21, 1872. Hanson was a farmer in Dover and Farmington, where the following children were born.* Children:

272. i. David Sands, b. 9/22/1822.

ii. Adeline A., b. 5/1824; m. 3/16/1846, Freeman P. Howe; d. 12/21/1900. Four children.

iii. Ephraim K., b. 4/18/1826; m. 6/1853, Eliza A. Lord; d. 1/2/1908. No ch. Shoemaker, Farmington.

273. iv. Charles Clarence, b. 1829.

v. Edmund, b. 1834; m. 12/6/1865, Agnes (LaBonte) Locke. No children.

274. vi. Harrison F., b. 1836.

vii. Lorenzo D., b. 5/24/1839; m. Ella Stewart. A farmer and lumberman in New Durham, NH.

viii. Henry Clay, b. 8/1/1841; d. unm. 4/5/1864 "blown up in a powder mill".

192. Jedediah Roberts (David[6], Nathaniel[5], Nathaniel[4], Nathaniel[3], Thomas[2], Thomas[1]), a farmer, son of David and Hannah

---

* Hardon, Vol. IV, pp. 113-9.

SEVENTH GENERATION

(Meader) Roberts, was born in Farmington, New Hampshire, April 25, 1801. Nothing else is known, except he had the following daughter, born in Farmington.* Child:

 i. Adeline, b. 1825; m. Freeman P. Howe. 1 ch.

193. Ira Roberts (John[6], George[5], Nathaniel[4], Nathaniel[3], Thomas[2], Thomas[1]), a carpenter, son of John and Mary (Davis) Roberts, was born in Middleton, New Hampshire, March 4, 1810 and died June 2, 1875. He married, firstly, Belinda T. Merritt, who was born in Massachusetts, December 28, 1819, and died August 2, 1860. Ira married, secondly, October 25, 1861, Caroline Celesta (Foss) Ricker, who was born in Middleton, October 28, 1823, and died January 31, 1899. Caroline was the daughter of John and Lydia (Wingate) Foss and the widow of Joshua A. Ricker. The first three children below, all by the first wife, were born in New Durham, New Hampshire. The remaining two, by the second wife, were born in Milton, New Hampshire.⁺ Children:

275. i. Edward Everett, b. 7/12/1841.

 ii. Winfield Adams, b. 5/15/1848; d. unm. 4/12/1911. An artisan in Farmington, NH.

 iii. Arthur Webster, b. 3/30/1850; d. unm. An artisan in Farmington.

 iv. Frederick Belknap, b. 3/25/1863; m. 10/10/1917, Mary Jane (Rayner)(Burke) Spaulding. Frederick, a lumber merchant, and Mary res. Milton in 1930.

 v. Sadie Bell, b. 1/6/1869. Living unm. Milton, 1930.

194. George Belknap Roberts (John[6], George[5], Nathaniel[4], Nathaniel[3], Thomas[2], Thomas[1]), son of John and Mary (Davis) Roberts, was born in Middleton, New Hampshire, December 9, 1819, and died June 11, 1896. He married Susan S. Folsom, the daughter of John and Susan (Jackson) Folsom. Susan was born in

---

 * Hardon, Vol. IV, p. 127.
 ⁺ Hardon, Vol. IV, pp. 110-1.

Tamworth, New Hampshire, April 18, 1817, and died December 4, 1895. George was a manufacturer in Rochester, New Hampshire. He was elected to the state legislature and served from 1855 to 1860. From 1869 on he was postmaster of Rochester, where the following children were born.* Children:

    i. Mary Ann, b. 1843; m. 10/24/1859, Isaac S. Cater. One child.

    ii. Sarah E., b. 10/22/1851; d. 3/29/1867.

195. John Davis Roberts (John^6, George^5, Nathaniel^4, Nathaniel^3, Thomas^2, Thomas^1), son of John and Mary (Davis) Roberts, was born in Middleton, New Hampshire, May 4, 1822, and died December 20, 1902. He married September 6, 1846, Lydia Buzzell Frost, the daughter of Nathaniel and Dorothy (Buzzell) Frost. Lydia was born in Middleton, September 10, 1818, and died November 16, 1893. John was a farmer and shoemaker in Middleton, where the following children were born.⁺ Children:

    i. a son, d. 5/3/1847.

    ii. Emma Sophia, b. 10/27/1848; d. unm. 6/4/1869.

    iii. Mary Ellen, b. 11/7/1850; d. 7/19/1853.

    iv. Nathaniel Frank, b. 1/10/1855; m. 6/12/1879, Helen Augusta Murch. No children. A postmaster in Farmington; living in 1933.

196. Alonzo Roberts (Aaron^6, Daniel^5, Aaron^4, Nathaniel^3, Thomas^2, Thomas^1), son of Aaron and Maria (Gage) Roberts, was born in North Wolfeboro, New Hampshire, May 7, 1830, and died in Chicago, Illinois, August 18, 1898. He married April 14, 1858, Elizabeth Ann Copp Maleham, the daughter of Joseph and Rachel (Horn) Maleham. Elizabeth was born in Wakefield, New Hampshire, August 17, 1832, and died in Chicago, September 20, 1912. Alonzo was a merchant in Lacon, Illinois, where the

---

   * Hardon, Vol. IV, p. 112.
   ⁺ Hardon, Vol. II, p. 142.

SEVENTH GENERATION

following children were born.# Children:

    i. Nellie R., b. 5/3/1862; d. 1/12/1869.

276.   ii. Charles Aaron, b. 3/12/1865.

    iii. Mary Elizabeth, b. 5/3/1869; d. 8/5/1870.

197. Andrew Torr Roberts (Alonzo^6, Daniel^5, Aaron^4, Nathaniel^3, Thomas^2, Thomas^1), son of Alonzo and Mary (Torr) Roberts, was born in Dover, New Hampshire, February 2, 1828, and died March 15, 1909. He married January 1, 1856, Ann Elizabeth Roberts, the daughter of Aaron and Mary (Bennett) Roberts. Ann was born in Dover, June 30, 1838, and died November 27, 1912. Andrew was a farmer and brick maker in Dover, where the following children were born.+ Children:

277.   i. Clarence Herman, b. 2/12/1857.

    ii. Arabella Lizzie, b. 4/3/1863; m. 12/31/1889, Harry Mason. One child. Living in Dover in 1930.

    iii. Emma Zanette, b. 8/14/1866; m. 8/14/1891, Elwin A. Reed.

198. Aaron Roberts (Alonzo^6, Daniel^5, Aaron^4, Nathaniel^3, Thomas^2, Thomas^1), a mason, son of Alonzo and Mary (Torr) Roberts, was born in Dover, New Hampshire, May 30, 1829, and died there, or near there, January 2, 1900. He married Ann Eliza Arnold, the daughter of James and Dina (Williams) Arnold. Ann Eliza was born in Providence, Rhode Island, May 4, 1833, and died April 3, 1904. The following children were born in Dover.# Children:

    i. Hannah Maria, b. 5/30/1854; m. 4/24/1871, John H. Henderson. Living in Dover in 1930. Two ch.

278.   ii. Preston Fremont, b. 11/2/1856.

---

* Hardon, Vol. IV, p. 128.
+ Hardon, Vol. IV, p. 130.
# Hardon, Vol. IV, p. 131-2.

DESCENDANTS OF THOMAS & REBECCA ROBERTS

279.
    iii. William Aaron, b. 9/24/1860.

    iv. George, b. 10/18/1867; m. 12/22/1892, Harriet B. Morrill; d. 6/7/1893. No children. A designer of dress fabrics in Dover.

    v. Annie Alberta, b. 6/11/1875; m. 9/11/1897, Frederick W. Neal. No ch. Res. Dover in 1930.

199. Daniel William Roberts (Alonzo[6], Daniel[5], Aaron[4], Nathaniel[3], Thomas[2], Thomas[1]), a farmer, son of Alonzo and Mary (Torr) Roberts, was born in Dover, New Hampshire, March 29, 1833, and died there, or near there, January 19, 1879. He married April 18, 1858, Lucy Wentworth, the daughter of Isaac and Lucy (Twombly) Wentworth. She was born in North Rochester, New Hampshire, December 12, 1830, and died February 11, 1911. Their only child was born in Dover.* Child:

    i. Eva Lucy, b. 8/11/1867; m. 10/19/1901, Albert J. West; d. 6/30/1928. No children.

200. Stephen Roberts (Thomas[6], James[5], Moses[4], Nathaniel[3], Thomas[2], Thomas[1]), son of Thomas and Elizabeth (Roberts) Roberts, was born in New Durham, New Hampshire, July 27, 1820, and died November 6, 1883. He married April 14, 1860, Mary Hannah Peaslee, the daughter of Elijah and Abigail (Gove) Peaslee. Mary Hannah was born April 2, 1832, and died July 11, 1900. Stephen may have been married previously and had two daughters, Mary Ann and Mary Elizabeth, who were born in Somersworth, New Hampshire, July 7, 1846 and July 31, 1848. Stephen graduated from Dartmouth College (1851) and went west to pursue a career in teaching, in Le Grand, Iowa, and in Lake City, Minnesota, where the following children (along with four who died in infancy) were born.+ Children:

    i. Abigail Peaslee, b. 10/4/1860; living unm. in San Jose, CA (1930).

---

    * Hardon, Vol. II, p. 171.
    + Hardon, Vol. II, pp. 174-5 & Vol. IV, p. 36.

SEVENTH GENERATION

    ii.   Edwin Lindly, b. 8/15/1865; d. unm. 7/31/1914.

    iii. Elizabeth Clarice, b. 4/22/1868; d. unm. 12/25/1895.

201. Thomas Elwood Roberts (Thomas^6, James^5, Moses^4, Nathaniel^3, Thomas^2, Thomas^1), son of Thomas and Elizabeth (Roberts) Roberts, was born in New Durham, New Hampshire, November 8, 1836, and died in New Hampshire, July 17, 1892. His wife's name was Hannah J.; and they had two children born in Farmington, New Hampshire.* Children:

    i.   Lydia E., b. 1870; d. 5/9/1871.

    ii. Albert E., b. 10/27/1876(?); d. 9/13/1871(?).

202. Charles White Roberts (Jeremiah^6, James^5, Moses^4, Nathaniel^3, Thomas^2, Thomas^1), a farmer, son of Jeremiah and Love (Wingate) Roberts, was born in Sandwich, New Hampshire, March 1, 1822, and died October 1, 1900. He married December 1, 1850, Almira Varney, the daughter of Andrew and Susan (Footman) Varney. Almira was born in Dover, New Hampshire, August 3, 1829, and died July 8, 1882. The following children were born in Dover.⁺ Children:

    i.   Ellen Frances, b. 5/11/1852. Residing unm. in Dover in 1930.

    ii. Susan Amanda, b. 2/10/1859; d. 8/3/1868.

203. John Meder Roberts (Jeremiah^6, James^5, Moses^4, Nathaniel^3, Thomas^2, Thomas^1), son of Jeremiah and Love (Wingate) Roberts, was born in Sandwich, New Hampshire, November 19, 1824, and died in 1911. He married Helena Mills. This family lived in Muscatine, Iowa and Eugene, Oregon.# Children:

---

  * Hardon, Vol. IV, p. 37.
  ⁺ Hardon, Vol. II, p. 177.
  # Hardon, Vol. IV, p. 135-8.

280.   i. Charles Edwin, b. 1852.

ii. Elnora, b. 10/22/1854; d. infancy.

iii. George Herbert, b. 11/29/1855; m. 11/30/1910, Lavinia Solendia Knapp; living in 1930.

iv. Mercy, b. 12/5/1862; d. infancy.

v. Anna, b. 7/11/1869; d. infancy.

vi. Mary Adeline, b. 2/21/1866; m. 12/24/1883, Charles H. Vandenburg. Three children. Living in Cottage Grove, OR in 1930.

vii. Gertrude Helena, b. 1/9/1874; m. James I. Jones. Five children.

204. Daniel W. Roberts (Jeremiah[6], James[5], Moses[4], Nathaniel[3], Thomas[2], Thomas[1]), son of Jeremiah and Love (Wingate) Roberts, was born in Sandwich, New Hampshire, January 19, 1842. He married Louisa Atwood. This family moved to Iowa, where they took up farming, at Muscatine, where the following children were born, and at Oskaloosa.* Children:

i. Gilbert Jeremiah, b. 1866; m. Kathleen -----. Living in Ceres, CA in 1930.

ii. Arthur, d. in infancy.

iii. Adeline, d. in infancy.

iv. J. Clifford, m. Mabel -----; d. 10/1933. No children. A teacher in Whittier, CA.

v. Fred, an osteopathic physician in Des Moines, IA in 1930.

vi. Caroline M., res. unm., Long Beach, CA in 1930.

281.   vii. William L.

205. Amos K. Roberts (Stephen[6], James[5], Moses[4], Nathaniel[3],

---

* Hardon, Vol. IV, pp. 140-2.

SEVENTH GENERATION

Thomas², Thomas¹), a store keeper and farmer, son of Stephen and Love (Canney) Roberts, was born in Rochester, New Hampshire, December 19, 1835 and died in 1907 of apoplexy. He married December 15, 1857, Ann Mary Tuttle, who was born December 15, 1835, and died April 8, 1887, of consumption. This family lived in Dover, Skowhegan, Maine, Rochester, New Hampshire, and Brookfield, Massachusetts.* Children:

    i. Flora Belle, b. 1860, Dover; m. Metcalf Richardson, 1883; d. 1850. Four children.

    ii. Ceolia Josephine, b. 10/21/1861; m. Charles H. Bennett, 7/26/1878; d. 12/4/1902. Three children.

206. George Roberts (George⁶, John⁵, Alexander⁴, John³, Thomas², Thomas¹), son of George and Mary (Roberts) Roberts, was born in New Hampshire, in 1819. He married Lucy A. Davis, the daughter of Walter and Susan (Dexter) Davis. She was born in Boston, Massachusetts, in April of 1829, and died October 30, 1887. George was a farmer in Somersworth, New Hampshire. This family also lived in Boston, where the first child was born.⁺ Children:

    i. George H., b. 6/29/1848; d. 5/12/1907. A farmer in Franklin, NH.

    ii. Adelaide, b. 1850.

    iii. Walter, b. 1854.

    iv. Charles, b. 1856.

    v. Willis, b. 1859.

207. Alexander Roberts (George⁶, Thomas⁵, Alexander⁴, John³, Thomas², Thomas¹), a stationary engineer, son of George W. and Sarah (Woodhouse) Roberts, was born in Rochester, New Hampshire, in 1832, and died May 16, 1874. He married Caroline Hayes Plummer, the daughter of William and Pamela (Waldron) Plummer. Caroline was born November 1, 1837, and died May 16,

---

* Hardon, Vol. IV, p. 41; Wilson, pp. 19, 28 & 39-40.
⁺ Hardon, Vol. IV, p. 145.

1874. Alexander, Caroline, and their two daughters perished in the Mill River flood at Williamsburg, Massachusetts, May 16, 1874. The first child, and perhaps others, were born in Rollinsford, New Hampshire.* Children:

282. i. George William, b. 8/21/1859.

 ii. Nettie, b. 1867; d. 5/16/1874.

 iii. Olivette J., b. 1872; d. 5/16/1874.

208. George Thomas Roberts (George[6], Thomas[5], Alexander[4], John[3], Thomas[2], Thomas[1]), son of George W. and Sarah (Woodhouse) Roberts, was born in Rochester, New Hampshire, November 9, 1836. He married at South Berwick, Maine, May 2, 1862, Lydia E. Smith.† Child:

 i. George W. Living in 1930 in Boston, a lawyer and member of the City Council.

---

* Hardon, Vol. IV, pp. 146-7.
† Hardon, Vol. III, p. 1 & Vol. IV, p. 148.

EIGHTH GENERATION

209. Reuben Davis Roberts (George[7], Joseph[6], George[5], William[4], John[3], John[2], Thomas[1]), son of George and Hannah (Davis) Roberts, was born in Cape Elizabeth, Maine, November 4, 1798, and died in Portland, Maine, October 27, 1851.

He married, firstly, April 10, 1822, Mary Ann Flagg Baker, the daughter of Thomas and Mary (Cullis) Baker. Mary Ann was born in or near Portland, May 20, 1803. Reuben married, secondly, about 1839, Rachel Webster, the daughter of Benjamin and Mary (Waite) Webster. Rachel was born in Freeport, Maine, August 1, 1812, and died in Portland, January 9, 1841. Reuben married, thirdly, in Portland, October 24, 1841, Julia Ann Webster, the daughter of Benjamin and Lydia (Soule) Webster. Julia Ann was born in Freeport, August 9, 1807, and died in South Paris, Maine, May 20, 1893. The first four children below were by the first wife, Mary Ann, and the fifth was by the second wife, Rachel. All were born in Portland.

Reuben owned a bakery in Portland, which he took over from his first father-in-law. He was also licensed to sell beer, wine and spirits. Reuben was a member of the Chestnut Street Methodist Church in Portland.* Children:

    i. Amanda M., b. 12/24/1825; d. 8/28/1827.

    ii. Amanda, b. 7/9/1828; m. Lorenzo De M. Ling; d. 3/10/1851. One child.

    iii. Benjamin Tappan, b. 8/16/1830. Killed at the Battle of Fredericksburg, 11/9/1862.

    iv. Ezra Kellogg, b. 12/13/1832; d. unm., killed 1878 in Chicago, by a moving train. A sea captain.

283.   v. William Webster, b. 11/14/1840.

210. Benjamin Roberts (George[7], Joseph[6], George[5], William[4], John[3], John[2], Thomas[1]), son of George and Hannah (Davis) Roberts, was born in Cape Elizabeth, Maine, August 2, 1803, and died in Geneva, Illinois, in February, 1886.

He married in Portland, Maine, April 24, 1825, Clarissa Mitchell,

---

* Underhill, Vol. I, pp. 1182-5.

the daughter of John Hayes and Hannah (Bowdoin) Mitchell. Clarissa was born in Freeport, Maine, September 23, 1800, and died in Geneva, Illinois, in April of 1888. She was described as being five feet tall and of dark complexion.

Benjamin took up the cabinet-making trade, and later was listed as a carriage maker. In 1836 Benjamin and Clarissa sold their small house in Portland and moved to Boston, where Benjamin pursued a career as a chaise maker, a wheelwright, and a carriage maker. In 1850 they moved back to Portland to care for Benjamin's mother. After the mother's death they moved to Winona, Minnesota, to be near their eldest son George, and then to Geneva, Illinois, to be near their daughter. Benjamin is described as a little above average in height, with black eyes and black hair. The following children were born in Portland.* Children:

284. i. George Henry, b. 10/7/1827.

ii. Mary Caroline, b. 8/7/1829; m. 8/10/1852, Edward Alonzo Small, in Portland.

iii. Andrew Rose, b. 8/27/1835. About 1854 he went to the far West and was never heard from again, "supposed that he was killed by the Indians."

211. Millet Wentworth Roberts (James^7, Love^6, Love^5, Love^4, Thomas^3, John^2, Thomas^1), son of James and Hepsibah (Thompson) Roberts, was born in New Hampshire or Maine, June 29, 1837, and died June 17, 1916. He married September 20, 1859, Hannah Ann Butler, the daughter of Thomas and Hannah (Lord) Butler. Hannah Ann was born in Sanford, Maine, March 3, 1838, and died September 28, 1916. Millet was a farmer and shoemaker in Milton, New Hampshire, and Acton, Maine, where the following children were born.⁺ Children:

285. i. Frank (twin), b. 2/16(or 26?)/1860.

ii. Fanny (twin), b. 2/16(or 26?)/1860; m. 6/24/1886, Robert S. Pike. Living in 1930.

---

* Underhill, Vol. I, pp. 1187-93.
⁺ Hardon, Vol. III, pp. 23-4.

EIGHTH GENERATION

      iii. Hannah, b. 5/1/1862; m. 10/3/1887, Gilbert I. Lowe. Living in Salmon Falls, NH in 1930.

      iv. Wintie, b. 6/19/1866; d. 8/17/1868.

      v. Wentworth Thomas, b. 4/10/1869; d. unm. 9/3/1891. A clerk in Acton, ME.

286. vi. James Ezekiel, b. 3/19/1874.

      vii. Bessie Maud, b. 2/17/1884; m. 11/20/1915, Alfred W. Lewis. No children. Res. Acton, ME, 1930.

212. Loring True Roberts (Love^7, Love^6, Love^5, Love^4, Thomas^3, John^2, Thomas^1), son of Love and Sarah (True) Roberts, was born in Wayne, Maine, September 24, 1814, and died in Paris, Maine, March 11, 1905. He married, firstly, February 19, 1843, Mary Jane Virgin, the daughter of William and Nancy (Eaton) Virgin, and, secondly, Julia Bishop. Mary Jane was born in Rumford, Maine, May 15, 1818, and died January 20, 1856. Julia was born in Leeds, Maine, June 13, 1825, and died in Greenwood, Maine, April 5, 1902. Loring was a farmer and saw-miller in Wayne, where the three children with Mary Ann were born, and in Greenwood, where the only child with Julia was born.* Children:

      i. Ronello F., b. 1/8/1844; d. 1900. A farmer in Chattanooga, TN and a manufacturer in Chicago.

      ii. Emeline Hardy, b. 5/25/1846; m. 11/26/1871, Winfield S. Starbird; d. 11/24/1927.

      iii. Mariette Jane, b. 3/14/1849; m. 12/31/1874, Nicholas T. Sinclair; d. 11/14/1902.

287. iv. John Charles Fremont, b. 9/18/1861.

213. William Harrison Roberts (Love^7, Love^6, Love^5, Love^4, Thomas^3, John^2, Thomas^1), a cabinet maker, son of Love and Sarah (True) Roberts, was born in Wayne, Maine, November 8, 1819, and

---

* Hardon, Vol. III, pp. 30-1.

DESCENDANTS OF THOMAS & REBECCA ROBERTS

died there or near there, August 27, 1905. He married September 3, 1844, his first cousin, Mary B. Lowd, the daughter of Wentworth and Hannah (Roberts) Lowd and the granddaughter of Love (No. 69) Roberts. The last five of the following children were born in Wayne, with the first being born in Worchester, Massachusetts, and the second in Acton, Maine.* Children:

      i. Sarah Ellen, b. 7/5/1847; m. (1) 11/22/1882, Frank Ridley, (2) Frank Storer; d. 10/28/1915.

      ii. Wendell Phillips, b. 7/26/1849; m. Estella Norris; d. 9/13/1908. An undertaker in Readfield, ME.

288.   iii. Edgar Wentworth, b. 10/8/1851.

      iv. Levi True, b. 12/16/1853; d. 3/3/1854.

289.   v. William Love, b. 1/7/1855.

290.   vi. Frank Herbert, b. 6/25/1858.

291.   vii. Nathan Lewis, b. 3/24/1861.

214. Charles Ellery Fordyce Roberts (Love⁷, Love⁶, Love⁵, Love⁴, Thomas³, John², Thomas¹), son of Love and Mary (Phillips) Roberts, was born in Wayne, Maine, February 27, 1826, and died April 12, 1906. He married March 18, 1854, Ann Maria Libby, the daughter of Ebenezer and Emeline (Harding) Libby. Ann Maria was born in Scarboro, Maine, May 8, 1832, and died December 16, 1886. Charles was a carpenter and undertaker in Wayne, where the first three children below were born, and in North Livermore, Maine, where the remaining child was born.⁺ Children:

      i. Evelyn Harding, b. 5/31/1855; m. (1) 6/13/1875, David L. Chenery, (2) 10/13/1917, John F. Otis; d. 11/24/1925.

      ii. Mary Emeline, b. 10/9/1859; m. 5/26/1878, Edmund P. Ladd. No children.

---

* Hardon, Vol. III, pp. 32-3.
⁺ Hardon, Vol. III, pp. 33-4.

EIGHTH GENERATION

 iii. Elizabeth Rounds, b. 3/8/1861; m. 6/5/1880, Clinton R. Babb.

 iv. Caroline Whitney, b. 3/6/1873; m. 4/4/1890, Albert C. Bradbury; d. 4/24/1903.

215. Horace Roberts (James[7], Peter[6], Love[5], Love[4], Thomas[3], John[2], Thomas[1]), son of James Wakefield and Martha (Hill) Roberts, was born in Lyman, Maine, August 5, 1815, and died in the 1890's. Nothing else is known about this family other than they lived in Everett, Massachusetts, and had the following son.[*] Child:

 i. George A. Son Ralph of Everett, MA.

216. Jacob Waterhouse Roberts (James[7], Peter[6], Love[5], Love[4], Thomas[3], John[2], Thomas[1]), son of James Wakefield and Martha (Hill) Roberts, was born in Lyman, Maine, June 24, 1818, and died September 26, 1896. He married June 20, 1847, Safronia Porter Ricker, the daughter of Aaron and Phoebe (Fall) Ricker. She was born in Lebanon, Maine, August 13, 1822, and died July 25, 1904. Jacob was a wholesale grocer in Reading, Massachusetts, and Charletown, Massachusetts, where the following children were born.[+] Children:

292.	i.	Jacob Francis, b. 7/10/1849.
	ii.	William Henry, b. 1/18/1851; d. 1854.
293.	iii.	Walter Hill, b. 4/22/1855.
294.	iv.	Herbert Howard, b. 9/17/1857.
295.	v.	Arthur Everett, b. 6/22/1861.

217. Charles Hill Roberts (James[7], Peter[6], Love[5], Love[4], Thomas[3], John[2], Thomas[1]), a farmer, son of James Wakefield and Martha (Hill) Roberts, was born in Lyman, Maine, November 27, 1818, and died November 23, 1896. He married Mary Jane Fall, who was born in Old Town, Maine, in 1827, and died some time after 1896. The following children were born in Lyman or Dayton,

---

[*] Hardon, Vol. III, p. 54.
[+] Hardon, Vol. III, p. 55.

DESCENDANTS OF THOMAS & REBECCA ROBERTS

Maine.* Children:

  i. Abigail Hill, b. 4/13/1848; m. John F. Perkins, of Bath, ME.

296. ii. Edson.

  iii. Dennis, d. unm. 12/27/1904. A farmer in Waterboro, ME.

  iv. Henry H. A teamster in West Hollis, ME.

297. v. Charles Edwin.

  vi. Horace, b. 1858. A carpenter in Saco, ME in 1930. Had one daughter - Ethel May.

  vii. Jacob. A mariner in New York City.

  viii. Lucy.

298. ix. Amos.

  x. Flora M., b. 1867; m. -----Chase of Gardiner, ME. One child.

218. James Wakefield Roberts (James[7], Peter[6], Love[5], Love[4], Thomas[3], John[2], Thomas[1]), son of James Wakefield and Martha (Hill) Roberts, was born in Lyman, Maine, June 12, 1825. Nothing else is known about him, except that he had the following children.[†] Children:

  i. John A.

  ii. James (twin), living in Reading, MA in 1930.

  iii. William S.(twin), of Reading, MA.

219. Peter Stillings Roberts (James[7], Peter[6], Love[5], Love[4], Thomas[3], John[2], Thomas[1]), a wholesale provision dealer, son of James Wakefield and Martha (Hill) Roberts, was born in Lyman, Maine, October 21, 1827, and died May 21, 1904. He married

---

 * Hardon, Vol. III, pp. 56-69.
 † Hardon, Vol. III, p. 59.

EIGHTH GENERATION

Harriet L. Emerson, who was born June 5, 1832, and died January 6, 1901. The following children were born in Charlestown, Massachusetts.* Children:

    i. Harriet Ella, b. 1855; m. Clarence Delfendahl; d. 1893. One child.
    ii. Martha Etta, b. 1861; d. 3/16/1866.
    iii. Ida Florence, b. 1865; d. 1/3/1868.
    iv. Howard Emerson, b. 1865; d. 5/7/1865.

220. Benjamin Dudley Roberts (James^7, Peter^6, Love^5, Love^4, Thomas^3, John^2, Thomas^1), son of James Wakefield and Martha (Hill) Roberts, was born in Lyman, Maine, December 18, 1839, and died October 12, 1909. He married June 6, 1870, Tyra Ann Huntress, the daughter of James Knight and Eunice (Knight) Huntress. Tyra Ann was born in Waterboro, Maine, March 14, 1848, and was living in Biddeford, Maine, in 1930. The following children were born in Lyman.⁺ Children:

    i. Mabelle Huntress, b. 5/25/1872; m. (1) 9/12/1893, Frank W.H. Kendrick of Dayton, ME, (2) 10/22/1928, George E. Clark of Newfields, NH.
    ii. James Howard, b. 11/6/1878. A farmer, living unm. in Biddeford, ME in 1930.

221. Alonzo Roberts (Joseph^7, Peter^6, Love^5, Love^4, Thomas^3, John^2, Thomas^1), a farmer, son of Joseph Dennett and Rhoda (Fall) Roberts, was born in Lyman, Maine, February 21, 1832, and died January 29, 1917.

Alonzo was married four times. His first wife was Emily Gould, the daughter of James and Abigail (Waterhouse) Gould. She was born in 1833 and died in 1856, shortly after their first child was born. The second wife was Hannah Melissa Nason, the daughter of Durrell and Rosanna (Haley) Nason. She was born in Cornish, Maine, October 2, 1840, and died in 1863, having left no children.

---

    * Hardon, Vol. III, p. 60.
    ⁺ Hardon, Vol. III, p. 62.

The third marriage, February 2, 1868, was to Viola Jane Hill, the daughter of Isaiah and Elizabeth Jane (Deering) Hill. Viola Jane was born in Hollis (now Dayton), Maine, July 10, 1847, and died August 22, 1885, leaving three children. The final marriage, May 17, 1890, was to a cousin, Elizabeth Mary Roberts, the daughter of Ivory and Nancy C. (Fall) Roberts, and the neice of Alonzo's mother, and granddaughter of Peter (No. 70) Roberts.* Children:

        i.   Martha Emily, b. 12/29/1855; m. 12/29/1880, Frederick J. Pilsbury; d. 5/1/1924.

299.   ii.   Herman Ellery, b. 12/20/1870.

300.   iii. Porter Alonzo, b. 5/16/1880.

301.   iv. Arthur Leon, b. 9/11/1882.

222. George Henry Roberts (John[7], Peter[6], Love[5], Love[4], Thomas[3], John[2], Thomas[1]), son of John and Abigail A. (Conant) Roberts, was born in Lyman, Maine, in 1842. He married January 1, 1864, Mary Hemingway, who was born in Acton, Maine. The following children were born in Lyman. George was a teacher and postmaster in Springvale, Maine. During the Civil War he served as a lieutenant in the 27th and the 9th Maine Volunteer Infantry.⁺ Children:

        i.   Lila, b. 1865.

        ii. T. Henry, b. 1867.

223. Luke Roberts (John[7], Peter[6], Love[5], Love[4], Thomas[3], John[2], Thomas[1]), son of John and Abigail A. (Conant) Roberts, was born in Lyman, Maine. Nothing else is known about him, except that he had the following children.# Children:

        i.   William of Kennebunk, ME.

---

    * Hardon, Vol. III, pp. 72-3.

    ⁺ Hardon, Vol. III, p. 79; Whitman, William E. S. & True, Charles H. *Maine in the War for the Union...* Lewiston, Maine: Nelson Dingley, Jr. & Co., 1865, p. 589.

    # Hardon, Vol. III, p. 82.

EIGHTH GENERATION

    ii. Lewis.

    iii. Alice, m. -----Warren of Kennebunk. Liv. 1930.

224. John H. Roberts (Nahum[7], Peter[6], Love[5], Love[4], Thomas[3], John[2], Thomas[1]), son of Nahum and Sarah (Hemmenway) Roberts, was born in Alfred, Maine, October 8, 1831, and died December 21, 1898. He married, firstly, in May of 1859, Louisa Southard, and, secondly, Edwina Phelps. The children below were by the first wife. John H. was referred to as "Col. Roberts". He entered Civil War service in 1861 as a second lieutenant in Company F of the 8th Maine Infantry. In late 1863 he accepted command of Company M of the 2nd Maine Cavalry. His rank at that time was captain.* Children:

    i. Lillian Louise, m. Stuart R. Hayman of Wellesley Hills, MA. Living in 1930.

    ii. Gertrude M., living unm. in Wellesley Hills, 1930.

    iii. Martha Brown. Living in 1930.

225. Philander Roberts (Nahum[7], Peter[6], Love[5], Love[4], Thomas[3], John[2], Thomas[1]), son of Nahum and Sarah (Hemmenway) Roberts, was born in Alfred, Maine, November 3, 1833, and died somewhere in California. He married in Alfred, December 19, 1861, Caroline K. Treadwell.* Children:

    i. Clarence H., b. 9/25/1862.

    ii. Myrtle, b. 9/24/1864.

    iii. Elizabeth, b. 5/5/1868; d. 8/25/1868.

    iv. Mary Charlotte, b. 1/19/1871.

226. William Henry Harrison Roberts (Nahum[7], Peter[6], Love[5], Love[4], Thomas[3], John[2], Thomas[1]), son of Nahum and Sarah (Hemmenway) Roberts, was born in Alfred, Maine, November 2, 1840, and died June 17, 1926. He married October 24, 1867, Mary

---

* Hardon, Vol. III, p. 84; Whitman and True, pp. 193 & 564.
† Hardon, Vol. III, p. 85.

DESCENDANTS OF THOMAS & REBECCA ROBERTS

E. Walcott, who was born September 4, 1847. The following children were born in Somerville, Massachusetts.* Children:

    i. Helen Walcott, b. 12/30/1869; m. -----Orne of Seattle, WA. Living in 1930.

    ii. Mabel Frances, b. 2/2/1871; m. George West of Seattle, WA. Living in 1930.

    ii. Mary Elizabeth, b. 9/13/1874; m. -----Symonds of Seattle, WA. Living in 1930.

227. Luke Hemmenway Roberts (Nahum^7, Peter^6, Love^5, Love^4, Thomas^3, John^2, Thomas^1), a farmer, son of Nahum and Sarah (Hemmenway) Roberts, was born in Alfred, Maine, August 6, 1843, and died January 10, 1910. He married May 22, 1873, Celeste Cummings Morris, the daughter of Charles R. and Mary A. (Harding) Morris. Celeste was born in Newfield, Maine, March 2, 1849, and died September 27, 1912. The following children were born in Alfred.⁺ Children:

302.   i. Charles William, b. 3/28/1875.

    ii. Louis Eugene, b. 2/25/1880; m. 9/29/1903, Nellie M. Abbott. A mechanic in Lynnfield, MA, in 1930. No children.

    iii. Alice Kendall, b. 1/21/1889; m. 4/3/1913, Ernest R. Warren of Kennebunk. Living in 1930.

228. Albert F. Roberts (Nahum^7, Peter^6, Love^5, Love^4, Thomas^3, John^2, Thomas^1), son of Nahum and Sarah (Hemmenway) Roberts, was born in Alfred, Maine, December 12, 1845. He married Susan Stearns. Nothing else is known about this family, other than the fact they had the following children.# Children:

    i. Edith.

    ii. Millicent.

---

    * Hardon, Vol. III, pp. 86-7.
    ⁺ Hardon, Vol. III, p. 87.
    # Hardon, Vol. III, p. 88.

EIGHTH GENERATION

  iii. Marian.
  iv. Edward.

229. Nahum Frank Roberts (Nahum[7], Peter[6], Love[5], Love[4], Thomas[3], John[2], Thomas[1]), son of Nahum and Sarah (Hemmenway) Roberts, was born in Alfred, Maine, February 5, 1849, and died November 17, 1897. He married Adeline Glines. This family lived in Charlestown, Massachusetts, and Detroit, Michigan.[*] Child:

  i. Raymond.

230. Willie Crosby Roberts (Dimon[7], Peter[6], Love[5], Love[4], Thomas[3], John[2], Thomas[1]), a farmer, son of Dimon and Martha (Hemmenway) Roberts, was born in Lyman, Maine, January 29, 1853, and died January 21, 1879. He married Eliza C. Smith, the daughter of Eugene and Louise (Harris) Smith. Eliza was born January 14, 1854. Their only child was born in New York City.[+] Child:

  i. Dimon Eugene, b. 7/16/1878; m. Margaret Kaiser. A clerk of the U.S. Circuit Court of Appeals, in White Plains, NY in 1930.

231. John Weston Roberts (James[7], Timothy[6], John[5], Timothy[4], Thomas[3], John[2], Thomas[1]), son of James and Mercy (Wentworth) Roberts, was born in Milton, New Hampshire, March 27, 1810. He was married in Milton, in November of 1833, to Margaret Nutter, the daughter of Matthias and Sarah (Wentworth) Nutter. This family lived in Lincoln, Maine.[#] Children:

  i. Timothy, b. 1835. A shoemaker in Natick, MA.
  ii. Charles Francis, b. 1837.
  iii. James Benton, b. 1839.

232. James Cutts Roberts (James[7], Timothy[6], John[5], Timothy[4], Thomas[3], John[2], Thomas[1]), a farmer, son of James and

---

[*] Hardon, Vol. III, p. 89.
[+] Hardon, Vol. III, p. 94.
[#] Hardon, Vol. III, pp. 100-1.

DESCENDANTS OF THOMAS & REBECCA ROBERTS

Mercy (Wentworth) Roberts, was born in Milton, New Hampshire, March 27, 1810, and died March 3, 1865. He married Lydia J. Scates, the daughter of John and Mary Scates. She was born in Milton, April 22, 1807, and died May 3, 1866. The following children were born in Milton.* Children:

 i. Amos M., b. 6/7/1835; d. 8/10/1907. A grocer in Milton. No children.

 ii. Mary E., b. 1840; d. unm. 7/7/1879.

 iii. Clara A., b. 1844; m. 4/16/1868, George A. Hatch; d. 11/24/1928.

 iv. Charles P., b. 3/1846; d. 9/6/1849.

 v. John S., b. 10/17/1848; m. Susan Pearl; d. 1/22/1907. A farmer and shoemaker in Farmington, NH.

233. Owen Swain Roberts (James[7], Timothy[6], John[5], Timothy[4], Thomas[3], John[2], Thomas[1]), son of James and Mercy (Wentworth) Roberts, was born in Milton, New Hampshire, April 4, 1813, and died January 6, 1853. He married in 1838 Harriet L. Foss, the daughter of William and Mary (Downs) Foss. She was born in Milton in 1814, and died in 1895. Owen was a manufacturer in Somersworth.⁺ Children:

 i. James Woodbury, b. 1839; d. 8/28/1855.

 ii. Everett F., b. 1841; d. 1855.

 iii. Charles O., b. 1843; m. 9/17/1867, Nellie C. Parker.

 iv. Sarah E., b. 1846; d. unm. 1865.

 v. Rosetta, b. 1849; m. 2/3/1868, John H. James; d. 1876.

234. Beard Page Roberts (James[7], Timothy[6], John[5], Timothy[4],

---

 * Hardon, Vol. III, p. 102.
 ⁺ Hardon, Vol. III, p. 103.

EIGHTH GENERATION

Thomas³, John², Thomas¹), son of James and Mercy (Wentworth) Roberts, was born in New Hampshire, June 26, 1815, and died in November of 1890. He married, firstly, Sarah Merrill, who was born in 1808 and died June 24, 1858, and, secondly, April 5, 1860, Mary E. (Swett) Fernald, the daughter of Benjamin Swett. Mary was born in Limington, Maine, in 1827. Beard married, thirdly, April 19, 1862, Sarah J. Emerson, the was born in Candia, New Hampshire, in 1826, the daughter of John and Clarissa (Fitts) Emerson, and, fourthly, Nettie M. -----, who bore the child listed below. Beard was a railway station agent and a traveling agent in Milton, and South New Market, New Hampshire.* Child:

    i. Lena M., m. 6/12/1895, Charles E. Ham of Farmington, NH.

235. David Ballard Roberts (John⁷, Timothy⁶, John⁵, Timothy⁴, Thomas³, John², Thomas¹), son of John and Mary Ann (Adams) Roberts, was born in Boston, Massachusetts, December 21, 1820, and died in Hanover, Massachusetts, November 15, 1893. He married Agnes Hughes, who was born in England in 1824, the daughter of Frederick and Margaret (Hughes) Hughes. Agnes died April 21, 1858. The first child below was born in Bangor, Maine, the remainder in Boston.⁺ Children:

    i. Lucy Adams, b. 9/29/1846; d. unm. Marshfield, MA, 6/3/1865.

303.   ii. Coolidge Sutton, b. 1/11/1849.

    iii. Mary Anne, b. 9/27/1851; d. unm. 10/13/1928.

    iv. Katherine, b. 10/1854; m. Homer P. Lewis, 12/26/1878; d. 10/13/1880. No children.

236. Charles Wentworth Roberts (Amos⁷, Timothy⁶, John⁵, Timothy⁴, Thomas³, John², Thomas¹), son of Amos Main and Charlotte Barker (Rich) Roberts, was born in Bangor, Maine, October 22, 1828 and died March 23, 1898.

He married June 20, 1867, June Pierce, the daughter of Waldo

---

* Hardon, Vol. III, p. 104.
⁺ Hardon, Vol. III, p. 107.

Treat and Hannah Jane (Hills) Pierce. June was born in Bangor, July 9, 1840, and died July 7, 1906. The following two children were born in Bangor.

Charles Wentworth obtained his A.B. degree from Bowdoin College in 1851, and followed his father's occupation, lumber merchant. He entered service in the Civil War as a colonel in the 2nd Maine Volunteer Infantry and attained the rank of brevet Brigadier General. After the War Charles became active in politics and was twice nominated by the Democrat Party for governor of Maine, in 1870, and again in 1875. From 1887 to 1891 he was collector of customs.* Children:

    i. Charlotte, b. 7/2/1871; res. unm., Bangor in 1930.

    ii. Jane Pierce, b. 9/27/1874; res. unm., Bangor, 1930.

237. Joseph J. Roberts (Jonathan[7], Joseph[6], John[5], Timothy[4], Thomas[3], John[2], Thomas[1]), a farmer, the son of Jonathan Dame and Lydia (Jones) Roberts, was born in or near Farmington, New Hampshire, October 28, 1810, and died in Alton, New Hampshire, April 13, 1835. He married in Farmington, November 1, 1830, Sarah Ann Knight, who was born in Farmington, in 1810. The following children were born in Farmington.† Children:

    i. Lydia Ellen, b. 9/17/1831; m. 12/10/1848, George Edwin (No. 240) Roberts; d. 4/8/1900.

    ii. Mary Ann, b. 1834.

238. David S. Roberts (Jonathan[7], Joseph[6], John[5], Timothy[4], Thomas[3], John[2], Thomas[1]), son of Jonathan Dame and Lydia (Jones) Roberts, was born in or near Farmington, New Hampshire, April 6, 1813. He married February 5, 1834, Sarah Frye. The following children were born in Farmington. This family also lived in Boston.# Children:

    i. Lydia, m. Alonzo Briggs.

---

    * Hardon, Vol. III, p. 112.
    † Hardon, Vol. III, p. 117.
    # Hardon, Vol. III, pp. 117-8.

EIGHTH GENERATION

    ii.   Sarah, m. Frank Goodwin.

    iii. Dedie, m. Charles Pierce.

    iv. Herbert.

239. Joseph Augustus Roberts (John[7], Joseph[6], John[5], Timothy[4], Thomas[3], John[2], Thomas[1]), son of John and Sarah Abigail (Wingate) Roberts, was born in Farmington, New Hampshire, September 23, 1826, and died August 31, 1904. He married Phebe Ella Chesley, the daughter of John Chesley. She was born in New Durham, New Hampshire, in 1828, and died April 16, 1885. Joseph was a shoecutter and shoe dealer in Farmington. He was elected selectman of the town in 1854. The following children were born in Farmington.* Children:

304.   i. William Wingate, b. 3/7/1850.

       ii. Ella Agnes, b. 5/9/1866; m. 3/10/1897, Ralph E. Davis of Providence, RI; d. 3/6/1930.

240. George Edwin Roberts (John[7], Joseph[6], John[5], Timothy[4], Thomas[3], John[2], Thomas[1]), a shoe manufacturer, son of John and Sarah Abigail (Wingate) Roberts, was born in Farmington, New Hampshire, April 5, 1829, and died November 2, 1890. He married December 10, 1848, Lydia Ellen Roberts, a first cousin once removed. She was the daughter of Joseph J. (No. 237) and Sarah Ann (Knight) Roberts. The following children were born in Farmington.⁺ Children:

    i. Ellen Georgianna, b. 1849; m. 1/31/1870, Moses H. Greene of Haverhill, MA. No children.

    ii. Horatio Gates, b. 3/19/1852; d. unm. 3/24/1895.

241. Henry Laurens Roberts (John[7], Joseph[6], John[5], Timothy[4], Thomas[3], John[2], Thomas[1]), a shoe manufacturer, son of John and Sarah Abigail (Wingate) Roberts, was born in Farmington, New Hampshire, October 18, 1831, and died January 30, 1885. He

---

* Hardon, Vol. III, p. 120.
⁺ Hardon, Vol. III, p. 120.

married January 27, 1856, Anna Maria Elizabeth Towle, the daughter of Philip and Deborah (Fernald) Towle. Anna Maria was born in Winslow, Maine, June 22, 1836, and died April 7, 1915. The following children were born in Farmington.* Children:

    i. Ida Anne, b. 8/24/1857; m. 10/28/1874, Albert M. Trefethan; living in 1930.

    ii. Abigail Ellura, b. 10/25/1862; d. unm. 10/15/1896.

305.   iii. Frank Henry, b. 2/21/1867.

    iv. John Philip Bartlett, b. 5/3/1876; m.(1) 9/6/1903, Luella Tanner, (2) 1/31/1914, Ethel M. (Colby) Blouin. A shoecutter in Farmington in 1930.

242. Noah Horn Roberts (John[7], John[6], Thomas[5], Timothy[4], Thomas[3], John[2], Thomas[1]), a farmer, son of John Love and Rebecca Pinkham (Horn) Roberts, was born in West Lebanon, Maine, October 11, 1831, and died in Brookfield, Maine, March 31, 1917. He married December 18, 1855, Achsa Stanton Dixon, the daughter of Frederick and Caroline (Stanton) Dixon. Achsa was born in Lebanon, Maine, March 3, 1837, and died in Chester, Maine, May 6, 1928. The following children were born in Lebanon.⁺ Children:

306.   i. Charles Frederick, b. 8/4/1860.

    ii. Caroline Rebecca, b. 12/6/1861; m. 8/14/1880, Lester L. Churchill; d. 6/10/1903.

    iii. John Harrison, b. 6/2/1865; m. 5/27/1900, Elizabeth I. (Layne) Stearns; living in 1930. A lumber merchant in Dover.

307.   iv. William Pitt, b. 2/14/1867.

    v. James Stanton, b. 1/7/1872; m. 11/15/1916, Elizabeth B. Stewart. A graduate of Harvard and a physician in Chester, NH. Living in 1930.

---

* Hardon, Vol. III, p. 121.
⁺ Hardon, Vol. III, pp. 137-8.

EIGHTH GENERATION

    vi. Luther Hayes (formerly Martin Luther), b. 7/26/1873; m. Edith G. (Dixon) Swain. Liv. 1930.

243. Henry Kirkwood Roberts (John^7, John^6, Thomas^5, Timothy^4, Thomas^3, John^2, Thomas^1), son of John Love and Rebecca Pinkham (Horn) Roberts, was born in West Lebanon, Maine, October 3, 1845, and died May 8, 1926. He married March 16, 1867, Ellen Augusta Kimball, the daughter of Moses L. and Hannah (Eastman) Kimball. Ellen was born in Dover, New Hampshire, July 9, 1846, and died April 6, 1875. Henry married, secondly, in 1877, Mabel Rosina Hill, the daughter of Lyman H. and Annie L. (Hanscom) Hill. Mabel was born in Epping, New Hampshire, December 12, 1846, and died August 29, 1895. Henry was a farmer and carpenter in Rochester, New Hampshire, where the following children were born. The first four were by the first wife and the last six by the second wife.* Children:

308.   i. Fred Herbert, b. 1/22/1868.

        ii. Mary Bertha, b. 10/16/1870; m. 11/27/1925, George L. Perkins; living in 1930. No children.

        iii. George Henry, b. 9/17/1873; living unm. in 1930. A railroad yardman in Rochester.

        iv. Ellen Augusta, b. 4/6/1875; m.(1) 4/6/1892, Forrest E. Gerrish of Madbury, NH, (2) 3/27/1894, Alonzo F. Allender of Parsons, WV. Living in 1930.

        v. Edith Valma, b. 1/17/1878; m. 6/6/1900, Walter B. Howard of Brockton, MA. Living in 1930. No children.

        vi. Harold Kirkwood, b. 7/20/1879; d. unm. 11/24/1900.

        vii. Ivy Alice (twin), b. 3/23/1881; m. 12/22/1909, Charles C. Rogers. Living in 1930. One child.

---

* Hardon, Vol. III, pp. 139-140.

viii. Inez Annie (twin), b. 3/23/1881; m. 2/21/1906, William T. Hayes. Living in 1930. Three ch.

309.   ix. Ernest Linwood, b. 9/1885.

x. Edgar Stanwood, b. 6/17/1888; living unm. 1930. An artisan in Farmington.

244. Herman Winfield Roberts (John^7, John^6, Thomas^5, Timothy^4, Thomas^3, John^2, Thomas^1), son of John Love and Rebecca Pinkham (Horn) Roberts, was born in West Lebanon, Maine, May 5, 1847, and died September 5, 1892.

Herman was married three times. On May 7, 1867, he married Emma A. Snow, who was born September 7, 1850, and died October 22, 1870. She had no children. The second wife was Helen Clarkson, the daughter of Thomas and Martha Jane (Frisbee) Clarkson. Helen was born in Kittery, Maine, and died August 31, 1881. She had the first child listed below, born in Rochester, New Hampshire. Finally, on December 12, 1882, in Providence, Rhode Island, Herman married Sarah Rebecca Palmer, the daughter of William and Ellen N. (Berkeley) Palmer. Sarah was born in Lisbon, New Hampshire, April 4, 1856, and died in Seekonk, Massachusetts, November 12, 1929. Sarah had the second child shown below, born in Farmington, New Hampshire. Herman was a miller, grain dealer, and a town officer in Farmington.*
Children:

i. Nora Clarkson, b. 4/22/1881; m. 4/13/1912, Royal O. Ballard of Waterford, CA. A graduate of the NH State Normal School, living in 1930. No ch.

ii. Ellen, b. 7/8/1888; m. 6/5/1921, Joseph Butterworth of Seekonk, MA. A graduate of the RI School of Design, living in 1930. Two ch.

245. Thomas Herbert Roberts (William^7, Thomas^6, Timothy^5, Timothy^4, Thomas^3, John^2, Thomas^1), son of William Jones and Ellen (Hyde) Roberts, was born in Rochester, New Hampshire, September 10, 1852, and died April 19, 1929. He was married

---

* Hardon, Vol. III, p. 141.

EIGHTH GENERATION

twice, but only his second one, of December 30, 1900, is known. This was to Harriet Ann Wilkinson, the daughter of Isaiah and Lucy Dennett (Hayes) Wilkinson. She was born August 4, 1869, and died some time after 1930. Thomas was a stationary engineer in Rochester. The one child by his first wife below was born in Portsmouth, New Hampshire.* Child:

310. i. Everett Anson, b. 4/6/1888.

246. Joseph Roberts (Joseph[7], Benjamin[6], Benjamin[5], Samuel[4], Hatevil[3], John[2], Thomas[1]), son of Joseph D. and Mercy (Chandler) Roberts was born March 5, 1829, in Roberts Island, Yarmouth, Nova Scotia, and died September 27, 1897, in Glenwood, Yarmouth, Nova Scotia. He married January 26, 1853, Lydia Ann Spinney, the daughter of Daniel and Lydia (Nickerson) Spinney. She was born in Central Argyle, Yarmouth, Nova Scotia, June 15, 1832, and died December 2, 1914. Lydia is buried in the Argyle Baptist Cemetery there.† Children:

     i. Emily Spinney, b. 11/17/1854; m. Rufus Hines; d. 1881, bur. Argyle Old Cemetery. Three children.

     ii. Alonzo Palmer, b. 3/23/1857; d. 4/1874, lost at sea on the schooner *Sarah C. Pyle*.

311. iii. Delancy Amos, b. 3/16/1858.

312. iv. Joseph Martin, b. 4/14/1863.

247. Reuben Roberts (Reuben[7], Paul[6], Samuel[5], Samuel[4], Hatevil[3], John[2], Thomas[1]), son of Reuben and Jane (Roberts) Roberts, was born in Newfield, Maine, August 7, 1807, and died in 1891. He married in Boston, Massachusetts, Jane Litch, the daughter of John and Jerusha (Lincoln) Litch. Jane was born in Lunenburg, Massachusetts, and died in February of 1898. Reuben was a farmer, and lived variously in Boston, Springfield, Vermont, Middletown, Connecticut, and Brookline, Massachusetts. The following child was born in Boston. There may have been others.#

---

* Hardon, Vol. III, p. 144.
† Notes of Clayton H. Roberts.
# Hardon, Vol. III, p. 152.

DESCENDANTS OF THOMAS & REBECCA ROBERTS

Child:

313. i. George Litch, b. 12/30/1836.

248. Simeon Brock Roberts (Aaron[7], Aaron[6], Samuel[5], Samuel[4], Hatevil[3], John[2], Thomas[1]), son of Aaron and Elizabeth (Fernald) Roberts, was born in Rollinsford, New Hampshire, January 18, 1850, and died September 30, 1932. He married September 13, 1871, Lydia Jane Shackford, the daughter of Joseph and Eliza (Palmer) Shackford. Lydia was born in Eaton, New Hampshire, in October of 1851, and died February 6, 1915. Simeon was a hotel manager in Rollinsford and a farmer/postmaster in South Berwick, Maine, where he was elected as a member of the state legislature. The following children were born in Rollinsford.[*]

Children:

i. Mayhew Tristram, b. 8/13/1872; m. Gertrude A. Russell. A farmer in Scotfield, Alberta in 1930.

314. ii. William Edward, b. 7/7/1874.

iii. Lena Mabel, b. 11/14/1875; m. 5/26/1894, Herbert F. Berry of Lawrence, MA (1930).

iv. Aaron Milton, b. 6/25/1878; m. 2/22/1902, Myra M. Chick. A station agent in South Berwick, ME.

315. v. Herbert Arthur, b. 6/18/1880.

vi. Ernest Raymond, b. 7/21/1882. A hotel manager in Rollinsford in 1930. Unmarried.

vii. George Roland, b. 2/6/1888; m. 4/28/1906, Delia Marshall. An amusement house operator in Redondo Beach, CA in 1930.

249. Samuel E. Roberts (Caleb[7], Benjamin[6], Nathan[5], Samuel[4], Hatevil[3], John[2], Thomas[1]), son of Caleb and Rhoda (Horn) Roberts, was born in Rochester, New Hampshire, in 1826, and died

---

[*] Hardon, Vol. III, pp. 159-60; Scales, John. *History of Strafford County, New Hampshire and Representative Citizens.* Chicago: Richmond-Arnold Publishing Co., 1914, pp. 632-3.

EIGHTH GENERATION

August 16, 1895. He married Patience Comfort Ackerman, who was born in 1834. Samuel was a farmer in Rochester and Alexandria, New Hampshire, where the following children were born.* Children:

    i. Eva Annette, b. 9/6/1859; m. 12/25/1879, Everett L. Calef. Living in Rochester in 1930.

    ii. William H., b. 5/4/1861; m. 10/21/1917, Martha J. Andrews. A farmer in Rochester in 1930.

    iii. Elmira Jane, b. 12/5/1862; m. James Roma. Living in Rochester in 1930. No children.

316.   iv. Herman C., b. 6/21/1864.

    v. Elizabeth, d. in infancy.

250. Benjamin Roberts (Caleb[7], Benjamin[6], Nathan[5], Samuel[4], Hatevil[3], John[2], Thomas[1]), a farmer, son of Caleb and Rhoda (Horn) Roberts, was born in Rochester, New Hampshire, July 5, 1827, and died January 5, 1900, and is buried in the Roberts-Henderson Cemetery, on the easterly side of the Farmington Road, about two miles north of Rochester. He married December 21, 1851, Mary Esther Place, the daughter of Jonathan and Abigail (Henderson) Place. Mary was born in Farmington, New Hampshire, July 23, 1834, and died November 3, 1918, and is also buried in the Roberts-Henderson Cemetery. The first three children below were born in Farmington, the other in Wakefield, New Hampshire.⁺ Children:

317.   i. John Place, b. 1/28/1852.

318.   ii. Horace Herbert, b. 12/3/1854.

319.   iii. Henry Benjamin, b. 2/19/1857.

    iv. Frank Jonathan, b. 8/13/1863; m. (1) Alta Warren, (2) Harriet Bryant; d. 11/2/1899. No children. A shoe worker in Haverhill, MA.

---

* Hardon, Vol. III, pp. 169-70.
⁺ Hardon, Vol. III, pp. 171-2.

251. Ernest Upham Roberts (Tobias[7], Jonathan[6], Thomas[5], Joshua[4], Hatevil[3], John[2], Thomas[1]), son of Tobias and Judith Frances Upham (Cogswell) Roberts, was born in Northwood, New Hampshire, October 29, 1855, and died February 8, 1878. He married in December 1873, Katherine Gerry. Ernest was a navy yard employee in Kittery, Maine.* Children:

    i. Ralph Newell of Worchester, MA. Living in 1930.

    ii. Adeline Naomi, d. unm. 1902. An actress.

252. Edwin Jonathan Roberts (George[7], Jonathan[6], Thomas[5], Joshua[4], Hatevil[3], John[2], Thomas[1]), son of George Seward and Eliza Ann (Bunker) Roberts, was born in Barnstead, New Hampshire, July 5, 1842, and died in Arlington, Massachusetts(?), October 8, 1911. He married March 29, 1864, Sarah Elizabeth Daniels, the daughter of Nathaniel and Mary Ann Daniels. Sarah was born in Lee, New Hampshire, July 10, 1840, and died March 24, 1898. Edwin was a farmer in Warrenburg, Illinois. The following two children were born in Illinois.⁺ Children:

320.   i. Harry Edwin, b. 6/3/1866.

    ii. Ernest Everett, b. 11/6/1870, Illini, IL; d. 7/3/1871.

253. George Franklin Roberts (George[7], Jonathan[6], Thomas[5], Joshua[4], Hatevil[3], John[2], Thomas[1]), son of George Seward and Eliza Ann (Bunker) Roberts, was born in Barnstead, New Hampshire, March 25, 1848, and died March 21, 1914. George married June 11, 1874, Ella Sophia Thayer, the daughter of William B. and Prudence S. (Burchard) Thayer. Ella Sophia was born in Quincy, Illinois, August 22, 1848, and died March 16, 1916. He was apparently born Franklin George, but preferred it the other way around. George was a prominent homeopathic physician in Minneapolis, Minnesota. Among his many achievements were the presidency of the Minneapolis Homeopathic Medical Society and the Minnesota State Institute of Homeopathy. He was also a

---

    * Hardon, Vol. IV, pp. 4-5.
    ⁺ Hardon, Vol. IV, p. 6.

EIGHTH GENERATION

professor of gynecology at the University of Minnesota.* Children:

321. i. William Burchard, b. 5/19/1875.

ii. Edna Thayer, b. 8/3/1877, Waterloo, IA. Living unm. in Minneapolis in 1930.

iii. a child, d. in infancy in Minneapolis.

254. Everett Lemuel Roberts (George^7, Jonathan^6, Thomas^5, Joshua^4, Hatevil^3, John^2, Thomas^1), son of George Seward and Eliza Ann (Bunker) Roberts, was born in Barnstead, New Hampshire, August 8, 1851, and died April 10, 1932. He married May 21, 1874, Anna Belle Clark, the daughter of Bradbury and Mary (Proctor) Clark. Anna Belle was born in Pittsfield, New Hampshire, February 20, 1853, and died November 3, 1928. Everett was a salesman in Lexington, Nebraska, and also lived in Warrensburg, Illinois, where their first two children were born, and in Bloomington, Illinois, where the remainder of the children were born.⁺ Children:

i. a son, d. in infancy.

ii. Bertha Mabel, b. 5/10/1880. A beauty specialist in Lexington, NE in 1930. Unmarried.

iii. Maude Adelaide, b. 6/30/1883; m. 3/15/1906, Alfred J. Betzer. A postal clerk in Lexington, NE.

iv. Grace Anna, b. 3/1/1885. A nurse in Fresno, CA in 1930, unmarried.

322. v. George Bradbury, b. 3/6/1890.

vi. Ruth, b. 11/11/1896; m. 1/10/1917, Elmer F. Zimmerman. Living in 1930.

255. Tobias Roberts (Joshua^7, Tobias^6, Joshua^5, Joshua^4, Hatevil^3, John^2, Thomas^1), a blacksmith, son of Joshua and Sarah (Scruton) Roberts, was born in Strafford, New Hampshire,

---

* Hardon, Vol. IV, p. 7.
⁺ Hardon, Vol. IV, pp. 7-8.

November 30, 1839, and died March 9, 1906. He married August 2, 1868, Lucy A. Pease, the daughter of Daniel and Jerusha (Hall) Pease. Lucy was born in New Bedford, Massachusetts, November 3, 1847, and died May 5, 1885.* Children:

323.	i.	Eugene Charles, b. 5/31/1869.
	ii.	Edwin Pease, b. 8/30/1870; m. 12/25/1897, Elizabeth A. Berry. A blacksmith and machinist in Haverhill, MA in 1930. No children.
	iii.	Grace Genevieve, b. 1/14/1873; m. 1/19/1891, Lovell W. Berry. Living in 1930.
324.	iv.	Harry Arthur, b. 8/30/1876.
325.	v.	Laurel Tobias (twin), b. 9/24/1881.
	vi.	Lucy Isabelle (twin), b. 9/24/1881. Living unm. in Dover, NH in 1930.
	vii.	Edith Adelaide, b. 4/22/1884; m. 5/6/1902, Hervey A. Scruton of Berwick, ME. Living in 1930. Two children.

256. Sewall Trevett Roberts (Richard^7, Joseph^6, Joseph^5, Joseph^4, Joseph^3, John^2, Thomas^1), son of Richard and Hannah (Willey) Roberts, was born in New Durham, New Hampshire, February 21, 1822, and died May 24, 1894.

He was married three times. His first marriage, December 18, 1850, was to Eliza Ellen Heard (or Hurd), the daughter of Jesse and Hannah (Berry) Heard. Eliza was born in Dover, New Hampshire, November 26, 1833 and died March 2, 1858. The first two children listed below were by Eliza. Sewall married, secondly, March 30, 1859, the widow Mary Ellen (Savage) Edson, the daughter of Benjamin and Lois (Davis) Savage. Mary Ellen was born in New Durham, March 22, 1830, and died June 10, 1861. The third child below was by Mary Ellen. Thirdly, Sewall married on June 3, 1862, Ann Eliza Beacham, the daughter of John C. and Olive (Young) Beacham. Ann Eliza was born in Wolfeboro, New

---

* Hardon, Vol. IV, pp. 16-7.

EIGHTH GENERATION

Hampshire, January 19, 1836, and died January 24, 1921. The remaining three children below were by Ann Eliza. Sewall was a farmer in Alton, New Hampshire, where his six children were all born.* Children:

      i. Orin Winfield, b. 6/8/1852; d. 7/16/1857.

     ii. Octavia Heard, b. 6/19/1854; m. 8/16/1874, Oliver J.M. Gilman; d. 11/16/1927. No children.

326. iii. Sewell Edson, b. 8/27/1860.

327. iv. John Pike, b. 12/10/1864.

     v. Eliza Ellen, b. 5/10/1868; m. 2/11/1890, John N. Tash; living in 1930. No children.

     vi. Annie Maria, b. 4/22/1876; m. 7/2/1912, Irving W. Slack of Punta Gorda, FL & Ocean Park, ME. Living in 1930, Annie Maria was an 1899 graduate of Bates College and a Doctor of Osteopathy (American School of Osteopathy, 1906).

257. Samuel Woodbury Roberts (Richard[7], Joseph[6], Joseph[5], Joseph[4], Joseph[3], John[2], Thomas[1]), son of Richard and Hannah (Willey) Roberts, was born in New Durham, New Hampshire, January 8, 1825, and died December 6, 1912. He married April 15, 1853, Elizabeth Smith, the daughter of John and Sarah (Ambrose) Smith. Elizabeth was born in Ossipee, New Hampshire, May 5, 1829, and died September 29, 1910. Samuel graduated from Dartmouth in 1853 and entered practice as a physician in Wakefield, New Hampshire, where the following children were born.⁺ Children:

      i. Clara Elizabeth, b. 1/25/1855; d. unm. 7/10/1880. A school teacher.

---

  * Hardon, Vol. IV, pp. 28-9.
  ⁺ Hardon, Vol. IV, pp. 29-30.

DESCENDANTS OF THOMAS & REBECCA ROBERTS

      ii. Mary Egeton, b. 5/13/1861; m. 8/18/1882, Horatio Knox of Providence RI (1930).

328.   iii. John Smith, b. 11/25/1864.

      iv. Henry Ambrose, b. 7/13/1868; d. unm. 1/19/1901. Graduated Dartmouth (1890), a Boston physician.

258. Richard Roberts (Richard[7], Joseph[6], Joseph[5], Joseph[4], Joseph[3], John[2], Thomas[1]), son of Richard and Hannah (Willey) Roberts, was born in New Durham, New Hampshire, May 12, 1830, and died December 29, 1918. He married, firstly, Mary E. Evans, the daughter of Dudley and Rebecca (Bickford) Evans. She was born in Alton, New Hampshire, June 10, 1831, and died August 28, 1864, leaving no children. Richard married, secondly, Augusta Catherine (Marston) Jackman, the daughter of Elijah and Ann (Pickering) Marston, and the widow of William Henry Jackman. Augusta was born in Newington, New Hampshire, March 3, 1839, and died August 14, 1902. The children below were hers. Richard was a shoemaker and farmer in Alton, Newburyport, Massachusetts, where the first two children were born, and in Newmarket, New Hampshire, where the remainder were born.[*] Children:

      i. Fred Richard, b. 4/16/1866; d. in infancy.

      ii. Harriet May, b. 8/9/1867; living unm. in Washington, DC in 1930.

      iii. Clara Bell, b. 7/27/1869; d. unm. 1/15/1898.

329.   iv. Richard Sewall Woodbury, b. 4/13/1877.

259. Allen Roberts (Nathaniel[7], James[6], Joseph[5], Joseph[4], Joseph[3], John[2], Thomas[1]), son of Nathaniel and Sarah (Wentworth) Roberts, was born in Alton, New Hampshire, in 1817, and died March 20, 1897. He married in Alton, February 16, 1843, Cynthia Coldbath, the daughter of George and Mary (Knight) Coldbath. She was born in Alton, March 5, 1817, and died November 28, 1895. Allen was a farmer in Alton, where the following child was born.[+]

---

[*] Hardon, Vol. IV, p. 30-1.
[+] Hardon, Vol. IV, p. 34.

EIGHTH GENERATION

Child:

    i.   Sarah Frances, b. 1843; d. 1857.

260. **Charles Samuel Roberts** (John[7], Hanson[6], Joseph[5], Stephen[4], Joseph[3], John[2], Thomas[1]), son of John and Mary Jane (Banks) Roberts, was born in Chelsea, Massachusetts, October 3, 1859, and died November 9, 1920. He married December 10, 1884 his fourth cousin, Ida Florence Gage, the daughter of Gerry R. and Abigail B. (Tuttle) Gage. She was born in Dover, New Hampshire, March 24, 1862, and was living there in 1930. Charles was a farmer in Dover, where the following children were born.[*]
Children:

    i.   John Franklin, b. 3/1/1886; d. unm. 10/27/1922, Concord, NH. A stationary engineer.

    ii. George Edward, b. 3/18/1888; d. 6/22/1889.

    iii. Helen Charlotte, b. 7/20/1898; living unm. in Dover in 1930.

261. **Charles Andrew Roberts** (Oliver[7], Hanson[6], Joseph[5], Stephen[4], Joseph[3], John[2], Thomas[1]), son of Oliver L. and Myrtilla A. (Jackson) Roberts, was born in Boston, Massachusetts, December 23, 1857, and died June 22, 1929. He married April 19, 1879, Johanna Elizabeth Sullivan, the daughter of William and Mary (Collins) Sullivan. Johanna was born in Medford, Massachusetts, October 18, 1854, and was living there in 1930. Charles was a brush maker in Medford, where the following children were born.[+]
Children:

    i.   William, b. 3/1880; d. 1882.

    ii. Harriet Norma, b. 8/4/1881; m. 8/1/1906, Eliot L. Moses of Kalamazoo, MI. Living in 1930. 3 ch.

330.   iii. Oliver Frank, b. 6/24/1883.

262. **Jackson Roberts** (John[7], Stephen[6], John[5], Stephen[4],

---

[*] Hardon, Vol. II, p. 117 & Vol. IV, p. 80.
[+] Hardon, Vol. IV, pp. 81-3.

Joseph[3], John[2], Thomas[1]), son of John and Charlotte (Rhodes) Roberts, was born in Groton, Vermont, May 9, 1836, and died May 24, 1897. He was married in Ryegate, Vermont, January 1, 1867, to Margaret Jane Gibson, the daughter of William N. and Eleanor (Allen) Gibson. She was born in Ryegate, June 27, 1845, and died in Colorado Springs, Colorado, August 28, 1933. Jackson and Margaret first moved to Washington, Iowa, where he was mayor and where the following children were born. The family then moved to California where Jackson practiced as a lawyer in San Juan and was an associate judge of the Court of Sessions in Nevada City, California.* Children:

      i. Ida Charlotte, b. 1/10/1868; living unm. in Colorado Springs, CO in 1930.

      ii. Frank William, b. 11/24/1869; living unm. in Colorado Springs in 1930, a financier.

331.   iii. Carl Jackson, b. 5/20/1874.

263. John Hilton Roberts (Thomas[7], Nicholas[6], John[5], Stephen[4], Joseph[3], John[2], Thomas[1]), son of Thomas Heard and Eliza Jane (Hilton) Roberts, was born in Somersworth, New Hampshire, March 9, 1875, and was living in 1930. He married January 29, 1902, Alice Caverly Laskey, the daughter of Jonas S. and Sarah (Vinal) Laskey. Alice was born in Dover, New Hampshire, February 13, 1876, and was living in 1930. John was a farmer in Milton Mills, New Hampshire, and Acton, Maine, where the following children were born.+ Children:

      i. a daughter, b. 1/1/1905; d. 1/2/1905.

      ii. Luther Hilton, b. 8/18/1906; a farmer living in Milton Mills in 1930, unm.

264. Stephen Herbert Roberts (Oliver[7], Oliver[6], John[5], Stephen[4], Joseph[3], John[2], Thomas[1]), son of Oliver Ayer and Emily Wilbor (Botsford) Roberts, was born in New Bedford, Massachusetts, November 7, 1874, and was living in 1930. He

---

    * Hardon, Vol. IV, p. 53.
    + Hardon, Vol. IV, p. 74.

EIGHTH GENERATION

married January 2, 1901, Sarah Amelia Jones, the daughter of William and Sarah Amelia (Everett) Jones. Stephen attended Antioch College and worked as a vice president of State Street Trust Company in Boston, Massachusetts. The following children were born in Melrose Highlands, Massachusetts.* Children:

    i. a child, d. young.

    ii. Eleanor, b. 10/26/1903; m. (1) Henry W. Hardy of Newton, MA, (2) L. Porter Dickenson of Honolulu, HI; living in 1930. One child.

332. iii. Gardner Brewster, b. 1/16/1907.

265. Walter Scott Roberts (Hiram[7], Stephen[6], John[5], Ebenezer[4], Joseph[3], John[2], Thomas[1]), son of Hiram Rollins and Ruth (Ham) Roberts, was born in Rollinsford, New Hampshire, January 21, 1842, and died September 8, 1921. He married Marietta Nichols, who was born in Westport, New York, and died March 12, 1905. Walter was a banker in Postville, Iowa.+ Child:

    i. Libbie R., m. -----Marquardt. Seven children.

266. Hall Roberts (Hiram[7], Stephen[6], John[5], Ebenezer[4], Joseph[3], John[2], Thomas[1]), son of Hiram Rollins and Ruth (Ham) Roberts, was born in Rollinsford, New Hampshire, March 7, 1844, and died September 16, 1916, apparently in Iowa. He married April 23, 1866, Maria Ortentia Easton, the daughter of Harvey and Sarah (Hume) Easton. Maria was born in Martinsburg, New York, January 24, 1846, and died July 29, 1923. Hall was a grain dealer in Postville, Iowa, where the following children were born.# Children:

333. i. Harvey Easton, b. 12/2/1871.

    ii. Bessie Ella, b. 11/22/1875; m. 6/17/1903, Otto J. Blessin of Galesburg, IL. Living in Los Angeles, CA in 1930. One child.

---

  * Hardon, Vol. IV, p. 79.
  + Hardon, Vol. IV, pp. 89 & 94-5.
  # Hardon, Vol. IV, pp. 90 & 96.

iii. Ruth, b. 10/30/1882; m. 12/31/1907, Herbert A. Templeton of Portland, OR. A graduate of Grinnell College; res. Oregon, 1930. 4 ch.

267. Joseph Doe Roberts (Hiram^7, Stephen^6, John^5, Ebenezer^4, Joseph^3, John^2, Thomas^1), son of Hiram Rollins and Ruth (Ham) Roberts, was born in Rollinsford, New Hampshire, November 12, 1848, and died January 7, 1923. He married in Wells, Maine, July 31, 1873, Addie Littlefield, the daughter of Thomas B. and Elizabeth (Jones) Littlefield. She was born in Wells, June 10, 1854, and was living in South Berwick, Maine, in 1930. Joseph raised Holstein cattle in Rollinsford and served as president of Rollinsford State Bank. In 1895 he was elected to the state legislature. The following children were born in Rollinsford.*
Children:

	i.	Elizabeth Gertrude, b. 8/11/1874; m. 6/9/1898, Charles G.F. Coker of Salem, MA. Four children.
	ii.	Rollins, b. 10/28/1875; d. 8/27/1880.
334.	iii.	John Harry, b. 7/16/1877.
	iv.	Edith Adelaide, b. 4/28/1880; living unm. in 1930, a professor of botany at Vassar College.
	v.	Roland Edward, b. 7/11/1883; d. 12/25/1889.
	vi.	Hiram Hall (twin), b. 5/23/1888; m. 1/6/1912, Catherine C. Pinkham. A farmer in Rollinsford.
	vii.	Ruth May (twin), b. 5/23/1888; m. 1/20/1913, Charles H. Dodge of South Berwick, ME; d. 1/20/1920. Three children.
335.	viii.	Joseph Clarence, b. 12/18/1890.
	ix.	Clara Helen, b. 1/7/1894; m. 3/31/1921, Wilbur A. Henderson of Dover, NH. Living 1930. 2 ch.

---

* Hardon, Vol. IV, pp. 91-2 & 97-8.

EIGHTH GENERATION

    x.   Dorothy Deborah, b. 1/21/1900; living unm. in Chicago, IL in 1930.

268. Francis Wayland Roberts (Hiram[7], Stephen[6], John[5], Ebenezer[4], Joseph[3], John[2], Thomas[1]), son of Hiram Rollins and Ruth (Ham) Roberts, was born in Rollinsford, New Hampshire, December 16, 1851, and died September 13, 1931. He married December 25, 1871, Abigail Morton, the daughter of Albert H. and Cynthia (Waldron) Morton. She was born in Rollinsford, February 12, 1852, and died June 27, 1920. Francis attended Dartmouth College, and then removed to Postville, Iowa, and finally, Seattle, Washington, where he worked in the banking industry.[*] Children:

    i.   Lillian Estelle, b. 12/2/1873, Dover, NH. Living unm. in Seattle, WA in 1930. An 1895 graduate of Grinnell College.

336.   ii.   Fred Morton, b. 3/16/1880.

    iii.   Helen Waldron, b. 2/23/1890; m. 7/2/1913, Clayton A. Shinstrom of Redmond, WA. A 1911 graduate of Grinnell College. Four children.

269. Moses Roberts (William[7], Stephen[6], John[5], Ebenezer[4], Joseph[3], John[2], Thomas[1]), son of William Hall and Clarissa (Hall) Roberts, was born in Rollinsford, New Hampshire, June 7, 1832, and died January 18, 1908. He married February 8, 1862, Lydia Maria Hussey, the daughter of Benjamin and Sabrina (Bunker) Hussey. Lydia was born in Somersworth, New Hampshire, March 15, 1839, and died January 18, 1908. The following children were born in Rollinsford. Moses was a farmer in Rollinsford, where he and Lydia were both killed in a railroad accident.[+] Children:

    i.   Cora Luella, b. 3/19/1863; d. 4/3/1873.

337.   ii.   William Hall, b. 4/20/1866.

270. Franklin Kimball Roberts (Jeremiah[7], Jeremiah[6], Ichabod[5], Ebenezer[4], Joseph[3], John[2], Thomas[1]), son of Jeremiah and

---

[*] Hardon, Vol. IV, p. 93.
[+] Hardon, Vol. IV, p. 100.

Alma (Roberts) Roberts, was born in Waterboro, Maine, in 1840, and died in 1926. He married November 22, 1866, Sarah A. Nason. Franklin was a veteran of the Civil War. He was a real estate manager and a Baptist minister in Buffalo, New York, where the following children were living in 1930.[*] Children:

    i. Mildred Sarah, an unm. teacher.

    ii. Alma Lucretia, an unm. teacher.

    iii. Grace May, an unm. music teacher.

271. James Arthur Roberts (Jeremiah[7], Jeremiah[6], Ichabod[5], Ebenezer[4], Joseph[3], John[2], Thomas[1]), son of Jeremiah and Alma (Roberts) Roberts, was born in Waterboro, Maine, March 8, 1847. He married, firstly, in June of 1871, Minerva Pineo, the daughter of David and Amelia (Hall) Pineo. Minerva was born in Calais, Maine, November 27, 1843, and died October 1, 1883. The first child shown below was hers. James married, secondly, December 11, 1884, Martha Dresser, the daughter of Richard and Mary A. Dresser, of Auburn, Maine.

James served in the 7th Maine Volunteer Light Artillery. After the War he graduated from Bowdoin College in 1870, and went on to attain a masters degree in 1885 and an LL.D. in 1898. He worked as a teacher and a school principal. He removed to Buffalo, New York, was a lawyer there from 1876 to 1894 and served there as a state assemblyman for two terms and as state comptroller from 1893 to 1902. He was a real estate manager in New York City and president of the New York State Historical Association.[+] Children:

338.   i. Joseph Banks, b. 11/18/1873.

    ii. Amelia M.; m. Frank St.J. Sidway. 3 ch.

272. David Sands Roberts (Hanson[7], David[6], Nathaniel[5], Nathaniel[4], Nathaniel[3], Thomas[2], Thomas[1]), son of Hanson and Eleanor C. (Kimball) Roberts, was born in Farmington, New Hampshire, September 22, 1822, and died October 27, 1910. He married in Farmington, November 25, 1847, Sabrina Lord, the

---

    [*] Hardon, Vol. IV, p. 106.
    [+] Hardon, Vol. IV, pp. 107-9; Little, Vol. III, p. 1635.

EIGHTH GENERATION

daughter of Isaac and Eliza (Hussey) Lord. Sabrina was born in Acton, Maine, in May of 1825, and died June 24, 1891. David was a farmer and shoemaker in Andover, Massachusetts, and Farmington, where the following children were born.* Children:

	i.	Eliza Ellen(or Eleanor), b. 4/1/1848; m. 5/12/1867, Elihu Varney; living in Alton, NH, in 1930. One child.
	ii.	Adeline Amanda, b. 6/11/1849; m. 9/21/1867, Albert W. Dame; d. 5/10/1901.
339.	iii.	Winfield Scott, b. 7/17/1851.
	iv.	Lydia Augusta, b. 3/25/1853; m. 11/13/1869, Benjamin E. Wentworth; d. 3/30/1931.
	v.	Idella May, b. 6/30/1855; m. 9/7/1873, David T.P. Chamberlain; d. 12/4/1881.
340.	vi.	Henry Sands, b. 6/15/1858.
	vii.	Josie St.Clair, b. 5/15/1862; d. 9/27/1863.
	viii.	Caroline Josephine, b. 1/31/1864; d. unm. 8/4/1886. A teacher.

273. Charles Clarence Roberts (Hanson[7], David[6], Nathaniel[5], Nathaniel[4], Nathaniel[3], Thomas[2], Thomas[1]), son of Hanson and Eleanor C. (Kimball) Roberts, was born in Farmington, New Hampshire, in 1829, and died in Minnesota, January 16, 1904. He married Susan Lamb Roberts, daughter of Thomas (No. 118) and Elizabeth (Roberts) Roberts. Susan was born February 8, 1834, in New Hampshire. Charles was a shoemaker. This family removed to Red Wing, Minnesota. Susan was described by a descendant as a very brilliant woman who spoke several languages and taught English to Norwegian immigrants in Goodhue County, Minnesota.⁺ Children:

---

* Hardon, Vol. IV, pp. 113-4 & 120-4.
⁺ Hardon, Vol. IV, p. 117; research notes of Karen Hanson Messer.

> i. Clarence C., b.c. 1853; d. 8/8/1905.
> ii. Addie Ellen, b.10/6/1869; m. John E. Weekes; d. 10/7/1919, in Missouri. Three children.
> iii. Isabel, d. aged 13.
> 341. iv. Nathan Charles, b. 2/7/1873, Belvidere, MN.
> v. Emma Mabel, b. 3/28/1874, Belvidere, MN; d.9/4/1966, Los Gatos, CA.
> iv. Elwood, b. 7/18/1876, Belvidere, MN; d.12/21/1965, San Jose, CA.

274. Harrison F. Roberts (Hanson[7], David[6], Nathaniel[5], Nathaniel[4], Nathaniel[3], Thomas[2], Thomas[1]), son of Hanson and Eleanor C. (Kimball) Roberts, was born in Farmington, New Hampshire, in 1836. He married August 28, 1866, Abigail Horn, the daughter of Barzillai and Lucy Horn. Abigail was born in Rochester, New Hampshire, in 1847. Harrison was a farmer. This family removed to Casselton, (North or South?) Dakota. There may have been other children, besides the one shown below.* Child:

> i. Charles.

275. Edward Everett Roberts (Ira[7], John[6], George[5], Nathaniel[4], Nathaniel[3], Thomas[2], Thomas[1]), son of Ira and Belinda T. (Merritt) Roberts, was born in New Durham, New Hampshire, July 12, 1841, and died January 20, 1911. He married December 16, 1871, Emma L. Jones, the daughter of John and Mary J. Jones. She was born in Middleton, New Hampshire, in 1854. Edward was a shoemaker in Middleton, where their only child was born, and a farmer in Barrington, New Hampshire.✝ Child:

> i. Linnie May, b. 1878; d. 2/1881.

276. Charles Aaron Roberts (Alonzo[7], Aaron[6], Daniel[5], Aaron[4], Nathaniel[3], Thomas[2], Thomas[1]), son of Alonzo and Elizabeth A.C. (Maleham) Roberts, was born in Lacon, Illinois,

---

* Hardon, Vol. IV, p. 118.
✝ Hardon, Vol. IV, p. 110.

EIGHTH GENERATION

March 12, 1865, and died March 16, 1928. He married September 24, 1890, Cora Jane Hicks, the daughter of Philip and Sarah (Damon) Hicks. Cora Jane was born in Chicago, Illinois, April 16, 1864, and died March 10, 1913. Charles was a merchant in Chicago, where the following children were born.[*] Children:

   i. Agnes Elizabeth, b. 8/24/1891; m. 3/1913, Harold W. Wolff of Bronxville, NY. Three children.

342. ii. Shepherd McGregor, b. 4/19/1893.

277. Clarence Herman Roberts (Andrew[7], Alonzo[6], Daniel[5], Aaron[4], Nathaniel[3], Thomas[2], Thomas[1]), son of Andrew Torr and Ann Elizabeth (Roberts) Roberts, was born in Dover, New Hampshire, February 12, 1857, and died April 7, 1905. He married September 27, 1879, Mary Rounds Gage, the daughter of Moses and Sarah E. (Marston) Gage. Mary was born in Dover, February 22, 1860, and was living in 1930. Clarence was a painter in Dover, where the following child was born.[+] Child:

   i. Alice P., b. 2/23/1881; d. 5/20/1885.

278. Preston Fremont Roberts (Aaron[7], Alonzo[6], Daniel[5], Aaron[4], Nathaniel[3], Thomas[2], Thomas[1]), son of Aaron and Ann Eliza (Arnold) Roberts, was born in Dover, New Hampshire, November 2, 1856, and was living in 1930. He married January 25, 1897, Annie Louise Mayo, the daughter of Annie Lovell (Higgins) Mayo. Annie Louise was born in Boston, Massachusetts, October 21, 1866, and was living in 1930. Preston was a mason in Dover, where the following children were born.[#] Children:

343. i. James Arnold, b. 8/2/1901.

   ii. Edith Louise, b. 10/17/1903; d. 5/27/1904.

279. William Aaron Roberts (Aaron[7], Alonzo[6], Daniel[5], Aaron[4], Nathaniel[3], Thomas[2], Thomas[1]), son of Aaron and Ann Eliza (Arnold) Roberts, was born in Dover, New Hampshire, September 24, 1860, and died in April of 1915. He married August

---

[*] Hardon, Vol. IV, p. 128.
[+] Hardon, Vol. IV, p. 130.
[#] Hardon, Vol. IV, p. 132.

16, 1882, Alice Ann Fallows, the daughter of Matthew and Mary A. (Preston) Fallows. Alice Ann was born in Fall River, Massachusetts, August 3, 1861, and was living in 1930 in Nahant, Massachusetts. William was a mason in Dover, where the following child was born.* Child:

   344.   i.   Frank Ernest, b. 7/19/1885.

280. Charles Edwin Roberts (John[7], Jeremiah[6], James[5], Moses[4], Nathaniel[3], Thomas[2], Thomas[1]), son of John Meder and Helena (Mills) Roberts, was born in 1852 and died in February of 1933. He married Bertha Enderson, who was born in England and was living in Los Gatos, California, in 1930. This family lived in Eugene, Oregon, where the first three children were born, and in Los Gatos, where the remainder were born.+ Children:

         i.   Myrtle.

         ii.   Clarence, of Seattle, WA.

         iii. Edith.

         iv. Edna, m. Floyd Curtis of Los Gatos, CA.

   345.   v.   Herbert E.

         vi. Edwin, living unm. in Los Gatos, CA in 1930.

281. William L. Roberts (Daniel[7], Jeremiah[6], James[5], Moses[4], Nathaniel[3], Thomas[2], Thomas[1]), son of Daniel W. and Louisa (Atwood) Roberts, was born in Muscatine, Iowa, and was living, apparently, in Modesto, California, in 1930. He married Mabel Cleaver, who was also living in 1930.# Children:

         i.   Cleaver.

         ii.   William.

282. George William Roberts (Alexander[7], George[6], Thomas[5], Alexander[4], John[3], Thomas[2], Thomas[1]), son of Alexander

---

    * Hardon, Vol. IV, p. 132.
    + Hardon, Vol. IV, pp. 136-9.
    # Hardon, Vol. IV, p. 142.

EIGHTH GENERATION

and Caroline Hayes (Plummer) Roberts, was born in Rollinsford, New Hampshire, August 21, 1859, and died May 30, 1914. He married June 3, 1885, Ella Rose Gould, the daughter of Sheldon B. and Lucy (Peasley) Gould. Ella Rose was born in Rockville, Connecticut, June 24, 1858, and was living in Maxwell, Nebraska, in 1930. This family moved firstly to Springfield, Vermont, where the following five children were born, and then to Maxwell, Nebraska, where George was a rancher.* Children:

        i. Caroline Waldron, b. 5/2/1886; m. (1) 8/4/1910, Ira E. Sage, (2) 5/23/1930, Ralph Graham. Living in 1930. No children.

346.   ii. Paul Henley, b. 8/6/1891.

        iii. George William, b. 7/2/1893; a rancher in Maxwell in 1930, unmarried.

347.   iv. Rodney McKay, b. 11/17/1898.

        v. Mildred Elizabeth, b. 10/21/1900; m. 7/31/1931, Henry T. Ross of Lincoln, NE. 1 child, poss. more.

---

* Hardon, Vol. IV, pp. 146-7.

NINTH GENERATION

283. William Webster Roberts (Reuben[8], George[7], Joseph[6], George[5], William[4], John[3], John[2], Thomas[1]), son of Reuben Davis and Rachel (Webster) Roberts, was born in Portland, Maine, November 14, 1840, and was living in Westbrook, Maine, in the early 1900's. He married September 3, 1862, in Medford, Massachusetts, Arabella Waterman, the daughter of Eben and Sarah (Rogers) Waterman. Arabella was born in Pembroke, Massachusetts, and was living in Westbrook, Maine, in the early 1900's. This family lived in Cincinnati, Ohio for a time in the 1860's, where their first child was born. By 1870 they were back in Maine. William worked in the stationery business in Portland and had his own business there. He was a member of the Odd Fellows Lodge, the Knights of Pythias, the Elks and the Masons. He and his family attended the Congress Square Universalist Church in Portland.*
Children:

    i. Lora Josephine, b. 10/24/1867; d. 9/14/1886; unm.

348. ii. George Clinton, b. 1/23/1871.

    iii. Alice McLellan, b. 7/10/1876; m. 4/24/1901, Alan O. Goold. At least one child.

284. George Henry Roberts (Benjamin[8], George[7], Joseph[6], George[5], William[4], John[3], John[2], Thomas[1]), son of Benjamin and Clarissa (Mitchell) Roberts, was born October 7, 1827, in Portland, Maine, and died in Minneapolis, Minnesota, August 8, 1905. He married July 27, 1856, in Portland, Sarah Melvina Small, the daughter of Joseph P. and Pamelia (Dolly) Small. Sarah was born in Readville, Maine, September 2, 1833, and was living in Minneapolis in 1908. This family moved to Winona, Minnesota to take up farming, shortly after their marriage. Their first son was born there. Their second son was born in Utica, Minnesota.⁺
Children:

349. i. Benjamin Edward, b. 3/21/1858.

---

  * Underhill, Vol. I, pp. 1185-6.
  ⁺ Underhill, Vol I, pp. 1192-3.

DESCENDANTS OF THOMAS & REBECCA ROBERTS

  ii. George Henry, b. 3/24/1860; m. 4/11/1889, Margaret Florence Butler. Lived in Minneapolis. No children.

285. Frank Roberts (Millett[8], James[7], Love[6], Love[5], Love[4], Thomas[3], John[2], Thomas[1]), son of Millett Wentworth and Hannah Ann (Butler) Roberts, was born in Acton, Maine, February 16 (or 26?), 1860, and died October 7, 1911. He married Grace Tibbetts, who was born in Somersworth, New Hampshire, and was living in Kennebunkport, Maine, in 1930. Frank was a salesman in Somersworth and Boston. Later the family lived in Kennebunkport, where the following child was born.* Child:

  i. Kenneth, a journalist in Kennebunkport in 1930.

286. James Ezekiel Roberts (Millett[8], James[7], Love[6], Love[5], Love[4], Thomas[3], John[2], Thomas[1]), son of Millett Wentworth and Hannah Ann (Butler) Roberts, was born in Acton, Maine, March 19, 1874, and died December 5, 1926. He married September 27, 1892, Bertha Gerrish, the adopted daughter of John E. and Jane (Gilman) Gerrish. Bertha was born in Acton, Maine, September 2, 1876, and was living in Sanford, Maine, in 1930. James was a machinist in Sanford, Gonic (Connecticut?), where their first four children were born and Glenville, Connecticut, where their fifth child was born.⁺ Children:

  i. James Louis, b. 5/31/1895; m. 8/11/1924, Marion Whitehouse. A weaver in Sanford in 1930.

  ii. Earle Frank, b. 3/22/1903. He was living in Sanford in 1930, unmarried, a clerk.

  iii. Rita Elizabeth, b. 3/3/1905; m. 11/11/1927, Roscoe C. Varney. Res. Sanford, 1930. 1 ch, poss. more.

  iv. Kenneth Frederick, b. 11/11/1906; m. 9/5/1925, Mabel Rogers. Res. Sanford in 1930, a salesman.

---

 * Hardon, Vol. III, pp. 23 & 25.
 ⁺ Hardon, Vol. III, pp. 24 & 27.

NINTH GENERATION

v. Harold Jay, b. 8/18/1909; living unmarried in Sanford in 1930, a weaver.

287. John Charles Fremont Roberts (Loring[8], Love[7], Love[6], Love[5], Love[4], Thomas[3], John[2], Thomas[1]), son of Loring True and Julia (Bishop) Roberts, was born in Greenwood, Maine, September 18, 1861, and died September 28, 1898. He married October 5, 1881, Abigail S. Emmons, the daughter of Daniel H. and Christiana (Emmons) Emmons. Abigail was born in Kennebunkport, Maine, June 21, 1861, and was living in Locke Mills, Maine in 1930. After John died she married January 1, 1901, Austin John Joseph Hayes of Greenwood. John was a farmer in Greenwood, where the following children were born.* Children:

    i. Susan Smith, b. 3/6/1886; m. (1) 11/2/1901, Pearl M. Whitman, (2) 9/17/1911, Frederick E. Tubbs. Living in 1930. Six children.

350.   ii. Elias Thomas, b. 2/26/1893.

351.   iii. Loring John, b. 1/24/1895.

288. Edgar Wentworth Roberts (William[8], Love[7], Love[6], Love[5], Love[4], Thomas[3], John[2], Thomas[1]), son of William Harrison and Mary B. (Lowd) Roberts, was born in Wayne, Maine, October 8, 1851, and died in Vienna, Maine, July 31, 1919. He married in Lawrence, Massachusetts, November 13, 1873, Emma Rebecca Hatch, the daughter of Israel and Rebecca F. (Lawrence) Hatch. Emma was born in Madison, New Hampshire, September 5, 1852, and was living in Dover, New Hampshire, in 1930. Edgar was a mechanic in Wayne, where their first four children were born, and in North New Portland, Maine, where the remainder were born.⁺ Children:

352.   i. George Royal, b. 12/4/1873.

    ii. Mary Helen, b. 12/26/1875; living unm. in Auburn, ME in 1930, a registered nurse.

---

* Hardon, Vol. III, pp. 31 & 39-40.
⁺ Hardon, Vol. III, pp. 32 & 42-3.

iii. Berthua Lillian, b. 5/23/1877; d. unm. 8/27/1910.

iv. Ruby Pearl, b. 8/18/1886; m. 3/1910, Seth H. Fish; d. 11/4/1915. One child.

v. Alvah Edgar, b. 3/3/1892; m. 2/19/1914, Bertha (Mace) Lincoln; living on the original Roberts farm in Dover, NH in 1931.

353.   vi. Clyde Harold, b. 10/6/1894.

289. William Love Roberts (William⁸, Love⁷, Love⁶, Love⁵, Love⁴, Thomas³, John², Thomas¹), son of William Harrison and Mary B. (Lowd) Roberts, was born in Wayne, Maine, January 7, 1855, and was living in 1930. He married, firstly, December 25, 1880, Cora Jane Hewitt, the daughter of Asa and Amanda (Norton) Hewitt. Cora Jane was born in Livermore, Maine, January 7, 1857, and died July 16, 1904.   William married, secondly, March 5, 1906, Edith May Parsons, the daughter of Emery and Abigail Ann (Mitchell) Parsons. William was an undertaker in Canton, Maine, and Needham, Massachusetts. The first two children below are by Cora Jane and the third by Edith May.* Children:

i. Guy, b. 10/9/1881, Norway, ME; d. 5/25/1889.

ii. Winnie, b. 4/17/1883, Readfield, ME; d. 6/11/1889.

iii. Wilma Emery, b. 12/1/1907, Canton, ME; living unm. in Needham, MA in 1930.

290. Frank Herbert Roberts (William⁸, Love⁷, Love⁶, Love⁵, Love⁴, Thomas³, John², Thomas¹), son of William Harrison and Mary B. (Lowd) Roberts, was born in Wayne, Maine, June 25, 1858, and died February 27, 1916. He married, firstly, January 18, 1881, Eva May Ladd, the daughter of Nathaniel and Drusilla (Elliot) Ladd. Eva May was born in Abbott, Maine, January 7, 1861, and died May 18, 1893. Frank married, secondly, September 15, 1894, Eunice Ellen (Carver) Foster, the daughter of James and Mary (Fish) Carver and the widow of Clark Foster. Eunice was

---

* Hardon, Vol. III, pp. 32 & 44.

NINTH GENERATION

born in Leeds, Maine, April 20, 1857, and died in Vienna, Maine, April 15, 1920. Frank was a farmer. The first child below, by Eva May, was born in Brockton, Massachusetts, the second, also by Eva May, was born in Wayne, and the third, by Eunice, was also born in Wayne.* Children:

354. i. Leslie Freeman, b. 12/9/1882.

      ii. Alice Julia, b. 7/25/1885; m. 9/4/1910, Linn F. Playse of Hopkinton, MA; living in 1930. No ch.

355. iii. Merton Ellingwood, b. 1/16/1898.

291. Nathan Lewis Roberts (William^8, Love^7, Love^6, Love^5, Love^4, Thomas^3, John^2, Thomas^1), son of William Harrison and Mary B. (Lowd) Roberts, was born in Wayne, Maine, March 24, 1861, and died in Readfield, Maine, June 2, 1913. He married June 16, 1883, Inza Graves, the daughter of Osgood and Ellen (Bishop) Graves. Inza was born in Wayne, November 3, 1867, and died in Auburn, Maine, May 12, 1894. Nathan was a farmer in Wayne, where the following children were born.⁺ Children:

      i. Fred D., b. 3/1/1884; d. 2/11/1885.

356. ii. Leon Chester, b. 10/28/1886.

292. Jacob Francis Roberts (Jacob^8, James^7, Peter^6, Love^5, Love^4, Thomas^3, John^2, Thomas^1), son of Jacob Waterhouse and Safronia P. (Ricker) Roberts, was born in Charlestown, Massachusetts, July 10, 1849, and died January 24, 1924. He married October 4, 1875, Ada Annet Dam, the daughter of Joseph S. and Mary J. (Pursell) Dam. Ada Annet was born in Harrington, Maine, April 12, 1851, and died July 17, 1893. Jacob was a bookkeeper in Reading, Massachusetts, and Winchester, Massachusetts, where the following children were born.# Children:

      i. Elmer Linwood, b. 3/24/1879; d. 6/13/1880.

---

* Hardon, Vol. III, pp. 33 & 45.
⁺ Hardon, Vol. III, pp. 33 & 46.
Hardon, Vol. III, pp. 55 & 64.

ii. Edna May, b. 1/3/1881; m. 9/6/1907, John Mead Adams, of Cambridge, MA; d. 4/5/1913. One ch.

293. Walter Hill Roberts (Jacob[8], James[7], Peter[6], Love[5], Love[4], Thomas[3], John[2], Thomas[1]), son of Jacob Waterhouse and Safronia P. (Ricker) Roberts, was born in Charlestown, Massachusetts, April 22, 1855, and was living in 1930. He married October 25, 1883, Alice Souther Daniels, the daughter of Charles E. and Frances Maria (Billings) Daniels. Alice was born in Charlestown, June 22, 1858, and died February 4, 1933. Walter graduated from Harvard in 1877, and attended law school there. He was an attorney in Boston.[*] Child:

357.   i.   Paul Billings, b. 2/3/1893, Melrose, MA.

294. Herbert Howard Roberts (Jacob[8], James[7], Peter[6], Love[5], Love[4], Thomas[3], John[2], Thomas[1]), son of Jacob Waterhouse and Safronia P. (Ricker) Roberts, was born in Charlestown, Massachusetts, September 17, 1857, and died April 11, 1928. He married October 30, 1895, Florence Mabel Cummings, the daughter of Horace L. and Abigail L. (Curry) Cummings. Florence was born in Mechanic Falls, Maine, January 14, 1866, and was living in Reading, Massachusetts, in 1930. Herbert graduated from Harvard in 1878, and was a wholesale grocer in Reading, where the following child was born.[+] Child:

i.   Ruth Cummings, b. 3/19/1898. A Boston Univ. graduate (1920), res. Reading, MA, unm. in 1930.

295. Arthur Everett Roberts (Jacob[8], James[7], Peter[6], Love[5], Love[4], Thomas[3], John[2], Thomas[1]), son of Jacob Waterhouse and Safronia P. (Ricker) Roberts, was born in Charlestown, Massachusetts, June 22, 1861, and died September 11, 1932. He married October 23, 1889, Clara Augusta Norris, the daughter of Edward J. and Clarissa Ann (Norton) Norris. Clara was born in Charlestown, and was living in 1930. Arthur was treasurer of Blackstone Savings Bank in Boston, and later lived in Reading.[#]

---

[*] Hardon, Vol. III, pp. 55 & 64.
[+] Hardon, Vol. III, pp. 55 & 64.
[#] Hardon, Vol. III, pp. 55 & 65.

NINTH GENERATION

Children:

    i.   Marjorie, b. 12/27/1890, Somerville, MA; m. 1/30/1915, Dean Peabody; d. 3/18/1916. No ch.

    ii.   Emma Norris, b. 8/14/1892, Reading, MA; d. 3/6/1894.

296. Edson Roberts (Charles^8, James^7, Peter^6, Love^5, Love^4, Thomas^3, John^2, Thomas^1), son of Charles Hill and Mary Jane (Fall) Roberts, was born in Maine, and died March 29, 1932. He was a farmer in Biddeford, Maine, and also lived in New York City, where the following children were born. The name of his spouse is not recorded.* Children:

    i.   Minnie Edson, living in 1930.

    ii.   Florence, living in 1930.

    iii.   Edson, living unm. in Biddeford in 1930.

297. Charles Edwin Roberts (Charles^8, James^7, Peter^6, Love^5, Love^4, Thomas^3, John^2, Thomas^1), son of Charles Hill and Mary Jane (Fall) Roberts, was born in Maine. He removed to Cheyenne, Wyoming, where he worked in automobile repair. Nothing else is known about this family, except for the following child.$^+$ Child:

    i.   Charles Hill, an auto repairer in Cheyenne, WY.

298. Amos Roberts (Charles^8, James^7, Peter^6, Love^5, Love^4, Thomas^3, John^2, Thomas^1), son of Charles Hill and Mary Jane (Fall) Roberts, was born in Maine, and was living in Hollis, Maine, in 1930. Nothing else is known about this family, except for the following child.$^\#$ Child:

    i.   Harry Carleton, living in Augusta, ME in 1930.

299. Herman Ellery Roberts (Alonzo^8, Joseph^7, Peter^6, Love^5, Love^4, Thomas^3, John^2, Thomas^1), son of Alonzo and Viola Jane (Hill) Roberts, was born in Lyman, Maine, December 20, 1870.

---

  * Hardon, Vol. III, pp. 56 & 66.
  $^+$ Hardon, Vol. III, pp. 57 & 67.
  $^\#$ Hardon, Vol. III, pp. 58 & 69.

He married, firstly, October 6, 1898, Alice Augusta Dennett, the daughter of Simon and Minerva (Kimball) Dennett. Alice was born in Lyman, September 10, 1876, and died August 23, 1903. Herman married, secondly, June 29, 1905, Gertrude May Greenleaf, the daughter of George W. and Ann Greenleaf. Gertrude was born in Wentworth, New Hampshire, September 17, 1876, and was living in 1930. Herman married, thirdly, in Portsmouth, New Hampshire, July 29, 1931, Elsie Louise Zinck, the daughter of Nathaniel and Louise (Naugler) Zinck. Elsie was born in La Have, Nova Scotia, September 26, 1897. The child below is by the first wife. Herman was a wholesale grocer in Alfred, Maine.* Child:

   i. Norman Dennett, b. 8/23/1903, Braintree, MA; m. 12/25/1932, Mathilda (Taylor) Hoeye. They lived in El Paso, TX.

300. Porter Alonzo Roberts (Alonzo^8, Joseph^7, Peter^6, Love^5, Love^4, Thomas^3, John^2, Thomas^1), son of Alonzo and Viola Jane (Hill) Roberts, was born in Lyman, Maine, May 16, 1880, and was living in 1930. He married in Alfred, Maine, June 26, 1906, Emma Payson Tripp, the daughter of Charles and Lucy (Gile) Tripp. Emma was born in Alfred, August 26, 1884, and was living in 1930. Porter was an accountant in Portland, Maine, where the following children were born.⁺ Children:

   i. Charles Alonzo, b. 11/17/1909; living unm. in Portland in 1930.

   ii. John Kenneth, b. 6/16/1913; a student at Kirksville College of Osteopathy in 1930.

   iii. David Lloyd, b. 11/28/1927; living in 1930.

301. Arthur Leon Roberts (Alonzo^8, Joseph^7, Peter^6, Love^5, Love^4, Thomas^3, John^2, Thomas^1), son of Alonzo and Viola Jane (Hill) Roberts, was born in Lyman, Maine, September 11, 1882, and died October 11, 1927. He married April 30, 1907, Winnefred Emerson, the daughter of Charles S.D. and Sidney (Smith)

---

 * Hardon, Vol. III, pp. 73 & 76.
 ⁺ Hardon, Vol. III, pp. 73 & 76.

NINTH GENERATION

Emerson. Winnefred was born in Lyman, July 8, 1888, and was living there in 1930. Arthur was a lumberman in Lyman, where the following children were born.* Children:

    i. Eleanor Viola, b. 7/19/1908; m. 8/29/1928, Joseph L. Howard of Boston; living in 1930. Three children, poss. others.

    ii. Emily Janice, b. 5/30/1910; m. 10/15/1932, Randolph G. Canedy of Portland, ME; living in 1930. One child, poss. others.

    iii. Arthur Leon, b. 4/23/1913; a student at the University of Maine in 1930.

    iv. Marion Emerson, b. 1/1/1918; a student at Thornton Academy in 1930.

302. Charles William Roberts (Luke[8], Nahum[7], Peter[6], Love[5], Love[4], Thomas[3], John[2], Thomas[1]), son of Luke Hemmenway and Celeste C. (Morris) Roberts, was born in Alfred, Maine, March 28, 1875, and died December 19, 1915. He married July 25, 1899, Isabelle Jordan Nash, the daughter of Orrin G. and Juliette (Jordan) Nash. Isabelle was born in Cumberland Centre, Maine, December 18, 1868, and died June 29, 1933. Charles was a farmer in Kennebunk, Maine, where the following child was born.⁺ Child:

    i. Elsie Louise, b. 11/20/1901; m. 7/25/1933, Nelson B. Hall.

303. Coolidge Sutton Roberts (David[8], John[7], Timothy[6], John[5], Timothy[4], Thomas[3], John[2], Thomas[1]), son of Davis Ballard and Agnes (Hughes) Roberts, was born in Boston, Massachusetts, January 11, 1849, and died February 17, 1904. He married June 16, 1875, Annie Dudley, the daughter of Charles S. and Isabel (Roby) Dudley. Annie was born in Cambridge, Massachusetts, and was living in 1930. Coolidge was an importer and lived for some time in Buenos Aires, Argentina, where the following children were

---

    * Hardon, Vol. III, pp. 73 & 77.
    ⁺ Hardon, Vol. III, pp. 87 & 91.

born.* Children:

  i. Edith Caswell, b. 1877; m. 4/30/1907, George P. Dike of Auburndale, MA; living in 1930.

  ii. Cecile, b. 1880; m. 6/5/1912, Ellery C. Stowell of Washington, DC; living in 1930. Three children.

304. William Wingate Roberts (Joseph^8, John^7, Joseph^6, John^5, Timothy^4, Thomas^3, John^2, Thomas^1), son of Joseph Augustus and Phebe E. (Chesley) Roberts, was born in Farmington, New Hampshire, March 7, 1850, and died February 7, 1933. He married January 1, 1880, Eloise Annie Flanders, the daughter of Samuel B. and Marcia A. (Brown) Flanders. Eloise was born in Danbury, New Hampshire, February 21, 1857, and died November 28, 1897. William was a druggist in Farmington, where the following children were born.⁺ Children:

358. i. George L., b. 12/29/1886.

  ii. Helen, b. 12/21/1890; living unm. in Arlington, MA in 1930, a teacher.

305. Frank Henry Roberts (Henry^8, John^7, Joseph^6, John^5, Timothy^4, Thomas^3, John^2, Thomas^1), son of Henry Laurens and Anna M.E. (Towle) Roberts, was born in Farmington, New Hampshire, February 21, 1867, and died March 16, 1907. He married September 24, 1891, Gertrude Estella Lund, the daughter of James B. and Ada E. (Cookson) Lund. Gertrude was born in Warren, New Hampshire, August 15, 1872, and died October 8, 1897. Frank was an artisan in Farmington, where the following child was born.# Child:

  i. Gertrude Lurline Estelle, b. 10/1/1897; m. 6/27/1920, Roland G. Kimball of Freeport, ME; living in 1930. Three children.

306. Charles Frederick Roberts (Noah^8, John^7, John^6, Thomas^5, Timothy^4, Thomas^3, John^2, Thomas^1), son of Noah Horn

---

 * Hardon, Vol. III, pp. 107-9.
 ⁺ Hardon, Vol. III, pp. 120 & 123.
 # Hardon, Vol. III, pp. 121 & 124.

NINTH GENERATION

and Achsa S. (Dixon) Roberts, was born in Lebanon, Maine, August 4, 1860, and died May 22, 1924. He married, firstly, February 18, 1886, Eva E. Nute, the daughter of Jeremy O. and Martha E. (Felch) Nute. Eva was born in Farmington, New Hampshire, September 9, 1866, and was living in Boston, Massachusetts, in 1930. Charles married, secondly, June 1, 1900, Jane Eaton, the daughter of Samuel S. and Mary E. (Perry) Eaton. Jane was born in Wakefield, New Hampshire, August 5, 1870, and was living in Los Angeles, California, in 1930. The child below was by the first wife. Charles studied medicine at Dartmouth College and then practiced as a physician in Sanbornville and Chester, New Hampshire, and in Los Angeles.* Child:

359.   i. Rex Nute, b. 1/21/1890, Sanbornville, NH.

307. William Pitt Roberts (Noah^8, John^7, John^6, Thomas^5, Timothy^4, Thomas^3, John^2, Thomas^1), son of Noah Horn and Achsa S. (Dixon) Roberts, was born in Lebanon, Maine, February 14, 1867, and was living in 1930. He married January 14, 1902, Mary Diana Blanchard, the daughter of Melvin B. and Lounetta F. (Hall) Blanchard. Mary Diana was born in Dover, New Hampshire, June 20, 1868, and was living in 1930. William was a merchant in Dover, where the following child was born.⁺ Child:

   i. William Hall, b. 3/15/1910; d. 3/21/1910.

308. Fred Herbert Roberts (Henry^8, John^7, John^6, Thomas^5, Timothy^4, Thomas^3, John^2, Thomas^1), son of Henry Kirkwood and Ellen A. (Kimball) Roberts, was born in Rochester, New Hampshire, January 22, 1868, and died in Strafford, New Hampshire, May 16, 1925. He married June 6, 1906, Bessie Winnifred Evans, the daughter of Abram and Josephine E. (Page) Evans. Bessie was born in Haverhill, Massachusetts, August 2, 1874, and was living in 1930 in Lynn, Massachusetts. Fred was a surveyor and farmer in Rochester, where the following child was born.# Child:

---

   * Hardon, Vol. III, pp. 137 & 142.
   ⁺ Hardon, Vol. III, pp. 138 & 142.
   # Hardon, Vol. III, pp. 139 & 142.

i. Merton Urban, b. 8/25/1907; living unm. in Fisher's Island, NY in 1930.

309. Ernest Linwood Roberts (Henry[8], John[7], John[6], Thomas[5], Timothy[4], Thomas[3], John[2], Thomas[1]), son of Henry Kirkwood and Mabel R. (Hill) Roberts, was born in Rochester, New Hampshire, in September of 1885, and was living in 1930. He married June 18, 1913, Cora Ethel Pinkham, the daughter of George F. and Cora E. (Cate) Pinkham. Cora Ethel was born in Rochester, July 23, 1883, and died September 1, 1932. Ernest was a stationary engineer in Rochester, where the following children were born.*
Children:

i. Richard Lovell, b. 8/4/1915; living unm. in 1930.

ii. Dorothy, b. 10/4/1919; living in 1930.

310. Everett Anson Roberts (Thomas[8], William[7], Thomas[6], Timothy[5], Timothy[4], Thomas[3], John[2], Thomas[1]), son of Thomas Herbert Roberts, was born in Portsmouth, New Hampshire, April 6, 1888, and was living in 1930. He married October 26, 1920, Geneva Payne, the daughter of Charles H. and Earla (Sullivan) Payne. Geneva was born in Sonora, Kentucky, November 23, 1896, and was living in 1930. Everett was a safety engineer in Chicago, Illinois. The following children were born in Louisville, Kentucky.⁺
Children:

i. Frances Earline, b. 2/22/1922; living in 1930.

ii. Everett Lee, b. 12/22/1924; living in 1930.

311. Delancy Amos Roberts (Joseph[8], Joseph[7], Benjamin[6], Benjamin[5], Samuel[4], Hatevil[3], John[2], Thomas[1]), son of Joseph and Lydia Ann (Spinney) Roberts, was born in Nova Scotia, March 16, 1858, and died December 22, 1945, of coronary arteriosclerosis, in Dorchester, Massachusetts. He married August 21, 1878, in Glenwood, Nova Scotia, Edna Josephine Whitehouse, the daughter of Benjamin J. and Ophelia J. (Ricker) Whitehouse. She was born in Glenwood, December 17, 1859, and died December 4, 1916, of

---

* Hardon, Vol. III, p. 140.
⁺ Hardon, Vol. III, pp. 144 & 147.

NINTH GENERATION

pulmonary tuberculosis, in North Reading, Massachusetts. This family migrated to Boston, July 5, 1881, arriving on the steamer *Dominion*. The first two children below were born in Glenwood, the remainder in Boston or Dorchester.* Children:

    i. Alice Maud, b. 10/27/1878; m. Richard H. Blood, 8/18/1911; d. 8/13/1919.

    ii. Bertha Annabel, b.9/29/1883; d.1896, Glenwood, NS.

    iii. Sarah Helen, b. 2/25/1888; m. Lyman L. Hale, 10/11/1911; d. 2/19/1978, FL, bur. Manlius, NY. Four children.

    iv. Jesse Nina, b. 3/30/1891; d. 11/28/1916.

360. v. Robert Whitehouse, b. 1/25/1893.

361. vi. Waldo Preston, b. 7/29/1896.

362. vii. Clayton Hartley, b. 11/28/1899.

312. Joseph Martin Roberts (Joseph[8], Joseph[7], Benjamin[6], Benjamin[5], Samuel[4], Hatevil[3], John[2], Thomas[1]), son of Joseph and Lydia Ann (Spinney) Roberts, was born in Nova Scotia, April 14, 1863, and died January 27, 1918. Joseph was married three times, firstly, in Glenwood, Nova Scotia, to Sarah Helen Whitehouse, April 11, 1887, secondly, to Lillian Ruth Wentworth, March 1, 1892, and thirdly, to Melvina Whitehouse. Sarah Helen was born in 1866 and died in 1887, and was the mother of the first child shown below. Lillian Ruth was born in 1872 and died in 1909, and was the mother of the other six children. Melvina was born in 1865.⁺ Children:

    i. Alonzo Joseph Martin, b. 1887; d. 1888.

    ii. Clifton Wood, b. 1894.

    iii. a child b. & d. 1898.

---

* Clayton H. Roberts notes.
⁺ Clayton H. Roberts notes.

363. iv. Victor Wentworth, b. 1899.

v. Elsie, b. 1903; d. 1906.

vi. Howard Franklin, b. 1908.

vii. Ruth Retta, b. 1908.

313. George Litch Roberts (Reuben^8, Reuben^7, Paul^6, Samuel^5, Samuel^4, Hatevil^3, John^2, Thomas^1), son of Reuben and Jane (Litch) Roberts, was born in Boston, Massachusetts, December 30, 1836, and died in Brookline, Massachusetts, April 29, 1929. He married Hinda Barnes, the daughter of Duane and Cynthia (Turner) Barnes. Hinda was born in Middletown, Connecticut, in June of 1839, and died in May of 1909. George graduated from Wesleyan College in 1859 and practiced law in Boston.* Children:

364. i. Odin, b. 1/22/1867.

ii. Harold, b. 4/8/1869; living unm. in Upper Montclair, NJ in 1930.

314. William Edward Roberts (Simeon^8, Aaron^7, Aaron^6, Samuel^5, Samuel^4, Hatevil^3, John^2, Thomas^1), son of Simeon Brock and Lydia J. (Shackford) Roberts, was born in Rollinsford, New Hampshire, July 7, 1874, and died March 29, 1917. He married April 18, 1907, Jane (Emerson) Smith, the daughter of Frank W. and Isabelle W. (Eaton) Emerson, and the former wife of Ernest B. Smith. Jane was born in Atkinson, New Hampshire, September 4, 1878, and was living in Dover, New Hampshire, in 1930. William was a shoe worker in Dover.⁺ Child:

i. Paul Ramon, b. 3/24/1912, Rollinsford, NH; m. 8/6/1932, Alice May La Belle; a cook in Northwood, NH in 1930.

315. Herbert Arthur Roberts (Simeon^8, Aaron^7, Aaron^6, Samuel^5, Samuel^4, Hatevil^3, John^2, Thomas^1), son of Simeon Brock and Lydia J. (Shackford) Roberts, was born in Rollinsford, New

---

* Hardon, Vol. III, pp. 152-4.
⁺ Hardon, Vol. III, pp. 159 & 163.

NINTH GENERATION

Hampshire, June 18, 1880, and was living in 1930. He married December 24, 1901, Lily Porter, the daughter of James and Eliza (Moore) Porter. Lily was born in Trowbridge, England, October 9, 1883, and was living in 1930. Herbert was an iron molder in Rollinsford.* Children:

- 365. i. Harold Clifton, b. 10/30/1902.
- 366. ii. Ernest Arthur, b. 7/13/1904.
- iii. James Porter, b. 7/23/1908; a hotel clerk in Rollinsford, unm. in 1930.
- iv. Mildred Helen, b. 2/19/1910; living in Rollinsford in 1930, a teacher.
- v. Elinor Elizabeth, b. 6/24/1916; living in 1930.

316. Herman C. Roberts (Samuel^8, Caleb^7, Benjamin^6, Nathan^5, Samuel^4, Hatevil^3, John^2, Thomas^1), son of Samuel E. and Patience Comfort (Ackerman) Roberts, was born in Alexandria, New Hampshire, June 21, 1864, and died February 1, 1931. He married Susanna Warbrick, who was born in Liverpool, England, March 14, 1867, and died June 12, 1925. Herman was a farmer in Rochester, where the following children were born.⁺ Children:

- i. Angeline Anstrus, 5/14/1891; m. 6/28/1911, Winifred R. Chalmers; d. 7/10/1917. No children.
- ii. Etta Elizabeth, b. 7/27/1893; m. 7/15/1910, Walter E. Hayes; res. East Rochester, NH, 1930. 3 ch.
- iii. Clyde Samuel, b. 8/4/1904; m. 6/15/1929, Gertrude L. Witham; d. 5/16/1930. No children.

317. John Place Roberts (Benjamin^8, Caleb^7, Benjamin^6, Nathan^5, Samuel^4, Hatevil^3, John^2, Thomas^1), son of Benjamin and Mary Esther (Place) Roberts, was born in Farmington, New Hampshire, January 28, 1852, and died July 30, 1927. He married, firstly, Clara Irene Tibbetts, the daughter of Silas C. and Lois

---

* Hardon, Vol. II, p. 166 and Vol. III, p. 159.
⁺ Hardon, Vol. III, pp. 170 & 175.

(Grace) Tibbetts. Clara was born in New Durham, New Hampshire, March 27, 1861, and died August 2, 1906. John married, secondly, April 22, 1916, Lillian Alma (Rollins) (Willey) Hayes, the daughter of Solomon and Lucinda (Tufts) Rollins and the widow of -----Willey. She was also the former wife of Seth Walker Hayes. Lillian was born in New Durham, in 1860. The children below are by Clara. John was a train man and a farmer in Farmington, where the following children were born.[*] Children:

    i. Ethel Gertrude, b. 4/3/1882; m. (1) 6/2/1906, Guy H. Stoddard, (2) 12/27/1930, James H. Bannon; living in 1930. No children.

    ii. Helen Hayes, b. 11/15/1885; m. 4/20/1919, Willis C. Hanson; living in 1930. One child.

367.   iii. Harry Fletcher, b. 8/10/1886.

318. Horace Herbert Roberts (Benjamin[8], Caleb[7], Benjamin[6], Nathan[5], Samuel[4], Hatevil[3], John[2], Thomas[1]), son of Benjamin and Mary Esther (Place) Roberts, was born in Farmington, New Hampshire, December 3, 1854, and died March 4, 1921. He married September 30, 1881, Mary E. Noyes, the daughter of James B. and Sybil (Wentworth) Noyes. Mary was born in Anawan, Illinois, November 21, 1855, and died in December of 1931. Horace was a farmer in Farmington, where the following children were born.[+] Children:

368.   i. Carl Noyes, b. 10/13/1886.

    ii. Perley James, b. 6/17/1891; m. 10/4/1915, Rachel S. Grimes; living in 1930, a chemist in Waverly, MA. A graduate of Dartmouth (1912).

319. Henry Benjamin Roberts (Benjamin[8], Caleb[7], Benjamin[6], Nathan[5], Samuel[4], Hatevil[3], John[2], Thomas[1]), son of Benjamin and Mary Esther (Place) Roberts, was born in Farmington, New Hampshire, February 19, 1857. He married, firstly, Ella Blakeley, the daughter of Johnson Blakeley, and,

---

[*] Hardon, Vol. III, pp. 171 & 176.
[+] Hardon, Vol. III, pp. 171 & 178.

NINTH GENERATION

secondly, April 29, 1914, Edna G. (Pillsbury) York, the daughter of Daniel and Elizabeth (Roberts) Pillsbury, and the former wife of ---- York. Edna was born in Newbury, Massachusetts, in 1866. Henry was a shoe finisher in Haverhill, Massachusetts, and Farmington, where the following child was born.* Child:

    i. Nellie Blanche.

320. Harry Edwin Roberts (Edwin[8], George[7], Jonathan[6], Thomas[5], Joshua[4], Hatevil[3], John[2], Thomas[1]), son of Edwin Jonathan and Sarah E. (Daniels) Roberts, was born in Metamore, Illinois, June 3, 1866, and died in St. Louis, Missouri, July 16, 1932. He married November 13, 1894, Abigail Morrill Eaton, the daughter of Thomas Eaton. Abigail was born in Illini, Illinois, August 11, 1874. Harry was a farmer in Warrensburg, Illinois, and Illini, where the following child was born.+ Child:

    i. Lawrence Bailey, b. 7/13/1897; d. 12/13/1914.

321. William Burchard Roberts (George[8], George[7], Jonathan[6], Thomas[5], Joshua[4], Hatevil[3], John[2], Thomas[1]), son of George Franklin and Ella Sophia (Thayer) Roberts, was born in Lacon, Illinois, May 19, 1875, and was living in 1930. He married June 22, 1904, Elizabeth Brant, the daughter of Clark Thompson and Ellen (Matson) Brant. Elizabeth was born in Chariton, Iowa, and was living in 1930. William was a lieutenant in the U.S. Medical Corp in World War I. He was a physician in Minneapolis, Minnesota.# Children:

    i. Dorothy, b. 10/17/1906; m. 4/7/1929, Francis P. Whiting; living in 1930. Two ch., poss. more.

    ii. Elizabeth, b. 4/2/1909; d. 3/1910.

    iii. George F., b. 6/7/1911; living in 1930.

322. George Bradbury Roberts (Everett[8], George[7], Jonathan[6], Thomas[5], Joshua[4], Hatevil[3], John[2], Thomas[1]), son of Everett Lemuel and Anna Belle (Clark) Roberts, was born in

---

  * Hardon, Vol. III, pp. 171 & 178.
  + Hardon, Vol. IV, pp. 6 & 10.
  # Hardon, Vol. IV, pp. 7 & 10.

Bloomington, Illinois, March 6, 1890, and was living in 1930. He married November 6, 1919, Barbara Ozello Roth, the daughter of John and Annie T. (Heinrich) Roth. Barbara was born in Woodville, California, May 29, 1894, and was living in 1930. George was a foreman in a gasoline refinery in El Segundo, California.* Child:

    i. Keith Everett, b. 6/17/1923, Los Angeles, CA.

323. Eugene Charles Roberts (Tobias^8, Joshua^7, Tobias^6, Joshua^5, Joshua^4, Hatevil^3, John^2, Thomas^1), son of Tobias and Lucy A. (Pease) Roberts, was born May 31, 1869, and died December 8, 1899. He married in June of 1888, Bertha Jane Berry, the daughter of Lovell F. and Melissa A. (Hartford) Berry. Bertha was born in Strafford, New Hampshire, August 28, 1868, and was living in 1930. Eugene was a blacksmith in Strafford.⁺ Child:

    i. Charles Arthur, b. 12/12/1890; d. 6/1/1891.

324. Harry Arthur Roberts (Tobias^8, Joshua^7, Tobias^6, Joshua^5, Joshua^4, Hatevil^3, John^2, Thomas^1), son of Tobias and Lucy A. (Pease) Roberts, was born August 30, 1876, and was living in 1930. He married Ida Dorry Berry, the daughter of Lovell R. and Melissa A. (Hartford) Berry. Ida was born in Strafford, New Hampshire, and was living in 1930. Harry was a blacksmith in Rochester, New Hampshire, where the following children were born.# Children:

    i. Beulah May, b. 5/19/1907; m. 6/25/1927, Gerald E. Towle of Haverhill, MA. Two children.

    ii. Carlyle Berry, b. 6/12/1917; living in 1930.

325. Laurel Tobias Roberts (Tobias^8, Joshua^7, Tobias^6, Joshua^5, Joshua^4, Hatevil^3, John^2, Thomas^1), son of Tobias and Lucy A. (Pease) Roberts, was born September 24, 1881, and was living in 1930. He married December 17, 1904, Lillian Albertha Bickford, the daughter of Charles E. and Cora I. (Shorey) Bickford. Lillian

---

    * Hardon, Vol. IV, pp. 8 & 11.
    ⁺ Hardon, Vol. IV, pp. 16 & 21.
    # Hardon, Vol. IV, pp. 17 & 22.

NINTH GENERATION

was born in Rochester, New Hampshire, March 12, 1882, and was living in 1930. Laurel was a blacksmith in Rochester, where the following child was born.* Child:

    i. Lillian Isabelle, b. 6/16/1906; living unm. in 1930.

326. Sewell Edson Roberts (Sewall^8, Richard^7, Joseph^6, Joseph^5, Joseph^4, Joseph^3, John^2, Thomas^1), son of Sewall Trevett and Mary Ellen (Savage) Roberts, was born in Alton, New Hampshire, August 27, 1860, and died November 18, 1928. He married March 17, 1886, Ella Sophia Trask, the daughter of William P. and Lydia (Butler) Trask. Ella was born in Lake Darling, Nova Scotia, October 12, 1858, and was living in Alton, in 1930. Sewell was a farmer in Alton, where the following children were born.$^+$ Children:

369.   i.   George Fillmore, b. 11/24/1887.

370.   ii.   Charles Edson, b. 5/18/1893.

327. John Pike Roberts (Sewall^8, Richard^7, Joseph^6, Joseph^5, Joseph^4, Joseph^3, John^2, Thomas^1), son of Sewall Trevett and Ann Eliza (Beacham) Roberts, was born in Alton, New Hampshire, December 10, 1864, and was living in 1930. He married, firstly, January 12, 1887, Lillie Ann Bagley, the daughter of Orlando J. and Mary (Watson) Bagley. Lillie Ann was born in Somersworth, New Hampshire, October 16, 1861, and died December 29, 1917. John married, secondly, September 28, 1920, Susan (Townsend) Cross, the daughter of Obediah and Nancy A. (Gamage) Townsend, and the widow of William M. Cross. Susan was born in West Bowdoin, Maine, May 1, 1866, and was living in 1930. John attended Bates College, and was a clergyman in Lisbon Falls, Maine. The following child was born in Alton.$^\#$ Child:

    i. Mary Lillian, b. 9/19/1892; living unm. in Providence, RI in 1930, a graduate of Bates College (1915) and a teacher.

---

    * Hardon, Vol. IV, pp. 17 & 22.
    $^+$ Hardon, Vol. IV, pp. 28 & 32.
    $^\#$ Hardon, Vol. IV, pp. 29 & 32.

328. John Smith Roberts (Samuel[8], Richard[7], Joseph[6], Joseph[5], Joseph[4], Joseph[3], John[2], Thomas[1]), son of Samuel Woodbury and Elizabeth (Smith) Roberts, was born in Wakefield, New Hampshire, November 25, 1864, and was living in 1930. He married May 20, 1893, Sarah Naomi Moulton, the daughter of Herschel and Mary Eliza (Thompson) Moulton. Sarah was born in Wakefield, October 26, 1865, and was living in 1930. John was a farmer in Wakefield, where the following child was born.* Child:

    i. Samuel Woodbury, b. 8/2/1906; m. 4/9/1932, Hilda Ruth Garton of Providence, RI; living in Springfield, MA in 1930, a graduate of N.H. State College (1927) and a design engineer.

329. Richard Sewall Woodbury Roberts (Richard[8], Richard[7], Joseph[6], Joseph[5], Joseph[4], Joseph[3], John[2], Thomas[1]), son of Richard and Augusta C. (Marston) Roberts, was born in New Market, New Hampshire, April 13, 1877, and was living in 1930. He married September 14, 1904, Jane C. Ames, the daughter of Charles E. and Rose Ames. Jane was born in Richmond, New Hampshire, in 1878, and was living in 1930. Richard was a graduate of Bates College (1901) and an optometrist in Whitinsville, Massachusetts.⁺ Children:

    i. Elizabeth, b. 4/18/1908; d. in infancy.

    ii. Marion, b. 7/19/1909. A graduate of Boston U.

330. Oliver Frank Roberts (Charles[8], Oliver[7], Hanson[6], Joseph[5], Stephen[4], Joseph[3], John[2], Thomas[1]), son of Charles Andrew and Johanna Elizabeth (Sullivan) Roberts, was born in Boston, Massachusetts, June 24, 1883, and was living in 1930. He married February 29, 1908, Mildred Austin Clapp, the daughter of Frank and Faustena (Austin) Clapp. Mildred was born in Damariscotta, Maine, March 4, 1885, and was living in 1930. Oliver was an insurance manager in Santa Monica, California.# Children:

---

    * Hardon, Vol. IV, pp. 30 & 33.
    ⁺ Hardon, Vol. IV, pp. 30 & 33.
    # Hardon, Vol. IV, pp. 81 & 83.

NINTH GENERATION

    i. Faustena Austin, b. 4/26/1909, Malden, MA; m. 9/19/1931, John E. Fradd; living in San Diego, CA in 1931. One child, poss. more.

    ii. Priscilla, b. 12/27/1910, Chicago, IL; living unm. in Santa Monica, CA in 1930.

331. Carl Jackson Roberts (Jackson[8], John[7], Stephen[6], John[5], Stephen[4], Joseph[3], John[2], Thomas[1]), a financier, son of Jackson and Margaret J. (Gibson) Roberts, was born in Washington, Iowa, May 20, 1874, and was living in 1930. He married in Willis, Michigan, September 28, 1904, Alice Maud Hoover, the daughter of John M. and Mary (Roblin) Hoover. Alice was born in Kent County, Ontario, Canada, and was living in 1930.* Child:

    i. Mary Hoover, b. 10/27/1908; m. 8/10/1932, Ray N. Berry. A graduate of Iowa Univ. (A.B. 1930 and A.M. 1931).

332. Gardner Brewster Roberts (Stephen[8], Oliver[7], Oliver[6], John[5], Stephen[4], Joseph[3], John[2], Thomas[1]), son of Stephen Herbert and Sarah A. (Jones) Roberts, was born in Melrose Highlands, Massachusetts, January 16, 1907, and was living in 1930. He married Virginia Haigis, who was born in Virginia and was living in 1930. Gardner was a sales manager in Boston, Massachusetts, where the following (and possibly others) child was born.⁺ Child:

    i. Virginia, b. 7/1931.

333. Harvey Easton Roberts (Hall[8], Hiram[7], Stephen[6], John[5], Ebenezer[4], Joseph[3], John[2], Thomas[1]), son of Hall and Maria O. (Easton) Roberts, was born in Postville, Iowa, December 2, 1871, and was living in 1930. He married January 3, 1924, Florence Marston, the daughter of Adelbert C. and Nettie (Kerr) Marston. Florence was born in Postville, December 2, 1891, and was living in 1930. Harvey was a graduate of Grinnell College (1893), and a grain dealer in Postville, where the following child (and possibly

---

* Hardon, Vol. IV, pp. 53 & 62.
⁺ Hardon, Vol. IV, p. 79.

other children) was born.* Child:

    i.   Hall, b. 10/15/1927; living in 1930.

334. John Harry Roberts (Joseph[8], Hiram[7], Stephen[6], John[5], Ebenezer[4], Joseph[3], John[2], Thomas[1]), son of Joseph Doe and Addie (Littlefield) Roberts, was born in Rollinsford, New Hampshire, July 16, 1877, and was living in 1930. He married April 17, 1918, Mary Martha Wright, the daughter of William and Mary (Greenway) Wright. Mary Martha was born in Dover, New Hampshire, December 8, 1887, and died December 22, 1922. John was a farmer in Rollinsford. The child below was born in Dover.⁺ Child:

    i.   Clyde Thomas, b. 1/13/1919; living in 1930.

335. Joseph Clarence Roberts (Joseph[8], Hiram[7], Stephen[6], John[5], Ebenezer[4], Joseph[3], John[2], Thomas[1]), son of Joseph Doe and Addie (Littlefield) Roberts, was born in Rollinsford, New Hampshire, December 18, 1890, and was living in 1930. He married September 10, 1912, Mary Louise Armstrong, the daughter of Daniel N. and Matilda M. (Banks) Armstrong. Mary was born in York, Maine, April 17, 1885, and was living in 1930. Joseph was a farmer in Rollinsford. The following children were born in Dover.# Children:

    i.   Ormond, b. 6/13/1913; living in 1930.

    ii.   Louise, b. 12/24/1914; living in 1930.

336. Fred Morton Roberts (Francis[8], Hiram[7], Stephen[6], John[5], Ebenezer[4], Joseph[3], John[2], Thomas[1]), son of Francis Wayland and Abigail (Morton) Roberts, was born in Postville, Iowa, March 16, 1880, and was living in 1930. He married June 17, 1908, Edith Christine Swan, the daughter of George and Antoinette (Cold) Swan. Edith was born in Reinbeck, Iowa, September 2, 1883, and was living in 1930. Fred graduated from Grinnell College (1899) and Harvard Law School (1903). He practiced in Seattle,

---

   * Hardon, Vol. IV, pp. 90 & 96.
   ⁺ Hardon, Vol. IV, pp. 91 & 98.
   # Hardon, Vol. IV, pp. 92 & 98.

NINTH GENERATION

Washington, where the following children were born.* Children:

    i. James Morton, b. 7/11/1909; d. in an accident 12/20/1932. Graduated from Stanford Univ. Law School in 1931.

    ii. Ruth, b. 6/11/1912; living unm. in 1930.

    iii. Mary Frances, b. 7/6/1914; living in 1930.

337. **William Hall Roberts** (Moses^8, William^7, Stephen^6, John^5, Ebenezer^4, Joseph^3, John^2, Thomas^1), son of Moses and Lydia M. (Hussey) Roberts, was born in Rollinsford, New Hampshire, April 20, 1866, and was living in 1930. He married June 28, 1905, Lila Lizette Burgess, the daughter of Vernon and Evora (Messer) Burgess. Lila was born in Kennebunk, Maine, April 1, 1881, and was living in 1930. William was a lawyer and clerk of the Superior Court in Dover, New Hampshire, where the following children were born.⁺ Children:

    i. Wade Hanson, b. 2/20/1907; living unm. in 1930. A graduate of the Univ. of N.H. (1930).

    ii. Wilma Lila, b. 9/10/1913; living in 1930.

338. **Joseph Banks Roberts** (James^8, Jeremiah^7, Jeremiah^6, Ichabod^5, Ebenezer^4, Joseph^3, John^2, Thomas^1), son of James Arthur and Minerva (Pineo) Roberts, was born in Waterboro, Maine, November 18, 1873, and was living in 1930. He married, firstly, April 20, 1903, Mary Van Rensselaer Ferris, the daughter of Morris P. and Mary L. (Douw) Ferris. Mary was born in Niagara Falls, New York, May 20, 1883, and was living in Ridgewood, New Jersey in 1930. Joseph married, secondly, February 12, 1921, Evelyn Bean, who was born in Marion, Ohio, and was living in 1930. The following children were by Mary. Joseph graduated from Bowdoin College in 1895 and earned his law degree at the University of Buffalo in 1899. He practiced law in Buffalo and New York City. He moved his family to Pueblo, Colorado in 1917. He was vice president of the American Carbide Company, a director

---

  * Hardon, Vol. IV, pp. 93 & 99.
  ⁺ Hardon, Vol. IV, pp. 100 & 102.

of various companies, and president of San Isabel Tours Company from 1921.* Children:

    i. Dorothy Douw, b. 5/28/1904, New York City; living unm. in 1930 in Ridgewood, NJ.

    ii. Morris Ferris, b. 7/26/1905, Garden City, NY; living unm. in 1930, a poultry farmer in Ridgewood, NJ.

    iii. James DePeyster, b. 9/9/1906, Hempsted, NY; d. 9/20/1906.

    iv. Margaret Livingston Dresser, b. 8/28/1908, Ridgewood, NJ; living there unm. in 1930.

339. Winfield Scott Roberts (David^8, Hanson^7, David^6, Nathaniel^5, Nathaniel^4, Nathaniel^3, Thomas^2, Thomas^1), son of David Sands and Sabrina (Lord) Roberts, was born in Farmington, New Hampshire, July 17, 1851, and died July 22, 1926. He married August 5, 1871, Oceana Fitzgerald Fall, the daughter of Otis and Rosillah (Evans) Fall. Oceana was born in Farmington, October 9, 1851, and died April 30, 1922. Winfield was a shoecutter in Farmington, where the following children were born.⁺ Children:

    i. Idella E., b. 11/1872; d. 7/24/1874.

    ii. Rosillah, b. 6/25/1880; m. 8/19/1906, Harry T. Jones; living in 1930. No children.

340. Henry Sands Roberts (David^8, Hanson^7, David^6, Nathaniel^5, Nathaniel^4, Nathaniel^3, Thomas^2, Thomas^1), son of David Sands and Sabrina (Lord) Roberts, was born in Farmington, New Hampshire, June 15, 1858, and was living in 1930. He married, firstly, April 23, 1883, Lelia Jameson Holland, the daughter of John and Emily S. (Welch) Holland. Lelia was born in Lewiston, Maine, June 15, 1863, and died December 29, 1888. Henry married, secondly, June 16, 1890, Belle Frances Davis, the daughter of Paine and Esther (Babcock) Davis. Belle was born in Warner, New

---

    * Hardon, Vol. IV, pp. 107 & 109.
    ⁺ Hardon, Vol. IV, pp. 114 & 123.

NINTH GENERATION

Hampshire, June 30, 1870, and was living in 1930. Henry graduated from Bates College with an A.B. in 1881 and an A.M. in 1885. He was a high school master in Farmington and the Superintendent of Schools in Suncock, New Hampshire.* Children:

371. i. David Sands, b. 4/9/1885, Lewiston, ME.

ii. Mildred Francis, b. 6/9/1891, Somersworth, NH. Graduate of Smith College (1913), a teacher, living unm. in Pasadena, CA.

372. iii. Fred Paine, b. 10/5/1892, Somersworth.

iv. Clive Malcolm, b. 9/5/1893, North Adams, MA; unm. druggist in Wolfeboro, NH in 1930.

v. Louise Davis, b. 5/12/1896, Belmont, MA; m. Frank L. Caton, 7/15/1923. Living in 1930.

341. Nathan Charles Roberts (Charles[8], Hanson[7], David[6], Nathaniel[5], Nathaniel[4], Nathaniel[3], Thomas[2], Thomas[1]), son of Charles Clarence and Susan (Lamb) Roberts, was born in Belvidere, Minnesota, February 7, 1873, and died in 1947. He married Anna Amelia Glanders. There is no further information on her.⁺ Children:

i. Esther Emma, b. 3/30/1913; m. Lawrence R. Smith, 1/23/1931; d. 5/27/1988, Tucson, AZ; bur. Mazeppa, MN. Two children.

ii. Elizabeth C., b. 5/15/1916, Havre, MT; m. George L. Schafer. Four children.

iii. George, b. 1921.

iv. Ed.

v. Charles.

342. Shepherd McGregor Roberts (Charles[8], Alonzo[7], Aaron[6], Daniel[5], Aaron[4], Nathaniel[3], Thomas[2], Thomas[1]), son of Charles Aaron and Cora Jane (Hicks) Roberts, was born in Chicago,

---

* Hardon, Vol. IV, pp. 114 & 125.
⁺ Messer notes.

DESCENDANTS OF THOMAS & REBECCA ROBERTS

Illinois, April 19, 1893, and was living in 1930. He married May 26, 1917, Marguerite Ione Dixon, the daughter of Frank and Violet (Hyde) Dixon. Marguerite was born in Chicago, July 29, 1892, and was living in 1930. Shepherd was a merchant in Chicago, where the following children were born, and a first lieutenant in the U.S. Ordinance Department.[*] Children:

    i. Charles Shepherd, b. 3/5/1919; living in 1930.

    ii. Shepherd McGregor, b. 1/31/1927; living in 1930.

    iii. John Hyde, b. 2/1/1932.

343. James Arnold Roberts (Preston^8, Aaron^7, Alonzo^6, Daniel^5, Aaron^4, Nathaniel^3, Thomas^2, Thomas^1), son of Preston Fremont and Annie Louise (Mayo) Roberts, was born in Dover, New Hampshire, August 2, 1901, and was living in 1930. He married June 26, 1926, Doris Bradway, the daughter of Frank and Josephine (Leonard) Bradway. Doris was born in Willimantic, Connecticut, February 3, 1901, and was living in 1930. James graduated from the University of New Hampshire in 1923 and worked as an actuary in Hartford, Connecticut, where the following children (and possibly others) were born.[+] Children:

    i. Joan Elizabeth, b. 6/9/1928; living in 1930.

    ii. Janet Carol (twin), b. 11/18/1931; d. 11/25/1931.

    iii. Ruth Bradway (twin), b. 11/18/1931; d.11/27/1931.

344. Frank Ernest Roberts (William^8, Aaron^7, Alonzo^6, Daniel^5, Aaron^4, Nathaniel^3, Thomas^2, Thomas^1), son of William Aaron and Alice Ann (Fallows) Roberts, was born in Dover, New Hampshire, July 19, 1885, and was living in 1930. He married May 23, 1908, Gertrude Bell, the daughter of William L. and Emma C. (Higgins) Bell. Gertrude was born in Winnepeg, Manitoba, Canada, February 22, 1887, and was living in 1930. Frank was a manager for the A. & P. Tea Company in Nahant, Massachusetts.

---

    [*] Hardon, Vol. IV, pp. 128-9.
    [+] Hardon, Vol. IV, pp. 132-3.

NINTH GENERATION

The following child was born in Lynn, Massachusetts.* Child:

 i. Ernest Bell, b. 3/29/1910; living unm. in 1930, a telegrapher in Nahant, MA.

345. Herbert E. Roberts (Charles^8, John^7, Jeremiah^6, James^5, Moses^4, Nathaniel^3, Thomas^2, Thomas^1), son of Charles Edwin and Bertha (Enderson) Roberts, was living in Los Gatos, California in 1930. He married Ruth Littlepage.⁺ Children:

 i. Rosemary.

 ii. Janet.

346. Paul Henley Roberts (George^8, Alexander^7, George^6, Thomas^5, Alexander^4, John^3, Thomas^2, Thomas^1), son of George William and Ella Rose (Gould) Roberts, was born in Springfield, Vermont, August 6, 1891, and was living in 1930. He married July 11, 1920, Edith Manila Oleson, the daughter of Mentz and Geolena (Svenson) Oleson. Edith was born in Neehah, Wisconsin, April 25, 1898, and was living in 1930. Paul graduated from the University of Nebraska in 1915 and served as a cavalry officer in World War I. After the War he worked in Washington, D.C., as an administrative officer in the research branch of the U.S. Forest Service.# Child:

 i. Rodney Gould, b. 12/24/1923, Albuquerque, NM.

347. Rodney McKay Roberts (George^8, Alexander^7, George^6, Thomas^5, Alexander^4, John^3, Thomas^2, Thomas^1), son of George William and Ella Rose (Gould) Roberts, was born in Springfield, Vermont, November 17, 1898, and was living in 1930. He married December 30, 1924, Emelyn Karen Anderson, the daughter of Matthew and Emily (Axling) Anderson. Emelyn was born in Gothenburg, Nebraska, November 6, 1901, and was living in 1930. Rodney graduated from the University of Nebraska in 1932, and was a teacher in Maxwell, Nebraska. The following children (and

---

 * Hardon, Vol. IV, pp. 132-3.
 ⁺ Hardon, Vol. IV, pp. 135-9.
 # Hardon, Vol. IV, p. 147.

possibly more) were born in Lincoln, Nebraska.* Children:
    i.   Rebecca Eloise, b. 11/7/1926; living in 1930.
   ii.   Rodney McKay, b. 9/6/1928; living in 1930.

---

* Hardon, Vol. IV, p. 147.

TENTH GENERATION

348. George Clinton Roberts (William^9, Reuben^8, George^7, Joseph^6, George^5, William^4, John^3, John^2, Thomas^1), son of William Webster and Arabella (Waterman) Roberts, was born in Portland, Maine, January 23, 1871. He married November 27, 1895, in Portland, Nancy Day Kimball. George learned the pharmacy business, but failing health obliged him to give up that calling and move to a small farm in Westbrook, Maine. The following children were born in Portland.* Children:

    i.   Pauline Alice, b. 10/1/1896.

    ii. Marian, b. 1/4/1900.

349. Benjamin Edward Roberts (George^9, Benjamin^8, George^7, Joseph^6, George^5, William^4, John^3, John^2, Thomas^1), son of George Henry and Sarah M. (Small) Roberts, was born in Winona, Minnesota, March 21, 1858. He married August 28, 1879, in Minneapolis, Minnesota, Sarah Elizabeth Rutledge, the daughter of John and Belinda (Whipps) Rutledge. Sarah was born in Fish Lake, Minnesota, April 19, 1858. Benjamin was a sheet metal worker in Minneapolis, where the following children were born.⁺ Children:

    i.   Sarah Mabel, b. 5/8/1881; m. 10/17/1900, Hugh R. Campbell. Three children.

    ii. Ralph Benjamin, b. 6/12/1884; d. 1/7/1890.

350. Elias Thomas Roberts (John^9, Loring^8, Love^7, Love^6, Love^5, Love^4, Thomas^3, John^2, Thomas^1), son of John Charles Fremont and Abigail S. (Emmons) Roberts, was born in Greenwood, Maine, February 26, 1893, and was living in 1930. He married October 18, 1913, Cecile Martin, the daughter of Pascoe and Nellie (Cole) Martin. She was born in Greenwood, October 19, 1897, and was living in 1930. Elias was a mill superintendent in Locke's Mill, Maine, where the following children were born.# Children:

---

   * Underhill, Vol. I, p. 1186.
   ⁺ Underhill, Vol. I, pp. 1192-3.
   # Hardon, Vol. III, pp. 31 & 40.

i. Reginald Thomas, b. 6/6/1915; living in 1930.

ii. Harriet Christiana, b. 4/8/1917; d. 4/23/1918.

iii. Gordon LeRoy, b. 5/22/1919; living in 1930.

iv. David Emmons, b. 6/15/1923; living in 1930.

351. Loring John Roberts (John^9, Loring^8, Love^7, Love^6, Love^5, Love^4, Thomas^3, John^2, Thomas^1), son of John Charles Fremont and Abigail S. (Emmons) Roberts, was born in Greenwood, Maine, January 24, 1895, and was living in 1930. He married November 18, 1912, Bertha Maude Corbett, the daughter of David T. and Arvilla M. (Swan) Corbett. Bertha was born in Greenwood, February 1, 1892, and was living in 1930. Loring was a mill foreman in Locke's Mill, Maine.* Children:

i. Wendell Fremont, b. 4/17/1914, West Paris, ME.

ii. Florence Arvella, b. 9/5/1916, Groveton, NH.

iii. Lee Wesley, b. 10/15/1919, Bethel, ME.

iv. William Edgar, b. 5/30/1923, Ineke's Mills, ME.

352. George Royal Roberts (Edgar^9, William^8, Love^7, Love^6, Love^5, Love^4, Thomas^3, John^2, Thomas^1), son of Edgar Wentworth and Emma R. (Hatch) Roberts, was born in Wayne, Maine, December 4, 1873, and was living in 1930. He married April 12, 1905, Mary Ellen McFarland, the daughter of Andrew P. and Clara E. (Kent) McFarland. Mary Ellen was born in Ellsworth, Maine, December 9, 1884, and was living in 1930. George was a farmer in Litchfield, Maine.⁺ Children:

i. Leah, b. 2/23/1907, Palmyra, ME; living unm. in Litchfield in 1930.

ii. William, b. 5/12/1915, Lewiston, ME.

353. Clyde Harold Roberts (Edgar^9, William^8, Love^7, Love^6, Love^5, Love^4, Thomas^3, John^2, Thomas^1), son of Edgar Wentworth

---

* Hardon, Vol. III, pp. 31 & 40.
⁺ Hardon, Vol. III, pp. 32 & 42.

TENTH GENERATION

and Emma R. (Hatch) Roberts, was born in North New Portland, Maine, October 6, 1894, and was living in 1930. He married June 3, 1922, Elizabeth Holt Allen, the daughter of Archie and Eliza Jane (Wylie) Allen. Elizabeth was born in West Manayunk, Pennsylvania, August 3, 1895, and was living in 1930. Clyde was a sheet metal worker in West Manayunk, where the following child was born.* Child:

    i. Florence May, b. 11/28/1923; living in 1930.

354. Leslie Freeman Roberts (Frank^9, William^8, Love^7, Love^6, Love^5, Love^4, Thomas^3, John^2, Thomas^1), son of Frank Herbert and Eva May (Ladd) Roberts, was born in Brockton, Massachusetts, December 9, 1882, and was living in 1930. He married May 2, 1906, Winifred Foster, the daughter of Arthur J. and Estella (Hayford) Foster. Winifred was born in Canton, Maine, November 26, 1886, and was living in 1930. Leslie was an undertaker in Richmond, Maine.⁺ Children:

    i. Carl Freeman, b. 11/5/1906, Farmington, ME; a clerk in Richmond, ME in 1930, unm.

    ii. Sherman Foster, b. 11/8/1910, Canton, ME; d. 9/19/1930.

355. Merton Ellingwood Roberts (Frank^9, William^8, Love^7, Love^6, Love^5, Love^4, Thomas^3, John^2, Thomas^1), son of Frank Herbert and Eva May (Ladd) Roberts, was born January 16, 1898, and was living in 1930. He married March 30, 1918, Sadie Collins, the daughter of Samuel and Ella (Bean) Collins. Sadie was born in Chesterville, Maine, August 8, 1896, and was living in 1930. Merton was an undertaker in Georgetown, Massachusetts.# Children:

    i. Frank Samuel, b. 4/25/1919, Vienna, ME.

    ii. Harold Arthur, b. 7/25/1922, Livermore Falls, ME.

    iii. Merton Ellingwood, b. 8/14/1924, Georgetown, MA.

---

  * Hardon, Vol. III, pp. 32 & 43.
  ⁺ Hardon, Vol. III, pp. 33 & 45.
  # Hardon, Vol. III, pp. 33 & 45.

356. Leon Chester Roberts (Nathan^9, William^8, Love^7, Love^6, Love^5, Love^4, Thomas^3, John^2, Thomas^1), son of Nathan Lewis and Inza (Graves) Roberts, was born in Wayne, Maine, October 28, 1886, and was living in 1930. He married October 19, 1907, Madeline Douglas, the daughter of Harry and Lottie M. (Ellis) Douglas. Madeline was born in Canton, Maine, August 7, 1890, and was living in 1930. Leon was an undertaker in Winthrop, Maine. The following children were born in Readfield, Maine.*
Children:

    i. Carleton Lewis, b. 9/29/1911; an undertaker in Winthrop, ME; unm.

    ii. Douglas Mitchell, b. 3/5/1913; living in 1930.

357. Paul Billings Roberts (Walter^9, Jacob^8, James^7, Peter^6, Love^5, Love^4, Thomas^3, John^2, Thomas^1), son of Walter Hill and Alice S. (Daniels) Roberts, was born in Melrose, Massachusetts, February 3, 1893, and was living in 1930. He married February 8, 1921, Doris Bailey MacKay, the daughter of Robert S.J. and Emily (Foote) MacKay. Doris was born in Cambridge, Massachusetts, January 12, 1900, and was living in 1930. Paul graduated with an A.B. from Harvard in 1914 and an LL.B. from there in 1917. He practiced law in Boston, Massachusetts.⁺ Child:

    i. Malcolm MacKay, b. 12/15/1921, Cambridge, MA.

358. George L. Roberts (William^9, Joseph^8, John^7, Joseph^6, John^5, Timothy^4, Thomas^3, John^2, Thomas^1), son of William Wingate and Eloise Annie (Flanders) Roberts, was born in Farmington, New Hampshire, December 29, 1886, and was living in 1930. He married June 21, 1909, Florence Isabelle Lougee, the daughter of Wilbur S. and Abigail J. (Berry) Lougee. Florence was born in Farmington, February 7, 1888, and was living in 1930. George was a druggist in Farmington, where the following child was born.# Child:

---

    * Hardon, Vol. III, pp. 33 & 46.
    ⁺ Hardon, Vol. III, pp. 55 & 64.
    # Hardon, Vol. III, pp. 120 & 123.

TENTH GENERATION

　　　i. Eloise Lucille, b. 4/5/1911; living unm. in 1930.

359. Rex Nute Roberts (Charles[9], Noah[8], John[7], John[6], Thomas[5], Timothy[4], Thomas[3], John[2], Thomas[1]), son of Charles Frederick and Eva E. (Nute) Roberts, was born in Sanbornville, New Hampshire, January 21, 1890, and was living in 1930. He married September 10, 1913, in Port Henry, New York, Martha Moore Heslin, the daughter of John and Alice (Moore) Heslin. Martha was born in Port Henry, April 10, 1886, and died April 10, 1916. Rex was a credit manager in Los Angeles, California, where the following child was born.[*] Child:

　　　i. Alice Marie, b. 12/8/1915; living in 1930.

360. Robert Whitehouse Roberts (Delancy[9], Joseph[8], Joseph[7], Benjamin[6], Benjamin[5], Samuel[4], Hatevil[3], John[2], Thomas[1]), son of Delancy Amos and Edna Josephine (Whitehouse) Roberts, was born in Dorchester, Massachusetts, January 25, 1893, and died August 14, 1980, apparently in Bath, Maine. He married Grace Lightbody.[+] Child:

　　　i. Roberta, b. 1921; m. Arthur Bannister. Three ch.

361. Waldo Preston Roberts (Delancy[9], Joseph[8], Joseph[7], Benjamin[6], Benjamin[5], Samuel[4], Hatevil[3], John[2], Thomas[1]), son of Delancy Amos and Edna Josephine (Whitehouse) Roberts, was born in Dorchester, Massachusetts, July 29, 1896, and died in Plymouth, Massachusetts, June 22, 1964. He married Grace Bellows.[#] Child:

　　　i. Gwendolyn, m. Theodore Senger. One child.

362. Clayton Hartley Roberts (Delancy[9], Joseph[8], Joseph[7], Benjamin[6], Benjamin[5], Samuel[4], Hatevil[3], John[2], Thomas[1]), son of Delancy Amos and Edna Josephine (Whitehouse) Roberts, was born in Dorchester, Massachusetts, November 28, 1899, and died in Boston, Massachusetts, September 11, 1967. He is buried in Dorchester. He married Sally MacPherson, July 31, 1938, in

---

　　[*] Hardon, Vol. III, pp. 137 & 142.
　　[+] Clayton H. Roberts notes.
　　[#] Clayton H. Roberts notes.

Springfield, Massachusetts. The daughter of Angus J. and Annie MacPherson, she was born in Glen William, Prince Edward Island, Canada, November 20, 1899, and died in Plymouth, June 12, 1986. She is also buried in Dorchester. Sally changed her name from Sadie when she moved to the United States. She went to nursing school and became a registered nurse.* Child:

373.   i. Clayton Hartley, b. 2/22/1942.

363. Victor Wentworth Roberts (Joseph^9, Joseph^8, Joseph^7, Benjamin^6, Benjamin^5, Samuel^4, Hatevil^3, John^2, Thomas^1), son of Joseph Martin and Lillian Ruth (Wentworth) Roberts, was born in 1899. He married Iola G. Gray, who was born in 1897.⁺ Children:

    i. Kathleen Ruth, b. 1926; d. 1928.

    ii. Victor B., b. 1931.

364. Odin Roberts (George^9, Reuben^8, Reuben^7, Paul^6, Samuel^5, Samuel^4, Hatevil^3, John^2, Thomas^1), son of George Litch and Hinda (Barnes) Roberts, was born January 22, 1867, and was living in 1930. He married April 19, 1897, Ada Mead, the daughter of Sumner R. and Ada (Lawrence) Mead. Ada was born in Boston, Massachusetts, November 29, 1870, and was living in 1930. Odin graduated from Harvard with an A.B. in 1886 and an LL.B. in 1891, and practiced law in Boston. The following children were born in Dedham, Massachusetts.# Children:

    i. Sumner Mead, b. 1/25/1898; m. 1929, Elizabeth Converse; graduated from Harvard (1921); physician in Newton, MA in 1930.

    ii. Lloyd Garrison, b. 11/15/1902; d. 1903.

    iii. Frederick Mead, b. 10/3/1903; living unm. in Boston in 1930. Graduate of Harvard (1928).

    iv. Virginia, b. 6/23/1907; m. 7/9/1932, Philip H. Rhinelander; living in Boston in 1930.

---

* Clayton H. Roberts notes.
⁺ Clayton H. Roberts notes.
Hardon, Vol. III, pp. 152-3.

TENTH GENERATION

365. Harold Clifton Roberts (Herbert[9], Simeon[8], Aaron[7], Aaron[6], Samuel[5], Samuel[4], Hatevil[3], John[2], Thomas[1]), son of Herbert Arthur and Lily (Porter) Roberts, was born October 30, 1902, and was living in 1930. He married in September of 1927 Blanche Woodruff, the daughter of Edward and Blanche Woodruff. She was born in Patchogue, New York, and was living in 1930. Harold was a salesman in Wolfeboro, New Hampshire, where the following child (and possibly others) was born.* Child:

  i. Dodd Edward, b. 9/4/1930.

366. Ernest Arthur Roberts (Herbert[9], Simeon[8], Aaron[7], Aaron[6], Samuel[5], Samuel[4], Hatevil[3], John[2], Thomas[1]), son of Herbert Arthur and Lily (Porter) Roberts, was born July 13, 1904, and was living in 1930. He married December 19, 1924, Edith Cheney, the daughter of Herbert and Ada Cheney. Edith was born in South Berwick, Maine, September 29, 1903, and was living in 1930. Ernest was a clerk in Glen Cove, New York, where the following child (and possibly others) was born.⁺ Child:

  i. Ruth Elinor, b. 9/4/1927; living in 1930.

367. Harry Fletcher Roberts (John[9], Benjamin[8], Caleb[7], Benjamin[6], Nathan[5], Samuel[4], Hatevil[3], John[2], Thomas[1]), son of John Place and Clara I. (Tibbetts) Roberts, was born in Farmington, New Hampshire, August 10, 1886, and was living in 1930. He married, firstly, December 23, 1905, Edith F. Connor, the daughter of Charles E. and Florence (Miller) Connor. Edith was born in Farmington, December 13, 1886, and was living in 1930. Harry married, secondly, August 31, 1931, Helen Leva MacDonald, the daughter of Frederick and Margaret (McPhee) MacDonald. Helen was born in Wellington, Prince Edward Island, Canada, in 1902, and was living in 1930. Harry was a merchant in Gilford, New Hampshire.# Children:

  i. Charles Connor, b. 6/14/1906; m. 2/9/1930, Amelia Gertrude King; a salesman in Dover, NH in 1930.

---

* Hardon, Vol. II, p. 166 & Vol. III, p. 159.
⁺ Hardon, Vol. II, p. 166 & Vol. III, p. 159.
Hardon, Vol. III, pp. 171 & 176-7.

> ii. Marjorie Lucille, b. 5/15/1909; m. 9/2/1933, Leslie G. Rief.
>
> iii. Irene Janette, b. 7/10/1910; unm. 1930.
>
> iv. Shirley Lillian, b. 10/11/1911; m. 11/18/1933, George A. Minor of Springfield, MA.

368. Carl Noyes Roberts (Horace^9, Benjamin^8, Caleb^7, Benjamin^6, Nathan^5, Samuel^4, Hatevil^3, John^2, Thomas^1), son of Horace Herbert and Mary E. (Noyes) Roberts, was born in Farmington, New Hampshire, October 13, 1886, and was living in 1930. He married June 14, 1911, in Conway, New Hampshire, Gladys P. Knox, the daughter of Charles O. and Ida (Glidden) Knox. She was born in Boston, Massachusetts, June 23, 1892, and was living in 1930. Carl was a farmer in Rochester, New Hampshire. The following children were born in Conway.* Children:

> i. Millard Knox, b. 3/1/1913; living in 1930.
>
> ii. Ida Mary, b. 8/5/1915; living in 1930.
>
> iii. Carl Noyes, b. 6/29/1916; living in 1930.

369. George Fillmore Roberts (Sewell^9, Sewall^8, Richard^7, Joseph^6, Joseph^5, Joseph^4, Joseph^3, John^2, Thomas^1), son of Sewell Edson and Ella S. (Trask) Roberts, was born in Alton, New Hampshire, November 24, 1887, and was living in 1930. He married August 28, 1911, Mary Langley Burnham, the daughter of James W. and Lydia A. (Buzzell) Burnham. Mary was born in Durham, New Hampshire, April 27, 1889, and was living in 1930. George was a farmer in East Barnard, Vermont. He was a 1911 graduate of New Hampshire State College. All of the children listed below were living in 1930.⁺ Children:

> i. Henry Edson, b. 8/27/1912, Cornish, NH.
>
> ii. Charles Burnham, b. 10/26/1914, Cornish, NH.

---

* Hardon, Vol. III, pp. 171 & 178.
⁺ Hardon, Vol. IV, pp. 28 & 32.

TENTH GENERATION

    iii. Olive Carolyn, b. 3/25/1916, Plainfield, NH.
    iv. George Fillmore, b. 1/13/1918, Windsor, VT.
    v. Esther Burnham, b. 3/24/1919, Barnard, VT.
    vi. Woodbury Langdon, b. 7/2/1920, Barnard, VT.
    vii. Ella Octavia, b. 7/20/1922, Barnard, VT.

370. Charles Edson Roberts (Sewell^9, Sewall^8, Richard^7, Joseph^6, Joseph^5, Joseph^4, Joseph^3, John^2, Thomas^1), son of Sewell Edson and Ella S. (Trask) Roberts, was born in Alton, New Hampshire, May 18, 1893, and was living in 1930. He married October 16, 1920, Ella Rowe, the daughter of Walter and Josephine (Doyle) Rowe. She was born in Newburyport, Massachusetts, August 21, 1897, and was living in 1930. Charles attended New Hampshire State College and was a builder in East Alton, New Hampshire, where the fourth and fifth children below were born. The first three children were born in Wolfeboro, New Hampshire. The first four children were living in 1930.* Children:

    i. Leslie Edson, b. 8/7/1921.

    ii. Mary Josephine (twin), b. 12/13/1922.

    iii. Preston Trask (twin), b. 12/13/1922.

    iv. Irving Rowe, b. 2/15/1928.

    v. Ruth Frances, b. 1/8/1933.

371. David Sands Roberts (Henry^9, David^8, Hanson^7, David^6, Nathaniel^5, Nathaniel^4, Nathaniel^3, Thomas^2, Thomas^1), son of Henry Sands and Lelia J. (Holland) Roberts, was born in Lewiston, Maine, April 9, 1885, and was living in 1930. He married July 19, 1911, in Vergennes, Vermont, Mabel Field, the daughter of Luther and Emma (Roscoe) Field. She was born in Ferrisburg, Vermont, April 18, 1884, and was living in 1930. David was a creamery inspector in Lowville, New York. The children listed below were all living

---

* Hardon, Vol. IV, pp. 28 & 32.

in 1930.* Children:

 i. Emma Lelia, b. 6/29/1912, Vergennes, VT.

 ii. Mildred Jane, b. 5/22/1913, Malone, NY.

 iii. Holland Sands, b. 10/15/1915, Vergennes, VT.

372. Fred Paine Roberts (Henry^9, David^8, Hanson^7, David^6, Nathaniel^5, Nathaniel^4, Nathaniel^3, Thomas^2, Thomas^1), son of Henry Sands and Belle F. (Davis) Roberts, was born in Somersworth, New Hampshire, October 5, 1892, and was living in 1930. He married October 31, 1928, Evelyn Robinson, the daughter of Rodney F. and Cora F. (Davis) Robinson. She was born in Concord, New Hampshire, February 12, 1897, and was living in 1933. Evelyn graduated from Wellesley College in 1920. Fred was a store manager in Concord, where the following (and possibly other) children were born.⁺ Children:

 i. Sylvia, b. 12/23/1930.

 ii. Rodney Bradford, b. 9/10/1933.

---

 * Hardon, Vol. IV, pp. 114 & 125.
 ⁺ Hardon, Vol. IV, pp. 114 & 125.

ELEVENTH GENERATION

373. Clayton Hartley Roberts Jr. (Clayton^{10}, Delancy^9, Joseph^8, Joseph^7, Benjamin^6, Benjamin^5, Samuel^4, Hatevil^3, John^2, Thomas^1), son of Clayton Hartley and Sally (MacPherson) Roberts, was born in Boston, Massachusetts, February 22, 1942, and was living in Duxbury, Massachusetts, in 1992. He married November 28, 1969, in Camden, Maine, Barbara Louise Wilbur, the daughter of Harold G. and Elizabeth A. (Aylward) Wilbur. Barbara was born in Camden, January 16, 1943.* Child:

    i.   Kyle Bevan, b. 8/7/1973.

---

* Clayton H. Roberts notes.

FIRST GENERATION

At about the time of the death of Thomas Roberts of Dover, New Hampshire in 1674, another Roberts family was establishing roots in the adjoining town of Exeter, New Hampshire. Records which have survived from the 1600's in New Hampshire consist almost entirely of minutes of town meetings and court proceedings. Births, marriages and deaths generally went unrecorded. For a man of this era who was not in trouble with the law or a leader in town affairs, the best we can hope for is to catch a glimpse of his life story from the fragmentary records that have survived the centuries.

1. George Roberts was born possibly between 1640 and 1650 and died in or near Exeter, New Hampshire, in 1691, or perhaps 1692.

He married Mary Jones, the daughter of George and Mary Jones of Exeter, about 1670. She was born about 1650 and died "an ancient woman" in or near Exeter in about 1743.[*]

No record of George's birth or early life has been located, so where he came from and how he happens to appear in Exeter by 1674 are matters for conjecture. Perhaps he was a son of the shadowy Joseph Roberts, who was sent to New Hampshire, in 1632, by John Mason. (Was this the same Joseph Roberts who drowned there in 1664?)[+] Or, was he related to Thomas Roberts of Dover, in some way? There seems to be no evidence one way or the other.

George first appears in Hampton, New Hampshire (the seat of the court having jurisdiction over the Exeter area) in 1674 in connection with his legal action to recover one thousand white oak pipestaves removed from his possession by Richard Scammon, the proprietor of the Shrewsbury patent (a land grant covering the eastern side of Exeter in an area that became the town of Stratham in 1715/6). The court found against George. At the time Exeter was attempting to attract new residents by permitting them to harvest up to one thousand pipestaves of timber on unallocated and common town

---

[*] Noyes, Libby, & Davis, pp. 386 & 588.

[+] Noyes, Libby & Davis, pp. 383, 589, & 695; Holmes, Frank R. *Directory of the Ancestral Heads of New England Families 1620-1700.* Baltimore: Genealogical Publishing Co., 1984 (Originally published New York, 1923), p. cciii; Hotten, p. 150.

land. In view of the fact that boundaries and land titles were so unsettled in these early days, it is easy to imagine how George's harvesting efforts might have encroached on the Shrewsbury grant.*

George's father-in-law, George Jones, who owned a "plantation" in the area of the Shrewsbury patent also fought with the Scammons over timber rights. In 1678 the local court convicted him of breach of the peace and "evil carriage" toward the Scammons and bound him to good behavior; and, he was ordered to be fined or to be "wipped ten stripes tomorrow after lecture." In 1677 George Jones called another neighbor a "forsworn rogue and forsworn cur" and threatened him with a gun. Fifteen years earlier, "lately come into town", George Jones had been charged with punching John Harte's wife in the face and calling her a "devil and an old squaw".+

The last reference to George Roberts is found in a 1689/1690 petition of New Hampshire settlers to the colony of Massachusetts, asking that they be taken back under the latter's jurisdiction. Of the over 300 men whose names are on the petition, about 100 (including George) signed with a mark rather than a signature, thus indicating a probable lack of or low level of literacy.#

After George Roberts' death his widow Mary very soon married Nathaniel Folsom, a mill man of Exeter, and had two sons in the early to mid-1690's, Nathaniel Jr. and Israel. In 1699 Mary and Nathaniel Folsom sued Mary's sister, apparently over the estate of George Jones. (Mary was not named in her father's will). Some time around 1715-1720, after Nathaniel died, Mary again re-married, this time to Nicholas Norris of Exeter.**

We know of the following child by virtue of a reference in court records of 1741 that John Roberts, Nathaniel Folsom, Jr., and Israel Folsom were called upon by the town of Exeter to assist

---

    * *Records & Files of the Quarterly Courts of Essex Co., Mass.* Salem, Mass.: Essex Institute, 1916, Vol. V, p. 407; Bell, pp. 53, 61 & 116.

    + Noyes, Libby & Davis, pp. 383, 386 & 695; *Records & Files of the Quarterly Courts of Essex County, Mass.*, Vol. VI, pp. 340, 433 & 513 and Vol. V, p. 407; Hammond, Otis G., ed. *New Hampshire Court Files* (State Paper Series). Manchester, N.H.: State of New Hampshire, 1943, Vol. 40.

    # Massachusetts Archives, Book 35, p. 229. Cited in "Petition of New Hampshire Settlers", *New England Historical and Genealogical Register*, July 1854, pp. 233-5.

    ** Noyes, Libby & Davis, pp. 383, 386 & 695.

FIRST GENERATION

in the support of their elderly mother.* There may have been other children born to George and Mary, but it would appear that none, if any, reached their majority.⁺ Child:

2.　　i.　　John.

---

* New Hampshire Division of Records Maintenance and Archives. Provincial Court Records, files 10817 and 21715.

⁺ Needless to say, infant mortality was frightfully high at this time of history. A contemporary, Queen Anne of England, gave birth to 17 children, none of whom reached adulthood. Arguing against the existence of other adult children of George and Mary is the fact that there is no record in N.H. of any "stray" Robertses that could even possibly be connected to this family.

DESCENDANTS OF GEORGE & MARY ROBERTS

SECOND GENERATION

2. John Roberts (George[1]), son of George and Mary (Jones) Roberts, was born in Exeter, New Hampshire, or vicinity, about 1680, and died in Brentwood, New Hampshire, in 1750/1.[*] John married Elizabeth Magoon, daughter of Alexander & Sarah (Blake) Magoon.[+] She was born in New Hampshire about 1685 and died in Brentwood sometime after 1759.

John was listed on a 1712 roster of the Exeter militia. He worked as a weaver and owned a modest piece of land on the east side of town. When this section of Exeter broke off to form Stratham in 1715/6, John and Elizabeth were among the charter worshipers at the new meeting house. Records of the Stratham committee that established a permanent seating chart for the congregation yield important clues about the socio-religious status of the membership. John Roberts was assigned a seat just about in the middle of the men's section (the "uplong front seat"), indicating he was in good standing, although not one of the leaders of the group. Goodwife Roberts was seated in the "second long seat", in the women's section, also about an average placement.[#]

By 1723 the Roberts family, now numbering ten, moved to a presumably larger property on the Exeter/Kingston line. Most of the family became active in the Kingston church, where many of the children would be married and several of the grandchildren would be baptized between 1732 and 1750.

Fortunately, about the time the older children were forming families of their own, in the late 1730's, Elizabeth inherited from her parents a sizable tract of land in western Exeter. Elizabeth's father, Alexander Magoon, had previously inherited the property from his grandfather, Nicholas Lissen, the original grantee of 300 acres from the town of Exeter in 1648/9.

John Roberts made gifts of parts of the Lissen grant to his sons at various times. The remainder of it was bequeathed to his various

---

[*] Hammond, Isaac W., ed. *Probate Records of the Province of New Hampshire.* Concord, N.H.: The Rumford Press, 1915, Vol. 3, pp. 413-4.

[+] Noyes, Libby & Davis, p. 452; Rockingham County Deeds, Vol. 24, p. 64.

[#] Nelson, Charles B. *History of Stratham, New Hampshire 1631-1900.* Stratham: Town of Stratham, 1987, pp. 114-6.

225

sons, and much of it remained in Roberts hands into the early 1800's. From various legal descriptions, it would seem that this property was located in the mid-to-western part of the present town of Brentwood, between the Exeter River and the old Gordon Road (now closed). The property included a sawmill on the Exeter River, known as Black Rock, which John sold in 1738/9.[*]

John Roberts became a leading citizen of their new neighborhood and was active in promoting the establishment of Brentwood, served on committees to establish the line between Exeter and Brentwood and to build a new meetinghouse.[+]

In his will dated 1746 John names the children listed below. He left five shillings to each of his five eldest sons and to his daughter Mary, they having already received their portions. Elizabeth was bequeathed five pounds "old tennor money", she having already received part of her portion. Ann was to receive twenty pounds, his wife Elizabeth all the house goods and the use of 1/3 of the land for her life. The dwelling house, outbuildings and remaining property, comprising some twenty-nine acres, and debts were left to John's youngest son, Jonathan, who was named the executor of the will.

John signed the will with his mark rather than a signature, as was his custom with the many deeds he made over his lifetime. It can therefore be assumed that he was only partly literate, at best.[#] Of his sons, George and Alexander could sign their own names, but Jonathan and Benjamin could not.[**] Children:

3.	i.	John.
4.	ii.	Alexander.
5.	iii.	George.

---

[*] Rockingham County Deeds, Vol. 172, p. 24, Vol. 15, pp. 286-7, Vol. 17, p.453, Vol. 24, p. 64, Vol. 26, pp. 167-8, 225, & 483, Vol. 49, p. 545, Vol. 45, p. 501, Vol. 39, p. 42.

[+] Bell, p. 228; Brentwood Town Records, vol. 1.

[#] Hammond, ed., Vol. 3, pp. 413-4; Rockingham County Deeds, Vol. 172, p. 24.

[**] Literacy rates in the early 1700's in New Hampshire were not high, with perhaps 1/3 or more of adult males unable to write. See Lockridge, Kenneth A. *Literacy in Colonial New England*. New York: W. W. Norton, Inc., 1974.

SECOND GENERATION

6.   iv. Samuel.
7.   v. Benjamin.
        vi. Elizabeth, m. Ezekiel Smith, 3/11/1734, Kingston,NH*; d. Raymond, NH 1780(?).
        vii. Mary, m. Thomas Critchett, 5/9/1739, Kingston, NH.⁺
        viii. Ann, m. Henry Marsh, 6/2/1743, Kingston, NH.#
8.   ix. Jonathan, b. 1726-7.**

---

    * "Kingston First Church Records", *New Hampshire Genealogical Record*, Vol. II, No. 1 (July 1904), p.45.
    ⁺ Stackpole & Thompson, Vol. I, p. 81.
    # "Marriages Performed by Peter Coffin, Pastor of ye 2nd Church of Christ in Kingston, N.H." (an item of Kingston Church Records on LDS film 15563), p. 39.
    ** Badcock, Rev. Josiah. "Record of Deaths in Andover, N.H. 1782-1831"(item No. 2 of Andover records on LDS film 15552), p. 5.

DESCENDANTS OF GEORGE & MARY ROBERTS

THIRD GENERATION

3. John Roberts (John², George¹), son of John and Elizabeth (Magoon) Roberts, was born in or near Exeter, New Hampshire, between about 1700 and 1705. He died in Brentwood, New Hampshire in 1756.*
John married, by 1731, Abigail Gordon, daughter of Thomas and Elizabeth (Harriman) Gordon. She was born in Haverhill, Massachusetts, May 28, 1707 ⁺ and died sometime after 1759. John and Abigail lived on land in Brentwood received from his father. John Roberts, Jr., is listed as a local taxpayer as early as 1733. Along with his father he was part owner in a sawmill on the Exeter River, which they sold in 1740.# He was elected town surveyor and fence viewer in 1744/5 and selectman of Brentwood in 1746, and also served as constable for a time.**

In 1732 John "own'd ye covenant for ye baptism of his child John", but apparently he was not active in the church, because a list of members in 1736 lists only his wife Abigail. Abigail is also listed among charter members of the new parish church established in Brentwood in the late 1740's.⁺⁺

John acquired some lots in Meredith, New Hampshire, in 1750.## Two of his sons subsequently moved there and established large families. Abigail is mentioned in her father's will of 1757. Her bequest consisted of 75 pounds, "a cow, and a Smaul pot and a Tramel and a Pot hook and three Puter Plates."*** John Jr.'s estate was valued at 3,062 pounds. (This was somewhat above average for the time and place.)

---

* Hammond, ed., Vol. 6, p. 498.
⁺ Cobb, Blanche G. "The Gordon Family of Maine & New Hampshire", unpub., 1946.
Rockingham County Deeds, Vol. 17, p. 528, Vol. 26, p. 168; Holbrook, *1732 Census*.
** Brentwood Town Records, Vol. 1.
⁺⁺ "Kingston First Church Records", *N.H.G.R.*, Vol. III, p. 67; Brentwood Historical Society. *Brentwood's 225 Years*. Dover, N.H.: The Riding Press, c. 1967, p. 9; "Records of Congregational Church of Brentwood, N.H.", Vol. 1, p. 112; "Copy of the Records of Rev. Woodbridge Odlin" (an item of Exeter Church Records on LDS film 15558), p. 3;
Rockingham County Deeds, Vol. 69, p. 39.
*** Hammond, ed., Vol. 6, pp. 188 & 498.

DESCENDANTS OF GEORGE & MARY ROBERTS

The following children were born in Brentwood.* Children:

		i.	John, bapt. 5/14/1732; d. young?
9.		ii.	Joseph, b. 5/25/1740.
10.		iii.	Thomas, b. 1/9/1743.
		iv.	Joshua, b. 3/4/1745.
11.		v.	Alexander, b. 5/3/1747.

4. **Alexander Roberts** (John², George¹), son of John and Elizabeth (Magoon) Roberts, was born in or near Exeter, New Hampshire probably about 1710 and died in Brentwood, New Hampshire, in 1777.

He married in Kingston, New Hampshire, May 9, 1739, Lydia Judkins, a seamstress. She was the daughter of Daniel Giles of Raymond and widow of Benjamin Judkins. She died in Brentwood between 1784 and 1790. Lydia had a daughter by prior marriage, Susanna Judkins.⁺

Alexander was a taxpayer as early as 1733 and owned and lived on a number of parcels of land in Brentwood by 1740. In 1762 he deeded one-half of his residence to his daughter and son-in-law Samuel Johnson, who then moved in with the parents. In various deeds, he is described as a laborer or yeoman. Alexander and Lydia also owned land in Raymond.# At his death in 1777, he owned several small parcels of land, but his debts exceeded their value. His nephew Thomas Roberts, his son-in-law Samuel Johnson and widow Lydia served as co-administrators of the estate.**

In 1746 Sergeant Alexander Roberts and a company of Exeter

---

* Brentwood Town Records, p. 731. (These birth entries were made in the town book in the 1770's.)

⁺ Rockingham County Probate Records Docket No. 4376 OS; "Kingston First Church Records", *N.H.G.R.*, Vol. III, No. 1, p. 40; Judkins, Elizabeth L. "Job Judkins of Boston and his Descendants". Unpub., 1967.

Rockingham County Deeds, Vol. 88, pp. 544-6; Vol. 73, pp. 377-9; Vol. 86, p. 356; Vol. 64, p. 192; Vol. 69, p. 320; Vol. 82, p. 124; Vol. 107, p. 475; Vol. 79, p. 379; Vol. 105, p.125; Vol. 108, p. 173; Holbrook, *1732 Census.*

** Rockingham Co. Prob. Docket No. 4376 OS.

militiamen were ambushed by the Indians near the present city of Concord, New Hampshire. Alexander was captured, taken to Canada, but somehow managed to escape. Five of his comrades, including Lieut. Jonathan Bradley, were killed. The following year Alexander returned to Concord and was able to locate the skull of an Indian he had killed in the battle of the prior year. The General Assembly of New Hampshire awarded him a bounty of 15 pounds.*

Alexander signed the Association Test in 1776, a pledge of support to the Revolutionary War effort.⁺ He was elected surveyor of Brentwood in 1756. Alexander was a charter member of the Brentwood parish church formed in the mid to late 1740's. A Lydia Roberts was also a member and baptized in that church June 12, 1745, but this may be a reference to Alexander's daughter rather than his wife. Town records indicate that the "wife of Alexander Roberts" was excused from paying minister's rates, probably an indication that she was a Quaker.# Child:

 i. Lydia, m. Samuel Johnson.

5. **George Roberts** (John², George¹), son of John and Elizabeth (Magoon) Roberts, was born in or near Exeter, New Hampshire probably about 1710 and died in or near there probably about 1760.**

He married in Kingston, New Hampshire, November 15, 1733, Judith Kenniston, the daughter of Alexander and Elizabeth (Reed) Kenniston. She was baptized in Greenland, New Hampshire in

---

 * Bouton, Nathaniel. *The History of Concord. . .* Concord, N.H.: Benning W. Sanborn, 1856, pp. 156-8 and 165-7; Note that a John Roberts of Fremont, N.H. (near Exeter) had a son named Jonathan Bradley Roberts, born in 1794. See children under Benjamin No. 7.

 ⁺ *Miscellaneous Revolutionary War Documents of New Hampshire.* Manchester, N.H.: John B. Clarke Co., 1910, p. 20.

 # Brentwood Town Records, Vol. 1; "Records of Congregational Church of Brentwood, N.H.", Vol. II, p. 114; "Copy of the Records of Rev. Woodbridge Odlin", p. 2.

 ** Neither a birth nor a death record exists, so these dates are just a guess. The first notice of him is his marriage and the last is an appearance in 1756 to acknowledge two deeds. (Rockingham County Deeds, Vol. 60, p. 335, Vol. 100, pp. 427-8)

1713.*

It would appear that George, Judith and their young family initially lived on the eastern side of Exeter, perhaps with or near Judith's family in neighboring Greenland.+ George worked as a cordwainer (shoemaker), but the family had little, if any, property of its own and was very poor and constantly in debt. The sheriff attached items - a chair, a hat, an ax - at various times in satisfaction of small judgments.# There were some children born in the 1730's, but records, if any, have been lost. Moreover, it is not clear what church, if any, they attended at that time.

In 1740 George received as a gift twenty acres of land from his father in the western part of Exeter that became Brentwood in 1742. Perhaps the growing family moved to this property, since also in 1740 George and Judith became active in the church in nearby Kingston, where seven of their children were baptized between 1740 and 1750.**

---

* "Kingston First Church Records", *N.H.G.R.*, Vol.II,No.1, p.45; Noyes, Libby & Davis, p. 397; Lafler, Hazel E.K. *Ancestors and Descendants of Woodbury Kenerson*... Morristown, N.J.: Compton Press, 1977, pp. 8-9. See also Miles, Mrs. Byrd E. *John Keniston and His Descendants*. Privately published, no date, p. 75 (This work must be used with caution, due to a number of obvious errors.); "Marriages by Rev. Wm. Allen of Greenland, N.H.", *N.E.H. & G.R.*, Vol. 65, p. 35.

+ George is not among the Robertses who were petitioning Exeter in 1738 to set off the western end as the new town of Brentwood, but he is among Exeter residents who petitioned in 1739 to have the town annexed to Massachusetts. See *Town Papers of New Hampshire*, Vol. 9, pp. 252ff and Hurd, D. Hamilton. *History of Rockingham and Strafford Counties, N.H.* ... Philadelphia: J. W. Lewis, 1882, p. 263.

New Hampshire Provincial Court Records (Rockingham County Inferior Court of Common Pleas), files 10022, 13130, 13160, 13418, 13419, & 14141.

** Rockingham County Deeds, Vol. 49, p. 545; "Kingston First Church Records" *N.H.G.R.*, Vol. V, No. 3, pp. 107-112 & Vol. V, No. 4, p. 158. (It seems fairly certain from the records that these children were baptized in infancy and not in later childhood as was to become the practice in some congregations.)

It should be noted that from the settlement of Kingston, c. 1700, a part of the congregation there came from the part of Exeter that later became Brentwood, whose own church was not formed until the late 1740's. See

THIRD GENERATION

The Robertses were falling further behind on their bills, and the local shopkeeper obtained a judgment against them for 44 pounds in 1746. This legal problem apparently caused George to sell his twenty acres of land in 1747 for 260 pounds.* George seems to have owned no real estate after 1747 and left no estate at his death.

His signature and handwriting survive on a few deeds and promissory notes. He signed his name "Gorg Robeds". Children:

12.   i.   Joseph.⁺

      ii.   Anna (?), m. Joseph Eaton Kinaston 10/30/1757.#

      iii.   Judah, bapt. 1/25/1740.

13.   iv.   Jonathan, bapt. 10/11/1741.

      v.   Sarah, bapt. 9/18/1743. A Sarah Roberts was "warned to take her child and depart" Brentwood, 11/12/1765.**

      vi.   Elizabeth, bapt. 4/7/1745.

      vii.   Abigail, bapt. 4/15/1750.

      viii.   George, bapt. 4/15/1750.

14.   ix.   Eliphalet, b. 1748-49; bapt. 4/15/1750.

6. Samuel Roberts (John², George¹), son of John and Elizabeth

---

Hurd, p. 372.

    * N.H. Provincial Court Records, file 10738; Rockingham County Deeds, Vol. 37, p. 17.

    ⁺ There is no birth record for this individual and he is placed here because of a court accounting in 1765 (See page 248) that cites Eliphalet (No. 14) as his brother and a very strong family tradition that he and Jonathan (No. 13) were brothers. See further discussion under Joseph (No. 12).

    # "Kingston First Church Records" *N.H.G.R.*, Vol. III, No. 1, p.89.

    ** N.H. State Archives. Miscellaneous papers, Brentwood.

(Magoon) Roberts, was born in or near Exeter, New Hampshire about 1715 and apparently died there about 1785.

He married in Kingston, New Hampshire, May 7, 1736, Priscilla Langmaid. Their son Ezekiel was baptized there in 1751.

There is no record of land ownership by Samuel in the Exeter/Brentwood/Kingston area. However, he was living in Brentwood in 1767, when he was elected Tithingman of the town, and in 1776, when he signed the Association Test, pledging his support to the Revolutionary War effort. In 1780 he joined the "new" parish in Exeter and was elected moderator in 1783.* Child:

15.   i.   Ezekiel, bapt. 3/24/1751.

7. Benjamin Roberts (John², George¹), son of John and Elizabeth (Magoon) Roberts, was born in Exeter, New Hampshire, about 1718, and died in Brentwood, New Hampshire, in 1795.

His wife's name was Hannah, but nothing else is known about her. A spouse (unnamed) was living at Benjamin's death.

Benjamin's name first appears in public record in 1743, in connection with a petition to establish Brentwood as a separate parish. He was elected haward of Brentwood in 1746. In 1776 he signed the Association Test supporting the Revolutionary War effort.

He left no will. His insolvent estate was administered by his nephew Thomas (No. 10) Roberts. The inventory prepared by Thomas gives some idea of what a person of limited means might have owned at that time: "three acres of land with poor buildens thereon", "one old cow", "two sheep and two lambs", "one small swine", "one poor bed and beden", "iron wair one small pot", "one small kittle", "one old frying pan", "one old fire shovel and tongs", "one old acts and how", "old sieth irons and old fork", "red earthen wair", "one small stone jar", "tin wair", "glass", "one pair old cards", "one old saltmorter", "old wooden wair", "one old chist", "one old spinnen wheal", "four old chairs and old clothing", and

---

* "Kingston First Church Records", *N.H.G.R.*, Vol.II, No.1, p.46 & Vol. V, No. 4, p. 160; *Misc. Rev. War Docs. of N.H.*, p. 20; *Exeter Church Records 1755-1889*, pp. 45 & 69;   Brentwood town records, Vol. I, p. 731.

THIRD GENERATION

"one old table and old barrel".* Children:(?)

    i. John (?), m. Mary Hoit, 12/11/1783. They lived in Poplin (Fremont) and had Anna, b. 9/9/1784, John, b. 12/17/1786, James, b. 4/17/1789, Nathaniel Brown, b. 5/28/1791, Jonathan Bradley, b. 7/24/1794, Mary b. 9/26/1798, Dolly b. 4/6/1800.⁺

8. Jonathan Roberts (John², George¹), son of John and Elizabeth (Magoon) Roberts, was born in or near Exeter, New Hampshire in 1726 or 1727, and died in Andover, New Hampshire, May 10, 1798.

He married in Kingston, New Hampshire, December 10, 1747, Deliverance Smith, the daughter of David and Margaret (Goss) Smith. She was born in 1721 or 1722 and died, probably, in Andover, August 15, 1805.#

Jonathan was named executor of his father's will and inherited the family residence and farm in Brentwood in 1756. He sold this property in 1759.**

He may have served in the French and Indian War in 1760. Within the next few years he had taken up residence in the Salisbury/Andover area, where he operated a grist and sawmill at East Andover.⁺⁺ Jonathan was one of the original settlers listed in

---

    * Rockingham County Probate Docket No. 6114 OS; Rockingham County Deeds, Vol. 109, p. 24 & Vol. 90, p.5.; Brentwood Historical Society, *Brentwood's 225 Years*, p.4; Brentwood town records; *Misc. Rev. Docs. of N.H.*, p. 20.

    ⁺ Fremont, N.H. Town Records, 3663 part 202. Benjamin and John were taxpayers in Poplin(Fremont) 1789-1791.

    # "Kingston First Church Records", *N.H.G.R.*, Vol. III, No. 1, p. 43; Badcock, pp. 5 & 10; notes of Isabel T. Coburn. The death record refers to a "Mrs. Roberts", so there is some possibility this is a reference to someone else.

    ** Rockingham County Deeds, Vol. 172, p. 24.

    ⁺⁺ Dearborn, John J. *The History of Salisbury, N.H.* . . Manchester, N.H.: William E. Moore, 1890, p. 250. A Jonathan Roberts enlisted March 14, 1760, in Capt. Philip Johnson's company of Col. John Goffe's regiment. Dearborn seems to think this veteran is the Jonathan who settled in the Andover/Salisbury area. In 1760 Jonathan had a wife and several small children to support. It is more likely that this is the service record of his

1779.*

The first two children were born in Brentwood and the remainder either there or in the Andover/Salisbury area.⁺ Children:

  i. Lovy (or Lovina), bapt. 12/18/1748; m. Nathan Briggs.

  ii. Margaret, bapt. 7/30/1749. #

  iii. John (?), b. 1751.**

  iv. Dolly, m. Jeff Hancock.

16. v. Jonathan.

  vi. Ezra.

  vii. David.

---

nephew, Jonathan (No. 13), who was single and twenty years old at the time. Potter, Chandler E. *The Military History of the State of New Hampshire...* Concord, N.H.: Privately published, 1866, pp. 233 & 246-7.

 * Eastman, John R. *History of the Town of Andover, New Hampshire 1751-1906*. Concord, N.H.: Rumford Printing Co., 1910, pp. 285-6.

 ⁺ "Kingston First Church Records", *N.H.G.R.*, Vol. V, No.4, p.157; Eastman, pp. 285-6.

 # A Margaret Roberts had a son Samuel Sleeper Roberts born (out of wedlock?) in Andover, 8/13/1785. (See I.G.I.); Badcock (p. 32) lists the death in Andover of a Margaret Roberts (pauper) 8/6/1834.

 ** A John Roberts of Raymond (or Candia) served in the Rev. War. He was b. 1751 and d. near Grafton, N.H., 3/2/1829. His wife was Sarah. He was a miller and sold Raymond land in 1780 and moved to Andover, N.H., where he bought land from Jonathan Roberts (No. 16) in the same year. He sold a sawmill and other property in Andover in 1818 and moved to Grafton. Various children. See Hardon, "Roberts - Unconnected", Vol.I, p. 175.

FOURTH GENERATION

9. Joseph Roberts (John³, John², George¹), son of John and Abigail (Gordon) Roberts, was born in Brentwood, New Hampshire May 25, 1740, and died in Meredith, New Hampshire, June 12, 1812, and is buried, along with his wife, at the Smith Yard. He married, in Brentwood, Eunice Leavitt, July 16, 1761. She died May 16, 1815. Joseph was chosen tithingman of Brentwood in 1767 but yielded to his Uncle Samuel Roberts. This family apparently left Brentwood for Meredith about 1771, to settle on land previously acquired by Joseph's father. By 1776 Joseph was in Meredith to sign the Association Test to support the Revolutionary War effort and is honored by a marker in the Smith Yard put there by the Mary Butler Chapter of the Daughters of the American Revolution.* Children:

	i.	Abigail, b. 6/5/1762; m. Samuel Kelly.
17.	ii.	John, b. 8/18/1764.
	iii.	Eunice, b. 3/21/1767; m. William Mead. 11 ch.
18.	iv.	Joseph, b. 12/21/1770.
19.	v.	Joshua, b. 1779.
	vi.	Susana, m. -----Davis.

10. Thomas Roberts (John³, John², George¹), son of John and Abigail (Gordon) Roberts, was born in Brentwood, New Hampshire, January 9, 1743, and died there in 1821. He married (undoubtedly not as his first wife) Mary Sanborn, sometime after 1814. She was the daughter of Coffin and Hannah (Hilliard) Sanborn of Hampton Falls. Mary was born in 1761 and died in 1832. Her marriage to Thomas Roberts was her second of three marriages, the first being to Jonathan Marston of Brentwood, who died in 1814, and the third being to John Brown. Thomas had at least two children, however

---

* Brentwood Town Records, Vol. 1, p. 731; Hanaford, Mary E.N. *Meredith, N.H. Annals and Genealogies*. Concord, N.H.: The Rumford Press, 1932, pp. 433-5; Hardon, "Roberts -Unconnected", Vol. II, p. 33; Holbrook, Jay M. *New Hampshire 1776 Census*. Oxford, Mass.: Holbrook Research Institute, 1976, p. 123; notes of David C. Dewsnap.

their names are not known.* Thomas acquired land in Brentwood from his Gordon relatives in 1760 and from his uncle Alexander Roberts in 1772. He administered the estates of his uncles Alexander and Benjamin. In 1776 he signed the Association Test in Brentwood, pledging thereby to support the Revolutionary War effort.# Children: (?)

    i. a child.

    ii. a child.

11. Alexander Roberts (John^3, John^2, George^1), son of John and Abigail (Gordon) Roberts, was born in Brentwood, New Hampshire May 3, 1747, and died in Sanborntown, New Hampshire in 1810. He went by "Sander". Sander married Sarah Leavitt, the daughter of John and Abigail Leavitt. By 1772 Alexander and his wife Sarah were in Sanbornton, where the birth of their first child was recorded. They were apparently back in Brentwood by 1776, because "Sander Roberts Jr." signed the Association Test there. Apparently, the family moved to Meredith by 1790, the census of which reports a family of six. All but the first child was born in Meredith.* Children:

20.   i. Leavitt, b. 12/30/1772.

    ii. Levi.

    iii. Thomas.

    iv. George.

---

    * *Heads of Families at the First Census... 1790.*

    # Brentwood Town Records, Vol. 1, p. 731; Sanborn, V.C. *Genealogy of the Family of Sanborne or Sanborn in England and America.* Concord, N.H.: The Rumford Press, 1899, p. 113. Rockingham County Deeds, Vol. 67, p. 266; Vol. 105, p. 125; Rockingham Co. Prob. Rec.; *Misc. Rev. War Docs. of N.H.*, p. 20.

    * Hardon, "Roberts-Unconnected", Vol. II, p. 149; Brentwood Town Records, Vol. 1, p. 731; notes of Esther C. Wyatt; I.G.I.; *Misc. Rev. War. Docs. of N.H.*, p. 20; 1790 Census.

FOURTH GENERATION

v. John(?).

12. **Joseph Roberts**, apparently the son of George (No.5) and Judith (Kenniston) Roberts, was probably born in or near Exeter, New Hampshire, about 1734. He purportedly died in Buckfield, Maine about 1805, but perhaps as late as 1810, and is said to have been buried there in the Lowell Cemetery.* There is no known record of Joseph's birth. There is, however, a 1765 court document which states that Eliphalet Roberts (No. 14) was his brother. Because of this citation and the very strong family tradition that Joseph was the older brother of Jonathan (No. 13) Roberts, it is assumed that he was the son of George and Judith.#

Joseph married Hannah Young about 1755. She was born in or near Exeter, December 25, 1740, and died in Buckfield in 1815 or 1816. She was probably the daughter of Daniel and Hannah (Lovering) Young, of Brentwood.⁺

The name Joseph Roberts appears in a 1755 petition recorded in the town minutes of Brentwood, New Hampshire, where his eldest son was born in 1756. (Brentwood was set off from Exeter in 1742.) He next surfaces in nearby Nottingham, where he sold his proprietorship rights in property in Sandwich, New Hampshire, in 1763. In 1765 he was a defendant in a suit by John Robinson to recover a debt of some seventy pounds "old tenor money". A judgment was obtained and the sheriff attached a hog and cross-cut

---

* Maine Old Cemetery Association, *Index of Revolutionary War Veterans Buried in Maine* (1977), p. 596. In 1991 a Roberts researcher tried but failed to locate this grave. If it is there it is undoubtedly unmarked.

Amorena (Roberts) Grant established that Joseph and Jonathan were brothers based on her correspondence with Otis Oakes Roberts, 1901-1902. Otis Oakes Roberts states that his father, Amos Roberts (1800-1886), and Jacob Roberts (1784-1856), who both grew up in Buckfield together, were second cousins. The record is clear that Amos was a grandson of Jonathan No. 13 and Jacob a grandson of Joseph No. 12.

⁺ Grant, Amorena (Roberts), *The Roberts Family: A Genealogy of Joseph Roberts of Windham, Maine*. Chicago: West Chicago Press Assoc., no date (c. 1902), pp. 2-9; notes of Frances R. Jones.

239

saw belonging to Joseph, in partial satisfaction of the debt.*

Joseph and his brother Jonathan both migrated from New Hampshire to Maine (Joseph probably in 1766 or 1767, Jonathan at the same time or perhaps as much as a handful of years earlier) first to the Windham/Standish area, then Buckfield. There is record of at least two sales of property in Buckfield between these two men.#

In 1775 Joseph, so it is said, joined the Revolutionary War effort when he was unable to persuade his 19-year-old son Joseph Jr. to stay home. Both are said to have been at the battle of Bunker Hill. He was probably a veteran of the French and Indian War, as well.+

After the Revolution Joseph and his brother Jonathan settled their large families in Buckfield, where they farmed adjacent properties in the northern part of town, in an area known as Federal Corners. Here Joseph was one of the original incorporators of the Baptist Society of Turner and Buckstown in 1791.** Children:

21.   i.   Joseph, b. 2/6/1756.

       ii.   Hannah, b.c. 1762; m. James Jordan, 1780. 12 ch.

       iii.   Sarah, b. 6/1764; m. Jotham Shaw; d. 3/4/1855. Ten children.

22.   iv.   Jonathan, b.c. 1766.

---

   * Brentwood Town Records, Vol 1, p. 97; New Hampshire Provincial Court Records, file 11775; Rockingham County Deeds, Vol. 80, p. 413.

   # Grant, p. 7; Cole, Alfred, & Whitman, Charles F., *A History of Buckfield, Oxford County, Maine, from the Earliest Explorations to the Close of the Year 1900*. Buckfield, Maine: Privately published, c. 1915, pp. 667-73; Cumberland County Deeds, Book 40, p. 232.

   + Cole & Whitman, pp. 48-9. See also Dole, Samuel T., *Windham in the Past*. Reprinted Windham, Maine: Windham Historical Society, 1974 (originally published c. 1916), pp. 520-1. A Joseph Roberts of Brentwood served under Captain Johnson in a 1760 march to Canada. An old list of Buckfield veterans compiled by Virgil Parris in the mid-1800's credits this Joseph with French & Indian War service. See also Potter, pp. 246-7.

   ** French, W.R. *A History of Turner, Maine from Its Settlement to 1886*. Portland, Maine: Hoyt, Fogg & Donham, 1887, pp. 119 & 164-5; Cole & Whitman, pp. 48-9.

FOURTH GENERATION

  v. Elizabeth, b. 1769; m. Thomas Irish, 7/25/1792; d. 1856. Seven children.
  vi. Mary, b. 1773; m. Richard Taylor, 4/23/1794. 8 ch.
23. vii. John, b. 1777.

13. Jonathan Roberts (George³, John², George¹), son of George and Judith (Kenniston) Roberts, was born in or near Exeter, New Hampshire about 1740, was baptized in nearby Kingston, New Hampshire, October 11, 1741, and died in Buckfield (or perhaps Brooks), Maine about 1815.*

He married Elizabeth Webb in Windham, Maine, April 1, 1768. She was the daughter of Samuel and Bethia (Farrow) Webb of Windham. She was baptized in Windham January 8, 1746/7.#

This Jonathan is probably the Jonathan Roberts of Brentwood who deserted while marching toward Canada in 1760, during the French and Indian War.⁺ Sometime in the early to mid-1760's, Jonathan, either accompanied by or followed within a couple of years by his older brother Joseph (No. 12) Roberts, left New Hampshire for Maine.**

Enlisting in the Revolutionary War from Windham, Jonathan served as a private in Capt. Nathan Merrill's Company, Col. Jonathan Mitchell's detachment on the Penobscot expedition from July 8, 1779 to September 25, 1779. It is also said that he was at Bunker hill in 1775 with his brother and nephew, the two Joseph

---

 * "Kingston First Church Records", *N.H.G.R.*, Vol. V., No. 2, p. 107. Miles and Blanche J. Roberts (see citation under Eliphalet Roberts No. 14) attribute this baptismal to Jonathan No. 16, who went to Tunbridge, Vermont. Although their interpretation cannot be proven incorrect beyond a shadow of a doubt, based on all of the admittedly incomplete puzzle pieces presented by this family, the author of this book emphatically stands by the construction of relationships as developed herein.
 # Dole, p. 553.
 ⁺ Potter, pp. 233 & 246-7. A Jonathan Roberts of Brentwood enlisted March 14, 1760 in Capt. Philip Johnson's Company of Col. John Goffe's Regiment. While on a march to Canada, he deserted June 7, 1760. Eastman thinks this is a reference to Jonathan (No. 8).
 ** Grant, pp. 6-7; Cole & Whitman, p. 668.

DESCENDANTS OF GEORGE & MARY ROBERTS

Robertses.[*]

After the Revolution, Jonathan and Elizabeth moved to Buckfield, Maine, where Jonathan was a farmer and trader, who often travelled widely on town and personal business. In Buckfield Jonathan and Elizabeth acquired a settling lot (#44) of 100 acres in 1781. In 1783 Jonathan acquired 50 acres in Windham, where his family was located at the time of the 1790 Census. That property was sold in 1793, and by 1800 this family was back in Buckfield. In 1802 Jonathan, now of Washington Plantation (later renamed Brooks), sold over 100 acres in Buckfield. By 1810 he and Elizabeth seem to be resident in Brooks, Maine, where a number of Robertses had recently settled. Jonathan is said to have been a member of the Baptist church and a staunch Federalist.[#]

Of the ten children listed below, the first seven were recorded as born in Windham, the last three in Buckfield.[+] Children:

24.   i.   Samuel, b. 2/5/1769.

       ii.   Susannah, b. 4/28/1771; m. Richard Anderson. One child.

25.   iii.   George, b. 4/26/1773.

       iv.   Jonathan, b. 7/17/1775.

26.   v.   James, b. 9/15/1777.

       vi.   Bethia, b. 9/17/1779; m. Benjamin Fobes (See Seth No. 27.); d. 1817-20. Four children.

       vii.   Judith, b. 10/6/1781; m. Zadock Fobes, 3/16/1797. Nine children.

---

[*] Commonwealth of Massachusetts. *Massachusetts Soldiers and Sailors of the Revolutionary War*. Boston: Wright & Potter Printing Co., State Printers, 1905, p. 408; Cole & Whitman, p. 48.

[#] Dole, pp. 520-1; Cole & Whitman, p. 675; Cumberland County Deeds, Book 34, p. 499, Book 64, p. 360, Book 57, p. 344, Book 38, p. 329. U. S. Census, Maine, 1790, 1800, & 1810.

[+] Hilton, Elizabeth H., "Roberts Family History"(unpub.), no date (c. 1985), pp. 4-7. The Buckfield town record book, p. 35.

FOURTH GENERATION

    viii. Betsey, b. 12/10/1783; m. Going Knight, 10/25/1812; d. 5/3/1860. One child.
27.   ix. Seth, b. 5/5/1786.
    x. Rebekah, b. 12/9/1788; m. Arza Fobes, 2/5/1811; d. 8/14/1854 Buckfield.

14. Eliphalet Roberts (George[3], John[2], George[1]), son of George and Judith (Kenniston) Roberts, was baptized in Kingston, New Hampshire April 15, 1750 and died in Strafford, Vermont, September 27, 1843 in his 95th year. He was buried in the Clough Cemetery.[*]

He married, firstly, Elizabeth West, daughter of Daniel and Elizabeth (Gordon) West. She was baptized in Kingston, New Hampshire, October 1, 1745 and died April 8, 1785. Eliphalet married, secondly, Sarah Sawyer, January 6, 1787, the daughter of Moses and Sarah (Pike) Sawyer, and the widow of Paul Chase, of Enfield, New Hampshire. She was born in Plaistow, New Hampshire, March 6, 1764 and died at Strafford, Vermont, February 24, 1840 (or 1848?) and was buried in the Clough Cemetery.[#]

Very little is known about his youth in New Hampshire, with only one public record on him coming to light. A court file from 1765 indicates that Joseph Roberts (No. 12) was in debt to John Robinson for a number of items, including 3 shilling and 7 pence worth of rum for "yr. bror. Elipht." (This may not tell us much about his drinking habits at age 17, since rum at that time was one of the most widely prescribed medicines, as well as an accepted

---

    [*] "Kingston First Church Records", *N.H.G.R.*, Vol. V, No.4, p.158. One source says that an Eliphalet of Strafford was from Connecticut. The dates of birth and death are different than shown here. Eliphalet Roberts is an unusual name, and it would be easy to jump to conclusions. There was an Eliphalet Roberts born in Connecticut, but the one who went to Strafford, Vermont, was undoubtedly from New Hampshire. See Knox, Grace L. & Ferris, Barbara B. *Connecticut Nutmeggers Who Migrated.* Bowie, Maryland: Heritage Books, 1988, p. 193.

    [#] Roberts, Blanche J. "Strafford, Vt. Records", unpub., 1984-5, p 539; Miles, pp. 77-8; Hammond, ed., *N.H. Probate*, Vol. 5, pp. 507-8.

DESCENDANTS OF GEORGE & MARY ROBERTS

beverage for persons of all ages.)*

Having a 100 acre farm there as early as 1774, Eliphalet was one of the first settlers of Strafford, Vermont. He enlisted in the Revolutionary cause in early 1777 and served at Ticonderoga.[#] The following petition signed by fourteen citizens of Strafford tells what happened next:

"Strafford April ye29, 1778

These may certify Any Gentlemen to whom it may concern that Eliphalet Roberts is an inhabitant of this town and that he did in July last desert his Countreys Cause and fled to the Enemy and their remaind til the Surrender of General Burgoin and Quick after that he returned to this town and Appeared to be very sorry for his Conduct made all the Recantations that could be thought proper He promises to be friendly for the future and to be subject to our laws to turn out and defend his Cuntry by arms if cald upon His conduct since he came home apears to be Agreable to his Confession and promises He has a large family of small children and if he should be stript of what little improvements he has theirs some danger of his famelyes being some charge to the State Therefore if the Honorable Counsil in their wisdom should see fit sofar to Restore him as to allow him the use of his land upon his good behavour for the future it would be lokt upon as an act of generosity and be well accepted by the town in general."[+]

Apparently the first eight children below are by Elizabeth and the remaining nine are by Sarah. It is said that Eliphalet had twenty-two children in all.[**] Children:

        i. Judith, b. 7/30/1772; m. Moses Hunt, 9/28/1794. Nine children.

28.   ii. Eliphalet, b. 8/22(or2?)/1774.

29.   iii. William, b. 6/18/1776.

---

   * New Hampshire Provincial Court Records, file 11775. See p. 248.

   # Miles, pp. 77-8; Holbrook, Jay Mack. *Vermont's First Settlers.* Oxford, Mass.: Holbrook Research Institute, 1982, p. 71.

   + Document at the Vermont Historical Society.

   ** Roberts, Blanche J., p. 539; Miles, pp. 77-8; notes of Bobbi (Roberts) Bryant and Jane Louise Verret.

FOURTH GENERATION

	iv.	Elsa, b. 7/30/1778; d. 4/24/1798.
30.	v.	Daniel West, b. 12/1/1780.
	vi.	Hannah, b. 5/11/1782; m. John Rowell, 11/2/1806; d. 4/27/1835. Four children.
	vii.	George, b. 6/25/1784; d. 12/1785.
	viii.	Mabel (?), b. 1785; prob. d. 1785.
31.	ix.	George, b. 6/11/1788.
	x.	Moses, b. 4/25/1791; d. 5/18/1791.
	xi.	Sarah Abigail, b. 3/9/1792; m. Sewell Ross, 1/12/1817; d. 10/31/1865.
	xii.	Lucinda, b. 8/1794; m. Noah Sargent, 1/26/1817 or 1818; d. 12/5/1864.
32.	xiii.	Moses, b. 5/9/1796.
	xiv.	Eunice, b. 7/29/1797; m. John Clogston, 11/28/1817; d. 11/17/1875.
	xv.	Elsie, b. 4/23/1800; m. (1) Amos Felton, Jr., 8/29/1828, (2) Cyrus Hill, 12/25/1841; d. 1/9/1892.
33.	xvi.	Stephen, b. 5/20/1803.
	xvii.	Bethia, m. (?) Nathan Prescott, 1842.

15. Ezekiel Roberts (Samuel[3], John[2], George[1]), son of Samuel and Priscilla (Langmaid) Roberts, was born in 1748-9 and was baptized in Kingston, New Hampshire, March 24, 1751. He died in Raymond, New Hampshire, August 6, 1831. He married Margaret Crusey, the daughter of John Crusey of Newcastle, New Hampshire. She died in Raymond, April 17, 1822. Ezekiel owned various parcels of land in Raymond. Apparently he had at least one

DESCENDANTS OF GEORGE & MARY ROBERTS

daughter in addition to the son listed below.* Child:

34. i. John, b. 1772-3.

16. Jonathan Roberts (Jonathan^3, John^2, George^1), son of Jonathan and Deliverance (Smith) Roberts, was born in or near Brentwood, New Hampshire, about 1755, and died in Tunbridge, Vermont, January 5, 1806.# His wife's name was Hannah; nothing else in known about her. It would appear that Jonathan migrated with his father to the Andover/Salisbury, New Hampshire area. A list of early settlers of New Breton, New Hampshire (the original name for Andover) lists both Jonathan Roberts and Jonathan Roberts Jr. as taxpayers in 1779. In 1780 Jonathan and Hannah Roberts of Salisbury sold land in Andover to John Roberts (probably a close relative, however no documented connection) of Andover. Presumably this family moved to Vermont at about this time. Jonathan's will of 1805 names the following children, who were to receive six shillings each, except for Daniel ($30) and Noah, who was to inherit the family real and personal property after his mother's death.+ Children:

35. i.   Jonathan, b. 1778.**

     ii. Betsey, m. John Wills, 3/27/1814.

36. iii. Daniel, b. 4/9/1785.

37. iv. John, b. 4/14/1787.

---

* "Kingston First Church Records", *N.H.G.R.*, Vol. V, No. 4, p. 160; Fullonton, Joseph. *The History of Raymond, N.H.* Dover, N.H.: Privately published, 1875, pp. 333 & 336; 1790 Census.

Roberts, Blanche J., Vol. 4, p. 552. (It should be noted that Blanche Roberts shows this Jonathan as the son of George No. 5. This author has concluded that the preponderance of the evidence indicates that Jonathan No. 13 was the son of George No. 5.)

+ Eastman, pp. 285-6; Hillsborough County Deeds, Book 65, pp. 61-2. For more information on John Roberts, see footnotes under Jonathan No.8; Probate record Randolph District, Vermont, Vol. 3, p. 96.

** From family Bible in possession of a descendant.

FOURTH GENERATION

38.
    v. Noah, b. 3/29/1789.
    vi. William, b. 6/12/1791.
    vii. Sally, m. Walter Caswell, 3/6/1814.
    viii. Hannah, m. Joseph Scribner, 6/15/1820.
    ix. Polly.

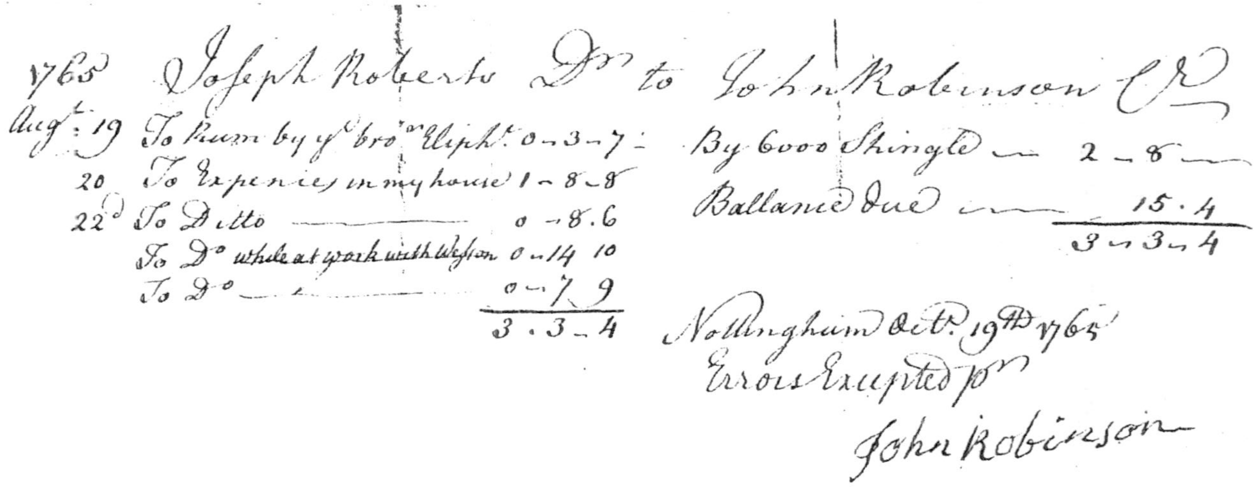

DESCENDANTS OF GEORGE & MARY ROBERTS

[Handwritten account, rotated sideways:]

1763 Joseph Roberts Dr to John Robinson Cr

Aug.t 19   To Rum by y.e bro.r Elijah   0 – 3 – 7
       To Expences at my house   1 – 8 – 8
20   To Ditto   0 – 8 – 6
22   To D.o while at work with Lifson 0 – 14 – 10
      To D.o   0 – 7 – 9
                                  ─────────
                                  3 – 3 – 4

By Cood Shingle   2 – 8 –
Ballance Due   15 – 4
                  ─────────
                   3 – 3 – 4

Nottingham Oct.r 19.th 1765
Errors Excepted p.r
                    John Robinson

(N.H. Provincial Court Records, file 11775).

FIFTH GENERATION

17. John Roberts (Joseph[4], John[3], John[2], George[1]), son of Joseph and Eunice (Leavitt) Roberts, was born August 18, 1764, apparently in Brentwood, New Hampshire. His first wife's name was Sally. They had the first three children listed below. John married (secondly?) Polly Sanborn, the daughter of Zadok and Susanna (Judkins) Sanborn of Brentwood, New Hampshire. Polly was born August 11, 1777. Susanna (Judkins) Sanborn was the step-daughter of Alexander (No.4.) Roberts. John is listed in 1790 among heads of household in Meredith, New Hampshire, where the following children were born.* Children:

    i. Susannah, b. 5/2/1787.

    ii. Daniel, b. 6/8/1789.

    iii. Eunice, b. 5/14/1791.

    iv. Sally, b. 9/28/1793.

    v. John (Sawyer?), b. 2/7/1797; m. Sarah Whitten (?)

    vi. Polly, b. 10/11/1799.

18. Joseph Roberts (Joseph[4], John[3], John[2], George[1]), son of Joseph and Eunice (Leavitt) Roberts, was born in Brentwood, New Hampshire December 21, 1770, died in Meredith, New Hampshire, January 20, 1849, and is buried in the Smith Yard there. His first wife was apparently named Polly. Another wife, Mary Davis, the daughter of William and Molly (Boynton) Davis, who was born in 1775 and died December 26, 1855, lies next to Joseph in the Smith Yard.⁺ Children:

    i. Mary (Polly), b. 8/27/1794; m. Joseph Mead. 3 ch.

    ii. William, b. 7/15/1796; d. 1799.

    iii. Eunice, b. 5/5/1798; m. 5/7/1821, Samuel Robie. Six children.

---

    * Brentwood Town Records, vol. 1, p. 731; Sanborn, p. 137; I.G.I., April 1988, pp. 7327-7346; 1790 Census; Hanaford, p. 433.

    ⁺ Hanaford, p. 435; Brentwood Town Records, vol. 1, p. 731; I.G.I., pp. 7327-7346; Dewsnap notes.

DESCENDANTS OF GEORGE & MARY ROBERTS

    iv. William Davis, b. 5/22/1801; m. 3/17/1823, Phebe Robie. Children?

    v. Sarah (or Sally), b. 12/8/1807; m. Nathaniel Sanborn, 12/25/1825. Nine children.

    vi. Susan Rosetta, b. 1/28/1812; m. Jacob J. Severance, 3/20/1845; d. 5/12/1896. Two children.

    vii. Olive Naomi, b. 1/26/1821; m. 7/17/1845, Elbridge G. Severance; d. 7/26/1892. Two children.

19. Joshua Roberts (Joseph[4], John[3], John[2], George[1]), son of Joseph and Eunice (Leavitt) Roberts, was born in 1779 and died about 1812. His wife's name was Elizabeth, or Betsey. This family lived in Meredith.[*] Children:

    i. Mary.

    ii. Elizabeth.

    iii. Polly, b. 8/28/1805.[+]

20. Leavitt Roberts (Alexander[4], John[3], John[2], George[1]), son of Alexander and Sarah (Leavitt) Roberts, was born in Sanbornton (or possibly Meredith or Brentwood), New Hampshire, December 30, 1772 and died there January 27, 1850, of "fever". He married Lovey Hawkins, who was born July 8, 1773 in Barnstead, New Hampshire, and died in Sanbornton, March 25, 1853. She is buried in the center of town in the Bean Road Cemetery, where Leavitt is also buried. Lovey was the daughter of John and Lydia (Bunker) Hawkins. This family lived for many years in Meredith, New Hampshire, and later in Sanborntown. The following children were born in either of those two towns, and some of them are buried in the Bean Road or the North Sanbornton Cemetery.[#] Children:

---

    [*] Hardon, "Roberts-Unconnected", Vol. II, p. 33.

    [+] I.G.I.

    [#] Hanaford, pp. 433-5; Hardon, "Roberts-Unconnected", Vol. II, pp. 58 & 159; I.G.I., pp. 7327-7346. Runnels, M.T. *History of Sanbornton,N.H.* Boston: Alfred Mudge & Sons, 1881, p. 599; Wyatt notes; Jackson, Ronald V., ed., *1850 Mortality Schedules - New Hampshire.* North Salt Lake City:

FIFTH GENERATION

	i.	John, b. 1793; m. Nancy Drake; d. July 23, 1867.
	ii.	Levi, b. 1795 (or 1798) ; m. Abiah Clement; d. 9/21/1864
	iii.	Phebe, b. 1799; d. 1866.
	iv.	Sanders, b. 10/1800; m. Sophronia Hawkins, 1/12/1825; d. 3/18/1847.(?)*
	v.	James, b. 1803 (or 1799); m. (1) Ann -----, (2) Nancy Chase, (3)? Elmira Clement; d. 1833.(?)⁺
39.	vi.	Calvin, b. 4/2/1807.
40.	vii.	Benjamin, b. 1802 (or 8/1809).
	viii.	Sally P., b. 1810; m. -----Bickford; d. 1836.
41.	ix.	Thomas, b. 9/11/1812.
	x.	Nancy C., b. 4/6/1813(or 8/27/1813); m. Madison Chase.
42.	xi.	George Washington, b. 10/10/1816.

21. Joseph Roberts (Joseph[4], George[3], John[2], George[1]), son of Joseph and Hannah (Young) Roberts, was born in Brentwood, New Hampshire February 6, 1756, and died in Brooks, Maine, January 10, 1843. He married on November 28, 1777, Esther Hamlin of Gorham, Maine. She was the daughter of Joseph Hamlin. Esther was born in Gorham, Maine, June 30, 1758, and died in Buckfield, Maine in 1800. Joseph and Esther had twelve children. After Esther died Joseph married, secondly, Margaret Hall, daughter of Hatevil and Ruth (Winslow) Hall, in 1801. Joseph and Margaret also had twelve children.

Joseph enlisted in the militia at Cape Elizabeth, Maine, May 15, 1775 and is said to have fought at the Battle of Bunker Hill. His

---

Accelerated Indexing Systems, Inc., 1987, p. 40.

  * James and Sanders (or Sanborn?) of the right ages appear as heads of household in the 1850 census for Meredith.
  ⁺ loc. cit.

DESCENDANTS OF GEORGE & MARY ROBERTS

official service record shows service in several regiments from 1775 through September 25, 1779, including service in the Bagaduce campaign on the Maine coast. He received pensions for his Revolutionary War service through various acts of Congress from 1818 to 1820 and again from 1831 to the date of his death. Joseph and Esther settled in Standish, Maine about 1780 and then lived in Buckfield, Maine, where Joseph was one of the original incorporators of the Baptist Society in 1791. In 1799 Joseph became the first white settler of Brooks, Maine. He and his family built the first saw mill there and later a grist mill. They manufactured wooden ware for many years. The first thirteen children below were born in Buckfield, the remainder in Brooks.*
Children:

	i.	Hannah, b. 2/20/1778; m. John Young, 1799; d. 1844. Ten children.
	ii.	Tabitha, b. 1/11/1780; m. James (No. 26) Roberts, 1799; d. 11/20/1868. Four children.
	iii.	Sarah, b. 5/6/1782; m. Shadrach Hall; d. 11/1859. Ten children.
43.	iv.	Isaac (twin), b. 5/10/1784.
44.	v.	Jacob (twin), b. 5/10/1784.
	vi.	Elizabeth, b. 2/2/1786; m. John Cates, 1804; d. 6/1832. Nine children.
45.	vii.	Gilman, b. 10/28/1788.
46.	viii.	Enoch, b. 3/27/1791.
	ix.	infant, b. 1793; d. 1793.
	x.	Esther, b. 3/20/1795; m. Daniel Hamilton, 1813; d. 1877. Thirteen ch.

---

* Grant, pp. 8-13; French, p. 119; Buckfield town record book, p. 19; Gould, Nathan. "Colonel Jonathan Mitchell's Cumberland County Regiment, Bagaduce Expedition 1779". *Collections and Proceedings of the Maine Historical Society*, 2nd Series, 10:52-80 & 143-77.

FIFTH GENERATION

	xi.	Lovina, b. 8/8/1797; m. Levi Bowen, 1818; d. 10/1856. Twelve children.
47.	xii.	Joseph, b. 11/2/1799.
	xiii.	Nathan, b. 2/5/1802; d. young.
48.	xiv.	Benjamin, b. 2/4/1804.
49.	xv.	John, b. 1/1806.
50.	xvi.	Alfred J., b. 10/21/1807.
	xvii.	Ruth, b. 1809; d. young.
	xviii.	Mary, b. 1811; d. young.
51.	xix.	Timothy T., b. 7/31/1812.
	xx.	Charles, b. 1/1814; m. Clarinda Havener; d. 1/6/1840.
52.	xxi.	Nathan Hall, b. 6/9/1815.
	xxii.	Mary, b. 1818; m. Calvin Fogg; d. 12/1893. 4 ch.
53.	xxiii.	Winslow, b. 3/8/1821.
54.	xxiv.	Rufus, b. 4/14/1823.

22. Jonathan Roberts (Joseph[4], George[3], John[2], George[1]), son of Joseph and Hannah (Young) Roberts, was born about 1766, probably in or near Windham, Maine, and died, apparently in Brooks, Maine in 1804. He married Prudence Willard, January 24, 1787 in Windham, Maine. She was born in March of 1767 and died December 20, 1843, apparently in Brooks, Maine. This family lived on Roberts Hill in Brooks for many years. After Jonathan died Prudence married Samuel King (or Kinsley?) May 25, 1806. Prudence and Samuel had no children.[*] Children:

55.	i.	Jotham, b. 12/28/1787.

---

[*] Grant, p. 128; Norwood, Seth W. *Sketches of Brooks (Me.) History*. Dover, N.H.: J.B. Page Printing Co., 1935, p. 14; Buckfield town records, p.9.

DESCENDANTS OF GEORGE & MARY ROBERTS

   ii. Lydia, b. 10/26/1789.

56. iii. Daniel, b. 12/30/1791.

   iv. Hannah, b. 12/22/1794 (or 12/23/1793?).

57. v. Willard, b. 3/27(or21?)/1796.

   vi. Cyrus, b. 3/29/1798; d. young.

   vii. Cyrus, b. 4/21/1803. Sailed from Boston in 1825 and never heard from again.

23. John Roberts (Joseph^4, George^3, John^2, George^1), son of Joseph and Hannah (Young) Roberts, was born in or near Windham or Buckfield, Maine in 1777. He married Miriam Irish of Buckfield. Along with his brothers, John and his family went to Brooks, Maine; but then, in 1812, they migrated west to Ohio. The following six children were born in Maine, the first two in Buckfield. Apparently, an additional six children were born in Ohio, or points west.* Children:

   i. John, b. 4/5/1800.

   ii. William, b. 11/19/1801.

   iii. Emerson, b. 1803.

58. iv. Sylvanus Irish, b. 11/9/1804.

   v. Charlotte.

   vi. Marjory.

24. Samuel Roberts (Jonathan^4, George^3, John^2, George^1), son of Jonathan and Elizabeth (Webb) Roberts, was born in Windham, Maine, February 5, 1769, and died in Brooks, Maine, between 1840 and 1850. He married in Falmouth, Maine, May 21, 1791, Abigail Wheeler of Cape Elizabeth, Maine, the daughter of John Wheeler, Jr., and his first wife (name unknown). She was born in 1769 and died in Brooks between 1850 and 1860. Samuel was an early settler in Brooks, on Gould Hill Road. He was a farmer and a

---

 * Grant, p. 138; Buckfield town records, p. 29.

FIFTH GENERATION

member of the Baptist church. The first six children were born in Windham or Turner, Maine, the remainder probably in Brooks.*
Children:

- 59. i. Jonathan, b. 3(or5?)/11/1792.
  - ii. Lydia, b. 6/14/1794
  - iii. Sally, b.c. 1796; m. Silvenus Eaton.
  - iv. George, b. 6/4/1796.
  - v. Elizabeth, b.c. 1798; unm.
- 60. vi. Samuel, b. 7/1800.
  - vii. son, b.c. 1802; d. young.
- 61. viii. Seth, b.c. 1804.
- 62. ix. Josiah, b.c. 1806.
- 63. x. Watson, b. 12/1809.
  - xi. daughter, b. 1811; d. young.

25. George Roberts (Jonathan[4], George[3], John[2], George[1]), son of Jonathan and Elizabeth (Webb) Roberts, was born in Windham, Maine, April 26, 1773, and died in Sangerville, Maine, March 10, 1852. He married in Turner, Maine, November 24, 1796, Mary Brown, daughter of Amos and Sarah (Cilley) Brown. Mary was born in Buckfield, Maine, October 20, 1780, and died in Sangerville, May 10, 1851. All children below were born in Buckfield.⁺ Children:

- i. Susannah, b. 6/13/1799; m. Howell Ryerson, 8/20/1817. Twelve ch.
- 64. ii. Amos, b. 10/6/1800.
- 65. iii. Ezra, b. 3/30/1802.

---

* Hilton, p. 5; Jones notes.
⁺ Hilton, pp. 5-6; Buckfield town record book, p. 39.

66.	iv.	George, b. 10/17/1803.
67.	v.	Jonathan, b. 7/21/1806.
	vi.	Sarah, b. 7/8/1808.
	vii.	Seth, b. 12/7/1810; m. Anna Young, 6/5/1834.
	viii.	Benjamin Brown, b. 10/19/1812; m. Eliza Brown, 7/1/1835.
	ix.	Alanson, b. 6/14/1814; m. Mary Burrill, 8/21/1836.
	x.	Mary Brown, b. 5/2/1816.
	xi.	Hannah P., b. 5/11/1818; m. George Chase, 11/25/1835.
	xii.	Mary Ann, b. 11/5/1823; m. Rufus Edgerly; d. 5/2/1899. Three ch.
	xiii.	Alice B., m. Micajah Swain, 4/7/1836.

26. James Roberts (Jonathan[4], George[3], John[2], George[1]), son of Jonathan and Elizabeth (Webb) Roberts, was born in Windham, Maine, September 15, 1777, and died in Waldo, Maine, in 1864. James married his first cousin once-removed, Tabitha Roberts, daughter of Joseph and Esther (Hamlin) Roberts, April 20, 1799, in Buckfield, Maine. She was born in Buckfield, January 11, 1780, and died November 20, 1868. James and Tabitha had two infants who died in infancy, in addition to the two children listed below. Tabitha, it is said, once killed an English soldier with a pitchfork as he was attempting to rustle their last cow.[*] Children:

    i. Esther, b. 1802; m. George Fogg, 11/20/1821; d. 1841. Six children.

---

[*] Hilton, p. 6; Grant, pp. 18-19. This would have been quite a feat for a girl of at most three years of age, if it occurred during the Revolution. Perhaps this story was told by Tabitha, but an older friend or relative was the combatant. Perhaps it occurred during the War of 1812, or perhaps it has no basis in fact. We will never know.

FIFTH GENERATION

68. ii. Eli, b. 2/19/1804.

27. Seth Roberts (Jonathan⁴, George³, John², George¹), son of Jonathan and Elizabeth (Webb) Roberts, was born in Buckfield, Maine, May 5, 1786, died in Peru, Maine, April 30, 1843, and is buried in the Knox Cemetery in Peru.* Seth married in Windham, Maine, January 9, 1814, Miriam Fobes, daughter of Benjamin and Anna (Gammon) Fobes.⁺ She was born in Maine in 1798 and died in Peru, October 17, 1858.# Seth and Miriam were fifth cousins, both being descendants of Thomas Holbrook, an early resident of Weymouth, Massachusetts.** Seth and Miriam were pioneer settlers in the plantation days of Peru. They lived in a log house on the tract of land east of the Daniel Fletcher farm, on the road leading to West Peru. The house stood on the north side of the road, on heights of land sloping east, on a very pretty and fertile swell of land. The Robertses "were honest, of good habits, good deportment, generous, hospitable, and good neighbors", in the words

---

* Town Records, Peru, Maine; Cole & Whitman, p. 675. Adams, Eloi A. *Madbury: Its People & Places*. Madbury, N.H.: Madbury Bicentennial Committee, 1968, pp. 84-6, reports that Seth Roberts, father of Jonathan Roberts of Madbury, was born in Wales about 1786. Ironically, this erroneous assertion is based on a small paper your present author prepared in the early 1960's. A neophite genealogist gave too much credence to the hazy memories and fuzzy family lore of his great aunts and uncles.

⁺ Hilton says that Miriam was the daughter of Jonah and Bethia (Drake) Fobes. Based on my own research into the Fobes family, I have concluded that Jonah and Bethia Fobes were almost certainly the parents of Benjamin and hence the grandparents of Miriam. The confusion may have arisen because Benjamin Fobes was both the father-in-law and the brother-in-law of Seth Roberts. See Turner, Hollis. *The History of Peru. . .From 1789 to 1911*. Augusta, Maine: Press of the Maine Farmer Pub. Co., 1911, p. 228. See also Fobes, Lawrence. *The Fobes Family in America*. Privately published, 1976, p. 38.

Town Records, Peru & Buckfield, Maine; U.S. Census, 1850.

** This statement based on my own research into collateral lines. Miriam has an interesting chart. Her maternal grandmother was a Lowell, from the well-known Massachusetts family of that name. She was a cousin of Henry David Thoreau. And her gr-gr grandparents Fobes are ancestors of Diana, the current (1992) Princess of Wales.

DESCENDANTS OF GEORGE & MARY ROBERTS

of a local historian. All of their children were born in Peru.[*] Seth Roberts served briefly during the War of 1812.[+] Children:

69.	i.	Benjamin, b. 5/9/1815.
70.	ii.	James, b. 2/25/1817.
	iii.	Anna, b. 9/7/1819; m. Henry E. Young, 5/14/1841; d. 8/25/1852. Five children.
	iv.	Elizabeth Webb, b. 1/11/1822; m. Charles G. Knox, 9/19/1840; d. 11/26/1901. Nine children.
71.	v.	Jonathan, b. 10/12/1824.
72.	vi.	William, b. 4/3/1827.
	vii.	Bethiah, b. 2/14/1829; m. Danville D. Knox, 11/6/1850; d. 11/11/1909. Eight children.
73.	viii.	Adrian Greenleaf, b. 2/25/1832.
	ix.	Nancy, b. 7/3/1834; d. 11/14/1837.
	x.	Miriam, b. 5/1/1837; m. -----Knox; d. 7/25/1903.
	xi.	Seth, b. 2/21/1840; d. during the Civil War while serving in the 5th Maine Regiment, Co. E.[#]

28. Eliphalet Roberts (Eliphalet[4], George[3], John[2], George[1]), a farmer, son of Eliphalet and Elizabeth (West) Roberts, was born in Strafford, Vermont, August 22(or2?), 1774, and died there March 19, 1854. He married Mary Evans in Strafford, December 7, 1797. She was born in New Hampshire, August 20, 1776, and died in Strafford, March 5, 1855.[**] Children:

	i.	Anna, b. 9/18/1798; m. Nathaniel Blanchard, 2/19/1826; d. 1/26/1855.

---

[*] Turner, pp. 117-8, 228-9 & 301.
[+] A list of Buckfield soldiers prepared in the mid-1800's by Virgil Parris.
[#] Civil War Records, National Archives, Washington.
[**] Roberts, Blanche J., p. 540.

FIFTH GENERATION

74.   ii. Eliphalet, b. 11/15/1801.

75.   iii. Zerah Norton, b. 10/20/1803.

       iv. John, b. 2/2/1806; m. (1) Lydia Gordon, 12/3/1829, (2) Caroline M. Avery, 2/2/1859.

       v. Elizabeth, b. 4/9/1808; m. Gershom Fox; d. Brattleboro, VT, 2/2/1887.

       vi. Mary, b. 7/7/1812; d. young.

       vii. Mary, b. 5/26/1814; m. (1) Joseph Cummings Lovejoy, (2) Roswell Morey.

       viii. Elsie O., b. 1/7/1818; m. Joseph Sargent, 4/25/1839; d. 1/24/1907. Ten children.

29. William Roberts (Eliphalet[4], George[3], John[2], George[1]), son of Eliphalet and Elizabeth (West) Roberts, was born in Strafford, Vermont, June 18, 1776 and died November 30, 1847. He married, firstly, Lena Percival, November 4, 1798, and, secondly, Orimel Morse, September 24, 1818, and thirdly, Mary (Tucker) Preston, March 16, 1829.* Children(?):

30. Daniel West Roberts (Eliphalet[4], George[3], John[2], George[1]), son of Eliphalet and Elizabeth (West) Roberts, was born in Strafford, Vermont, December 1, 1780, and died there in 1871. He married, firstly, Abigail Latham, May 3, 1804, secondly, Lydia English, March 8, 1847, and thirdly, Louisa (Johnson) Muzzey, May 19, 1852. Abigail died July 20, 1846, aged 62, Lydia died February 11, 1851, and Louisa died March 22, 1884, aged 76. The children below were born in Sharon, Vermont.⁺ Children:

76.   i. Royal, b. 5/22/1805.

77.   ii. Amplias, b. 8/18/1807.

---

   * Roberts, Blanche J., p. 539.
   ⁺ Roberts, Blanche J., p. 539; Kill & Russell, "Strafford Cemetery Records", p. 69; Bryant and Verret notes.

DESCENDANTS OF GEORGE & MARY ROBERTS

78.   iii.   James Lull, b. 4/1(or30?)/1809.
79.   iv.   West Daniel, b. 4/7/1811.
          v.   Abigail, b. 2/26/1813, m. Asa Dow.
          vi.   Elizabeth, b. 12/25/1814.
80.   vii.   Chester Merrill, b. 5/6/1817.
          viii.   Cordelia, b. 3/11/1819; m. Leonard Cook, 5/4/1835; d. 9/5/1893.
81.   ix.   Larkin, b. 2/3/1821.
          x.   Mary Adeline (twin), b. 6/27/1824; m. Lucian (No. 145) Roberts; d. 4/16/1863.
          xi.   Sarah Angeline (twin), b. 6/27/1824; m. Willis L. (No. 144) Roberts; d. 10/1/1867.
82.   xii.   Darius Witt, b. 7/7/1828.

31. George Roberts (Eliphalet[4], George[3], John[2], George[1]), son of Eliphalet and Sarah (Sawyer) Roberts, was born in Strafford, Vermont, June 11, 1788. He married Lavinia Jones, daughter of Ephraim and Betsey Jones, July 4, 1813.* Children:

          i.   Jerusha, b. 6/24/1814.
          ii.   George, b. 8/30/1815.

32. Moses Roberts (Eliphalet[4], George[3], John[2], George[1]), son of Eliphalet and Sarah (Sawyer) Roberts, was born in Sharon, Vermont, May 9, 1796 and died August 14, 1866. He married Catherine Davis, January 8, 1818. She was the daughter of Ashel and Nancy (Smith) Davis, and was born in Hubbardston, Massachusetts, February 3, 1793.⁺ Children:

          i.   Almira Maria, b. 1819(?); m. 11/15/1841, Robertson A. Clark. Five children.

---

     * Roberts, Blanche J., p. 543.
     ⁺ Roberts, Blanche J., p. 558; Bryant and Verret notes.

FIFTH GENERATION

83.   ii. Orlando Hartwell, b. 8/3/1824.

iii. Alden E., b. 1829(?), m. Sarah Sargent.

iv. Laura Alzina, m. Reubin Marsh. One child.

v. Francese Almira, b. 5/13/1831; m. 3/18/1847, Henry Willard Benton; d. 1/31/1904, Lebanon, NH.

vi. Harriet Louella, b. 11/14/1836; m. Henry Seavey Blake; d. 2/2/1912, Minneapolis, MN. One ch.

84.   vii. Joseph Johnson, b. 1836.

viii. Mary Ann E., m. 8/4/1859, William DeLoss Clough; d. 7/4/1900.

ix. Henry.

33. Stephen Roberts (Eliphalet^4, George^3, John^2, George^1), a farmer, son of Eliphalet and Sarah (Sawyer) Roberts, was born May 20, 1803, in Strafford, Vermont. He died December 13, 1866, apparently in Vermont. Stephen married, firstly, Clarissa Russell, July 10, 1825, in Strafford. He married, secondly, Alvira Fox, daughter of Charles and Margaret (Allen) Fox, about 1836. Alvira was born in Lyme, New Hampshire, and died in Strafford, about 1888.* Children:

85.   i. Stephen, b. 7/18/1838.

ii. Hannah, b.c. 1840; m. (1) Charles Kimball, 10/15/1865, (2) John H. Smith, 9/24/1870.

iii. Charles Frank, b.c. 1842; d.c. 1925.

iv. George, b. 5/19/1843; d. 5/5/1864. A Civil War casualty at the Battle of the Wilderness.

v. Elsy, b.c. 1846; m. Simon B. Harris, 1/10/1863.

vi. Lucinda, b.c. 1848; m. David K. Dike; d. 5/24/1915.

---

* Roberts, Blanche J., p. 564.

86. vii. West Daniel, b.c. 1849.

 viii. Sarah Elizabeth, b. 2/6/1850; m. Amos Kimball, 7/29/1866; d. 3/27/1892.

 ix. Amelia, b. 5/8/1851; d. 8/31/1859, of diptheria.

 x. Alnett, b. 3/1/1854; m. Oscar A.R. Packard, 10/10/1869.

 xi. Olive, b. 3/5/1855; m. Alonzo S. (No. 201) Roberts, 3/4/1879; d. 1/5/1937.

34. John Roberts (Ezekiel[4], Samuel[3], John[2], George[1]), son of Ezekiel and Margaret (Crusey) Roberts, was born in or near Raymond, New Hampshire in 1772 or 1773, and died there in 1859. The name of his first wife, who died March 18, 1829 aged 54, is not known. The second one, Mariam, died October 21, 1851, aged 76. This family lived in Raymond for many years. Their real estate in 1850 was valued at $ 100. There were eight children by the first wife, although four of them died at early ages and their names are not known. The last two children below are by the second wife.* Children:

87. i. Samuel, b. 1800.

88. ii. Thomas, b. 1802-3.

 iii. Daniel, b. 1807-8, m. Sarah J.D. -----. No ch. in 1850 census; d. 9/15/1861.

89. iv. William, b. 1813.

 v. Andrew J., b. 8/26/1830 (?); d. 8/29/1887. An unm. shoemaker in Candia, NH, 1850.

 vi. Sarah, b. 1831/2, m. Samuel S. Smart.(?)

35. Jonathan Roberts (Jonathan[4], Jonathan[3], John[2], George[1]), son of Jonathan and Hannah Roberts, was born in 1778, probably

---

* Fullonton, pp. 315 & 325-353; Hardon, "Roberts-Unconnected", Vol. I, p. 200; 1850 Census, Raymond, N.H.

FIFTH GENERATION

in New Hampshire, and died at Lowell, Vermont, July 1, 1845, and is buried in the Old Protestant Cemetery there. He married Olive Beede on January 21, 1802. The last three children below were born in Enosburg, Vermont, the remainder in Strafford.* Children:

      i. Azariah Beede, b. 9/18/1804, Strafford, VT; killed by a falling tree 2/2/1846, Lowell, VT.

90.   ii. Alba, b. 10/25/1806.

      iii. John Lord(?), b. 2/26/1809; d. young.

91.   iv. Dudley Avery, b. 4/12/1811.

      v. Charles, b. 7/27/1815; d. 11/22/1896.

      vi. John Lord, b. 3/18/1818; m. 6/30/1854, Hannah Williams, Fair Haven, VT.

      vii. Elizabeth, b. 6/25/1820; m. Ebenezer Dunham; d. 10/31/1891.

92.   viii. Jonathan Martin, b. 12/10/1822.

      ix. William Merrit, b. 8/10/1826; d. 10/5/1873.

93.   x. Andrew Jackson, b. 8/14/1829.

36. Daniel Roberts (Jonathan⁴, Jonathan³, John², George¹), son of Jonathan and Hannah Roberts, was born in Vermont, April 9, 1785, and died in the Randolph, Vermont poor house, August 9, 1860. He married in Strafford, Vermont, October 23, 1825, Hannah Maxfield. The two children below were born in Strafford.⁺ Children:

      i. Alonzo, b. 9/18/1826.

94.   ii. Daniel Azro, b. 5/4/1828.

37. John Roberts (Jonathan⁴, Jonathan³, John², George¹), son of Jonathan and Hannah Roberts, was born in Vermont, April 14,

---

* Notes of Rae D. Laitres; Miles, p. 76.
⁺ Roberts, Blanche J., p. 535.

DESCENDANTS OF GEORGE & MARY ROBERTS

1787. He married in Westmore, Vermont, Sarah Carr, June 6, 1810. The three children below were born in Strafford.* Children:

    i. Clarissa Tracy, b. 6/5/1816.

    ii. Amos P., b. 6/14/1818; m. (2) Hannah (Gilson) Keep, 2/1/1867.

    iii. Lucina, b. 6/6/1820.

38. Noah Roberts (Jonathan^4, Jonathan^3, John^2, George^1), son of Jonathan and Hannah Roberts, was born in Tunbridge, Vermont, March 29, 1789 and died of heart disease in Royalton, Vermont, May 23, 1860. His body lies in the North Royalton cemetery. He married, firstly, Polly Carr, December 4, 1809 in Strafford, Vermont, by the Rev. Aaron Buzzell. Polly was born March 9, 1790, the daughter of Bradbury and Mehitable (Preston) Carr. After Polly died in January of 1834, Noah married, secondly, Lucinda (Illsley) Vesper, in Norwich, by the Rev. Newell Culver. Lucinda died June 4, 1868 and is buried in Royalton.⁺ Children:

    i. Persis, b. 12/14/1809; m. -----Wetherbee.

95.   ii. Daniel Carr, b. 9/10/1811.

    iii. Hannah, b. 12/1/1813; m. David May, 6/21/1840.

    iv. Mary Pervilla, b. 10/6/1815.

    v. Louisa, b. 9/3/1817; d. 2/1830.

    vi. Roxalana, b. 1/1/1822; m. Royal Simonds; d. 12/30/1904.

    vii. Lucy, b. 5/11/1826.

    viii. Angeline Clarissa, b. 6/7/1828; m. Samuel Smith, (2?) -----Palmer; d. 9/25/1880.

    ix. John, b. 5/30/1832.

---

* Roberts, Blanche J., p. 550.
⁺ Roberts, Blanche J., p. 560.

SIXTH GENERATION

39. Calvin Roberts (Leavitt[5], Alexander[4], John[3], John[2], George[1]), son of Leavitt and Lovey (Hawkins) Roberts, was born in Meredith, New Hampshire, April 2, 1807, and died in Holderness, New Hampshire, July 29, 1849. He married Mary M. Whitten, June 21, 1829.[*] Child:

   96.   i.   Alfred, b. 2/17/1832.

40. Benjamin Roberts (Leavitt[5], Alexander[4], John[3], John[2], George[1]), son of Leavitt and Lovey (Hawkins) Roberts, was born in Meredith, New Hampshire, in 1809 (or 1802?). He died March 30, 1886, and is buried in the North Sanbornton (New Hampshire) Cemetery. He married Mary ("Polly") Leavitt of Sutton, Vermont, in 1836, in Sheffield, Vermont. She was born in 1804 or 1805. Benjamin was a blacksmith and a deacon in the Pine Hill Baptist Church. This family lived in Meredith and Sanborntown, New Hampshire.[+] Children:

       i.   Benjamin Franklin, b. 8/6/1839 (or 8/28/1840?); m. Lizzie E. Woodworth, 10/12/1880.

      ii.   Ellen P., b. 6/1/1844; d. 9/7/1846.

41. Thomas Roberts (Leavitt[5], Alexander[4], John[3], John[2], George[1]), son of Leavitt and Lovey (Hawkins) Roberts, was born in Meredith, New Hampshire, September 11, 1812, and died there December 1, 1887. He married Nancy C. Wiggin, the daughter of Winthrop and Hannah (or Kate?) Wiggin. Nancy was born in Meredith in 1813 and died there March 31, 1868.[#] Children:

       i.   Orrin Nason, b. 4/16/1838; d. 5/13/1926.

      ii.   George, b. 1840.

     iii.   Eben, b. 1842-3.

     iv.   James Franklin, b. 11/5/1852; d. 6/2/1900.

---

   [*] Hardon, "Roberts-Unconnected", Vol. 1, p. 32.

   [+] Hanaford, p. 434; Runnels, p. 599; 1850 Census, Sanbornton; Hardon, "Roberts-Unconnected", Vol. 1, p. 25.

   [#] Hanaford, p. 434; Hardon, "Roberts-Unconnected", Vol. II, p. 159; I.G.I.; 1850 Census, Meredith.

DESCENDANTS OF GEORGE & MARY ROBERTS

42. George Washington Roberts (Leavitt[5], Alexander[4], John[3], John[2], George[1]), son of Leavitt and Lovey (Hawkins) Roberts, was born in Meredith, New Hampshire, October 10, 1816. He died in North Sanbornton, New Hampshire, February 4, 1896 and is buried there. He married Lydia Cole Howland, October 24, 1837. She was born November 22, 1819 in Lisbon, New Hampshire, and died in North Sanbornton, August 14, 1897. She was the daughter of Benjamin and Dorcas (Spooner) Howland.[*] Children:

    i. Adaline M., b. 9/16/1838; m. Caleb Sargent, 3/17/1855; d. 2/28/1901. Three children.

    ii. Leavitt Sylvester, b. 9/11/1840; m. (1) Laura E. Burley, (2) Nora Liston. No children. Civil War Veteran.

    iii. Ellen P., b. 9/26/1846; d. 7/22/1926; m. Horace P. Howe. At least one child - George Howe.

    iv. Elizabeth Moses, b. 8/6/1849; m. Edward Carleton, 5/19/1870; d. 6/6/1903. Two children.

43. Isaac Roberts (Joseph[5], Joseph[4], George[3], John[2], George[1]), son of Joseph and Esther (Hamlin) Roberts, a twin, was born in Buckfield, Maine, May 10, 1784, and died in or near Brooks, Maine, October 4, 1862, of "paralysis". He married, firstly, Abigail Merrill of Hebron, Maine, in 1810, and secondly, after her death in 1834, Sarah Cobb of Limerick, Maine, in 1836. Sarah was born July 16, 1799, and died June 20, 1884. The two final children shown below were hers. This family lived for many years in Brooks, where the children below were all born. Having attended Hebron Academy, Isaac became a teacher of English grammar, and later a land agent and owner of a business in Belfast, Maine. He was an active member of the Freewill Baptist Church and later

---

    [*] Runnels, p. 599; 1850 Census, Sanbornton; research notes of Esther C. Wyatt.

SIXTH GENERATION

united with the Quakers.* Children:

97.   i.   Justin, b. 1811.

98.   ii.   Milton M., b. 1/4/1815.

         iii.   Clarkson B., b.c. 1818; m. Mary Nickerson; d. Los Angeles, CA, 10/1896. One child d. young.

         iv.   Addison J., b.c. 1822; d. Brooks, 1867; unm.

99.   v.   Isaac Pennington, b. 10/18/1826.

         vi.   Sophronia, d. young.

100.   vii.   Warren Norton, b. 5/2/1839.

44. Jacob Roberts (Joseph[5], Joseph[4], George[3], John[2], George[1]), a twin, son of Joseph and Esther (Hamlin) Roberts, was born in Buckfield, Maine, May 10, 1784, and died in North Vassalboro, Maine, March 15, 1856. He married, firstly, Huldah Myrick of Hebron, Maine, daughter of Beezaleel and Huldah (Moulton) Myrick. She was born in North Yarmouth, Maine, in 1793, and died April 6, 1845, of "paralysis". Jacob married, secondly, Abby Jenkins of Vassalboro, Maine, in March of 1852. Abby died in August of the same year. Jacob was a physician and practiced in Brooks, Maine for nearly forty years, before moving to Vassalboro, where he had a large practice as well. He was an advocate of homeopathic medicine and was very active in local politics, first as a Whig and later as an abolitionist. He followed the Quaker faith and was said to have had extensive investments in land and timber at times. Except for the eldest, who was born in Buckfield, the following children were all born in Brooks.⁺ Children:

101.   i.   Hamlin Myrick, b. 1811.

102.   ii.   Jacob Wellington, b. 11/29/1813.

---

* Buckfield town records, p. 19; Grant, pp. 11, 29-35.
⁺ Buckfield town records, p. 19; Grant, pp. 36-65.

DESCENDANTS OF GEORGE & MARY ROBERTS

	iii.	Amorena Deborah Theresa, b. 9/2/1815; m. Ezra Manter, 1836; d. 6/20/1852. No children.
103.	iv.	Barnabas Myrick, b. 10/17/1818.
104.	v.	Charles Linneus, b. 4/14/1821.
105.	vi.	Porteus Beezaleel, b. 7/27/1823.
	vii.	Emily Esther, b. 1825; d. 1834, froze to death on the way home from school.
	viii.	Phebe Young, b. 4/5/1828; m. William P. Miller, 1847; d. 9/1849. One child.
	ix.	Huldah Jane, b. 12/19/1830; m. Joseph H. Barrows, 3/25/1852; d. after 1902. Three children.
	x.	Ellen Cecilia, b. 5/27/1833; m. & div. Ezra Manter (her brother-in-law), 12/1852; d. 8/10/1901. No children.
	xi.	William Pinkney, b. 1/25/1836; m. (1) Susan A. Weeks, 1859, (2) Cora B. Ferris, 4/14/1888; went West to find a cure for his consumption, became a doctor in Chicago and later Janesville, WI; d. after 1902. No children.

45. Gilman Roberts (Joseph⁵, Joseph⁴, George³, John², George¹), son of Joseph and Esther (Hamlin) Roberts, was born in Buckfield, Maine, October 28, 1788, and died in Brooks, Maine, May 4, 1877. He married, firstly, Ann Leathers, who was born in Buckfield, April 1791 and died in 1829. Gilman married, secondly, in 1830, Susan Bachelder of Swanville, Maine, who was born in 1795 and died March 25, 1881. Ann had eight children and Susan four. This family lived and farmed in Brooks for many years, except for a few years in the 1850's spent in Bangor, Maine.*
Children:

| 106. | i. | Ahira, b. 2/12/1812. |

---

* Buckfield town records, p. 19; Grant, pp. 73-85.

SIXTH GENERATION

- ii. Caroline,b.c. 1813;m. Israel Elliot, 1839. 2ch.
- iii. Florilla Decker, b. 7/6/1815; m. Emerson Cilly, 1838; d. after 1902. Five children.
- iv. Sarah, b. 1819; m. Moses Page. Two ch. d.young.
- v. Margaret, b. 1821; d. 6/3/1878. No children.
- vi. Harriet, b. 7/4/1823; m. George W. Elliot, 10/13/1844. Lived in Rockford, MN. 2 Ch.
- vii. Edwin, b. 1825; drowned at young age.

107.
- viii. Ezra, b. 1827.
- ix. Hannah, b. 7/19/1831; m. Samuel Reynolds, 10/10/1851. One child.
- x. Miriam, b. 6/19/1833; m. (1) 1854, Renselaer Huxford, (2) 5/19/1883, John J. Jacques. 6 ch.
- xi. Almira, b. 7/19/1835; m. (1) William White, (2) John Ballou; d. Brooks, 7/2/1865. One child.
- xii. Clara, b. 4/12/1840; m. David Lowry; d. Brooks, 5/3/1874.

46. Enoch Roberts (Joseph[5], Joseph[4], George[3], John[2], George[1]), son of Joseph and Esther (Hamlin) Roberts, was born in Buckfield, Maine, March 27, 1791, and died in Brooks, Maine, July 25, 1858. He married Eleanor Leathers, who was born in Buckfield, February 1793 and died in Brooks, November 30, 1848. Later in life Enoch married Eliza Aborn of Knox, Maine, who was born about 1808 and died after 1902.[*] Children:

- i. Orena, d. aged c. 20.
- ii. Tabitha, b. 9/8/1815; m. George Gardner, 1/1/1839; d. 1/2/1896, Merrill, ME. Six children.

108.
- iii. Jacob, b. 3/4/1818.

---

[*] Buckfield town records, p. 19; Grant, pp. 84-89.

DESCENDANTS OF GEORGE & MARY ROBERTS

   iv. Mary, b. 5/12/1820; m. Samuel Hall, 1843; d. Castle Hill, ME, 1/27/1865. Eight children.

   v. Hannah, m. (1) James Wiggin, (2) -----Churchill; lived in Kansas. Four children.

109. vi. Gilman, b.c. 1825.

110. vii. Alfred, b.c. 1827.

   viii. Anna, b. 1830; m. Alfred F. Watson. Three ch.

   ix. Thomas Jefferson, b. 1832; d. 1834.

   x. Thomas Jefferson, b. 1835; d. 1875, Aroostook, ME; unm.

   xi. Eleanor, b. 1838; m. Joseph Files. Three children.

47. Joseph Roberts (Joseph^5, Joseph^4, George^3, John^2, George^1), son of Joseph and Esther (Hamlin) Roberts, was born in Buckfield, Maine, November 2, 1799, and died in Levant, Maine, October 26, 1885. He married Lydia Knight, daughter of Nathaniel and Sarah (Webb) Knight. Lydia was born in Falmouth, Maine, December 26, 1798, and died in Levant, January 19, 1894. Joseph was in the lumber business in Palmyra, Maine, and later farmed in Brooks, where he had grown up. He and his wife were active in the temperance movement, the Free Will Baptist Church, and the Free Soil and later Republican Party.* Children:

   i. Elizabeth Cates, b. 8/1/1825, Jackson, Maine; m. Milton (No. 98) Roberts, a cousin, 8/1/1843; d. 12/5/1895, in Minnesota. Four children.

   ii. Abigail Knight, b. 10/7/1829; m. Luther D. Spencer, 4/15/1852. One child.

   iii. Nathaniel Knight, b. 7/9/1832; d. 7/29/1875; unm. A Civil War Veteran (First Maine Cavalry, Co. A.), severely wounded and never fully recovered.

---

* Grant, pp. 103-6.

SIXTH GENERATION

48. Benjamin Roberts (Joseph[5], Joseph[4], George[3], John[2], George[1]), son of Joseph and Margaret (Hall) Roberts, was the first child born in Brooks, Maine, February 4, 1804. He died of starvation at Salisbury, North Carolina, while in a Confederate prisoner of war camp, November 23, 1864. He married on August 16, 1843, Nancy Cilley, who was born April 1, 1827, and was still living in Brooks, Maine, at the turn of the century. A millman and a farmer, Benjamin enlisted in Company I of the Fourth Maine Regiment, December 5, 1863.[*] Children:

    i. Delphina H., b. 6/7/1845; m. Wellington R. Stimpson, 9/11/1867. Five children.

    ii. Rose Ina, b. 7/7/1846; m. Stanley A. Perkins, 6/8/1866. Two children.

    iii. Leila J., b. 12/2/1847; d. 1/1884, Lewiston, ME.

111. iv. Charles H., b. 7/15/1853.

    v. Julia Almeda, b. 12/17/1854; m. Allen Daggett, 7/14/1872. Three ch.

49. John Roberts (Joseph[5], Joseph[4], George[3], John[2], George[1]), son of Joseph and Margaret (Hall) Roberts, was born in Brooks, Maine, January, 1806 and died in Minnesota, May, 1886. He married Harriet Jackson in 1834. Their first two children were born in Waldo, Maine, and the remaining ones in Brooks. John was a millwright by trade and was active in the temperance and Free Soil movements.[+] Children:

112. i. Sharon, b. 1/31/1836.

    ii. Augusta Ann, b. 8/8/1838; m. Reuben Harwood, 1885; d. 11/24/1901, Westboro, MA.

---

[*] Grant, pp. 107-8.
[+] Grant, pp. 109-11.

iii. Lenora Avilda, b. 4/2/1840; m. (1) 12/1859, Frank Knowles (k. Civil War), (2) 12/1887, Daniel P. Conover. Lived in Champlin, MN. Two children.

iv. Jay, b. 11/14/1842; d. 8/23/63 of "fever" contracted while serving with the 26th Maine Regiment in Louisiana. unm.

v. Eddie, d.c. 10 mo.

vi. Rose Alba, b. 10/14/1844; m. Clarendon Boody, 12/7/1865. Lived in St. Paul (MN?). Three ch.

113. vii. Everett W., b. 11/4/1846.

viii. Dora, b. 10/23/1850; m. (1) Edward Boody, (2) Frank Sanborn. Lived in West Somerville, MA. Two children.

50. Alfred J. Roberts (Joseph^5, Joseph^4, George^3, John^2, George^1), son of Joseph and Margaret (Hall) Roberts, was born in Brooks, Maine, October 21, 1807, and died there October 15, 1868. He married firstly, on October 10, 1831, Caroline Davis, daughter of Joseph Davis. She was born April 5, 1813, and died October 9, 1857. In 1860 Alfred married, secondly, his second cousin once removed, Sarah Roberts, the daughter of Watson (No. 63) Roberts. The first eleven children below are by Caroline and the last three by Sarah, who was born January 25, 1838, and died in Brooks, August 25, 1877. Alfred had extensive business interests in the Brooks area, not only owning large tracts of timber land but also owning and operating lumber mills. He was active in the temperance and free soil movements, and was said to have been a very strong person, both physically and mentally.* Children:

i. Adelaide S., b. 11/12/1832; unm.

ii. Mary Ann, b. 3/10/1835; m. 11/10/1853, Michael Chase. One child.

---

* Grant, pp. 112-4.

SIXTH GENERATION

- iii. Louise C., b. 8/3/1837; m. 6/21/1865, Otis Libby (a Civil War veteran). Two children.
- iv. Abbie D., b. 6/9/1839; m. 11/24/1862, Michael Chase; d. 10/14/1885. One child.
- v. Charles Alfred, b. 4/22/1842; d. 4/1/1846.
- vi. Edward, b. 12/3/1844; d. 2/5/1846.
- vii. Alfred, b. 1/10/1847; d. 3/15/1855.
- viii. Sarah Frances, b. 3/15/1849; m. 2/8/1877, Hollis Blackstone. Three children.
- ix. Ellen, b. 1/16/1852; m. 12/24/1871, James W. Jones. Two children.
- x. Isabel, b. 3/23/1855; m. 9/16/1891, Benjamin Robinson (a Civil War veteran).
- xi. William, b. 9/5/1857; d. 9/23/1858.
- xii. Laura, b. 3/20/1861; d. 4/20/1862.
- xiii. Alfred J., b. 7/28/1863; d. 2/28/1875.
- xiv. Henry M., b. 5/7/1865; d. 9/7/1867.

51. Timothy T. Roberts (Joseph[5], Joseph[4], George[3], John[2], George[1]), a farmer and miller, son of Joseph and Margaret (Hall) Roberts, was born in Brooks, Maine, July 31, 1812 and died there March 19, 1868. He married Nancy E. Gardner, March 18, 1835. She was born October 3, 1807 and died February 18, 1894.[*]
Children:

- 114. i. William Henry Harrison, 10/31/1835.
- ii. Manter Alverado, b. 10/1/1838; m. 1/25/1875, Mercy P. Silsby. Veteran of Civil War (19th Maine Reg.). Lived in Bangor, ME. Children?

---

[*] Grant, pp. 115-6.

	iii.	Marcia Ann, b. 11/30/1840; m. 3/22/1856, John Hall; d. 12/14/1889, Lowell MA. Two children.
115.	iv.	Oscar E., b. 6/7/1844.

52. Nathan Hall Roberts (Joseph^5, Joseph^4, George^3, John^2, George^1), son of Joseph and Margaret (Hall) Roberts, was born in Brooks, Maine, June 9, 1815 and died in Minneapolis, Minnesota, September 9, 1892. He married Elvira Irish, the daughter of Stephen Irish of Buckfield, Maine. She was born there in 1813 and died in October, 1872, in Minnesota. On April 25, 1874, Nathan remarried, to Mary Sophia Langham, who was born in Norway, May 14, 1846. This family moved to Minnesota about 1856 to take a government homestead there. Nathan was a very successful farmer and was a commissioner of Hennepin County for six years and later an alderman of the city of Minneapolis.* Children:

	i.	Arrington, b. 8/28/1842; m. (1) 7/3/1869, Jennette Ray, div., (2) Josephine Burnham, 1876. Ch.?
116.	ii.	Charles A., b. 4/5/1846.
	iii.	Mary, b. 4/15/1850; m. 12/22/1868, Isaac Layman (Civil War veteran). Lived in MN. Seven ch.
117.	iv.	John Nelson, b. 4/11/1876.
118.	v.	Guy Hall, b. 12/8/1877.

53. Winslow Roberts (Joseph^5, Joseph^4, George^3, John^2, George^1), son of Joseph and Margaret (Hall) Roberts, was born in Brooks, Maine, March 8, 1821, and died in Waterville, Maine, June 17, 1879. He was married three times. His first wife was Amelia Putnam, who died in June of 1849; his second wife was Cornelia Rand, who died in Framingham, Massachusetts, in January of 1864. Winslow and Cornelia had the first two children listed below. With his third wife, Maria Bangs, he had the remaining five children. Winslow taught school and also practiced law. He also owned a successful boot manufacturing company in Brooks and later Waterville. In September 1859 he was elected to the Maine State

---

* Grant, pp. 116-120.

SIXTH GENERATION

Legislature. He put aside all of those pursuits in 1861 to accept a commission as lieutenant in Company I and later as captain in Company D, Fourteenth Maine Regiment. In the latter part of 1863, he accepted a commission as a captain in the U.S. Coast Guard. After Winslow's death Maria and some of the children relocated to Minneapolis, Minnesota.* Children:

    i. Cora, b. 7/30/1855, Shrewsbury, MA; m. Wesley J. Maynard. Lived in Portland, ME. One child.

    ii. Ellen A., b. 4/7/1861, Brooks; m. Edward E. Sibley. One child.

    iii. Edward W., b. 12/20/1865, Brooks;m.10/19/1887, Grace Burwell of Minneapolis. Children?

    iv. Alice May, b. 5/5/1868, Brooks; d. 3/15/1873.

    v. James Alton, b. 10/23/1874, Waterville; m. Georgeanna Guptill of Minneapolis, 11/28/1900. Children?

119.   vi. Walter Henry, b. 2/15/1876, Waterville.

    vii. Mary Frances, b. 3/21/1879, Waterville. Lived in Minneapolis.

54. **Rufus Roberts** (Joseph^5, Joseph^4, George^3, John^2, George^1), son of Joseph and Margaret (Hall) Roberts, was born in Brooks, Maine, April 14, 1823, and died in Minneapolis, Minnesota, in May of 1900. He married Adeline Files, who was born in Thorndike, Maine, May 10, 1823. Their first five children were born in Brooks and the last one in Minneapolis. Rufus was a mill worker in Brooks, and later worked for the city of Minneapolis. During the Civil War he served as a second lieutenant in the Fourteenth Maine Regiment.⁺ Children:

    i. Juliette, b. 9/17/1846; m. A.E. Ayers, 1869. Lived in Minneapolis. Ten children.

---

  * Grant, pp. 120-3.
  ⁺ Grant, pp. 123-5.

	ii.	Ella (twin), b. 7/20/1850; d. 1851.
	iii.	Joseph (twin), b. 7/20/1850; d. 7/20/1850.
120.	iv.	Fred Leslie, b. 7/21/1854.
121.	v.	Frank H., b. 12/9/1860.
	vi.	Addie D., b. 8/4/1869; m. Frank Colville, Jr., 4/4/1890. Four children, poss. more.

55. Jotham Roberts (Jonathan^5, Joseph^4, George^3, John^2, George^1), a merchant and cabinet maker, son of Jonathan and Prudence (Willard) Roberts, was born in Buckfield, Maine, December 28, 1787, and died there April 30, 1865. He married, firstly, in 1810, Mary Richardson, who was born in 1792 or 1793, and died in Buckfield, March 4, 1850. His second wife was the Widow Lydia Doe (nee Doble), and the third was the widow Hannah Woodman (nee Walker), of Freeport, Maine.* Children:

	i.	Fidelia, b. 12/5/1811; m. Leonard Rowe. Five ch.
	ii.	Iantha, b. 5/13/1813, Vassalboro; m. John Totman, 2/13/1831; d. 10/3/1852, Clinton, ME. Ten ch.
	iii.	Prudence, b. 3/12/1815; d. 1848, Buckfield. A teacher, apparently unm.
	iv.	Orlando, b. 6/25/1817; m. -----Neal. Lived in Bridgeport, CT and Ohio. Ten children.
	v.	Aurelia, b. 4/24/1819; d. 1846, Buckfield.
	vi.	Addison, b. 1/29/1821; d. 1822.
	vii.	Loring, b. 12/28/1822; d. 1824.
122.	viii.	Thomas Loring, b. 5/6/1825.
	ix.	Rebecca, b. 3/16/1830, Buckfield; m. Sidney A. Allen, 5/1850; d. 9/1892, Auburn, ME. Three ch.

---

* Buckfield town records, p. 9; Grant, pp. 129-132.

SIXTH GENERATION

123.   x.   Albert Augustus, b. 1/13/1832.

56. Daniel Roberts (Jonathan[5], Joseph[4], George[3], John[2], George[1]), son of Jonathan and Prudence (Willard) Roberts, was born in Buckfield, Maine, December 30, 1791. He married Mary Haskell. They had ten children in all, six of whom died at early ages.[*] Children:

    i.   Clementine, m. Simon Thompson. Two children.

    ii. Cyrus, b. 1825; m. Abby Marriam. Lived in Lawrence, MA. Children?

    iii. John P., m. Widow Varney. Lived in Mapleton, ME. A Civil War Veteran. Children?

    iv. Caroline, m. F. Ball. Lived in Mapleton. 3 ch.

57. Willard Roberts (Jonathan[5], Joseph[4], George[3], John[2], George[1]), son of Jonathan and Prudence (Willard) Roberts, was born in Buckfield, Maine, March 27(or 21?), 1796, and died in Brooks, Maine, in July of 1867. He married Ruth Edwards, who was born in August of 1796 and died in June of 1867, in Brooks. She was a Quaker.[+] Children:

124.   i.   Alonzo, b. 10/1819.

    ii.   Willard, b. 1823; d. young.

    iii. Marsters, b. 1825; d. young.

125.   iv.   Daniel Edwards, b. 11/1828.

58. Sylvanus Irish Roberts (John[5], Joseph[4], George[3], John[2], George[1]), son of John and Miriam (Irish) Roberts, was born in Brooks, Maine, November 9, 1804, and died in Stockton, Maine, April 25, 1872. He married, firstly, Mary Jane Thompson of Brooks, who died February 7, 1842, and secondly, in 1844, Remember (Record) Warren, of Buckfield. There were four children by each union. Sylvanus spent his early life with relatives

---

[*] Buckfield town records, p. 9; Grant, p. 136.
[+] Buckfield town records, p. 9; Grant, pp. 136-7.

in Oxford County, Maine, and went to Ohio to live with his father for a time. He returned to Maine to build a mill in Waldo Plantation, Maine. Later this family owned a large farm in Stockton. Sylvanus was very active in the temperance movement and served as sheriff of Waldo County in 1855.* Children:

126.	i.	Orpheus.
	ii.	Daphne, m. (1) Frank G. Staples, (2) Ferdinand A. Maxwell, 10/6/1873. Five children.
	iii.	Urbana, m. J. Wilford Staples. Six children.
	iv.	Laurens, d. 1/25/1863, serving in the Civil War.
127.	v.	Lloyd.
128.	vi.	Lucullus.
	vii.	Jane A., m. (1) Eugene Waterman, (2) Jules McHamy. Lived in Glenville, CA. Three ch.
129.	viii.	Dexter.

59. Jonathan Roberts (Samuel[5], Jonathan[4], George[3], John[2], George[1]), son of Samuel and Abigail (Wheeler) Roberts, was born in Windham (or possibly Turner) Maine, March (or May?) 11, 1792. He married Susan. They lived in Brooks, Maine.† Children:

130.	i.	Josiah W., b.c. 1825/6.
	ii.	William H., b.c. 1829.
	iii.	Cyrus H., b.c. 1831.
131.	iv.	Almond B., b.c. 1835.
	v.	Abby A., b.c. 1837.
	vi.	Sarah L., b.c. 1839.

60. Samuel Roberts (Samuel[5], Jonathan[4], George[3], John[2], George[1]), a farmer, son of Samuel and Abigail (Wheeler) Roberts,

---

* Grant, pp. 138-142.
† Hilton, supplement, p. 1.

SIXTH GENERATION

was born in Turner, Maine, in July, 1800, and died in Brooks, Maine, June 23, 1862, and is buried in the Lower (or New) Cemetery there. He married, firstly, Margaret H. Clifford, in Unity, Maine, May 21, 1830. She was the daughter of Joseph T. and Elizabeth (Priest) Clifford. Margaret was born in Camden, Maine, October 8, 1805, and died in Brooks, Maine, in 1833-5. Samuel married, secondly, Catherine Fogg, in Brooks, Maine, March 29, 1835. She was the daughter of George and Lydia (Marr) Fogg. Catherine was born in Limington, Maine, November 27, 1792, and died in Brooks, Maine, July 29, 1863, and is buried near her husband.* Children:

132. i. Gilman III, b. 4/14/1831.

133. ii. Watson Clifford, b. 3/12/1833.

61. Seth Roberts (Samuel[5], Jonathan[4], George[3], John[2], George[1]), a farmer, son of Samuel and Abigail (Wheeler) Roberts, was born in Brooks, Maine, in 1804. He married, firstly, Mary Clifford, October 30, 1830, in Unity, Maine. Mary, the daughter of Joseph T. & Elizabeth (Priest) Clifford, was born in Northport, Maine, October 6, 1808, and apparently died about 1840. Seth married, secondly, Adeline McLaughlin, who was born in 1813.⁺ Children:

    i.   Nancy, b.c. 1833.

    ii. Ellen, b.c. 1836.

    iii. Jane, b.c. 1838.

    iv. Ezra, b.c. 1839; m. Susan -----.

    v.   Eli, b.c. 1841; m. Julia -----.

    vi. Julia A., b.c. 1843; m. Thomas Jefferson Clifford, 1/27/1865, Monroe, ME.

    vii. Horace, b.c. 1844.

---

   * Jones notes; Hilton, p.9.
   ⁺ Hilton, supplement p. 1; Jones notes.

viii. Amarina, b.c. 1848.

ix. Joseph A., b.c. 1849.

x. Triphena, b. 1851.

xi. Emily, b. 1853-4.

62. Josiah Roberts (Samuel^5, Jonathan^4, George^3, John^2, George^1), a farmer, son of Samuel and Abigail (Wheeler) Roberts, was born in Brooks, Maine about 1806, and died there September 21, 1881. Both he and his wife are buried in the McClure (or McLune?) Cemetery in Wentworth's field, on Route 7, in Brooks. He married Jane Jellison, who was born in Monroe, Maine, in 1813 and died August 28, 1846, in Brooks.* Children:

    i. Martha J., b. 1834; m. -----Kendall. 3 ch.

134.   ii. Jonathan D., b. 8/11/1835.

    iii. Catharine, b.c. 1836; m. -----Cilley; d. 4/21/1886. Three children.

135.   iv. Levi, b.c. 1837-8.

    v. Wellington, b. 1841; m. Nancy Pease. Six ch.

63. Watson Roberts (Samuel^5, Jonathan^4, George^3, John^2, George^1), son of Samuel and Abigail (Wheeler) Roberts, was born in Brooks, Maine, in December of 1809 and died there March 7, 1879, and is buried in a cemetery near A.R. Pilley's house. He married Mary -----, who was born in July of 1808 and died January 30, 1879, and is buried near her husband.⁺ Children:

    i. Hulda, b.c. 1836.

    ii. Sarah A.("Sally"), b. 1/25/1838; m. Alfred J. (No. 50) Roberts (a second cousin once removed), 1860; d. Brooks, 8/25/1877. Three children.

---

    * Hilton, supplement pp. 1-3; Jones notes; Cafferty, Edward H. *A Genealogical History of the Roberts Family* ... Privately published, 1991, p.6.

    ⁺ Hilton, pp. 9-10; Jones notes.

SIXTH GENERATION

      iii. Allen, b. 1839-1840; d. Brooks 9/25/1866.

      iv. Patience, b.c. 1843; m. William H. Roberts(?).

      v. Orville, b. 3/1844; d. Brooks 7/11/1849.

136.   vi. Alpheus, b.c. 1848.

64. **Amos Roberts** (George^5, Jonathan^4, George^3, John^2, George^1), son of George and Mary (Brown) Roberts, was born in Buckfield, Maine, October 6, 1800, and died October 23, 1886 in Dexter, Maine. He and his wife are buried in Mt. Pleasant Cemetery in Dexter. Amos married Christiana Ryerson, daughter of Luke and Sarah (Coombs) Ryerson, in Sumner, Maine, January 22, 1822. She was born November 20, 1804, and died October 23, 1887 in Dexter. The first six children below were born in Sumner, the last seven in Sangerville, Maine.* Children:

      i. Augusta, b. 2/22/1824; d. 4/16/1837.

137.   ii. Nathan F., b.10/2/1825.

      iii. George, b. 6/24/1827; d. 3/16/1833.

      iv. Andrew Jackson, b. 9/28/1828; m. (1) Sarah Morrill, 1/1/1857, (2) Faithful Bonney; d. 12/2/1865 Buckfield. 2 ch. d. young.

      v. Ezra, b. 7/2/1830; d. 3/18/1833.

      vi. Mariah B., b. 5/17/1832; m. William N. Jackson, Sangerville, 7/20/1854; d. Sangerville 3/5/1857. Two children.

138.   vii. George B.M., b. 4/7/1834.

139.   viii. Ezra, b. 3/6/1836.

140.   ix. Amos B., b. 10/8/1838.

---

* Hilton, pp. 10-11,15,35, & 55.

> x. Christiana A.B., b. 7/2/1840; m. (1) Henry J. Carle, (2) Jonathan Bishop, (3) William Bryant; d. Sangerville, 1/16/1910. Five children.

141. xi. Otis Oakes, b. 3/20/1842.

> xii. Prudence G., b. 4/3/1844; m.(1) George W. Leathers, Sangerville, 11/4/1865, (2) Sylvanus Dinsmore, (3) Charles Davis; d. Dexter, 1/16/1912. Three children.
>
> xiii. Simeon R., b. 11/5/1848; m. Mary F. Farnum; d. Corinna, ME, 12/3/1916. C. W. Veteran. No ch.

65. Ezra Roberts (George^5, Jonathan^4, George^3, John^2, George^1), son of George and Mary (Brown) Roberts, was born March 30, 1802 in Buckfield, Maine, and died November 8, 1880. He married, firstly, Rebecca -----, who was born in 1801-2 and died April 30, 1839, and secondly, Jane Billington Lancaster of Charleston, July 26, 1841, in Sangerville, Maine. Jane was born May 12, 1810, and died June 18, 1877. There may have been additional children, not mentioned below.* Child:

> i. Hannah Jane, b. 2/17/1842; m. 10/3/1860, Frederick Augustus Pottle. At least one child.

66. George Roberts (George^5, Jonathan^4, George^3, John^2, George^1), son of George and Mary (Brown) Roberts, was born in Buckfield, Maine, October 17, 1803. He married Miriam Hall in Windham, Maine, November 9, 1827.⁺ Children:

> i. Estelle, m. -----Page.
>
> ii. Abbie, b. 1/16/1844; m. Gustavus Savage; d. 4/22/1880, Milo, ME. Seven children.
>
> iii. (?) Nathan.

67. Jonathan Roberts (George^5, Jonathan^4, George^3, John^2, George^1), son of George and Mary (Brown) Roberts, was born in

---

* Hilton, p. 11.
⁺ Hilton, p. 56.

SIXTH GENERATION

Buckfield, Maine, July 21, 1806, and died in Foxcroft, Maine, August 14, 1861. He and his wife are buried in the Knowlton Cemetery in East Sangerville, Maine. He married Lois Arseneth Leathers, daughter of Enoch and Mary (Cilley) Leathers, in Sangerville, November 26, 1829. Lois was born in Brooks, Maine, July 27, 1810, and died in Dover, Maine, June 29, 1868.* Children:

    i. Jane, b. 8/25/1830; d. 8/25/1830.

    ii. Jonathan, b. 8/11/1831; d. 2/1/1832.

    iii. George Edward, b. 10/4/1832; d. 3/28/1834.

    iv. Mary Jane, b. 9/16/1834; m. William Stacey, 2/28/1853, Dover, ME; d. 4/26/1870. Three children.

    v. Willard Harris, b. 9/25/1836; d. 3/18/1854.

    vi. James Thompson, b. 12/2/1838; d. 2/28/1840.

    vii. James Thompson II, b. 11/2/1840; m. Carolyn Farnham, 9/6/1865, Dover; d. 4/12/1914. No children.

    viii. Rebekah Abigail, b. 12/31/1842; m. James Ingram, 9/25/1863, Taunton, MA; d. 10/1/1867. No children.

    ix. Amos Gilman, b. 10/25/1848; d. 8/26/1852.

68. Eli Roberts (James^5, Jonathan^4, George^3, John^2, George^1), son of James and Tabitha (Roberts) Roberts, was born in Buckfield, Maine, February 19, 1804, and died August 22, 1861.

He married Nancy Jones.⁺ Children:

    i. Elizabeth.

    ii. Esther.

    iii. Daniel.

    iv. Nancy.

    v. Sylvira.

---

* Hilton, p. 61.
⁺ Hilton, p. 6.

vi. Tabitha.

vii. Welthia.

viii. Hulda.

ix. Elithea.

x. Abbie.

xi. James.

69. Benjamin Roberts (Seth^5, Jonathan^4, George^3, John^2, George^1), son of Seth and Miriam (Fobes) Roberts, was born in Peru, Maine, May 9, 1815 and died September 23, 1860, apparently in Peru. He married, firstly, Mercy Tuttle, who died July 26, 1848, aged 33. The first six children listed below were hers. Benjamin married, secondly, Sarah W. Barstow, September 18, 1849, daughter of Robert Barstow. Sarah died December 23, 1893. Apparently this family farmed in Peru for many years. Their property was valued at $500 in 1850.* Children:

i. Nancy Ellen, b. 3/18/1838; m. Gilbert H. Bailey; d. 12/9/1862. One child.

ii. Mary Elizabeth, b. 10/31/1839.

iii. Rosanna, b. 9/1/1842.

iv. Angeline, b. 5/4/1844.

v. Lois, b. 10/26/1845; m. Stephen W. Gammon, 11/18/1865; d. 5/30/1880. Two children.

vi. Roscoe W., b. 1/12/1848; d. 2/15/1849.

vii. Roscoe Benjamin, b. 12/1850; m. Elizabeth Hickoke, 1/10/1886; d. 3/1/1901 in Peru. No children.

viii. Alice Melvina, b. 9/1853.

70. James Roberts (Seth^5, Jonathan^4, George^3, John^2,

---

* Town Records, Peru, Maine; Turner, pp. 60, 127 & 228-9; U.S. Census, 1850.

SIXTH GENERATION

George¹), son of Seth and Miriam (Fobes) Roberts, was born in Peru, Maine, February 25, 1817. He married Mary A. M. Putnam, June 25, 1837. This family apparently left Peru before 1850, since they do not show up there in the census of that year.* Children:

    i. David S., b. 8/25/1837.

    ii. Nancy Maria, b. 10/8/1840.

    iii. James Albert, b. 8/8/1843.

    iv. Ann Genette, b. 9/8/1846.

    v. Sarah Barstow, b. 7/8/1848.

71. Jonathan Roberts (Seth⁵, Jonathan⁴, George³, John², George¹), son of Seth and Miriam (Fobes) Roberts, was born in Peru, Maine, October 12, 1824, near Tumbledown Dick Mountain. He died in Madbury, New Hampshire, December 14, 1909, and lies buried in the family lot there. The family lot is located at the old Roberts place on Stage Road. "John" Roberts, as he was better known, married Avis Jane Bodge, daughter of Stephen T. and Sarah (Williams) Bodge. She was born June, 1825, in Durham, New Hampshire, and died in Madbury, August 13, 1903, and is also buried in the family lot.

Being the third son of a small farmer, John left Peru for New Hampshire before 1850. For the next twenty years John pursued a career as a shoe maker in Massachusetts; and he, Avis Jane and their four boys lived at various times in Woburn, Weymouth, Lowell and Abbington. By about 1873 the Robertses were back in New Hampshire, where they settled on Stage Road in Madbury. Avis Jane was sick the last twenty-five years of her life and they had two grandchildren to raise; so the couple stayed pretty close to their little hay farm. According to the recollections of a grandchild who grew up with him in Madbury, John Roberts was a six-footer, athletic, with dark eyes and high cheek bones. He was hard-working and well thought of in the community. He worked as a handyman

---

* Town Records, Peru, Maine; Turner, pp. 228-9.

in his later years and also played fiddle at local dances.* Children:

142.   i. John Edgar, b.c. 1852.

143.   ii. Charles Edwin, b. 1/8/1855.

        iii. Walton E., b. 8/21/1856; d.c. 1910, unm. (He didn't want anyone to know his age, so he destroyed all of the pages of family records in the family Bible.)

        iv. William E., b.c. 1858; unm.

72. William Roberts (Seth[5], Jonathan[4], George[3], John[2], George[1]), son of Seth and Miriam (Fobes) Roberts, was born in Peru, Maine, April 3, 1827, and died near there November 24, 1906. He married Mary -----, who was born in Ireland in 1830 and died in Peru, June 25, 1879. This family lived for many years in Peru Center in the old Hall store.⁺ Children:

        i. Mary Jane, b. 1855-6; m. Pliney B. Wing, 7/29/1882.

        ii. Nancy E., b. 1857-8; d. 1861-2.

        iii. Rosanna, d. in first year.

        iv. Susie, m. Samuel B. Kittridge; d. 11/29/1906. Seven children.

73. Adrian Greenleaf Roberts (Seth[5], Jonathan[4], George[3], John[2], George[1]), son of Seth and Miriam (Fobes) Roberts, was born in Peru, Maine, February 25, 1832. He married Lydia Salmon Bailey, the daughter of Samuel L. Bailey. Lydia was born in Peru, June 23, 1830.# Children:

---

    * Roberts, Theresa Avis, "The Roberts Family" (unpub. article), c. 1960; Abington, Mass. Town Records; Correspondence with Amy Roberts Mercier, c. 1965; Peru Town Records; New Hampshire Bureau of Vital Statistics. See also Adams's *Madbury: Its People & Places* (See notes under Seth No. 27.)

    ⁺ Peru Town records; Turner, p. 229.
    # Peru Town records; Turner, p. 59.

SIXTH GENERATION

    i.   Charlotte Ella, b. 3/4/1852; d. 10/18/1853.

    ii. Gilbert M., b. 11/20/1854.

74. Eliphalet Roberts (Eliphalet[5], Eliphalet[4], George[3], John[2], George[1]), son of Eliphalet and Mary (Evans) Roberts, was born in Strafford, Vermont, November 15, 1801, and died in Sharon, Vermont, June 20, 1882. He married, firstly, Jane Marden, October 2, 1822 in Strafford. Jane was the daughter of Joseph and Sarah Marden; she was born in Epsom, New Hampshire, September 28, 1799, and died June 22, 1866. Eliphalet married, secondly, Mary Anne (Root) Rogers, November 20, 1866, in Strafford. Mary Anne, the daughter of John and Martha Root, was born in Northampton, Massachusetts in 1814 and died in Norwich, Vermont, August 23, 1885.[*] Children:

144.   i.   Willis L., b. 7/3/1823.

145.   ii. Lucian, b. 7/25/1824.

146.   iii. Mansir Hamilton, b. 5/25/1826.

        iv. Jane Amelia, b. 2/25/1828.

        v. Marcialine Rosetta, b. 3/24/1829; m. Truman R. Marden, 11/1/1847.

        vi. Emeline, b. 4/7/1831; m. Darius T. Rowell, 11/23/1846; d. 12/31/1909, Lebanon, NH.

75. Zerah Norton Roberts (Eliphalet[5], Eliphalet[4], George[3], John[2], George[1]), son of Eliphalet and Mary (Evans) Roberts, was born in Strafford, Vermont, October 20, 1803. He died in Sudbury, Vermont, April 19, 1882, and is buried in Leicester Cemetery. He married Sarah N. Sanders, the daughter of Samuel and Fanny (Nichols) Sanders. Sarah was born in Orwell, Vermont, and died in Whiting, Vermont, February 8, 1892, aged 84 years, 11 months.[+] Children:

---

  [*] Roberts, Blanche J., p. 540.
  [+] Roberts, Blanche J., p. 568.

DESCENDANTS OF GEORGE & MARY ROBERTS

    i. Myron C., b. 1830; d. 11/11/1873.

147. ii. Henry Harrison, b. 1/16/1837.

    iii. Fanny A.,b. 1842; m. Charles E. Church; d. 1932.

  76. Royal Roberts (Daniel⁵, Eliphalet⁴, George³, John², George¹), son of Daniel West and Abigail (Latham) Roberts, was born in Sharon, Vermont, May 22, 1805, and died there April 8, 1884, and is buried in the West Hartford Cemetery. He married Lora Lull, the daughter of Samuel and Clarissa Lull, April 6, 1829. She was born April 4, 1812, and died May 11, 1897.* Children:

    i. Melissa Marcia, b. 11/7/1830; m. Roswell Newell Stetson, 1/21/1862; d. 10/10/1899.

    ii. Alcesta Clarissa, b. 9/7/1847; d. 1/13/1859.

  77. Amplias Roberts (Daniel⁵, Eliphalet⁴, George³, John², George¹), son of Daniel West and Abigail (Latham) Roberts, was born in Sharon, Vermont, August 18, 1807, and died there April 8, 1884. He married, firstly, Mary Elvira Booth, February 15, 1829, and secondly, Fanny Wells, the daughter of N.C. and Peggy (George) Wells, March 26, 1844. Mary died in childbirth August 2, 1842, aged 33. Fanny was born January 24, 1805, and died December 12, 1870.⁺ Children:

    i. Ansel Amplias, b. 7/24/1830.

148. ii. Daniel West, b. 1/25/1836.

    iii. Orilla, b.c. 1839.

    iv. infant, b.&d. 8/2/1842.

    v. Betsey A., b.c. 1845; d. 9/27/1860.

    vi. Helen Melissa, b.c. 1848; d. after 1870.

  78. James Lull Roberts (Daniel⁵, Eliphalet⁴, George³, John², George¹), son of Daniel West and Abigail (Latham) Roberts, was

---

 * Roberts, Blanche J., p. 563; Bryant and Verret notes.
 ⁺ Roberts, Blanche J., p. 529.

SIXTH GENERATION

born in Sharon, Vermont, April 1 (or 30?), 1809, and died in Strafford, Vermont, September 20, 1876. He married Betsey Wells, the daughter of Nicholas C. and Peggy (George) Wells, March 14, 1833. Betsey was born in Strafford, December 14, 1809, and died there January 3, 1885.* Children:

   i. Harriet E., b. 5/15/1835; m. Freeman Wolcott, 1/3/1854; d. 1/10/1899.

149. ii. George Wells, b. 4/4(or7?)/1837.

150. iii. Alba James, b. 10/25/1840.

   iv. Francis Rufus, b. 1846; d. 3/6/1852.

   v. Edgar F., b. 1852; m. (1) Ida Alexander, 10/5/1876, (2) Alice Folsom, 7/1/1886.

   vi. Betsey Ann, d. 9/22/1860.

   vii. infant.

79. West Daniel Roberts (Daniel^5, Eliphalet^4, George^3, John^2, George^1), son of Daniel West and Abigail (Latham) Roberts, was born in Sharon, Vermont, April 7, 1811. He married, firstly, Hannah Rowell, July 9, 1846, and, secondly, Juliana (Poland?) Stoddard, the widow of John Stoddard and the daughter of Ashbel and Experience (Poland?), January 4, 1849. Hannah, the daughter of John and Hannah (Roberts) Rowell, was born August 6, 1818. Juliana was born in Waitsfield, Vermont, January 28, 1819. Perrin below was by this second marriage.⁺ Children:

   i. twins.

151. ii. Perrin, b.c. 1850.

80. Chester Merrill Roberts (Daniel^5, Eliphalet^4, George^3, John^2, George^1), son of Daniel West and Abigail (Latham) Roberts, was born in Sharon, Vermont, May 6, 1817, and died in Hanover, New Hampshire, December 11, 1875, of liver disease. He married Sophia Ann Miller, the daughter of Alvah and Cynthia (Hunt)

 * Roberts, Blanche J., p. 549.
 ⁺ Roberts, Blanche J., p. 566.

DESCENDANTS OF GEORGE & MARY ROBERTS

Miller, in 1844. Sophia was born in Northampton, Massachusetts, July 22, 1819, and died in Hanover, October 30, 1905. The two children below were born in Sharon, Vermont.* Children:

 i. Cynthia Eliza, b. 3/8/1845; d. 4/11/1852.

 ii. Cynthia Sophia, b. 4/17/1853; m. (1) E.G. Jones, 7/26/1872, (2) Joseph B. Herd, 7/15/1914. 5 ch.

81. Larkin Roberts (Daniel^5, Eliphalet^4, George^3, John^2, George^1), son of Daniel West and Abigail (Latham) Roberts, was born in Sharon, Vermont, February 3, 1821, and died in Northfield, Vermont, November 21, 1878. He married Julia Adelia Wolcott, who was born in Eaton, New Hampshire, in 1828. After Larkin died Julia married, secondly, Leonard D. Cady.⁺ Children:

 i. Leslie M., b. 10/9/1858.

 ii. Arthur, b. 1/30/1860; d. 11/16/1865.

 iii. son, b. 12/13/1869.

 iv. Helen P., m. Albert P. Comstock, 3/14/1875.

82. Darius Witt Roberts (Daniel^5, Eliphalet^4, George^3, John^2, George^1), son of Daniel West and Abigail (Latham) Roberts, was born in Sharon, Vermont, July 7, 1828, and died there August 5, 1892, of Bright's disease. He married Katherine Taylor, the daughter of Julius and Elizabeth (Hunt) Taylor, in 1851. She was born in Northampton, Massachusetts, July 20, 1827, and died in Sharon, September 21, 1906.# Children:

 i. Anna Mira, b. 8/13/1855; m. P.G. Norris, 4/2/1876; d. 3/4/1938, Bradford, VT. 6 ch.

 ii. a daughter, b. 8/26/1859.

 iii. Elizabeth Abigail, b. 9/24/1864; m. Charles Avery, 9/24/1884; d. 1/17/1944, Sharon. 10 ch.

---

 * Roberts, Blanche J., p. 533.
 ⁺ Roberts, Blanche J., p. 555.
 # Roberts, Blanche J., p. 537.

SIXTH GENERATION

152. iv. Julius D., b. 10/8/1867.

83. Orlando Hartwell Roberts (Moses[5], Eliphalet[4], George[3], John[2], George[1]), son of Moses and Catherine (Davis) Roberts, was born in Royalton, Vermont, August 3, 1824, and died in Stockbridge, Vermont, November 14, 1886. He was a farmer. He married Laura Marinda Badger, the daughter of Virsel and Harriet (Lamphere) Badger, in Hartford, Vermont, May 17, 1846. After Laura died September 17, 1878, Orlando married, secondly, Julia (Angel) Paine, in 1880.* Children:

        i. Mary M., b.c. 1848; m. West Daniel (No. 86) Roberts, 10/20/1867; d. 4/12/1909, Stockbridge.

153. ii. Frank Orlando, b. 5/15/1852.

        iii. Effie, b.c. 1855; m. 4/2/1873, Joseph S. Clark.

        iv. Eliza, b.c. 1856; m. John Shattuck.

        v. Sarah Estella, b.c. 1857, Compton, Quebec; d. 11/17/1877, Stockbridge.

        vi. Hattie A., b.c. 1860, Compton, Quebec; d. 9/12/1874, Stockbridge.

        vii. Orlin, b.10/10/1863, Stockbridge; d. 11/18/1877.

        viii. Agnes, b.c. 1865; m. 7/4/1898, David J. Carney.

84. Joseph Johnson Roberts (Moses[5], Eliphalet[4], George[3], John[2], George[1]), son of Moses and Catherine (Davis) Roberts, was born in Vermont in 1836 and died in Brattleboro Retreat, Vermont, March 31, 1909, and was buried in the Taftsville Cemetery. He was married three times. His first wife was Delia Hubbard, the daughter of George and Sarah (Merrill) Hubbard. Two daughters were of this union. Joseph married, secondly, Phelina T. Bryant, August 22, 1857 (or possibly 1867 or 1877), who bore him two sons. Thirdly, he married Mary Golden, who was born in 1845,

---

* Bryant and Verret notes.

and died July 22, 1907, and is also buried in the Taftsville Cemetery.* Children:

    i. Ida May, b. 1861; m. Nelson E. Martin, 11/29/1884; d. Worchester, MA, 1924.

    ii. Sarah Merrill, b. 2/25/1866, Montpelier, VT; m. R.M.Chandler, 8/29/1885.

    iii. Guy, b. 1877; d. 1915, unm.

    iv. Joseph, unm.

85. Stephen Roberts (Stephen^5, Eliphalet^4, George^3, John^2, George^1), son of Stephen and Alvira (Fox) Roberts, was born in Strafford, Vermont, July 18, 1838, and died November 20, 1914. He married Mary N. Clark, the daughter of Lyman and Harriet N. (Brown) Clark, December 2, 1858. She was born July 18, 1838 (?) and died January 23, 1916.⁺ Children:

154.   i. Stephen, b. 3/15/1862.

    ii. Hattie E., b. 9/29/1863; m. Curtis Witcomb, 11/29/1883; d. 6/30/1948. Two children.

86. West Daniel Roberts (Stephen^5, Eliphalet^4, George^3, John^2, George^1), son of Stephen and Alvira (Fox) Roberts, was born in Vermont, in (or about) 1849 and died there, February 12, 1908, and is buried in the Mt. Pleasant Cemetery in Stockbridge, Vermont. He married his second cousin Mary M. Roberts, October 20, 1867. She was born in Hartland, Vermont, July 9, 1848 and died April 12, 1909, and was also buried in the Mt. Pleasant Cemetery. Mary was the daughter of Orlando Hartwell (No. 83) and Laura Marinda (Badger) Roberts.# Children:

    i. Abbie Francelia, b. 1869; d. 3/27/1874.

---

* Roberts, Blanche J., p. 554.
⁺ Roberts, Blanche J., p. 565.
Roberts, Blanche J., p. 566.

SIXTH GENERATION

    ii. Burton West, b. 5/30/1872; m. Harriet O. Counter, 10/20/1898; d. 11/14/1942, Woodstock, VT.

    iii. Ernest Carroll, b. 2/14/1881; d. 9/1/1884, croup.

87. Samuel Roberts (John^5, Ezekiel^4, Samuel^3, John^2, George^1), a laborer, son of John Roberts of Raymond, New Hampshire, was born there in or about 1800 and died there October 5, 1852. From the 1850 census we have his wife's name as Mary, who was born in 1804-5 in New Hampshire. The following children, all from the 1850 census, are presumably theirs. Their real estate was worth $ 400.* Children:

    i. John, b. 1821-2.

    ii. George W., b. 1824-5.

    iii. Smith S., b. 1826-7.

    iv. Mary A., b. 1828-9.

    v. Edmund, b. 1830-1.

    vi. Dwight, b. 1833-4.

    vii. Susan V., b. 1837-8.

    viii. Harriet M., b. 1839-40.

88. Thomas Roberts (John^5, Ezekiel^4, Samuel^3, John^2, George^1), a laborer, son of John Roberts of Raymond, New Hampshire, was born there in 1802-3 and died there July 17, 1869. From the 1850 Census of nearby Sandown, New Hampshire, we learn that his wife's name was Elisabeth. She was born in New Hampshire in 1800-1. The following children from the census are presumed to be theirs.+ Children:

    i. Isac, b. 1821-2.

    ii. Folsom, b. 1823-4.

---

    * Fullonton, pp. 325-353; 1850 Census, Raymond, N.H.
    + Fullonton, pp. 325-353; 1850 Census, Sandown, N.H.

iii. Sally, b. 1829-30.

iv. Elisabeth, b. 1830-1.

v. Abigail, b. 1833-4.

vi. Asa J., b. 1845-6.

89. William Roberts (John[5], Ezekiel[4], Samuel[3], John[2], George[1]), a laborer, son of John Roberts of Raymond, New Hampshire, was born there in 1813 and died there January 25, 1852. From the 1850 Census we have his wife's name as Sarah, who was born in New Hampshire, in 1811 or 1812. The following children from the census are presumed to be theirs. The family real estate was valued at but $ 100.* Children:

i. Eaton, b. 1838-9

ii. Blake, b. 1840-1.

iii. Elisa J., b. 1844-5.

iv. Owen, b. 1849-50.

90. Alba Roberts (Jonathan[5], Jonathan[4], Jonathan[3], John[2], George[1]), son of Jonathan and Olive (Beede) Roberts, was born in Strafford, Vermont, October 25, 1806, and died in Enosburgh, Vermont, June 23, 1865, as the result of a fall. He married Sophia -----.⁺ Child:

i. Henry, b. 1835, Enosburg; d. 12/21/1896, Montgomery, VT.

91. Dudley Avery Roberts (Jonathan[5], Jonathan[4], Jonathan[3], John[2], George[1]), son of Jonathan and Olive (Beede) Roberts, was born in Strafford, Vermont, April 12, 1811, and died January 7, 1871 in Sheldon, Vermont. He married Sophia E. Leach, November 23, 1836, in Enosburg, Vermont. She was born in 1816 and died July 28, 1845, in Enosburg, and is buried in the cemetery there. Dudley may have had a second wife named Wealthy, who

---

* Fullonton, pp. 325-353; 1850 Census, Raymond, N.H.
⁺ Roberts, Blanche J., p. 553; Laitres notes.

SIXTH GENERATION

was born in 1817 and was residing with the son below in 1883.*
Child:

 i. Albert D., lived in Williamstown, VT.

92. Jonathan Martin Roberts (Jonathan[5], Jonathan[4], Jonathan[3], John[2], George[1]), son of Jonathan and Olive (Beede) Roberts, was born in Enosburg, Vermont, December 10, 1822, and died while a prisoner of war in Andersonville, Georgia, September 7, 1864. He married Elizabeth (Weeks) Huggins, June 1, 1845 in Lowell, Vermont. Elizabeth was born in Bath, New Hampshire.⁺
Child:

 i. Ida Luella, b. 10/9/1861, Fairfax, VT.

93. Andrew Jackson Roberts (Jonathan[5], Jonathan[4], Jonathan[3], John[2], George[1]), son of Jonathan and Olive (Beede) Roberts, was born in Enosburg, Vermont, August 14, 1829. He married Eunice Dunham, who was born in Enosburg in 1836. Eunice married, secondly, Martin Wallace, December 5, 1904.#
Children:

 i. John L., b. 1856; m. 3/9/1880, Norwich, VT, Marcella N. Wallace. Both died in Randolph, VT.

 ii. Will C., b. 1858; m. 2/24/1880, Norwich, Helen (Goulet) Roger.

 iii. (?) Allen J., b. 4/28/1874, Washington, N.H.

94. Daniel Azro Roberts (Daniel[5], Jonathan[4], Jonathan[3], John[2], George[1]), a farmer, son of Daniel and Hannah (Maxfield) Roberts, was born in Strafford, Vermont, May 4, 1828, and died in Greensboro, Vermont, June 17, 1867. He married in Corinth, Vermont, Sarah A. Lowell, who was born in Brookfield, Vermont. The child below was born in Brookfield.** Child:

---

 * Roberts, Blanche J., p. 537; Laitres notes.
 ⁺ Roberts, Blanche J., p. 552; Laitres notes.
 # Roberts, Blanche J., p. 529.
 ** Roberts, Blanche J., p. 535.

i. Willie Sherman, b. 1/3/1864.

95. Daniel Carr Roberts (Noah[5], Jonathan[4], Jonathan[3], John[2], George[1]), son of Noah and Polly (Carr) Roberts, was born in Westmore, Vermont, September 10, 1811, and died in Northfield, Vermont, October 1, 1881. He married Eliza Fannie Steel, the daughter of James and Esther (Smith) Steel. She was born in Northfield, April 5, 1818, and died there, April 18, 1893.[*]
Children:

    i. Alice Maria, b. 1843; m. Simeon B. Chase, 9/13/1860; d. 9/7/1905.

    ii. Francis H., b.c. 1851; m. Eunice M. Latham, 5/27/1875.

    iii. Esther E., m. W. W. Spearin.

    iv. Ann O., m. Henry A. Culver.

    v. Mary R., m. Chandler Culver.

    vi. James H.

---

[*] Roberts, Blanche J., p. 535.

SEVENTH GENERATION

96. Alfred Roberts (Calvin[6], Leavitt[5], Alexander[4], John[3], John[2], George[1]), son of Calvin and Mary (Whitten) Roberts, was born in New Hampshire, February 17, 1832, and died August 13, 1926. He married September 6, 1862, Julia Ann Small, the daughter of Richard and Lydia (Eastman) Small. Julia Ann was born in Campton, New Hampshire, September 17, 1845, and died September 29, 1922. Alfred was a blacksmith in Gilford, New Hampshire.* Children:

    i. Melvin C., b. 10/3/1869; d. 11/7/1898. A stonecutter in Concord, NH.

    ii. Nathan Alfred, b. 1876; m. 4/22/1903, Dorothy Dodge Reynolds. An Engineer in Concord, NH.

97. Justin Roberts (Isaac[6], Joseph[5], Joseph[4], George[3], John[2], George[1]), son of Isaac and Abigail (Merrill) Roberts, was born in Brooks, Maine, in 1811, and died there in April of 1846. He married Mary Jane McLeod in 1836. She was born in 1813 and died in 1863.⁺ Children:

    i. Abigail Sara, b. 8/10/1838; m. Corydon G. Ireland(A Civil War Veteran), 3/15/1860. Lived in Lewiston, ME. Two children.

155.   ii. Charles Justin, b. 11/9/1843.

    iii. Hannah Maria, b. 1/27/1846; m. 9/23/1871, Chandler E. Wiggin; d. 3/20/1895. Children?

98. Milton M. Roberts (Isaac[6], Joseph[5], Joseph[4], George[3], John[2], George[1]), son of Isaac and Abigail (Merrill) Roberts, was born in Brooks, Maine, January 4, 1815, and died in Minneapolis, Minnesota, April 28, 1895. He married his first cousin Elizabeth Cates Roberts, the daughter of Joseph (No. 47) and Lydia (Knight) Roberts. She was born in Jackson, Maine, August 1, 1825, and died in Minnesota, December 5, 1895. A graduate of Hebron Academy, Milton was a school teacher in Brooks and later New

---

    * Hardon, "Roberts-Unconnected", Vol. 1, p. 32.
    ⁺ Grant, p. 30.

York. He was a wood-turner by trade and invented an improved turning lathe, a steam plow, and other items, some of which he patented. He was a Quaker, an abolitionist and a Freemason. Milton, Elizabeth and their family moved to Wisconsin and then to Minnesota in 1864.* Children:

 i. Victoria Elizabeth, b. 4/29/1844; d. 7/5/1849, Levant, ME.

 ii. Milton M., b. 4/22/1847, Levant. Lived in Minneapolis. Children?

 iii. Evelyn V., b. 11/5/1849, Levant; m. Frank Tippett,1870. Lived in Minneapolis. 1 ch.d.young.

 iv. Jessie L., b. 6/12/1862, Jefferson, WI. Lived in Minneapolis.

99. Isaac Pennington Roberts (Isaac[6], Joseph[5], Joseph[4], George[3], John[2], George[1]), son of Isaac and Abigail (Merrill) Roberts, was born in Brooks, Maine, October 18, 1826 and died, apparently in Wisconsin, after 1902. He married Harriet Stanley, November 25, 1852. She was born in Harrison, Maine, October 27, 1832. Isaac P. became a minister of the Methodist Church in 1857 and moved to Wisconsin in 1871 to pursue his career in religion.⁺ Children:

 i. Justin Everett, b. 10/10/1855; d. 9/21/1856.

 ii. Leslie Manter, b. 3/28/1857, Carmel, Me. Lived in Wisconsin, later New York. Children?

 iii. Selwyn Prentice, b. 2/1862; d. 8/26/1863.

 iv. Herbert Elwyn, b. 7/30/1864; d. 8/31/1867.

 v. a daughter, d. young.

 vi. a daughter, d. young.

100. Warren Norton Roberts (Isaac[6], Joseph[5], Joseph[4],

---

* Grant, pp. 31-2.
⁺ Grant, pp. 32-4.

SEVENTH GENERATION

George[3], John[2], George[1]), son of Isaac and Sarah (Cobb) Roberts, was born in Brooks, Maine, May 2, 1839, and died in Lowell, Massachusetts, January 1, 1902. He was married three times. His first wife was Mary E. Parsons. They were married in Brooks, February 19, 1862. Mary died April 10, 1863, leaving an infant son. Warren married, secondly, Lovisa (Turner) Roberts, widow of Gilman (No. 109) Roberts, in Brooks, October 29, 1864. Lovisa died in Lowell, January 11, 1891 (or 1883?). Finally, on April 10, 1892, Warren married Georgia A. Robinson, who died in Lowell, September 10, 1894. Warren Norton worked variously as a school teacher in Brooks, and later as a janitor and grocer in Lowell.[*]
Child:

    i. Willie M., b. 4/2/1863; d. Lowell, MA, 10/22/1888.

101. Hamlin Myrick Roberts (Jacob[6], Joseph[5], Joseph[4], George[3], John[2], George[1]), son of Jacob and Huldah (Myrick) Roberts, was born in Buckfield, Maine, in 1811, and died in Brooks, Maine, in June of 1856. He married Mary Ann Rich, the daughter of Joseph Rich, in 1835. After Hamlin died Mary Ann married Dexter Waterman in 1859, at Unity, Maine. She died in 1877 in East Dixfield, Maine. Hamlin was active in the Quaker church and the abolitionist movement. A life-long farmer in Jackson, Maine (next to his father's homestead in Brooks), he was a charter member of the Waldo County Agricultural Society.[+]
Children:

156.	i.	Allen Hamlin, b. 2/22/1836.
157.	ii.	Francis Alton, b. 8/9/1838.
	iii.	Emily, b. 1840; d. 1848.
	iv.	Nelson, b. 1842; d. 1848 (as a result of a block of granite house foundation falling on him).
158.	v.	Cassius Clay, b. 3/5/1845.

102. Jacob Wellington Roberts (Jacob[6], Joseph[5], Joseph[4],

---

[*] Grant, pp. 34-5.
[+] Grant, pp. 40-3.

George³, John², George¹), son of Jacob and Huldah (Myrick) Roberts, was born in Brooks, Maine, November 29, 1813 and died in Maine, December 18, 1849, apparently of over-exposure to mercury. He married Phebe Susan Abbot, the daughter of Isaac and Chloe Abbot of Jackson, Maine. She was born on Sears Island, Maine, May 24, 1818, and died in Brooks, December 26, 1844. Jacob married, secondly, in June of 1849, Jane Lippencott of South China, Maine. Jacob was educated at the Friends School in Providence, Rhode Island and worked as a teacher in various towns of Waldo and Knox counties, Maine. He was also a writer and a prominent debater for the Free Soil party. He was also active in the temperance and the abolitionist movement.* Children:

	i.	Edward Junius, b. 2/8/1837; d. 1/4/1838.
159.	ii.	Edward Junius, b. 2/10/1839.
160.	iii.	Freeman Myrick, b. 12/21/1840.
	iv.	Amorena, b. 11/5/1842; m. Lemuel C. Grant (a Civil War Veteran), 5/3/1869. Lived in Maine. She is the Amorena (Roberts) Grant (cited as "Grant"), whose book is the basis of some of this line of the Roberts family.

103. Barnabas Myrick Roberts (Jacob⁶, Joseph⁵, Joseph⁴, George³, John², George¹), son of Jacob and Huldah (Myrick) Roberts, was born in Brooks, Maine, October 17, 1818, and died in Stockton, Maine, December 20, 1896. He married Emeline Rich, the daughter of Joseph Rich and the sister of Mary Ann Rich, wife of Barnabas' older brother Hamlin. Emeline died in Stockton, Maine, December 19, 1893. Barnabas owned a general store in Brooks and was also a partner in a ship building business. He was also a teacher of Latin. His greatest interest, however, seems to have been politics. Active in first the Whig, then the Abolitionist parties, he was a founder of the Republican Party in Maine. He was a state senator for two years during the Civil War, a representative in the legislature for one year, collector of customs

---

* Grant, pp. 47-51.

SEVENTH GENERATION

for Belfast for four years, and postmaster of Stockton for four years.* Children:

    i. infant, b. 1/1844.

    ii. Ralph, b. 9/1845; d. 1857.

161.   iii. Charles Sumner, b. 8/21/1851.

    iv. Hamlin Myrick, b. 5/15/1853; lost at sea 12/1876.

162.   v. Woodbury Davis, b. 9/5/1855.

    vi. Ellen Cecilia, b. 6/18/1859; m. Franklin P. Flanders, 11/7/1899.

    vii. Frank, b. 1/1864; d. 8/2/1872.

104. Charles Linneus Roberts (Jacob^6, Joseph^5, Joseph^4, George^3, John^2, George^1), son of Jacob and Huldah (Myrick) Roberts, was born in Brooks, Maine, April 14, 1821 and died in Yates City, Illinois, May 20, 1896. He married Caroline P. Metcalf of North Vassalboro, Maine, who died in 1877. Charles was a school teacher, merchant, hotelkeeper and justice of the peace. Later he was postmaster of Yates City. He was educated at the Quaker School in Providence, Rhode Island, and was active in the abolitionist movement and the Republican Party.⁺ Children:

    i. Emma Lucelia, b. 11/10/1856; d. Yates City, 11/9/1866.

    ii. Carrie Louise, b. 5/4/1860; m. John E. Bear of Farmington, IL. Two children.

163.   iii. Charles Addison, b. 8/10/1862.

    iv. Georgia Anna, b. 8/10/1865, Yates City. Lived in Peoria, IL.

    v. Ellen Lois, b. 4/7/1868, Yates City. A school teacher in Peoria.

---

* Grant, pp. 52-3.
⁺ Grant, pp. 54-5.

DESCENDANTS OF GEORGE & MARY ROBERTS

    vi. Blanche Lenore, b. 9/7/1873, Yates City; m. Arthur J. Lawrence, 2/22/1898. Lived in Galesburg, IL. At least one son.

105. Porteus Beezaleel Roberts (Jacob^6, Joseph^5, Joseph^4, George^3, John^2, George^1), son of Jacob and Huldah (Myrick) Roberts, was born in Brooks, Maine, July 27, 1823, and died in Brooklyn, New York, March 4, 1888. He married Mary Ann Preckett of Lansingburg, New York, June 17, 1848. She was born in Feresham, Kent County, England, April 22, 1833. Porteus left Maine in 1848 for Illinois to teach school, but soon went to work for the railroads. He rose to great heights in the railroad industry, building street railroads in Cincinnati, Ohio, and Staten Island, New York. He became a large landowner in Iowa and Illinois, was a large operator in cotton, and was a broker in New York. Unfortunately, he was financially ruined in the great crash of "Black Friday".* Children:

    i. Manter Wellington, b. 4/12/1849; d. 4/26/1849, Richmond, IL.

164.   ii. Charles Wellington, b. 7/1/1850.

    iii. son, b. & d. 6/1852, Peoria, Ill.

    iv. Fanny Fern, b. 3/20/1854, Peoria; m. Arthur Bell of Brooklyn, NY, 4/10/1877. One child.

    v. Frank, b. 5/29/1856, Peoria; d. 4/1881.

    vi. Mary Ellen, b. 10/14/1858, Peoria. Lived in Boston.

    vii. son, b. 2/12/1860; d. 3/1860.

    iii. Sherman, b. 7/6/1862, Chicago; m. Anna Vanderbeck, 12/16/1894. Children?

    ix. son, b. & d. 11/1864, N.Y.

---

* Grant, pp. 57-9.

SEVENTH GENERATION

165. x. Campbell Myrick, b. 8/14/1865.

xi. Huldah Margaret, b. 10/13/1870, Brooklyn; m. Howard D. Hammond, 11/11/1897. At least two children.

166. xii. Lincoln Hamlin, b. 3/20/1877.

106. Ahira Roberts (Gilman^6, Joseph^5, Joseph^4, George^3, John^2, George^1), son of Gilman and Ann (Leathers) Roberts, was born in Brooks, Maine, February 12, 1812, and died in North Dakota, November 26, 1894. He married Mary Ann Durgin of Rumford, Maine. She was born May 13, 1814 and died December 20, 1854.* Children:

i. Albert G., b. 1/6/1840; d. 9/6/1840.

ii. Hannah Catherine, b. 12/6/1841; m. Sylvester Frederick, 2/17/1865. Four children.

167. iii. Samuel Gilman, b. 3/10/1843.

168. iv. Albert, b. 7/28/1844.

v. Llewellyn, b. 12/6/1847; d. 10/24/1872.

vi. Frank, b. 4/15/1848; d. in 1864 in Andersonville P.O.W. camp; served in the 30th Maine Reg.

vii. Ahira A., b. 3/15/1850; d. 9/27/1852.

169. viii. Augustus, b. 4/15/1852.

107. Ezra Roberts (Gilman^6, Joseph^5, Joseph^4, George^3, John^2, George^1), son of Gilman and Ann (Leathers) Roberts, was born in 1827, in or near Brooks, Maine, and died there in 1900. He married Lydia Wentworth of Knox, Maine. Ezra was a veteran of the Civil War.⁺ Child:

170. i. Freeman Otis, b. 9/11/1856.

---

* Grant, pp. 73-9.
⁺ Grant, p. 83.

DESCENDANTS OF GEORGE & MARY ROBERTS

108. Jacob Roberts (Enoch⁶, Joseph⁵, Joseph⁴, George³, John², George¹), son of Enoch and Eleanor (Leathers) Roberts, was born in Brooks, Maine, March 4, 1818, and died there April 14, 1889. He married Cynthia Badger, who was born November 17, 1824, and died April 21, 1900.* Children:

    i. Abbie F., b. 8/30/1846; d. 6/12/1863.

    ii. Mary M., b. 11/10/1847; m. Manly Ellis, 7/4/1865; d. 3/1/1892. Lived in Monroe, ME. Five children.

    iii. Ann C., b. 5/21/1849; d. 3/15/1859.

    iv. Hattie C., b. 9/2/1850; m. Albert Jenkins, 10/12/1873. Lived in Monroe, ME. Six children.

    v. Henry L., b. 7/19/1852. "Went west."

    vi. William J., b. 1/28/1856. "Went west."

171. vii. Herbert F., b. 7/18/1858.

172. viii. Melvin W., b. 2/23/1862.

173. ix. George Atwood, b. 10/23/1865.

109. Gilman Roberts (Enoch⁶, Joseph⁵, Joseph⁴, George³, John², George¹), son of Enoch and Eleanor (Leathers) Roberts, was born in Brooks, Maine, about 1825 and died there November 28, 1863. He married, firstly, Abigail Wilson of Waldo, Maine, and, secondly, Lovisa Turner, who died in Lowell, Massachusetts, January 11, 1883 (or 1891?). Gilman and Lovisa apparently had but one child.⁺ Child:

    i. Alfreda L., b. 4/24/1862.

110. Alfred Roberts (Enoch⁶, Joseph⁵, Joseph⁴, George³, John², George¹), son of Enoch and Eleanor (Leathers) Roberts, was born in Brooks, Maine, about 1827 and died in an army hospital in 1863,

---

  * Grant, pp. 85-6.
  ⁺ Grant, p. 88.

SEVENTH GENERATION

while serving his country in the Civil War. He married Emily Dean.* Children:

    i. Edwin.

    ii. Alice.

111. Charles H. Roberts (Benjamin^6, Joseph^5, Joseph^4, George^3, John^2, George^1), son of Benjamin and Nancy (Cilley) Roberts, was born in or near Brooks, Maine, July 15, 1853, and apparently died after 1901. He married Julia Douglas of Morrell, Maine, June 23, 1872.$^+$ Child:

    i. Stanley J., b. 10/17/1873, Brooks; m. Lillian Woodbury of Knox, ME, 12/23/1893. Children?

112. Sharon Roberts (John^6, Joseph^5, Joseph^4, George^3, John^2, George^1), son of John and Harriet (Jackson) Roberts, was born January 31, 1836, in Waldo, Maine, and apparently died after 1901. He married Ann Mary Boody of Jackson, Maine, who died October 29, 1898.# Children:

    i. Edith Gertrude, b. 2/27/1859; m. Wilbur Barker. Lived in Brooks. One child.

    ii. Maud, b. 9/1869; m. Frank Hogan. Lived in Thorndike, ME. Three children.

113. Everett W. Roberts (John^6, Joseph^5, Joseph^4, George^3, John^2, George^1), son of John and Harriet (Jackson) Roberts, was born in Brooks, Maine, November 4, 1846, and apparently died after 1901. He married, firstly, in April of 1870, Mellissa A. Munson, who died in Minnesota, February 20, 1889, and, secondly, Mrs. Viola Phelps (nee Rutledge). Only the final child below is by Viola.** Children:

---

    * Grant, p. 88.
    + Grant, p. 108.
    # Grant, p. 109.
    ** Grant, p. 111.

i. Bert, b. 2/1872, MN; m. Verna Hanson. One son b.4/13/1897.

ii. child, b. & d. 1874.

iii. John, b. & d. 1878.

iv. Frank, b. 1886.

v. Nellie, b. 10/1888.

vi. Mary H., b. 7/22/1895.

114. William Henry Harrison Roberts (Timothy[6], Joseph[5], Joseph[4], George[3], John[2], George[1]), son of Timothy T. and Nancy E. (Gardner) Roberts, was born in or near Brooks, Maine, October 31, 1835, and died after 1901. He married Esther B. Rand of Thorndike, Maine, August 6, 1856.* Children:

174.   i. Forrest K., b. 2/9/1860.

       ii. Elmer G., b. 1/12/1862; m. Estelle Card. Lived in Brooks. One child died in infancy.

175.   iii. Edna M., b. 12/6/1865.

115. Oscar E. Roberts (Timothy[6], Joseph[5], Joseph[4], George[3], John[2], George[1]), son of Timothy T. and Nancy E. (Gardner) Roberts, was born in Corinna, Maine, June 7, 1844, and died after 1901. He married Romilia A. Clements in Knox, Maine, November 23, 1867. She was born in Waldo, Maine, May 4, 1851. Oscar served in the Nineteenth Maine Regiment during the Civil War. After the War they moved to Lynn, Massachusetts, where Oscar took up cabinet making.⁺ Children:

i. Emma F., b. 4/22/1869, Brooks.

ii. Lizzie E., b. 10/21/1877, Belfast, ME.

iii. Willie O., b. 12/14/1880, Belfast; d. 6/1/1882.

116. Charles A. Roberts (Nathan[6], Joseph[5], Joseph[4], George[3],

---

* Grant, p. 115.
⁺ Grant, pp. 115-6.

SEVENTH GENERATION

John², George¹), son of Nathan Hall and Elvira (Irish) Roberts, was born in Brooks, Maine, April 5, 1846, and died after 1901. He married Matilda Moran of Minneapolis, Minnesota, June 28, 1868. This family settled in Leonard, North Dakota.[*] Children:

    i. Will, b. 3/21/1869. A farmer in Sanborn, MN.

    ii. Lee, b. 1871; m. Grace Gurley. A lumber merchant in Fargo, ND. At least two children.

    iii. Charles, b. 1876. Commander of a lake steamer.

117. John Nelson Roberts (Nathan⁶, Joseph⁵, Joseph⁴, George³, John², George¹), son of Nathan Hall and Mary Sophia (Langham) Roberts, was born in Minnesota, April 11, 1876. He married Jessie Shugars, September 20, 1899. John served in a Minnesota regiment in the Spanish American War. This family lived in Minneapolis and probably had more children than the one listed below.[+] Child:

    i. Beatrice Marietta, b. 5/14/1901.

118. Guy Hall Roberts (Nathan⁶, Joseph⁵, Joseph⁴, George³, John², George¹), son of Nathan Hall and Mary Sophia (Langham) Roberts, was born in Minnesota, December 8, 1877. He married Dora L. Shipton, July 28, 1896. Guy served in the Spanish American War and then enrolled in Harvard University. He and Dora probably had additional children not listed below.[#] Child:

    i. Mercedes Alexander, b. 9/23/1901; d. 9/28/1901.

119. Walter Henry Roberts (Winslow⁶, Joseph⁵, Joseph⁴, George³, John², George¹), son of Winslow and Maria (Bangs) Roberts, was born in Waterville, Maine, February 15, 1876. He married Mary Elizabeth Harvey, March 7, 1900. She died May 2, 1901. Walter served in the Spanish American War, in the Hospital

---

  [*] Grant, pp. 118-20.
  [+] Grant, pp. 118-120.
  [#] Grant, p. 120.

DESCENDANTS OF GEORGE & MARY ROBERTS

Corps. in the Phillipines.* Child:

    i. Lillian Marie, b. 1/4/1901.

120. Fred Leslie Roberts (Rufus^6, Joseph^5, Joseph^4, George^3, John^2, George^1), son of Rufus and Adeline (Files) Roberts, was born in Brooks, Maine, July 21, 1854. He married in 1876 and later divorced Josie Briley. They had two children. Fred remarried in 1892, to Emma Mitchell. They had five children.$^+$ Children:

    i. Leslie Perry, b. 5/1/1878; m. May Hoffman, 7/8/1897. At least one child - Earl, b. 8/15/1898.

    ii. Gladys May, b. 6/11/1883. Lived with mother in Pueblo, CO.

    iii. Emma Hay, b. 12/1892, Morris, MN.

    iv. son, d. 1893.

    v. Inez, b. 7/3/1895.

    vi. Lillian, b. 3/29/1896.

    vii. child, d. 8/10/1899.

121. Frank H. Roberts (Rufus^6, Joseph^5, Joseph^4, George^3, John^2, George^1), son of Rufus and Adeline (Files) Roberts, was born in Brooks, Maine, December 9, 1860. He married firstly on March 24, 1884, Sadie Kessler of Rockford, Minnesota, who died March 20, 1885. Frank then married Annie E. Sutherland, June 3, 1886.$^\#$ Children:

    i. Howard Leroy, b. 7/24/1887.

    ii. Hazel Viola, b. 4/3/1890.

122. Thomas Loring Roberts (Jotham^6, Jonathan^5, Joseph^4,

---

    * Grant, p. 123.
    $^+$ Grant, pp. 123-5.
    $^\#$ Grant, p. 125.

SEVENTH GENERATION

George³, John², George¹), son of Jotham and Mary (Richardson) Roberts, was born in Brooks, Maine, May 6, 1825, and died before 1902. He married Nancy Ellen Perry, October 6, 1850. She was the daughter of Barney Perry of Turner, Maine. Nancy was born in 1822 and died in Auburn, Maine, December 26, 1897. Thomas served in the Sixteenth Maine Regiment in the Civil War and was active in the Grand Army of the Republic after the War.* Child:

    i. Mary, b. 8/9/1851, Turner, ME; m. George G. Gifford.

123. Albert Augustus Roberts (Jotham⁶, Jonathan⁵, Joseph⁴, George³, John², George¹), son of Jotham and Mary (Richardson) Roberts, was born in Brooks, Maine, January 13, 1832, and died in Turner, Maine, March 12, 1901. He married Maria Louisa Woodman of Freeport, Maine, December 18, 1853. Born March 25, 1831, she was the daughter of Jonathan Woodman, of Freeport. Maria died after 1901. Albert was a contractor and a builder and a member of the I.O.O.F. in Turner, Maine. During the Civil War he served in the Twenty-third Maine Volunteers, mostly as an ambulance driver.⁺ Children:

    i. Alice Prudence, b. 10/20/1854, Buckfield; m. William C. Chadbourne, 4/27/1888. Res. Turner.

    ii. Howard Augustus, b. 6/14/1857, Buckfield; m. Margaret F. Soule, 3/7/1899. Lived in Turner.

    iii. Albion Woodman, b. 7/14/1863. Lived in Turner.

    iv. Alberta Maria, b. 9/6/1867, Buckfield. A teacher in Turner.

    v. Thomas Arthur, b. 10/27/1873, Lewiston, ME. Graduated Bates College 1899. A school principal.

    vi. Charles Gilman (an adopted son), b. 9/16/1873.

---

* Grant, p. 132.
⁺ Grant, pp. 132-5.

124. Alonzo Roberts (Willard[6], Jonathan[5], Joseph[4], George[3], John[2], George[1]), son of Willard and Ruth (Edwards) Roberts, was born in or near Brooks, Maine, in October of 1819 and died in June of 1894. He married Eunice Stevens, who died in February, 1897.[*] Children:

    i. Carrie Isabel, b. 6/1862; m. Hamlin Rich. 1 ch.

    ii. George Bean, b. 5/1864; m. Carrie M. Crane. One child- Doris Albertine, b. 5/1896.

    iii. Ruth Willard, b. 2/1867; m. Hiram Michaels. Lived in Belfast, ME. One child.

125. Daniel Edwards Roberts (Willard[6], Jonathan[5], Joseph[4], George[3], John[2], George[1]), son of Willard and Ruth (Edwards) Roberts, was born in or near Brooks, Maine, in November of 1828 and died in December of 1863. He married Mary Severance.[+] Child:

    i. Mary Ruth.

126. Orpheus Roberts (Sylvanus[6], John[5], Joseph[4], George[3], John[2], George[1]), son of Sylvanus Irish and Mary Jane (Thompson) Roberts, was born in Waldo, Maine, and died in July 1863, at the battle of Gettysburg, during the Civil War. He married Cementhe E. Staples of Prospect (later renamed Stockton), Maine.[#] Children:

    i. Dianna E.

    ii. Delora J., d. in infancy.

127. Lloyd Roberts (Sylvanus[6], John[5], Joseph[4], George[3], John[2], George[1]), son of Sylvanus Irish and Remember (Record) Roberts, was born in or near Stockton, Maine. He married Ella Griffin of Searsport, Maine. Lloyd served in the U.S. Navy during the Civil War. This family lived in Sherman Mills, Maine, where the

---

[*] Grant, pp. 136-7.
[+] Grant, p. 137.
[#] Grant, p. 138.

SEVENTH GENERATION

following two children were born.* Children:

    i. Lottie.

    ii. Edmund.

128. Lucullus Roberts (Sylvanus^6, John^5, Joseph^4, George^3, John^2, George^1), son of Sylvanus Irish and Remember (Record) Roberts, was born in or near Stockton, Maine, and died in Somerville, Massachusetts, May 7, 1901. He married Jennie Houston of Searsport, Maine. Lucullus was a machinist in Stockton, where their first two children were born, and later in Somerville, where their third child was born.⁺ Children:

    i. Bessie A.

    ii. Edward.

    iii. Marian Alice.

129. Dexter Roberts (Sylvanus^6, John^5, Joseph^4, George^3, John^2, George^1), son of Sylvanus Irish and Remember (Record) Roberts, was born in or near Stockton, Maine. He married Belle Libby of Carmel, Maine, where this family took up residence and their two children were born.# Children:

    i. Harry.

    ii. Helen.

130. Josiah W. Roberts (Jonathan^6, Samuel^5, Jonathan^4, George^3, John^2, George^1), son of Jonathan and Susan Roberts, was born in Brooks, Maine, in 1825-6. He married Joanna -----, who

---

  * Grant, p. 139.
  ⁺ Grant, p. 139.
  # Grant, p. 139.

was born in 1826.* Child:

    i. Mary, b. 1860.

131. Almond B. Roberts (Jonathan^6, Samuel^5, Jonathan^4, George^3, John^2, George^1), son of Jonathan and Susan Roberts, was born in Brooks, Maine, about 1835. He married Cassandra McDonald, who was born in 1847-8.$^+$ Children:

    i. Alice M., b. 1869.

    ii. Georgia, b. 1869.

    iii. Ida Florence, b. 1870; m. George Cilley.

132. Gilman Roberts III (Samuel^6, Samuel^5, Jonathan^4, George^3, John^2, George^1), son of Samuel and Margaret H. (Clifford) Roberts, was born in Brooks, Maine, April 14, 1831, and died in Waldo, Maine, April 26, 1915. He married three times. He married in March 1855 Cynthia Austin, daughter of Winslow and Mary Ann (Lane) Austin. She was born in Pownal, Maine, February 22, 1829 and died in Brooks, Maine, September 1, 1859 and is buried in South Brooks "on the home place". Gilman married next March 25, 1860, Harriet A. Dingee (or Dinger) of Calais, Maine, who was born in 1842. Finally, before 1880, he married Lucy Ellen ----, who was born in March of 1830. Gilman and his family resided in Waldo, Maine, where they farmed. When he died in 1915, it is said he had no surviving children or spouse.$^\#$ Children:

    i. Marietta, b. 12/28/1855; d. 9/26/1877; unm.

    ii. Lucy Ellen, b. 11/23/1858; d. 8/23/1859.

    iii. Cynthia, b. 1862.

    iv. Lewis E., b. 1864.

---

* Hilton, supplement p. 1.
$^+$ Hilton, supplement, p. 1.
$^\#$ Jones notes.

SEVENTH GENERATION

 v. Linneus A., b. 1868.

 vi. Ada F., b. 1876; m. 1897 Isaac G. Sanborn. 2 ch.

133. Watson Clifford Roberts (Samuel[6], Samuel[5], Jonathan[4], George[3], John[2], George[1]), son of Samuel and Margaret H. (Clifford) Roberts, was born in Brooks, Maine, March 12, 1833 and died in Chico, California, September 16, 1917 and is buried in Chico Cemetery. He married, firstly, in Concord, New Hampshire, July 5, 1855, Olive Melissa Cummings, daughter of the Rev. Jonathan and Abigail E. (Quimby) Cummings. Olive was born in Newport, Vermont, October 7, 1837, and died in Chico, March 27, 1900 and is buried in Chico Cemetery. Watson married, secondly, in Chico, January 2, 1901, the widow Hannah M. ("Patty") Patridge. She was born in Illinois in 1853 and died in Chico, March 5, 1909 and is also buried in Chico Cemetery. Watson had been a "bound boy" and apparently left home as soon as he came of age. He served in the Civil War. Watson and Olive came to Calfornia together in 1874 via train. At Butte Meadows, Watson was a hotel proprietor and in Chico a harnessmaker. He also had orchard holdings in Tehama County. In his last eight years he became a Seventh Day Adventist and turned over all of his property in exchange for life-time care.* Children:

176. i. Eugene Roswell, b. 4/22/1856.

  ii. Georgie Etta, b. 11/7/1857, Concord, NH; m. Chico, 10/7/1880, George Edward Vadney; d. Chico, 6/7/1911. Six children.

  iii. Abby Isabel, b. 8/29/1859, Warner, NH; m. Chico, 3/28/1881, Frederick Hoffman; d. Chico 10/8/1889. Three children.

  iv. Laura Anna, b. 7/6/1866, Effingham, NH; d. Chico, 10/31/1883.

134. Jonathan D. Roberts (Josiah[6], Samuel[5], Jonathan[4], George[3], John[2], George[1]), son of Josiah and Jane (Jellison) Roberts,

---

 * Jones notes; Hilton supplement, pp. 3-6.

was born in Brooks, Maine, August 11, 1835, died in Belfast, Maine, June 10, 1913, and is buried in the Brooks Lower Cemetery. On November 11, 1855, he married Sarah J. Stimpson, who was born August 3, 1836 and died December 2, 1923, in Belfast.[*] Children:

	i.	Mary F., b. 1859; m. David Seeking; d. 12/18/1901.
177.	ii.	James S., b. 12/8/1861.
178.	iii.	Henry G.(or C.?), b. 12/1863.
179.	iv.	Cyrus H., b. 7/11/1865.
	v.	a child, b. 1867; d. young.
	vi.	Phebe E., b. 11/30/1869; m. Larrin Small; d. 3/22/1964.
	vii.	John I., b. 1870-1, m. Abbie Parsons; d. 8/23/1902. One son.
	viii.	Emery J., b. 1/14/1873; m. (1) Mattie Gilbert, (2) Ada Greenlaw, (3) Clara Burgess; d. 1949.
180.	ix.	Frank H., b. 3/27/1874.
	x.	Everett, b. 8/1/1876; d. 1881.
	xi.	Jane, b. 1878; d. young.
	xii.	Clara, b. 3/17/1879; m. John Harvey; d. 1901. Three children.
181.	xiii.	George S., b. 12/30/1880.

135. Levi Roberts (Josiah[6], Samuel[5], Jonathan[4], George[3], John[2], George[1]), son of Samuel and Jane (Jellison) Roberts, was born in Brooks, Maine in 1837 or 1838, died October 14, 1901 in Waldo, Maine, and is buried in the Harding Cemetery there. He married, firstly, October 25, 1861, Mary E. Jellison of Monroe,

---

[*] Hilton supplement, p. 1; Jones notes; Cafferty, pp. 189-202.

SEVENTH GENERATION

Maine, secondly, Lucy Holmes (or Ford?) (b.c. 1852), thirdly, June 24, 1883, Mrs. Mary A. McFarland of Monroe, and fourthly, in 1887 or 1888, Rachel Ella Harvey. Rachel was born in 1872 and died July 13, 1920. Levi was a trapper, farmer and a logger. He served in the Civil War. The first two children below are by Lucy and the remaining three by Rachel Ella.* Children:

182.	i.	William E., b. 1872.
183.	ii.	Frederick L., b. 3/3/1876.
184.	iii.	Leslie Burton, b. 2/1888.
185.	iv.	Ernest Tucker, b. 4/5/1890.
186.	v.	Raymond Renworth, b. 12/1892.

136. Alpheus Roberts (Watson^6, Samuel^5, Jonathan^4, George^3, John^2, George^1), son of Watson and Mary Roberts, was born in Brooks, Maine, about 1848. He married Emma F. Sylvester.⁺ Children:

187.   i. Raymond Sylvester, b. 8/21/1894.

         ii. Sidney, lived in Winslow, ME.

137. Nathan F. Roberts (Amos^6, George^5, Jonathan^4, George^3, John^2, George^1), son of Amos and Christiana (Ryerson) Roberts, was born in Sumner, Maine, October 2, 1825. He died in Dexter, Maine, November 21, 1896 and is buried in Mt. Pleasant Cemetery there. He married Augusta Parshley in Sangerville, Maine, April 2, 1850. She was born in 1827 and died in 1915. Nathan was a shoemaker, selectman of Dexter and postmaster of Dexter from 1892 to 1896.# Children:

         i. Fred E., b. 1850; d. 1851.

188.   ii. Frank W., b. 12/6/1850.

---

    * Hilton supplement, p. 2; Jones notes; Cafferty, p. 7.
    ⁺ Hilton, pp. 9-10; Jones notes.
    # Hilton, p. 13.

	iii.	Elmer Nathan, b. 1852; d. 1902. To Ontario, OH.
189	iv.	Charles D., b. 1855.
	v.	Mary, b. 7/11/1858; m. John W. Haines, 1/14/1880; d.12/1/1947, Augusta, ME. 3 ch.

138. George B. M. Roberts (Amos⁶, George⁵, Jonathan⁴, George³, John², George¹), son of Amos and Christiana (Ryerson) Roberts, was born in Sangerville, Maine, April 7, 1834. He died in Chicago, Illinois, from the effects of war wounds suffered during the Civil War, September 30, 1866. He married Hannah Jane Ramsdell, in Sangerville, Maine, January 31, 1856. She was born in Garland, Maine, December 1, 1836 and died in Roxbury, Massachusetts, February 16, 1920. George enlisted January 6, 1865 in Co. F, Coast Guard Infantry and was mustered out July 7, 1865.* Children:

190.	i.	George Brinton, b. 10/17/1857.
191.	ii.	Frederick Parkhurst, b. 1858.
	iii.	a daughter, d. in infancy.

139. Ezra Roberts (Amos⁶, George⁵, Jonathan⁴, George³, John², George¹), son of Amos and Christiana (Ryerson) Roberts, was born in Sangerville, Maine, March 6, 1836. He died in Dexter, Maine, July 4, 1900 and is buried in Mt. Pleasant Cemetery, along with his first wife and daughter. He married, firstly, Almeda Russell, in Dexter, July 28, 1860. Almeda was born July 2, 1838 and died in Dexter, May 23, 1897. Ezra apparently married, secondly, Elmira Leathers, who died in 1924. Albert Dudley was apparently a child of the second marriage.⁺ Children:

    i. Winnie L., d. in infancy.

    ii. Albert Dudley, of Palo Alto, Calif. Had a son David Ezra Roberts.

140. Amos B. Roberts (Amos⁶, George⁵, Jonathan⁴, George³,

---

* Hilton, p. 16.
⁺ Hilton, p. 23.

SEVENTH GENERATION

John[2], George[1]), son of Amos and Christiana (Ryerson) Roberts, was born in Sangerville, Maine, October 8, 1838. He died in Stony Creek, Connecticut, October 21, 1926, and is buried in the Damascus Cemetery in Branford, Connecticut. Amos was married four times. He first married (and later re-married) in Dexter, Maine, April 5, 1860, Rebecca J. Pullen, who was born in 1839 and died in 1887 and is buried in Mt. Pleasant Cemetery in Dexter, Maine. The first three children below were Rebecca's. Amos' second wife was Julie -----, who was the mother of Christiana below. His third wife was Kittendean ("Kittie") Ayers Record, who was born in New York state and died in Branford, July 5, 1951 or 1952, and is buried in the Damascus Cemetery. Kittie was the daughter of ----- and Margaret Ayers Record. Sadie and Hazel below were Kittie's daughters.

Amos Roberts enlisted in the Civil War from Dexter, August 29, 1862, in Co. B, 20th Maine Volunteer Regiment. He fell ill at Antietam and was discharged. Later he re-enlisted in the 3rd Maine Battalion and served two more years. After the War he was commander of the Mason Rogers Post of the Grand Army of the Republic in Stony Creek. He was also a member of the Seaside Lodge, I.O.O.F.* Children:

192.	i.	William Otis, b. 1/20/1859.
193.	ii.	Adrian, b. 11/24/1864.
	iii.	Lametta Eva, b. 1867; m. Adoniram H. Fassett; d. 1926. 2 children.
	iv.	Christiana, m. -----Pearley; d. Waterbury, CT.
	v.	Sadie, b. 8/16/1887; m. (1) 1/2/1905, Frank Hoffman, div.,(2) 5/17/1922, Addison Beckwith, div., (3) 4/9/1949, George Mortimer. Lived to over 90 years old in the New Haven, CT area. Five children.

---

* Hilton, p. 24.

vi. Hazel, b. 6/10/1890; m. 10/16/1907, Alexander M. Greenvall; d. 7/20/1965, Stony Creek,CT.1 ch.

141. Otis Oakes Roberts (Amos^6, George^5, Jonathan^4, George^3, John^2, George^1), son of Amos and Christiana (Ryerson) Roberts, was born in Sangerville, Maine, March 20, 1842, and died in Dexter, Maine, February 8, 1930, and is buried in Mt. Pleasant Cemetery.

Otis married, firstly, January 23, 1864, in Sangerville, Emelda Davis, who died November 21, 1864. Next, he married May 18, 1865 in Dexter Rosella Morgan Twombly, who died in May of 1875. Otis married, thirdly, Louise Achsa Hussey Edgerly on May 27, 1876 in Detroit, Michigan. Louise was the daughter of Leonard and Sarah Hinkley Hussey, was born in Orono, Maine, February 19, 1853 and died in Dexter, September 8, 1938.

Otis was the first man in Dexter to enlist in service on May 28, 1861 in Co. H, 6th Maine Volunteer Infantry. He rose to the rank of second lieutenant and received the Medal of Honor for capturing the flag of the 8th Louisiana Regiment in hand-to-hand combat at Rappahanock Station, Virginia, in November of 1863. He was discharged on disability February 11, 1865 due to the amputation of one-half of his foot. A cobbler, shopkeeper and farmer, Otis was a rabid Republican who always voted a straight ticket.* Children:

194.   i. Otis Jackson, b. 3/1/1877.

    ii. Kate Emelda, b. 4/24/1878; m. Arthur Elwell Inman, Dexter, 4/23/1900; d. Dexter, 9/11/1960. Four children.

    iii. Eula Rose, b. 11/17/1879; m.(1) 8/8/1895, Frank A. Hager, div., (2) 3/26/1908, Fred S. Hill, (3) 11/17/1938, Chester L. Hussey; d. 12/3/1956. Seven children.

    iv. Jessie Louise, b. 11/9/1884; m. 7/2/1904, Duane Kower; d. 6/22/1960. Two children.

---

* Hilton, p. 43.

SEVENTH GENERATION

195. v. Winfield Twombly, b. 11/24/1889.

142. John Edgar Roberts (Jonathan[6], Seth[5], Jonathan[4], George[3], John[2], George[1]), son of Jonathan and Avis Jane (Bodge) Roberts, was born in Massachusetts about 1852. He married Eva Gertrude Fernald of Dover, New Hampshire. John and Eva were separated and their two children went to live with John's parents in Madbury.* Children:

  i. Amy, b. 9/1887; m. Oliver J. Mercier of Westerly, RI; d.c. 1987, buried at old Roberts place on Stage Road, Madbury. Lived in Wells, ME. 1 adopted son.

196. ii. Charles Edwin, b.c. 1890.

143. Charles Edwin Roberts (Jonathan[6], Seth[5], Jonathan[4], George[3], John[2], George[1]), son of Jonathan and Avis Jane (Bodge) Roberts, was born in Weymouth, Massachusetts, January 8, 1855. He died in Omaha, Nebraska, January 14, 1925, and was buried in West Lawn Cemetery there.

He married in Bethany (now Portis), Kansas, October 12, 1879, Theresa Vine, daughter of William and Elizabeth (Terrill) Vine. She was born near Platteville, Wisconsin, January 27, 1858, died in Omaha, March 10, 1940, of a heart attack suffered while riding a street car to church, and was buried in West Lawn Cemetery.

Charles left his father's farm at the age of about twelve to learn to be a house painter. On March 19, 1878, at the age of 23, he was in Boston to enlist for five years in the cavalry to fight the Indians out West in the Bannock War. He was assigned to C.C. Carr's Company I of the 1st Regiment. After suffering a hernia caused by being thrown from a horse, Charles was honorably discharged at Camp Halleck, Nevada, November 16, 1878. He, and later his widow, received a small disability check from the War Department for the rest of their lives.

Apparently the West appealed to the young Roberts, for he was

---

  * 1960's correspondence with Amy (Roberts) Mercier and 1992 correspondence with Fern (Roberts) Williams.

homesteading a tree claim in Smith County, Kansas, within a few months of his discharge. Here Charles married Theresa, who had come to Kansas from Wisconsin with a preacher's family in a covered wagon. Theresa was to operate a millinery store in Kansas. By 1884 the Robertses had moved to Montfort, Wisconsin, the home of Theresa's parents. They moved finally to Omaha, Nebraska, in 1889. Here Charles worked as a contractor, painter, and paper hanger.

Charles E. Roberts was five feet, nine and one-half inches tall and had fair hair and blue eyes. Naming their first two sons after Presidents Garfield and Arthur, Charles and Theresa were both staunch Republicans.* Children:

197.	i.	Roderick Garfield, b. 6/21/1881.
198.	ii.	Charles Arthur, b. 8/18/1884.
199.	iii.	Harry Edgar, b. 3/27/1886.
	iv.	Theresa Avis, b. 10/17/1887; unm.; d. 1/1980. A school teacher in Omaha.
	v.	Myra Florence, b. 10/25/1895; m. 7/2/1921, David W. Barrow, div. 8/25/1933. Four children. Still living in Omaha in 1990.

144. Willis L. Roberts (Eliphalet[6], Eliphalet[5], Eliphalet[4], George[3], John[2], George[1]), a farmer, son of Eliphalet and Jane (Marden) Roberts, was born in Sharon, Vermont, July 3, 1823, and died in Strafford, Vermont, April 28, 1895. He married, firstly, a first cousin once removed, Sarah Angeline Roberts, February 26, 1843. Sarah was the daughter of Daniel West (No. 30) and Abigail (Latham) Roberts, and was born June 27, 1824, and died in Sharon, October 1, 1867. Willis married, secondly, February 11, 1868, Julia Ann (Hall) Alger, who was born June 15, 1829, in Worcester, Vermont, and died March 3, 1920, in Strafford.+ Children:

---

* Roberts, Theresa Avis, "Roberts Family"; Dept. of War records, National Archives, Wash. D.C.; misc. family papers.
+ Roberts, Blanche J., p. 568.

SEVENTH GENERATION

200.	i.	Nelson C., b. 4/4/1845.
	ii.	Augusta M., b. 2/20/1847; m. Marcus Richardson, 9/2/1877; d. 10/2/1882. One child died young.
201.	iii.	Alonzo S., b. 9/14/1853.
	iv.	Royal E., b. 4/3/1858; d. 1/6/1859,"lung fever".
	v.	Frederick E., b. 11/11/1861; d. 3/29/1863.
202.	vi.	Frederick Ransom, b. 10/22/1865.
	vii.	Jennie E., b. 12/10/1868; d. 3/25/1886.
	viii.	Eva Alger, m. Franklin B. Quimby.

145. Lucian Roberts (Eliphalet^6, Eliphalet^5, Eliphalet^4, George^3, John^2, George^1), a farmer, son of Eliphalet and Jane (Marden) Roberts, was born July 25, 1824, in Sharon, Vermont, and died there April 18, 1889, and is buried in the Pine Hill Cemetery. He married, firstly, a first cousin once removed, Mary Adeline Roberts, September 25, 1845. Mary was the daughter of Daniel West (No. 30) and Abigail (Latham) Roberts, and was born June 27, 1824. Lucian married, secondly, in Sharon, June 30, 1863, Electa Mehitable Blanchard, who was born February 3, 1840, and died in Sharon, March 28, 1916. After Lucian died Electa married Olin Chamberlin, July 20, 1906.* Children:

203.	i.	Franklin B., b. 7/23/1847.
204.	ii.	Curtis Barrett, b. 1849.
205.	iii.	Calvin Blanchard, b. 8/3/1851.
	iv.	Mary Angeline, b. 10/17/1853; m. (1) Charles Tracy, 1/25/1882, (2) Lewis D. Coit, 6/29/1903; d. 9/16/1926. Three children.
	v.	Susan Maria, b. 1856; m. Charles Waterman, 9/26/1877; d. 6/18/1888. One child.

---

* Roberts, Blanche J., p. 557.

DESCENDANTS OF GEORGE & MARY ROBERTS

      vi.   Judith M., b. 2/3/1859; m. Nelson Hubbard, 11/6/1876. 2 ch.

     vii.   Rosabelle, b. 11/29/1861; m. Henry Wilcox, 10/4/1884.

    viii.   Adeline Loella, b. 10/1/1864; m. Herman Barrows, 2/15/1886, Lebanon, NH.

206.   ix.   John, b. 10/1/1866.

       x.   Alice, b. 1/27/1869; m. Arthur S. Hapgood, 11/29/1892; d. 5/31/1927, Whitman, MA, heart attack.

207.   xi.   Charles, b. 5/5/1872.

146. **Mansir Hamilton Roberts** (Eliphalet[6], Eliphalet[5], Eliphalet[4], George[3], John[2], George[1]), a farmer and shoemaker, son of Eliphalet and Jane (Marden) Roberts, was born in Strafford, Vermont, May 25, 1826, and died there May 22, 1899. He married Sarah B. Richardson, the daughter of Aurora and Cynthia (Hunt) Richardson, March 3, 1849. She was born in Northampton, Massachusetts, in 1830, and died in 1914.* Children:

       i.   Augustus A., b. 12/26/1849; d. 3/30/1852.

      ii.   Catherine, b. 1/1/1851; d. 3/30/1851.

208.   iii.   Augustus Harland, b. 2/8/1853.

      iv.   Sarah (?) Josephine, b. 1856; m. (1) William Howard, 7/11/1876, (2) William Rowe, 8/13/1907, (3) Joe Bean, 3/8/1909; d. 1923, Newport, NH.

       v.   Julia Ann, b. 4/17/1862; m. William Fred Carter, 12/25/1887.

      vi.   Gertrude S., m. Rush Hawkins.

147. **Henry Harrison Roberts** (Zerah[6], Eliphalet[5], Eliphalet[4],

---

* Roberts, Blanche J., p. 558.

SEVENTH GENERATION

George³, John², George¹), son of Zerah Norton and Sarah (Sanders) Roberts, was born in Sudbury, Vermont, January 16, 1837, and died in Leicester, Vermont, August 8, 1915. He married Sabina L. (Rossiter) Sawyer, who was born January 25, 1837, and died May 17, 1923.* Children:

209.   i. Glenn Arthur, b. 9/1/1861.

        ii. Benjie Stuart, b. 8/25/1863; d. 5/20/1893.

        iii. Gertrude, b. 12/15/1873; d. 3/3/1877.

        iv. Zerah Norton, b. 3/5/1881.

148. Daniel West Roberts (Amplias⁶, Daniel⁵, Eliphalet⁴, George³, John², George¹), son of Amplias and Mary (Booth) Roberts, was born January 25, 1836, and died July 13, 1913 in Pomfret, Vermont, and was buried in the Hewittville Cemetery. He married Lucy M. Shepard, August 25, 1862, the daughter of Spalding and Mary Shepard. Lucy was born June 9, 1834, in Coventry, Vermont, and died April 25, 1900 in Pomfret, and is also buried in the Hewittville Cemetery. Daniel West was a farmer and breeder of pure blood Atwood Merino sheep, Jersey cattle, and Hambletonian horses. He served in Company G of the 16th Regiment of Vermont Volunteers in the Civil War.⁺ Child:

210.   i. Albertus Royal, b. 3/9(or 19?)/1870.

149. George Wells Roberts (James⁶, Daniel⁵, Eliphalet⁴, George³, John², George¹), a teamster and farmer, the son of James Lull and Betsey (Wells) Roberts, was born in Strafford, Vermont, April 7 (or 4?), 1837, and died there March 2, 1904. He married, firstly, Olive Josephine Kendall, the daughter of Jotham and Clarissa Kendall, March 10, 1859. George married, secondly, March 25, 1865, Miriam Swift, the daughter of Joseph and Nancy (Seavey) Swift. Olive was born July 4, 1841, and died in Strafford, September 19, 1861. Miriam was born April 12, 1841, and died in

---

* Roberts, Blanche J., p. 547.
⁺ Roberts, Blanche J., p. 536.

DESCENDANTS OF GEORGE & MARY ROBERTS

Strafford, June 5, 1919.* Children:

    i. Carlie Josephine, b. 8/5/1861; m. Frank E. Carter, 12/15/1884; d. 6/11/1907, Hanover, NH. Two ch.

    ii. Fred G., b. 5/12/1865; m. Harriet Benjamin, 4/2/1889; d. 9/27/1934. One child.

    iii. Nellie, b. 12/29/1866; d. 1/23/1877.

    iv. Harriet May, b. 3/6/1869; d. 10/12/1872.

    v. Gertrude R., b. 6/17/1871; m. Willis Estes, 11/23/1892; d. 4/17/1924.

    vi. Fannie May, b. 7/21/1874; m. Harvey B. Ordway, 9/27/1892; d. 2/4/1913.

    vii. Della Frances, b. 9/11/1879; m. (1) Frank Colby, 8/26/1898, (2) Elmer Nugent, 9/10/1919; d. 1/17/1950.

150. Alba James Roberts (James[6], Daniel[5], Eliphalet[4], George[3], John[2], George[1]), son of James Lull and Betsey (Wells) Roberts, was born in Strafford, Vermont, October 25, 1840, and died in Enfield, New Hampshire, April 18, 1904. He married in Strafford, Laura Ingraham, the daughter of Jer. and Eunice (Carpenter) Ingraham, March 27, 1864. Laura was born in Victory, Vermont, August 13, 1846, and died in Hartford, Vermont, March 16, 1884.⁺ Children:

    i. Francis R., b. 8/29/1865; m. Lizzie J. Donaghy, 12/10/1886; d. 4/6/1902.

    ii. Willis G., b. 6/27/1871; d. 8/7/1933.

    iii. Jenny Lind, b. 10/15/1872; m. Charles Hutchins, 11/21/1899.

    iv. female child, b. & d. 1/15/1875.

---

  * Roberts, Blanche J., p. 544.
  ⁺ Roberts, Blanche J., p. 527.

SEVENTH GENERATION

    v. Bessie Maud, b. 2/3/1876; m. Fred Paquin, 11/21/1899; d. 7/6/1938.

    vi. Winona May, b. 7/11/1881; d. 11/8/1881.

151. Perrin Roberts (West[6], Daniel[5], Eliphalet[4], George[3], John[2], George[1]), son of West Daniel and Julianna (Stoddard) Roberts, was born in Warren, Vermont, about 1850. He married Caroline Gould, the daughter of Waltz Conant and Mary (Morris) Gould, April 5, 1873. Caroline was born in Lyme, New Hampshire.[*] Child:

    i. Nora May, b. 8/28/1878.

152. Julius D. Roberts (Darius[6], Daniel[5], Eliphalet[4], George[3], John[2], George[1]), son of Darius Witt and Katherine (Taylor) Roberts, was born in Sharon, Vermont, October 8, 1867, and died in West Norwich, Vermont, October 8, 1934, and was buried in the Beaver Meadow Cemetery there. He married, firstly, Verna M. Lackey, April 29, 1908. They were divorced in 1920. Julius married, secondly, Edith May (Henry) Edmunds, August 23, 1929. Verna married, secondly, Henry Shepard. Verna was born October 9, 1882 and died September 17, 1932.[+] Child:

    i. Julius Jr., b. 5/2/1909; m. Stella Labelle, 9/8/1937. Five children. Lived in South Strafford, VT.

153. Frank Orlando Roberts (Orlando[6], Moses[5], Eliphalet[4], George[3], John[2], George[1]), son of Orlando Hartwell and Laura Marinda (Badger) Roberts, was born in Vermont, May 15, 1852, and died in Bethel, Vermont, March 31, 1928. He is buried in the Fairview Cemetery in Bethel. He was a farmer.

Frank was married four times. His first wife, and mother of the first four children listed below, was Emma Luce, the daughter of Alpha and Mary (Amell) Luce. Frank and Emma were married November 9, 1873, in Stockbridge, Vermont. After Emma died January 25, 1884, Frank married Lutheria Crossman. Lutheria was

---

    [*] Roberts, Blanche J., p. 561.
    [+] Roberts, Blanche J., p. 554.

the daughter of Amos Holt and Polly B. (Wheat) Crossman. Frank was Lutheria's second husband, the first being Charles Pinney and the third being John Duffany. Frank and Lutheria had one child - Carl Jackson. His other marriages were in 1889, to Hattie Almira Clark (the daughter of Alexander and Almira (Roberts) Clark), with whom he had one child who died in infancy, and in 1927, to Leota Maud Rogers.[*] Children:

      i. George Eugene, b. 2/3/1875; m. 4/28/1896, Mary (Mina) Fredette; d. 2/27/1937, Woodstock, VT.

      ii. Mary Lillian, b. 9/1/1876; m. 12/16/1899, Glenn E. Foster.

      iii. Stella Sarah, b. 3/12/1878; m. 5/15/1894, James Monroe French; d. 9/18/1924.

      iv. Edwin Orrin, b. 12/26/1879; d. 8/30/1882.

211.   v. Carl Jackson, b. 10/27/1885.

      vi. Myrtie Jane, b. 1890; d. 1890.

154. **Stephen Roberts** (Stephen^6, Stephen^5, Eliphalet^4, George^3, John^2, George^1), son of Stephen and Mary N. (Clark) Roberts, was born in Vermont, March 15, 1862, and died there July 18, 1938. He married Lillian M. Jenks, June 15, 1895. This family lived in Norwich, Vermont, where the following two children were born.[+] Children:

      i. Ray Daniel, b. 6/4/1896.

      ii. Glen Edward, b. 3/3/1908.

---

    [*] Bryant and Verret notes.
    [+] Roberts, Blanche J., p. 565.

EIGHTH GENERATION

155. Charles Justin Roberts (Justin[7], Isaac[6], Joseph[5], Joseph[4], George[3], John[2], George[1]), son of Justin and Mary Jane (McLeod) Roberts, was born in Brooks, Maine, November 9, 1843 and died there April 13, 1892. He married Maranda W. Warren, March 20, 1864, in China, Maine. Charles served in Company I of the Fourteenth Maine Infantry during the Civil War.[*] Children:

    i. Alberta, b. 6/30/1866, Brooks; d. 8/20/1869.

    ii. Lelia, b. 3/9/1868, Brooks; d. 8/17/1869.

    iii. Melzar, b. 9/20/1871, Belfast, ME; d. 4/11/1892.

    iv. Evie E., b. 1/14/1877, Searsport, ME.

156. Allen Hamlin Roberts (Hamlin[7], Jacob[6], Joseph[5], Joseph[4], George[3], John[2], George[1]), son of Hamlin Myrick and Mary Ann (Rich) Roberts, was born in Jackson, Maine, February 22, 1836, and died after 1901, apparently in Illinois. He married Kate Weatherhead of Pawtucket, Rhode Island, in 1863. Allen was educated at New Hampton Seminary in New Hampshire and taught school in Maine, Massachusetts, and Rhode Island. In 1857 he moved to Illinois, where he worked for the railroad and later had a stock business in Council Bluffs, Iowa, and Chicago.[+] Child:

    i. Katie, d. Chicago aged 9.

157. Francis Alton Roberts (Hamlin[7], Jacob[6], Joseph[5], Joseph[4], George[3], John[2], George[1]), son of Hamlin Myrick and Mary Ann (Rich) Roberts, was born in Jackson, Maine, August 9, 1838, and died in Waterville, Maine, May 26, 1892. He married Mary F. Huzzy of China, Maine, in December of 1861. Francis was educated at New Hampton Seminary in New Hampshire and Dartmouth College. Graduating in 1861 from Hahnemann Homeopathic College in Philadelphia, he took up the practice of

---

    [*] Grant, pp. 30-1.

    [+] Grant, p. 41.

medicine. Francis practiced most of his career in North Vassalboro and Waterville, Maine. He was also a horse breeder.* Child:

    i. Emily, d. 1873, age 3.

158. Cassius Clay Roberts (Hamlin^7, Jacob^6, Joseph^5, Joseph^4, George^3, John^2, George^1), son of Hamlin Myrick and Mary Ann (Rich) Roberts, was born in Jackson, Maine, March 5, 1845, and died after 1905, apparently in Illinois.

    He married three times. His first wife was Paulina E. Colcord, the daughter of Josiah and Jane (Berry) Colcord, of Stockton, Maine. They were married December 31, 1868, and the two daughters listed below were hers. Paulina died November 30, 1875, and Cassius married, secondly, on January 5, 1898, Margaret Bennett, the daughter of James J. Bennett, of Clyde, Illinois. Margaret died August 28, 1899, and Cassius married, thirdly, Katherine T. Harlan, of Louisville, Kentucky. The son listed below is by her.

    Cassius had a very colorful career as a soldier, politician and newspaperman. In August of 1861, at the age of 16 he enlisted in the Tenth Maine Infantry. Later he served with the First Maine Heavy Artillery. Rising through the ranks to captain, he saw service in the Shenandoah Valley, Louisiana, and at Appomattox Courthouse in 1865, where he witnessed Lee's surrender. After the War Cassius graduated from Eastman's Business College in Poughkeepsie, New York, and returned to Maine to form a partnership in the shipbuilding industry and operated a general store in Stockton. In Stockton he was chairman of the board of selectmen for three years and was elected in 1878 to the Maine State Senate. In 1880 he moved to Boston to take up a commission business and a job as a political reporter for the *Boston Globe*. In 1884 the Robertses moved to Chicago where Cassius had a grocery business and published and edited the *Chicago Opinion*. About 1900 he became superintendent of several post office stations in Chicago. He was active in the Grand Army of the Republic and

---

    * Grant, p. 42.

EIGHTH GENERATION

several social and fraternal organizations.* Children:

   i. Parepa Rosa, b. 8/7/1869;m. William I. Bennett.

   ii. Paulina E., b. 8/15/1875; m. James J. Lawler, 2/13/1897.

   iii. Cassius Philip, b. 7/29/1899; d. 6/22/1901, from ingesting gasoline administered by a deranged nurse.

   iv. Cassius Harlan, b. 3/13/1905.

159. Edward Junius Roberts (Jacob^7, Jacob^6, Joseph^5, Joseph^4, George^3, John^2, George^1), son of Jacob Wellington and Phebe Susan (Abbot) Roberts, was born in Brooks, Maine, February 10, 1839, and died, apparently in Maine, sometime after 1901. He married Emma Evans of Dixmont, Maine, November 15, 1865. Edward graduated from Philadelphia Dental College in 1865. He practiced in Vassalboro, Maine, and then, beginning in 1870, in Augusta, Maine. He was a founding member of the Maine Dental Association, active in the Methodist Church, and a member of the Masons and the Knights Templar.* Children:

   i. Arthur Wellington, b. 8/20/1868, North Vassalboro.

   ii. Lottie Adelia, b. 9/11/1873; d. 10/14/1873.

   iii. Orville Leslie, b. 10/12/1874, Augusta, where he was in practice as a dentist.

160. Freeman Myrick Roberts (Jacob^7, Jacob^6, Joseph^5, Joseph^4, George^3, John^2, George^1), son of Jacob Wellington and Phebe Susan (Abbot) Roberts, was born in South Jackson, Maine,

---

* Little, George T. *Genealogical and Family History of the State of Maine.* New York: Lewis Historical Publishing Co., 1909. Vol. III, pp. 1639-40; Grant, pp. 43-6.

* Grant, pp. 48-9.

December 21, 1840, and died, apparently in Maine, after 1901. He married Aurelia Julana York, February 1, 1866. She died September 11, 1899, aged fifty-five. Freeman enlisted in Company F, Fourth Maine Infantry, to serve in the Civil War. He participated in First Bull Run, Gettysburg, the Wilderness, and Cold Harbor, among other battles. After the war he farmed in Jackson and later Newport, Maine.* Children:

    i. Ella Mabel, b. 2/14/1870; m. Oscar R. Emerson, 12/8/1896. Lived in Monson, ME.

    ii. Anna, b. 9/21/1871; d. 8/24/1872.

    iii. Junius Everett, b. 2/14/1875; m. Blanche Whittum. A high school principal in Presque Isle, ME. At least one child - Edward Freeman, b. 10/14/1901.

    iv. Bertha Myra, b. 7/3/1877; d. 12/10/1880.

    v. Amorena Gertrude, b. 5/14/1880; m. Bela Burrill, 6/2/1900. Lived in Newport, ME. At least one ch.

161. Charles Sumner Roberts (Barnabas^7, Jacob^6, Joseph^5, Joseph^4, George^3, John^2, George^1), son of Barnabas Myrick and Emeline (Rich) Roberts, was born in Jackson, Maine, August 21, 1851, and died in Stockton, Maine, February 16, 1882. He married Faustina Marden of Stockton, Maine, January 18, 1877.⁺ Child:

    i. Alton, b. 3/9/1880.

162. Woodbury Davis Roberts (Barnabas^7, Jacob^6, Joseph^5, Joseph^4, George^3, John^2, George^1), son of Barnabas Myrick and Emeline (Rich) Roberts, was born in Stockton, Maine, September 5, 1855, and died, apparently in Washington state, after 1901. He married Evelyn Cheney of Stockton, June 14, 1879. She was born July 10, 1856. This family moved to Chehalis, Washington about 1885.# Children:

---

    * Grant, pp. 49-50.
    ⁺ Grant, p. 53.
    # Grant, p. 53.

EIGHTH GENERATION

 i. Fred Barnabas, b. 6/18/1885.

 ii. Edward Cheney, b. 3/28/1892.

 iii. Eldon Woodbury, b. 7/1/1897.

163. Charles Addison Roberts (Charles[7], Jacob[6], Joseph[5], Joseph[4], George[3], John[2], George[1]), son on Charles Linneus and Caroline P. (Metcalf) Roberts, was born in Yates City, Illinois, August 10, 1862. He married Mary Wolcott of Quincy, Illinois, June 5, 1889. Charles worked for the railroad in Elmwood, Illinois, until his election as a Republican to the office of clerk of the probate court of Peoria County in 1898.[*] Children:

 i. George Seacord, b. 1/9/1891.

 ii. Isabel, b. 4/15/1893; d. 4/5/1899.

 iii. Wolcott, b. 9/1/1897.

164. Charles Wellington Roberts (Porteus[7], Jacob[6], Joseph[5], Joseph[4], George[3], John[2], George[1]), son of Porteus Beezaleel and Mary Ann (Preckett) Roberts, was born in Bunker Hill, Illinois, July 1, 1850. He married Sarah Angeline Lusk, October 1, 1879. Charles was a farmer and doctor in Mechanicsville, Iowa.[+] Children:

 i. Mary Blanche, b. 7/18/1880.

 ii. Grace, b. 11/9/1882; d. 11/14/1889.

 iii. Porteus Henry, b. 3/4/1885.

 iv. Cora Belle, b. 12/6/1888.

 v. Bertha Palmer, b. 11/12/1894.

165. Campbell Myrick Roberts (Porteus[7], Jacob[6], Joseph[5], Joseph[4], George[3], John[2], George[1]), son of Porteus Beezaleel and Mary Ann (Preckett) Roberts, was born in New York, August 14, 1865. He married Mattie Morris, June 17, 1891.[#] Children:

---

[*] Grant, p. 55.
[+] Grant, p. 58.
[#] Grant, p. 59.

i. Arthur Campbell, b. 4/11/1892.

  ii. Emmet Livingston, b. 5/21/1896.

166. Lincoln Hamlin Roberts (Porteus[7], Jacob[6], Joseph[5], Joseph[4], George[3], John[2], George[1]), son of Porteus Beezaleel and Mary Ann (Preckett) Roberts, was born in Brooklyn, New York, March 20, 1877. He married Nettie Morris, April, 1897. There may have been children in addition to those listed below.[*] Children:

  i. Jennette Adele, b. 3/20/1898.

  ii. Milton Lincoln, b. 3/10/1899; d. 7/1/1899.

  iii. Howard, b. 1900; d. 3/1901.

167. Samuel Gilman Roberts (Ahira[7], Gilman[6], Joseph[5], Joseph[4], George[3], John[2], George[1]), son of Ahira and Mary Ann (Durgin) Roberts, was born in Maine, March 10, 1843. He married Mrs. Jennie Baldwin, October 18, 1872. Samuel served in the Seventeenth Massachusetts Regiment during the Civil War. In 1871 he moved to Fargo, North Dakota, where he became an attorney.[+] Children:

  i. Frank Augustus, b. 8/22/1874; d. 11/19/1876.

  ii. child, b. 12/7/1876; d. 12/8/1876.

  iii. Ruth, b. 12/2/1878; m. Gilbert W. Haggert, 11/21/1900. Lived in Fargo.

168. Albert Roberts (Ahira[7], Gilman[6], Joseph[5], Joseph[4], George[3], John[2], George[1]), son of Ahira and Mary Ann (Durgin) Roberts, was born in Brooks, Maine, July 28, 1844, and died apparently in North Dakota, after 1901. He married Isabella M. McKinley, the daughter of William McKinley, March 9, 1868. Albert enlisted in Company C of the Twentieth Regiment of Maine Volunteers in 1862. He suffered a head wound at Cold Harbor and permanently lost all hearing in his right ear. After the War he attended Poughkeepsie Business College, where he graduated in

---

[*] Grant, p. 59.
[+] Grant, pp. 73-5.

EIGHTH GENERATION

1866. Shortly thereafter he headed west and located in Greenwood, Minnesota, where he farmed and taught school. As a Republican he served two years in the state legislature. By 1883 this family had migrated to Devil's Lake, North Dakota, where they were engaged in extensive farming and cattle raising. Albert was active in the Grand Army of the Republic and the Masons.* Children:

    i. Mae Bethia, b. 7/16/1869, Lake Sarah, MN; m. George A. Ruhberg, 12/25/1890. One child.

    ii. Hallie, b. 1871; d. in infancy.

    iii. Olive, b. 1873; d. aged 7.

    iv. Floyd John (twin), b. 7/14/1876; graduated from medical department of Hamline University, Minneapolis, in 1899. Sent by U.S. government to North Dakota to help with eradication of smallpox.

    v. Lloyd Albert (twin), b. 7/14/1876. A teacher and farmer in Devil's Lake.

    vi. Roy Ralph, b. 9/14/1880; d. 8/26/1900.

    vii. Ruth Muriel, b. 8/12/1883. A teacher in ND.

169. Augustus Roberts (Ahira^7, Gilman^6, Joseph^5, Joseph^4, George^3, John^2, George^1), son of Ahira and Mary Ann (Durgin) Roberts, was born in Maine, April 15, 1852. He married Florence Chambers in December of 1879. Augustus was a county judge in Fargo, North Dakota.⁺ Children:

    i. Edwin Abbott, b. 12/7/1880.

    ii. Jay, b. 9/18/1883; d. 5/13/1884.

170. Freeman Otis Roberts (Ezra^7, Gilman^6, Joseph^5, Joseph^4, George^3, John^2, George^1), son of Ezra and Lydia (Wentworth) Roberts, was born in Maine, September 11, 1856. He married Mary Olivia Larrabee, who was born April 6, 1856.#

---

* Grant, pp. 75-8.
⁺ Grant, p. 79.
Grant, p. 83.

Children:

    i. Charles Arthur, b. 1/13/1881.

    ii. William Winworth, b. 10/27/1884.

    iii. Hattie May, b. 7/31/1886.

    iv. Freeman Edwin, b. 6/13/1888.

    v. Frank Gilman, b. 9/2/1890.

    vi. Chester Allen, b. 1/28/1895.

    vii. Carrie Gertrude, b. 5/17/1896.

171. Herbert F. Roberts (Jacob^7, Enoch^6, Joseph^5, Joseph^4, George^3, John^2, George^1), son of Jacob and Cynthia (Badger) Roberts, was born in Maine, July 18, 1858, and died there March 28, 1900. He married Hattie Briggs of Monroe, Maine, March 21, 1881.* Children:

    i. Delia L., b. 5/7/1882.

    ii. Harry W., b. 6/2/1884.

    iii. Hovey L., b. 4/8/1893.

172. Melvin W. Roberts (Jacob^7, Enoch^6, Joseph^5, Joseph^4, George^3, John^2, George^1), son of Jacob and Cynthia (Badger) Roberts, was born in Maine, February 23, 1862. He married Annie Hall, the daughter of Enoch Hall of Brooks, Maine.⁺ Children:

    i. Celia Maud, b. 5/30/1886, Brooks.

    ii. Earle Melvin, b. 4/27/1893, Monroe, ME.

173. George Atwood Roberts (Jacob^7, Enoch^6, Joseph^5, Joseph^4, George^3, John^2, George^1), son of Jacob and Cynthia (Badger) Roberts, was born in Maine, October 23, 1865. He married Lilla V. Austin of Lemoine, Maine, June 20, 1889, in Union, Maine. This family lived in North Cambridge,

---

    * Grant, pp. 85-6.

    ⁺ Grant, p. 86.

EIGHTH GENERATION

Massachusetts.* Children:

    i. Heleaa Belle, b. 4/5/1890, Union, ME.

    ii. Hazel Dell, b. 5/12/1892, Portland, ME.

    iii. Jessie Maria, b. 1/31/1899, Union, ME.

174. Forrest K. Roberts (William⁷, Timothy⁶, Joseph⁵, Joseph⁴, George³, John², George¹), son of William Henry Harrison and Esther B. (Rand) Roberts, was born in Brooks, Maine, February 9, 1860. He married Mabel Penney.⁺ Children:

    i. Claire E., b. 7/3/1890.

    ii. Olive G., b. 2/3/1894.

175. Edna M. Roberts (William⁷, Timothy⁶, Joseph⁵, Joseph⁴, George³, John², George¹), son of William Henry Harrison and Esther B. (Rand) Roberts, was born in Brooks, Maine, December 6, 1865. He married Julia Wentworth. They resided in Quincy, Massachusetts.# Children:

    i. Tomasita Margarita, b. 4/26/1889.

    ii. William Harrison, b. 8/29/1891.

    iii. Esther Myrtle, b. 10/5/1893.

    iv. Edward Nathaniel, b. 10/5/1897.

176. Eugene Roswell Roberts (Watson⁷, Samuel⁶, Samuel⁵, Jonathan⁴, George³, John², George¹), son of Watson Clifford and Olive Melissa (Cummings) Roberts, was born in Concord, New Hampshire, April 22, 1856, and died in Alaska about 1912. He married Sierra Nevada Fleming on January 1, 1888, in Forest Ranch, California. "Vada", the daughter of George and Isaphena (Carver) (Walker) Fleming, was born in Chico, California, January 23, 1868, and died in Pacific Grove, California, August 3, 1953. Her ashes lie in the El Carmelo Urn Garden in Pacific

---

* Grant, p. 86.
⁺ Grant, p. 115.
Grant, p. 115.

Grove. Eugene worked for many years as a lumberman and machinist and then owned and operated shoe repair shops in Chico, Oroville, and Oakland, California. At nights he studied law and later practiced in Oakland. He was also a fiddler at country dances, and that is how he met his wife. The first four children below were born in Chico, the last in Oroville.* Children:

      i. Anna May, b. 11/30/1888; m. Oakland, 7/21/1911, Charles E. Davis; d. San Jose, CA 11/8/1915. 2 ch.

      ii. Etta Eugenia, b. 1/15/1891; m. Oakland, 6/19/1910, James T. Rye; d. San Jose, 3/21/1960. Three ch.

      iii. Charles Watson, b. 12/16/1892; m. (1) San Jose, 12/20/1914, Olga K. Carlson, (2) Reno, NV, 1/28/1964, Betty Ford, a widow; d. Walnut Creek, CA, 7/9/1973. No children.

212.   iv. Walter Clifford, b. 8/1/1895.

      v. Richard Henry, b. 11/10/1900; d. Oakland 11/24/1905 of spinal meningitis.

177. James S. Roberts (Jonathan[7], Josiah[6], Samuel[5], Jonathan[4], George[3], John[2], George[1]), son of Jonathan and Sarah (Stimpson) Roberts, was born in Brooks, Maine, December 8, 1861, and died in Medway, Massachusetts, July 7, 1936, and is buried in Belfast, Maine. He married, firstly, Emma Ames, and, secondly, July 5, 1884, Rosa B. Sweet. Rosa was born in Knox, Maine, March 8, 1866, and died in Thomaston, Maine, December 15, 1919.⁺ Children:

      i. Grace E., b. 4/1885; m. Ralph Emmons; d. 7/13/1946. No children.

      ii. Emma, b. 9/29/1887; m. Perley Barry; d. 8/12/1975. Three children.

---

    * Hilton supp. pp. 4-5; Jones notes.
    ⁺ Cafferty, p. 189-190.

EIGHTH GENERATION

213.   iii. Wellington J., b. 8/1888 (or 1889?).

214.   iv. Lawrence James, b. 1/5/1891.

215.   v. Maurice E., b. 8/2/1895.

216.   vi. Arthur B., b. 12/10/1897.

178. Henry C. (or G.?) Roberts (Jonathan[7], Josiah[6], Samuel[5], Jonathan[4], George[3], John[2], George[1]), son of Jonathan and Sarah (Stimpson) Roberts, was born in Brooks, Maine, in December of 1863, and died in December of 1949. He married Amanda E. Swett, who was born in Knox, Maine, June 26, 1864, and died in Brooks, August 4, 1950.* Child:

  i. Gladys G., b. 10/12/1892; unm.

179. Cyrus H. Roberts (Jonathan[7], Josiah[6], Samuel[5], Jonathan[4], George[3], John[2], George[1]), son of Jonathan and Sarah (Stimpson) Roberts, was born in Brooks, Maine, July 11, 1865, and died in Belfast, Maine, October 24, 1948. He married, firstly, Addie Peavey, December 20, 1891. She and two children died at child birth. Cyrus married, secondly, Florence May Woodbury, who was born in Knox, Maine, September 21, 1889, and died in Belfast, Maine, February 20, 1962. The first child below is Addie's, and the remainder Florence's.[+] Children:

217.   i. Luther Earl, b. 9/20/1895.

  ii. Edna Hazel, b. 6/23/1908; d. 9/27/1912.

  iii. Thelma Ruby, b. 4/17/1917; m. Clyde Page. Living in Belfast, ME. Three children.

  iv. Horatio Walter, b. 8/2/1921; d. 10/30/1923.

180. Frank H. Roberts (Jonathan[7], Josiah[6], Samuel[5], Jonathan[4], George[3], John[2], George[1]), son of Jonathan and Sarah

---

* Cafferty, p. 195.
+ Cafferty, pp. 195-6 & 199.

(Stimpson) Roberts, was born in Maine, March 27, 1874, and died in Swanville, Maine, in 1955. He married Elizabeth Roberts.* Child:

 218. i. Frank Herbert, b. 5/24/1917.

181. George S. Roberts (Jonathan^7, Josiah^6, Samuel^5, Jonathan^4, George^3, John^2, George^1), son of Jonathan and Sarah (Stimpson) Roberts, was born in Maine, December 30, 1880, and died in Belfast, Maine, in 1962. He married Mary Rennie, who was born in Abadine, Scotland, May 11, 1884, and died November 22, 1948.⁺ Children:

 i. Clarence, b. 1902.

 ii. Everard, b. 12/1/1903; d. 1954.

 iii. Phebe, b. 9/20/1905; m. John Brown. One child.

 iv. Evelyn, b. 7/1/1907.

 v. Claribel, b. 4/15/1915; m. Robert Gould; d. 3/3/1961, Bangor, ME. Five children.

182. William E. Roberts (Levi^7, Josiah^6, Samuel^5, Jonathan^4, George^3, John^2, George^1), son of Levi and Lucy (Holmes?) Roberts, was born in Maine in 1872, and died in Monroe, Maine, in 1927. He married Adelia Seeking, who was born in Swanville, Maine, October 16, 1881, and died in 1955.# Child:

 i. Lucy C.(or G.?), b. 3/1899; m. Louis A. Stubbs. Three children.

183. Frederick L. Roberts (Levi^7, Josiah^6, Samuel^5, Jonathan^4, George^3, John^2, George^1), son of Levi and Lucy (Holmes?) Roberts, was born in Carmel, Maine, March 3, 1876, and died October 5, 1940. He married Edith M. Page, July 14, 1908, in Providence, Rhode Island.** Children:

---

 * Cafferty, p. 201.
 ⁺ Cafferty, pp. 202-3.
 # Cafferty, p. 206.
 ** Cafferty, p. 206.

EIGHTH GENERATION

    i. Laura M., b. 5/4/1910; m. Kenneth G. Lambie.

    ii. Alice P., b. 1/23/1912; m. Howard Whipple.

184. Leslie Burton Roberts (Levi[7], Josiah[6], Samuel[5], Jonathan[4], George[3], John[2], George[1]), son of Levi and Rachel Ella (Harvey) Roberts, was born in Orneville, Maine, in February of 1888, and died in Swanville, Maine, November 17, 1962. He married Daisy Howard, who was born in Belfast, Maine, September 24, 1886, and died in Swanville, August 22, 1964. This family lived in Bucksport, Searsmont and Swansville, Maine.* Children:

	i.	Leslie, b. 9/29/1907; unm.; d. 6/15/1990.
	ii.	Maxine, b. 7/25/1909; m. Ralph Richards; d. 3/27/1988. Lived in East Belfast, ME. 3 ch.
	iii.	Irish, b. 9/10/1911; m. (1) Chester Richards, div., (2) George Frattarilla. Four children.
	iv.	Waneta (Wanda), b. 5/23/1913; m. (1) Kermit Leeman, (2) Bernard Eveslage; d. 1959. Lived in Belfast, ME. Four children.
219.	v.	Claude, b. 10/20/1914.
	vi.	Marguerite, b. 10/8/1916; m. Fred Floyd. Living in Swanville, ME. Six children.
	vii.	Arline, b. 2/3/1920; m. Elmer Walker; d. 6/11/1985. Lived in Swanville, ME. 3 ch.
220.	viii.	Stanley, b. 10/27/1921.
221.	ix.	Robert, b. 2/27/1924.
	x.	Daisy, b. 5/11/1926; m. Freeman Gushee. Living in Belfast, ME. Five children.

---

* Hilton supplement, p. 2; Notes of Ervin Roberts.

xi. Florence, b. 12/29/1928; m. 10/3/1946, Lonnie Griffin; d. 12/28/1980. Lived in Appleton, ME. Six children.

185. Ernest Tucker Roberts (Levi^7, Josiah^6, Samuel^5, Jonathan^4, George^3, John^2, George^1), son of Levi and Rachel Ella (Harvey) Roberts, was born in Orneville, Maine, April 5, 1890, and died in Morrill, Maine, November 2, 1953, and is buried in South Brooks, Maine. He married in Brooks, Maine, April 16, 1916, Agnes Cram, who was born in Brooks, Maine, July 13, 1900 and died in Portland, Maine, October 1, 1972. This family lived in Belfast, Brooks, and Morrell, Maine.* Children:

    i. Ernestine, b. 4/17/1918; m. 6/22/1940, George Riley; d. 6/12/1964. Went to North Carolina. 1 ch.

    ii. Levi, b. 5/30/1919; d. 7/3/1919.

    iii. Ella Mae, b. 9/22/1920; m. 8/10/1940, Guy Work. Living in Monroe, ME. Three children.

    iv. Frances, b. 3/23/1922; m. 4/26/1941, Robert Dolloff. Living in Monroe, ME. Six children.

    v. Marian (twin), b. 2/22/1924; m. 5/9/1945, Malcolm Wood. Living in Belfast, ME. Three children.

    vi. Mary (twin), b. 2/22/1924; d. 3/4/1925.

222. vii. Ervin, b. 4/29/1926.

    viii. Norma, b. 4/29/1928; m. 12/11/1948, Francis Woodbury. Living in Morrill, ME. 3 ch.

    ix. Lucille, b. 11/21/1931; m.(1) 10/5/1947, Paul Payne, div., (2) George Gatchell, (3) Neal Fox. Living in Corinth, ME. Seven children.

---

* Hilton supplement, p. 2; Notes of Ervin Roberts.

EIGHTH GENERATION

       x. Margaret, b. 8/7/1936; m. 9/16/1951, Hugh Littlefield. Living in Morrill, ME. Five children.

223.   xi. Roger Ernest, b. 1/7/1941.

186. Raymond Renworth Roberts (Levi^7, Josiah^6, Samuel^5, Jonathan^4, George^3, John^2, George^1), son of Levi and Ella (Harvey) Roberts, was born in Orneville, Maine, December 12, 1892 and died of a stroke, in Cranston, Rhode Island, May 24, 1942, and is buried in the Pocasset Cemetery there. He married Lena Maria Fenner, December 24, 1910, in Providence, Rhode Island. Lena was born September 23, 1889, in Johnston, Rhode Island, and died in Cranston, March 1, 1971, and is also buried in the Pocasset Cemetery. Raymond worked at a number of jobs in Cranston, teamster, motor car conductor, fireman and warehouseman.* Children:

      i. Evelyn Frances, b. 10/20/1911; m. John W. Schofield 1/1929; d. 1991. Two children.

      ii. Ella Dorothy, b. 8/1912; m. Gunnar Mortenson, 4/5/1930. Lived in Greenville, RI. Three children.

      iii. Ruth Olive, b. 6/14/1915; m. Ernest Boehm, 6/24/1935. Two children.

      iv. Lena May, b. 9/21/1919; m. William Simmons, 2/1938. Two children.

      v. Helen Louise, b. 4/13/1923; m. (1) John Coulthurst, div., (2) Earl Adams, 1/1/1956; d. 12/28/1979. One child.

      vi. Audrey Ernestine, b. 10/15/1927; m. Edward H. Cafferty, 6/29/1946. Three children. Live in Norwood, MA.

      vii. Lena.

187. Raymond Sylvester Roberts (Alpheus^7, Watson^6,

---

* Cafferty, pp. 7-9 and 228-9.

Samuel⁵, Jonathan⁴, George³, John², George¹), son of Alpheus and Emma (Sylvester) Roberts, was born in Brooks, Maine, August 21, 1894. He married in Brooks Nina Dickey, daughter of Walter and Grace (Jenkins) Dickey, a distant cousin.* Children:

    i. Ruth Havenner, b. 2/16/1922; m. (1) Arthur Mingo, Waterville, ME, div., (2) Skip Burns. Lived in Mountain Home, ID. No children.

224. ii. Raymond Sylvester, b. 3/12/1923.

225. iii. Edgar Frank, b. 4/11/1924.

226. iv. Edwin Ashley, b. 8/7/1925.

188. Frank W. Roberts (Nathan⁷, Amos⁶, George⁵, Jonathan⁴, George³, John², George¹), a shoe store owner, son of Nathan and Augusta (Parshley) Roberts, was born in Sangerville, Maine, December 6, 1850, and died in Brunswick, Maine, February 15, 1911. He married Abbie Eliza Stanwood, the daughter of Nathaniel and Ella Jane (Linscott) Stanwood. Abbie was born in Brunswick, Maine, April 14, 1855 and died there February 12, 1944.⁺ Children:

227. i. Willis Elmer, b. 9/17/1885.

228. ii. Frank Stanwood, b. 3/26/1893.

189. Charles D. Roberts (Nathan⁷, Amos⁶, George⁵, Jonathan⁴, George³, John², George¹), a shoe store owner, son of Nathan and Augusta (Parshley) Roberts, was born in Maine in 1855 and died there in 1923 and is buried in Mt. Pleasant Cemetery in Dexter. He married Lucy Grant, who was born in 1853 and died in 1903.# Child:

    i. Marguerite, b. 1/1/1894 (or 1898?); m. Charles Bradeen; d. 3/4/1949, Bangor, ME. Two children.

190. George Brinton Roberts (George⁷, Amos⁶, George⁵, Jonathan⁴, George³, John², George¹), son of George B. M. and

---

 * Hilton, pp. 9-10.
 ⁺ Hilton, p. 13.
 # Hilton, p. 13.

EIGHTH GENERATION

Hannah Jane (Ramsdell) Roberts, was born in Maine, October 17, 1857, and died in Old Town, Maine, December 3, 1918. He married in November 1878, Hannah Patten Weeks, who was born April 2, 1860 and died in Bucksport, Maine, October 2, 1919.* Children:

    i. Edith Lola, b. 1/8/1880; m. (1) 9/2/1913, Hugh K. Borland,(2)7/16/1924,Harvey A. Tompkins. No children.

    ii. Annie Lucretia, b. 7/16/1881; m. 9/12/1909, Herbert Sawyer; d. 1964. Four children.

229. iii. George Brinton, b. 4/11/1883.

230. iv. Wilbur Prescott, b. 11/6/1885.

    v. Ralph Clifford, b. 8/22/1888; m. 11/4/1909, Ethel Powers; d. 4/1/1961. No children.

231. vi. Forest Rupert, b. 2/12/1891.

232. vii. Merton Elmer, b. 5/6/1893.

    viii. Atlee Fitzhugh, b. 12/29/1899; d. 8/9/1900.

191. Frederick Parkhurst Roberts (George[7], Amos[6], George[5], Jonathan[4], George[3], John[2], George[1]), son of George B. M. and Hannah Jane (Ramsdell) Roberts, was born in Maine, in 1858. He died October 24, 1920 at Eagle Lake, Maine. He married, firstly, Marion Annie Pierce, the daughter of Albert and Joan (Rand) Pierce. Marion died in May of 1888. Frederick married, secondly, Lucy Bloodsworth, in Caribou, Maine, on November 22, 1892. She was born in 1871 and died in January of 1903.⁺ Children:

233. i. George Frederick, b. 1886.

    ii. Nina Belle, d. 8/1889.

234. iii. Earle Henry, b. 12/9/1893.

---

    * Hilton, p. 16.
    ⁺ Hilton, p. 17.

DESCENDANTS OF GEORGE & MARY ROBERTS

235.   iv.   William Lewis, b. 9/1(or 7?)/1896.

       v.   Katherine, b. 6/2/1901; m. (1) Rudolph Ashe, 11/5/1921, (2) Frederick Fogg, 4/27/1946. 2 ch.

192. William Otis Roberts (Amos^7, Amos^6, George^5, Jonathan^4, George^3, John^2, George^1), son of Amos B. and Rebecca J. (Pullen) Roberts, was born in Maine, January 20, 1859 and died May 9, 1931. He married Hattie Adel Hart, who was born May 10, 1860 and died January 8, 1928.* Children:

236.   i.   Stanley W., b. 7/11/1880, Dexter, ME.

      ii.   Eva Elizabeth, b. 2/25/1887; m. Albert Sutton, 5/11/1907; d. 9/1966. Six children.

      iii. Ida May, b. 2/24/1889; m. Frank J. Garborino. Three children.

      iv. Arthur L., b. 2/9/1891; d. 8/31/1891.

237.   v.   Menza Alfred, b. 5/17/1892.

193. Adrian Roberts (Amos^7, Amos^6, George^5, Jonathan^4, George^3, John^2, George^1), son of Amos B. and Rebecca J. (Pullen) Roberts, was born in Dexter, Maine, November 24, 1864, and died April 20, 1950 in Skowhegan, Maine, and is buried in the Southside Cemetery there. He married Hattie Devoll, the daughter of David A. and Olive B. Devoll, in Dexter, June 29, 1888. She was born March 25, 1871 and died December 3, 1935. Adrian and Hattie were divorced and Adrian married, secondly, Rose Turner, and thirdly, Alice Tucker. The first four children below were by Hattie and the last one by Rose.⁺ Children:

      i.   Ethel, b. 4/29/1890, Dexter; m. (1) Lester Libby, 9/5/1905, div., (2) Enoch Flewelling, 11/1/1919; d. 4/3/1957 or 1958, Skowhegan. Four children.

238.   ii.   Timothy Victor, b. 7/25/1892, Norridgewock, ME.

---

* Hilton, pp. 24-5.
⁺ Hilton, p. 25.

EIGHTH GENERATION

    iii. Harold E., b. 9/23/1894; d. 8/27/1895.

    iv. Calla, b. 4/16/1896, Skowhegan; m. (1) Herbert Huff, 8/11/1917, (2) Harry Bosworth, 12/2/1937; d. 3/17/1960, Skowhegan. Two children.

239.   v. Everett, b. 9/20/1902, Dexter.

194. Otis Jackson Roberts (Otis[7], Amos[6], George[5], Jonathan[4], George[3], John[2], George[1]), son of Otis Oakes and Louise (Hussey) Roberts, was born in Belgrade, Maine, March 1, 1877, and died at Dexter, Maine, January 17, 1965, and is buried in Mt. Pleasant Cemetery there. He married, firstly, Myrtle Estelle Farrar, May 16, 1898 at Dexter, Maine. She was born in Dexter July 12, 1877 and died March 14, 1906. Otis married, secondly, Marcia Alice Jackson at Dexter, on May 11, 1912. Born in Sangerville, Maine, November 20, 1883, she was the daughter of Charles and Adeline (Bridges) Jackson. Marcia died in Dover Foxcroft, Maine, November 21, 1979. Otis was a farmer and owned and operated Roberts' Dairy in Dexter. He was elected to the Maine State Legislature.* Children:

240.   i. Otis Jackson, Jr., b. 2/14/1914.

241.   ii. Omar Warren, b. 7/6/1921.

195. Winfield Twombly Roberts (Otis[7], Amos[6], George[5], Jonathan[4], George[3], John[2], George[1]), son of Otis Oakes and Louise (Hussey) Roberts, was born in New Haven, Connecticut, November 24, 1889, and died in Bangor, Maine, August 19, 1966, and is buried in Carmel, Maine. He was married three times. His first wife was Esther Mabel Seavey, the daughter of Cotton and Ellen Deborah (Felker) Seavey, who was born in Ripley, Maine, November 5, 1894, and died at Greenville Hospital, August 29, 1936, and was buried in Ripley. Winfield married secondly, November 19, 1937, Eva M. Hillman Day Todd, who was born October 31, 1894. They were divorced, and Winfield then married Christine Marie McLaughlin in Concord, New Hampshire, December 20, 1948. Christine was born in Carmel, Maine, July 27,

---

* Hilton, p. 44.

1905, the daughter of Harry McLaughlin. The three children below, all born in Dexter, Maine, were by Esther.* Children:

    i. Thelma Pearl, b. 7/28/1913; m. Norris W. Bennett. Three children.

242. ii. Wayne Seavey, b. 7/20/1923.

    iii. Arlene Ruth, b. 9/1/1925; d. 2/27/1933.

196. Charles Edwin Roberts (John[7], Jonathan[6], Seth[5], Jonathan[4], George[3], John[2], George[1]), son of John Edgar and Eva Gertrude (Fernald) Roberts, was born in or near Dover, New Hampshire, about 1890, and died in Wells, Maine, in 1964.+ Children:

    i. Lorraine.

    ii. Billy.

    iii. Earl.

    iv. Barbara, m. -----Perkins. Lived in Wells.

    v. Clifford. Lived in Biddeford, ME.

    vi. Clarence. Lived in Somersworth, NH.

    vii. Raymond. Lived in Somersworth.

    viii. Richard. Lived in Canton, MA.

    ix. Mary, m. -----Gould; res. No. Berwick, ME.

197. Roderick Garfield Roberts (Charles[7], Jonathan[6], Seth[5], Jonathan[4], George[3], John[2], George[1]), son of Charles Edwin and Theresa (Vine) Roberts, was born in Smith County, Kansas, June 21, 1881, and died in Seattle, Washington, May 16, 1958, of cancer, and his remains are at the Washelli Crematorium in Seattle.

He married on February 16, 1905, in Omaha, Nebraska, Myrtle Harris, the daughter of John Woodson and Clara (Hoagland) Harris. She was born in Hastings, Nebraska, November 12, 1884,

---

* Hilton, pp. 45-6.
+ 1960's correspondence with Amy Roberts Mercier.

EIGHTH GENERATION

and died in Seattle, August 13, 1965, of complications from stroke. Her remains are also at the Washelli Crematorium.

Rod worked as a railway clerk in Omaha and Denver, and then farmed in Hotchkiss, Colorado, from 1910 to 1915. Studying at night, he obtained his law degree from the University of Omaha in 1920. Instead of practicing law, however, he took a position with the railroad in Denver, and then moved his family to Seattle in 1924, where he worked for many years as a self-employed house painter and paper-hanger. During World War II he worked in a factory making gas masks. Myrtle worked for many years in the fabric department of Rhodes department store.

During his years with the railroad Rod was drawn to the Socialist movement led by Eugene V. Debs. By the 1920's, however, he had returned to his Republican roots and thereafter voted for the Democratic nominee for President only once (in 1932). Myrtle was a life-long Republican, like her father, whom she greatly admired.

Rod had always regretted not having gone on to college; and, even though he and Myrtle struggled financially during the Great Depression, they managed to see all of their children graduate from from the University of Washington.* Children:

243.   i. John Roderick, b. 11/30/1906, Omaha.

        ii. Charles Harris, b. 12/24/1908; d. 1909, polio.

        iii Jane, b. 11/1/1911, Denver; m. and div. John Wyatt Durham,II. Grad. U. of Wash., Masters in Botany. One child(Durham): John Wyatt III, a Harvard Ph.D. and professor at Kansas State U. Jane, J.W. III, his wife Ruth (Kebker) Durham, and adopted son David live in Hays, KS.

        iv. Myrtle Grace, b. 11/28/1919, Omaha; m. 7/2/1941, Andrew Boone Jacobsen (b. 11/4/1915, Seattle). A retired school teacher and a retired engineer respectively, they live in Scottsdale, AZ. Both graduated from the Univ. of Wash.

---

* Family records of the author.

Children(Jacobsen):

(1) Roderick Andrew, b. 11/1/1943, Cambridge, MA; m. & div. Siobhan Costello. Four children(Jacobsen): Samantha (two children-Amy & Heidi), Vanessa, Rick & Gillian. A graduate of Ariz. State Univ., with masters degrees from A.S.U. and Northeastern; a CPA in Phoenix, AZ.

(2) Thomas Andrew (author of this book), b. 7/9/46, Chicago, IL; m. 6/17/1982, Deborah Weinreb (b. 5/10/1955), a Calif. State Univ. graduate and a counselor and teacher. Two children (Jacobsen): Sara Faith (b. 4/20/1984) and Hilary Minda (b. 10/26/1988). They live in Corte Madera, CA. Tom graduated Phi Beta Kappa from the U. of Calif.-Berkeley, (major in history), has masters in business degrees from A.S.U. and Golden Gate Univ., and practices as a CPA in Larkspur, CA.

(3) Linda Mary, b. 3/4/1949, Seattle; m. Scott Loomis, an attorney. Two children(Loomis): Brenda Boone and Scott Jr. A doctorial graduate of the U. of Ariz. and school administrator in Tucson, AZ.

244.   v. William Arthur, b. 11/24/1922, Denver.

198. Charles Arthur Roberts (Charles[7], Jonathan[6], Seth[5], Jonathan[4], George[3], John[2], George[1]), son of Charles Edwin and Theresa (Vine) Roberts, was born in Montfort, Wisconsin, August 18, 1884. He died September 24, 1979, in Tampa, Florida. He married Meta Kleine, who was born in Santa Maria, California, September 29, 1889, and died in Tampa, June 15, 1976.

"Art" Roberts graduated from baking school in Minneapolis, Minnesota, but worked most of his life as a paperhanger and painting contractor. He was quite adventurous as a youngster,

EIGHTH GENERATION

hopping a freight train and travelling the rails at the age of 13. Later he rode his bicycle across the country. Art was known by the family as a real jokester, but he was also seriously interested in philosophy and religion. Meta attended the University of California and taught school in California and Florida for 34 years.* Child:

 i. Fern Meta, b. 10/23/1927, Denver, CO; m. Herbert Austin Williams (b. 2/22/1927), a graduate of the Univ. of Florida, and a retired agricultural chemist. Fern graduated from Florida State Univ. and later obtained a masters degree from Georgia State Univ. She taught school in Georgia for 34 years, earning a Freedom Foundation award and Teacher of the Year honors. She and Herbert were living in Atlanta, GA in 1993.

 Children(Williams):

 (1) Stephen Austin Williams, b. 11/3/1951, Ocala, FL. He earned B.S. and J.D. from the University of Georgia and practices law in Dalton, GA. He married Nancy Lampkin, a dentist in Dalton. Children(Williams): Jessica Haines (b. 11/26/1983), Peter Austin (b. 8/14/1986) & John Stephen(b. 3/1/1989).

 (2) Frank Leonard Williams, b. 12/20/1953, Gainesville, FL, unm., an electrical engineering consultant.

199. Harry Edgar Roberts (Charles[7], Jonathan[6], Seth[5], Jonathan[4], George[3], John[2], George[1]), son of Charles Edwin and Theresa (Vine) Roberts, was born in Montfort, Wisconsin, March 27, 1886, and died November 13, 1963. He married and divorced Ethel Christman.⁺ Child:

---

 * Notes of Fern (Roberts) Williams.
 ⁺ Avis Roberts, "The Roberts Family" (a typewritten article, c. 1960.)

i. Jennie, b. 10/18/1911; m.(1) -----Sutphen, (2) David Henry; two sons - Richard Charles Sutphen of Malibu, CA and Robert James Sutphen of Minneapolis.

200. Nelson C. Roberts (Willis[7], Eliphalet[6], Eliphalet[5], Eliphalet[4], George[3], John[2], George[1]), son of Willis and Sarah Angeline (Roberts) Roberts, a farm laborer, was born in Vermont, April 4, 1845, and died in Norwich, Vermont, April 4, 1880. He married Marcia Walbridge, September 2, 1877, the daughter of Levi and Susan (Silver) Walbridge.[*] Child:

i. Wavey, b. 9/15/1878; d. 10/31/1887.

201. Alonzo S. Roberts (Willis[7], Eliphalet[6], Eliphalet[5], Eliphalet[4], George[3], John[2], George[1]), son of Willis and Sarah Angeline (Roberts) Roberts, was born in Strafford, Vermont, September 14, 1853, and died in West Fairlee, Vermont, June 23, 1933, and is buried in the West Fairlee Cemetery. He married a first cousin twice removed, Olive Roberts, the daughter of Stephen (No. 33) and Alvira (Fox) Roberts, May 4, 1879. Olive was born in Strafford, March 5, 1855, and died in West Fairlee, January 5, 1937, and is buried in the cemetery there. The child below is described as the "illegitimate child of Harley J. Currier".[+] Child:

i. William Eugene, b. 2/3/1884; d. 1965, buried South Strafford Cemetery.

202. Frederick Ransom Roberts (Willis[7], Eliphalet[6], Eliphalet[5], Eliphalet[4], George[3], John[2], George[1]), son of Willis and Sarah Angeline (Roberts) Roberts, was born in Strafford, Vermont, October 22, 1865, and died in Vermont, February 1, 1938, and is buried in the South Royalton Cemetery. He married, firstly, Caroline Florence Slack, the daughter of Jefferson and Ellen (Belknap) Slack, March 11, 1888. Ransom married, secondly, Bertha Emily (Preston) March, September 30, 1919. Caroline was born August 23, 1863 and died January 12, 1915. Bertha was born in Strafford, November 18, 1864, and died in Royalton, October 21,

---

[*] Roberts, Blanche J., p. 560.
[+] Roberts, Blanche J., p. 528.

EIGHTH GENERATION

1932.* Children:

245.   i.   Irving R., b. 2/12/1891.

246.   ii.   Linwood Belknap, b. 10/11/1895.

247.   iii.   Stanley L., b. 10/14/1902(or 1903?).

        iv.   Vivian Florence, b. 4/24/1906; m. Thomas McKenzie, 9/30/1930. Lived in NC.

203. Franklin B. Roberts (Lucian^7, Eliphalet^6, Eliphalet^5, Eliphalet^4, George^3, John^2, George^1), son the Lucian and Mary Adeline (Roberts) Roberts, was born in Sharon, Vermont, July 23, 1847, and died there August 18, 1897, and is buried in the Pine Hill Cemetery there. He married Freedom Annette Sargent, the daughter of Joseph and Elsie (Roberts) Sargent, February 28, 1867. She was born in Strafford, June 5, 1842, and died in Lowell, Massachusetts, January 6, 1919, and is buried in the Point Cemetery. Franklin and Freedom were divorced June 14, 1878, and she married, secondly, George H. Bragg. Franklin was a farmer and, during the Civil War, served as a sharpshooter.⁺ Children:

        i.   Elsie Ella, b. 8/27/1868; m. (1) Elmer E. Rothwell, 9/15/1887, (2) -----Stewart. Five children.

        ii.   Nellie Annette, b. 6/14/1876, m. Andrew Mills.

204. Curtis Barrett Roberts (Lucian^7, Eliphalet^6, Eliphalet^5, Eliphalet^4, George^3, John^2, George^1), son of Lucian and Mary Adeline (Roberts) Roberts, was born in Sharon, Vermont, in 1849, and died in Lowell, Massachusetts, of tuberculosis, in 1905, and is buried in the Edson Cemetery in Lowell. He married Emily R. Hadley, the daughter of Thomas Delano and Roany (Goodale) Hadley, July 28, 1872, in Barnet, Vermont. Emily was born July 20, 1852 in Waterford, Vermont, and died in Woodsville, New Hampshire, October 15, 1931.# Children:

---

     *   Roberts, Blanche J., p. 542.
     ⁺   Roberts, Blanche J., p. 542.
     #   Roberts, Blanche J., p. 534.

i. Kate, b. 8/11/1873; m. Alfred Darby; d. 11/5/1932. Nine children.

ii. Walter, b. 9/29/1877; m. Henrietta Sylvia Woodbury.

205. Calvin Blanchard Roberts (Lucian^7, Eliphalet^6, Eliphalet^5, Eliphalet^4, George^3, John^2, George^1, son of Lucian and Mary Adeline (Roberts) Roberts, was born in Sharon, Vermont, August 3, 1851, and died there April 16, 1901, and is buried in the Pine Tree Cemetery. He married, firstly, Amanda Blanchard, the daughter of Isaac and Amanda (Rive) Blanchard, September 10, 1871, and, secondly, Harriet Arabella Ladd, the daughter of Orrin B. and Harriet (Brown) Ladd, August 21, 1888. Amanda was born May 30, 1855, in Pittsfield, and died in Sharon, December 15, 1886. Harriet was born August 27, 1862, and died in Sharon, March 4, 1918.* Children:

i. Mary A., b. 6/16/1872; d. 8/8/1887, consumption.

ii. Elihu Warren, b. 10/3/1874; d. 6/13/1892, diptheria.

iii. Bertha Amanda, b. 6/7/1876; m. Arthur W. Densmore, 11/28/1900; d. 10/4/1955.

248. iv. Baxter Walter, b. 11/2/1877.

v. Letty Ruby, b. 7/19/1880; m. Wilfred Edson, 9/7/1907; d. 5/11/1917.

vi. Jennie M., b. 11/22/1882; d. 6/18/1892, diptheria.

vii. Arthur Horace, b. 4/11/1884; d. 10/5/1884.

206. John Roberts (Lucian^7, Eliphalet^6, Eliphalet^5, Eliphalet^4, George^3, John^2, George^1), son of Lucian and Electa M. (Blanchard) Roberts, was born in Sharon, Vermont, October 1, 1866, and died there April 27, 1922, and is buried in the Pine Hill Cemetery. He married Daisy Sargent, the daughter of Alvora and

---

* Roberts, Blanche J., p. 531.

EIGHTH GENERATION

Martha (Bruce) Sargent, February 7, 1893. Daisy was born September 8, 1875, and died April 2, 1918, and is also buried in the Pine Hill Cemetery.* Child:

249.   i. Edward Baxter, b. 10/30/1893.

207. Charles Roberts (Lucian[7], Eliphalet[6], Eliphalet[5], Eliphalet[4], George[3], John[2], George[1]), son of Lucian and Electa M. (Blanchard) Roberts, was born Lucian Mark Roberts, May 5, 1872, in Sharon, Vermont, and died in Northfield, Massachusetts, April 23, 1957. He married Viola Stella Penn, the daughter of Fred and Harriet Jane (King) Penn, December 1, 1895. They were divorced October 15, 1925.⁺ Children:

    i. Celia Laura, b. 9/14/1895; m. (1) Putney Leslie Howe, 8/23/1914, div., (2) Albert Fountaine, 5/31/1950, Elkton, MD.

    ii. female, b. & d. 12/14/1901.

250.   iii. Clessant Charles, b. 5/1/1905.

251.   iv. Glenn Edward, b. 3/3/1908.

252.   v. Earl Foster, b. 5/1/1910.

208. Augustus Harland Roberts (Mansir[7], Eliphalet[6], Eliphalet[5], Eliphalet[4], George[3], John[2], George[1]), son of Mansir Hamilton and Sarah B. (Richardson) Roberts, a clerk and merchant, was born in Strafford, Vermont, February 8, 1853, and died in Hanover, New Hampshire, May 25, 1925. He married Mary Ann Richardson, the daughter of Fred and Amy (Willard) Richardson, July 24, 1876, in Hanover. Mary Ann was born in Goshen, Massachusetts, July 1, 1857, and died in Hanover, August 4, 1930.# Child:

    i. Amy S., b. 1876; m. Lionel H. Jones, 10/25/1906.

209. Glenn Arthur Roberts (Henry[7], Zerah[6], Eliphalet[5],

---

* Roberts, Blanche J., p. 532.
⁺ Roberts, Blanche J., p. 530.
Roberts, Blanche, J., p. 530.

Eliphalet⁴, George³, John², George¹), son of Henry Harrison and Sabina (Sawyer) Roberts, was born in Leicester, Vermont, September 1, 1861, and died in Castleton, Vermont, July 11, 1900. He was a physician. Glenn married Olive E.T. Attwood, the daughter of Frank C. and Sarah M. Attwood, June 27, 1882. Olive was born in Salisbury, Vermont, and died in Leicester, November 28, 1913, and is buried there.* Child:

    i. Harrison, b. 8/30/1886; d. 9/20/1914; unm.

210. Albertus Royal Roberts (Daniel⁷, Amphias⁶, Daniel⁵, Eliphalet⁴, George³, John², George¹), son of Daniel West and Lucy M. (Shepard) Roberts, was born in Sharon, Vermont, March 19 (or 9?), 1870, and died in Pomfret, Vermont, March 14, 1938, and is buried in the Hewittville Cemetery. He married Alice M. Gilbert, the daughter of Edwin A. and Agnes (Dean) Gilbert, March 14, 1900. Alice was born in Bridgewater, Vermont, May 31, 1880, and died September 16, 1958, and is also buried in the Hewittville Cemetery.⁺ Children:

    i. Lucy, res. Northfield, MA, in 1960.

    ii. Marion Beatrice, b. 6/22/1907; m. Wayne W. Wilson, 4/31/1930.

    iii. Daniel West, b. 2/17/1908; d. 7/14/1923

    iv. Florence Agnes, b. 9/2/1909; m. Sherman B. Manning, 9/9/1926; d. 4/27/1930. Two children.

253.   v. Edwin Gilbert, b. 1/9/1912.

211. Carl Jackson Roberts (Frank⁷, Orlando⁶, Moses⁵, Eliphalet⁴, George³, John², George¹), son of Frank Orlando and Lutheria (Crossman) Roberts, was born in Rochester, Vermont, October 27, 1885. He died there October 14, 1918, and is buried in the Fern Hill Cemetery. He was a farmer. Carl married Agnes Harriet Thresher, October 29, 1906, in Rochester. Agnes's parents were Nelson G. and Hattie Alice (Swinyer) Thresher. She was born

---

    * Roberts, Blanche J., p. 545.
    ⁺ Roberts, Blanche J., p. 528.

EIGHTH GENERATION

October 8, 1891, and died July 15, 1971, in Starksboro, Vermont, and is buried in the Fern Hill Cemetery. After Carl died, Agnes married, secondly, Louis Benjamin Phelps, in 1921.[*] Children:

      i. Neil Leo, b. 11/2/1907; m. 9/27/1937, Florence Dukett; d. 7/3/1959, Keene, NH.

      ii. Alice Harriet, b. 5/20/1909; m. 7/25/1927, Leonard Phelps; d. 7/16/1978, Starksboro, VT.

254.   iii. Richard Lester, b. 6/8/1911.

      iv. Frances Amy, b. 9/19/1913; m. Lynn Valyou.

      v. Ralph Vernon, b. 6/24/1915; m. 7/6/1935, Della Beatrice Valyou; d. 1989.

---

[*] Bryant and Verret notes.

NINTH GENERATION

212. Walter Clifford Roberts (Eugene[8], Watson[7], Samuel[6], Samuel[5], Jonathan[4], George[3], John[2], George[1]), son of Eugene Roswell and Sierra Nevada (Fleming) Roberts, was born in Chico, California, August 1, 1895, and died in Sacramento, California, November 6, 1984. He married, firstly, in Stockton, California, May 8, 1918, Margaret Boltzen. They were divorced; and Walter married, secondly, in Los Angeles, California, October 8, 1944, Dorothy Alice (Eliot) Martin.* Children:

    i. a son, b. 10/1919, Tracy, CA; d. at birth.

    ii. Dorothy Caryl, b. 10/17/1920, Tracy; m. & div. Edward J. Tingley; lives in Redondo Beach, CA. Three children.

    iii. Margaret Anne, b. 2/13/1922, Oakland, CA; m. Charles Grubb; lives in Palos Verdes Estates, CA. Three children.

213. Wellington J. Roberts (James[8], Jonathan[7], Josiah[6], Samuel[5], Jonathan[4], George[3], John[2], George[1]), son of James S. and Rosa B. (Sweet) Roberts, was born in Maine, in August of 1888 (or 1889?), and died, apparently in Belfast, Maine, in 1965. He married Addie May -----, who died in 1945.⁺ Children:

    i. Hazel, b. 10/21/1913; m. Ralph Copp; d. 2/23/1985. Two children.

    ii. Helen, b. 7/30/1915; m. William Smith. Lived in Bath, ME. One child.

255.   iii. Furber S., b. 8/26/1920.

214. Lawrence James Roberts (James[8], Jonathan[7], Josiah[6], Samuel[5], Jonathan[4], George[3], John[2], George[1]), son of James S. and Rosa B. (Sweet) Roberts, was born in Swanville, Maine, January 5, 1891, and died in Waterville, Maine, August (or May?) 10, 1961. He married Olive M. McCarty. Olive was born in Torrington,

---

* Jones notes.
⁺ Cafferty, pp. 189-90.

Connecticut, October 31, 1892, and died in Cushing, Maine, February 27, 1976.* Children:

256.   i. John Dimon, b. 12/15/1920.

    ii. Doris, b. 8/15/1922, Islesboro, ME; m. Wyman Hatch. Four children.

257.   iii. Ralph L., b. 6/11/1924.

258.   iv. Allen H., b. 5/6/1927.

215. Maurice E. Roberts (James^8, Jonathan^7, Josiah^6, Samuel^5, Jonathan^4, George^3, John^2, George^1), son of James S. and Rosa B. (Sweet) Roberts, was born in Swanville, Maine, August 2, 1895, and died in Millis, Massachusetts, April 16, 1944 or 1945. He married Esther Wiley, who was born in 1896 and died in 1983.⁺ Child:

    i. Herbert, lived in Rehoboth, MA.

216. Arthur B. Roberts (James^8, Jonathan^7, Josiah^6, Samuel^5, Jonathan^4, George^3, John^2, George^1), son of James S. and Rosa B. (Sweet) Roberts, was born in Belfast, Maine, December 10, 1897. He married Hazel Bridges, who was born in Rockland, Maine, October 10, 1901.# Children:

259.   i. Arthur Neil, b. 7/14/1919.

    ii. Rosa A., b. 7/8/1920; m. Vincent F. Renaud; lived in Swanville, ME. One child.

217. Luther Earl Roberts (Cyrus^8, Jonathan^7, Josiah^6, Samuel^5, Jonathan^4, George^3, John^2, George^1), son of Cyrus H. and Addie (Peavey) Roberts, was born in Belfast, Maine, September 20, 1895, and died there April 16, 1969. He married Georgia Small, who died in Belfast, March 15, 1964.** Children:

260.   i. Dennis, b. 2/23/1920.

---

* Cafferty, p. 191.
⁺ Cafferty, pp. 189 & 193.
Cafferty, p. 194-5.
** Cafferty, p. 196.

NINTH GENERATION

261.   ii.   Everett Ervin, b. 1/13/1922.

218. Frank Herbert Roberts (Frank^8, Jonathan^7, Josiah^6, Samuel^5, Jonathan^4, George^3, John^2, George^1), son of Frank H. and Elizabeth Roberts, was born in Belfast, Maine, May 24, 1917, and died there February 29, 1963. He married Jeanette Patterson, who was born July 24, 1913.* Children:

262.   i.   Roger Lloyd, b. 1/27/1936.

     ii.   Janice Marie, b. 8/21/1938; m. Robert Curtis. Three children.

263.   iii.   Norman, b. 4/2/1947.

219. Claude Roberts (Leslie^8, Levi^7, Josiah^6, Samuel^5, Jonathan^4, George^3, John^2, George^1), son of Leslie Burton and Daisy (Howard) Roberts, was born in Maine, October 20, 1914, and died there October 14, 1946. He married Shirley Clark. This family lived in Belfast, Maine.$^+$ Child:

     i.   Jacqueine, b. 9/20/1936; m. Robert Weaver. Living in Belfast, ME. Five children.

220. Stanley Roberts (Leslie^8, Levi^7, Josiah^6, Samuel^5, Jonathan^4, George^3, John^2, George^1), son of Leslie Burton and Daisy (Howard) Roberts, was born in Maine, October 27, 1921, and died there February 20, 1983. He married, firstly, Nillie Fuller, who was born in 1922 and died August 5, 1942. Stanley married, secondly, June Harford. This family lived in Swanville, Maine.$^\#$ Child:

264.   i.   Reginold, b. 7/5/1942.

221. Robert Roberts (Leslie^8, Levi^7, Josiah^6, Samuel^5, Jonathan^4, George^3, John^2, George^1), son of Leslie Burton and Daisy (Howard) Roberts, was born in Maine, February 27, 1924, and died there November 12, 1951. He married Ellen Duley. This family lived in Belfast, Maine.** Children:

---

* Cafferty, p. 201.
$^+$ Ervin Roberts notes.
$^\#$ Ervin Roberts notes.
** Ervin Roberts notes.

DESCENDANTS OF GEORGE & MARY ROBERTS

265.   i.   Garry, b. 6/6/1947.

266.   ii. Robert, b. 2/12/1950.

222. Ervin Roberts (Ernest[8], Levi[7], Josiah[6], Samuel[5], Jonathan[4], George[3], John[2], George[1]), son of Ernest Tucker and Agnes (Cram) Roberts, was born in Brooks, Maine, April 29, 1926. He married August 21, 1949, Viola Crosby, who was born in Exeter, Maine, November 24, 1925. This family lives in South Portland, Maine. Ervin is a genealogist and collected most of the material in this book related to his branch of the family.* Children:

   i.   Vicki, b. 7/5/1954.

   ii. Wendi, b. 6/14/1957; m. 10/26/1987, Clifford L. Verrill.

267.   iii. Ernest James, b. 6/26/1958.

223. Roger Ernest Roberts (Ernest[8], Levi[7], Josiah[6], Samuel[5], Jonathan[4], George[3], John[2], George[1]), son of Ernest and Agnes (Cram) Roberts, was born in Morrill, Maine, January 7, 1941. He married December 21, 1963, in Lisbon, Maine, Dawn Melville, who was born in Somerville, Massachusetts, June 30, 1942. This family is living in Morrill.⁺ Children:

   i.   Robin, b. 8/2/1964; m. Scott Mosher. One child.

   ii. Dana, b. 9/8/1966; m. 9/7/1991, Anne Elizabeth Shenett. Living in Knox, ME.

   iii. Paula, b. 11/27/1968. One child.

224. Raymond Sylvester Roberts, Jr. (Raymond[8], Alpheus[7], Watson[6], Samuel[5], Jonathan[4], George[3], John[2], George[1]), son of Raymond Sylvester and Nina (Dickey) Roberts, was born in Brooks, Maine, March 12, 1923. He married in Brooks, Shirley Avis Lowe, March 22, 1946. This family still lived in Brooks, as of the late

---

* Ervin Roberts notes.
⁺ Ervin Roberts notes.

NINTH GENERATION

1980's. The following children were born in Bangor, Maine.*
Children:

    i. Raymond Sylvester III, b. 2/2/1948.

268.   ii. Randall Frank, b. 9/4/1949.

    iii. Holley, b. 11/25/1952.

225. Edgar Frank Roberts (Raymond[8], Alpheus[7], Watson[6], Samuel[5], Jonathan[4], George[3], John[2], George[1]), son of Raymond Sylvester and Nina (Dickey) Roberts, was born in Brooks, Maine, April 11, 1924. He married Leota -----, of Bridgewater, Maine.⁺
Children:

    i. Sandra.

    ii. Diane.

226. Edwin Ashley Roberts (Raymond[8], Alpheus[7], Watson[6], Samuel[5], Jonathan[4], George[3], John[2], George[1]), son of Raymond Sylvester and Nina (Dickey) Roberts, was born in Brooks, Maine, August 7, 1925. He married Rita Smith of Torrington, Connecticut.# Children:

    i. Elaine (twin), m. -----Matches.

    ii. Sharon (twin).

227. Willis Elmer Roberts (Frank[8], Nathan[7], Amos[6], George[5], Jonathan[4], George[3], John[2], George[1], son of Frank W. and Abbie (Stanwood) Roberts, was born September 17, 1885 and died in March of 1960. He married Grace Marion Lunt, who was born August 19, 1888. Willis graduated from Bowdoin College in 1907 and attended the University of Maine Law School. He was a lawyer, court recorder and judge of the municipal court in Brunswick, Maine. He also ran his father's shoe store, which his wife carried on after his death.** Child:

---

  * Hilton, pp. 9-10.
  ⁺ Hilton, p. 10.
  # Hilton, p. 10.
  ** Hilton, p. 14.

i. Ruth, b. 5/10/1917; m. Payson V. Tucker, Jr. Three children.

228. Frank Stanwood Roberts (Frank[8], Nathan[7], Amos[6], George[5], Jonathan[4], George[3], John[2], George[1]), son of Frank W. and Abbie (Stanwood) Roberts, was born in Brunswick, Maine, March 26, 1893, and died July 30, 1974, in Atlanta, Georgia. He married Clare Ridley in Brunswick, February 9, 1918. She was born in Brunswick, October 9, 1895. Frank attended Bowdoin College and was a judge in Brunswick for many years.[*] Children:

269.   i. Frank Stanwood, b. 3/1/1922, Columbus, GA.

ii. Helen, b. 7/5/1925, Atlanta; m. 6/12/1948, Mason Whitney. Three children.

229. George Brinton Roberts, Jr.(George[8], George[7], Amos[6], George[5], Jonathan[4], George[3], John[2], George[1]), son of George Brinton and Hannah (Weeks) Roberts, was born in Plymouth, Maine, April 11, 1883, and died in Bridgewater, Maine, November 23, 1930. He married in Caribou, Maine, January 18, 1903, Jennie Kirkpatrick. She was born in Fort Fairfield, Maine, and died in Bangor, Maine, in May of 1966.[*] Children:

i. Juanita Pearl, b. 10/16/1903; m. Ray Thorne, 1/29/1925. 1 ch.

270.   ii. Sewell Wilbur, b. 10/25/1904.

230. Wilbur Prescott Roberts (George[8], George[7], Amos[6], George[5], Jonathan[4], George[3], John[2], George[1]), son of George Brinton and Hannah (Weeks) Roberts, was born November 6, 1885. He married Charlotte Bartlett, the daughter of Nathaniel and Ruth Bartlett, September 19, 1909. She was born in Burnham, Maine, December 10, 1887, and died in 1964.[#] Children:

i. Wilbur Prescott, b. 7/3/1915; m. Marie Spooner.

271.   ii. Dwane Bartlett, b. 10/9/1919.

---

[*] Hilton, p. 14.
[*] Hilton, p. 18.
[#] Hilton, p. 18.

NINTH GENERATION

231. Forest Rupert Roberts (George[8], George[7], Amos[6], George[5], Jonathan[4], George[3], John[2], George[1]), son of George Brinton and Hannah (Weeks) Roberts, was born February 12, 1891, and died November 12, 1949. He married, firstly, Gussie Yerxa, October 6, 1907. They were divorced; and Forest married, secondly, November 24, 1939, Beatrice Gilbert, the daughter of Henry R. and Nellie Moon (Hillam) Gilbert. Beatrice was born in Bar Harbor, Maine, June 16, 1903.* Child:

272.　　i. Forest Rupert, b. 11/14/1940.

232. Merton Elmer Roberts (George[8], George[7], Amos[6], George[5], Jonathan[4], George[3], John[2], George[1]), son of George Brinton and Hannah (Weeks) Roberts, was born May 6, 1893, and died at Mars Hill, Maine, January, 1926. He married Vena Libby, June 26, 1912. She was born March 1, 1893 and died July 20, 1956.⁺ Children:

　　i. George Merton, b. 2/27/1913; unm.

　　ii. Maxine, b. 11/3/1917; m. 8/24/1940, Walter W. Tweedie. 3 children.

233. George Frederick Roberts (Frederick[8], George[7], Amos[6], George[5], Jonathan[4], George[3], John[2], George[1]), son of Frederick Parkhurst and Marion Annie (Pierce) Roberts, was born in Abbot Village, Maine, in 1886, and died in Presque Isle, Maine, in 1967. He married Lillian E. Thomas in Fort Kent, Maine, in 1905. She was the daughter of John and Georgiena (Stevens) Thomas. Lillian was born in St. John, Maine, in 1889, and died in Presque Isle, February 22, 1964.# Children:

273.　　i. Lewellyn Thomas, b. 10/21/1906.

　　ii. Verna, b. 11/24/1911; m. Lawrence J. Hedrick. Three children.

274.　　iii. Glen W., b. 2/22/1916.

---

* Hilton, p. 18.
⁺ Hilton, b. 18.
Hilton, pp. 19-20.

275.   iv.   Frederick Parkhurst, b. 8/23/1920.

v.   Jessie Mae, b. 8/13/1921; m. Roland A. Nelson, 11/15/1946. One child.

234.   Earle Henry Roberts (Frederick^8, George^7, Amos^6, George^5, Jonathan^4, George^3, John^2, George^1), son of Frederick Parkhurst and Lucy (Bloodsworth) Roberts, was born in Maine, December 9, 1893, and died January 8, 1943. He married Ella Augusta Pinkham, the daughter of Asa and Ella Pinkham, September 1, 1920. She was born at Fort Kent, Maine, September 25, 1892, and died in Pittsburgh, Pennsylvania, in June of 1962.* Children:

276.   i.   Kenneth Pinkham, b. 7/14/??

277.   ii.   David Mark, b. 5/7/1923.

iii.   Ruth Mae, b. 3/10/??, m. Carleton H. Clark, 7/2/1949. Two ch.

235.   William Lewis Roberts (Frederick^8, George^7, Amos^6, George^5, Jonathan^4, George^3, John^2, George^1), son of Frederick Parkhurst and Lucy (Bloodsworth) Roberts, was born in Caribou, Maine, September 1 (or 7?), 1896, and died in Bangor, Maine, October 12, 1965, and is buried in Mt. Hope Cemetery there. He married Ruey Logan, April 8, 1934. William and Ruey had three children, all born in Bangor.⁺ Children:

i.   Julia Ann, b. 1/9/1937; m. Arthur Little. One ch.

ii.   Celia Ann, b. 2/6/1935.

iii.   Barbara Ann, b. 4/1/1941.

236.   Stanley W. Roberts (William^8, Amos^7, Amos^6, George^5, Jonathan^4, George^3, John^2, George^1), son of William Otis and Hattie (Hart) Roberts, was born in Dexter, Maine, July 11, 1880, and died November 19, 1957. He married, firstly, Etta E. Eldridge, who was born April 19, 1882, and died January 4, 1933. Secondly, Stanley

---

* Hilton, p. 21.
⁺ Hilton, p. 21.

NINTH GENERATION

married Mary Wyer, the daughter of Joseph and Mary Ann (Audsley) Wyer. Mary was born in England, June 5, 1883, and died at Albion, Maine, January 26, 1977.* Children:

- 278.
  - i. Herbert A., b. 9/9/1900.
  - ii. Hazel W., b. 2/17/1903; m. Edward Ireland, 9/1/1923. No children.
  - iii. Edith E., b. 5/22/1905, Sangerville, ME; m. Stanley Steeves, 6/2/1928. One child.
  - iv. Marian A., b. 2/16/1909; ensign in the U.S. Navy; m. Caleb F. Dyer, 6/16/1945. No children.
  - v. Edna H., b. 11/16/1910; d. 12/23/1910.
  - vi. Elsie M., b.10/22/1912, Dover-Foxcroft, ME; m. (1) C.Y. Lowry, 10/28/1943, (2) Bernard Berry; d. 7/30/1972. No children.
- 279.
  - vii. Ernest A., b. 1/16/1914.

237. Menza Alfred Roberts (William^8, Amos^7, Amos^6, George^5, Jonathan^4, George^3, John^2, George^1), son of William Otis and Hattie (Hart) Roberts, was born in Newport, Maine, May 17, 1892, and died in Salem, Massachusetts, June 16, 1943. He married Harriet Sheehan in November of 1916. She was born in Lynn, Massachusetts, January 15, 1894, and died in Salem, June 18, 1929. The children listed below were all born in Salem.$^+$ Children:

- 280.
  - i. Arthur Edwin, b. 10/28/1917.
  - ii. Francis, b. 1918; d. 1918.
  - iii. Leo Francis, b. 5/31/1920; unm.
  - iv. Eleanor Marian, b. 9/11/1921; m. Howard A. Jamisen, Jr., 12/19/1944. Three children.
  - v. Alfred M., b. 9/7/1926; unm.

---

* Hilton, pp. 26-7.
$^+$ Hilton, pp. 29-30.

vi. Harriet Edna, b. 6/14/1929; m. Leo Welton, 9/1/1951. Six children.

238. Timothy Victor Roberts (Adrian[8], Amos[7], Amos[6], George[5], Jonathan[4], George[3], John[2], George[1]), son of Adrian and Hattie (Devoll) Roberts, was born in Norridgewock, Maine, July 25, 1892, and died in Skowhegan, Maine, February 28, 1954, and is buried in the Southside Cemetery there. He married, firstly, Abbie Clara Colby, the daughter of George B. and Angie (Adams) Colby. Abbie was born in Moose River, Maine, March 28, 1894, and died in Skowhegan, May 12, 1968. After their divorce, Timothy married, secondly, Marian I. Robinson in Skowhegan, June 9, 1945. Timothy and Abbie had two sons; and Timothy and Marian had one son. Timothy served in World War I as a corporal in the So. M. 74th Inf., 12th Div.* Children:

281.   i. Victor Colby, b. 2/15/1912.

282.   ii. Adrian Everett, b. 3/26/1913.

        iii. Everett.

239. Everett Roberts (Adrian[8], Amos[7], Amos[6], George[5], Jonathan[4], George[3], John[2], George[1]), son of Adrian and Rose (Turner) Roberts, was born in Dexter, Maine, September 20, 1902. In 1987, he was still living, in New Hampshire. Everett married three times, the third time being to Leola Mae Crosby, who was born in Talmadge, Maine, in 1914. Everett was raised, although never adopted, by a Mr. and Mrs. Oscar Bennett. He apparently adopted the surname Bennett, since his numerous children are all listed as such.⁺ Children (Bennett):

        i. David.

        ii. Virene, m. Joseph Kursula; d. 1/1963. One son.

        iii. Everett, Jr., of Hamden, Me.

        iv. Carl, b. 8/9/1930; m. Leona Bashaw. Two children.

---

* Hilton, pp. 31-2.
⁺ Hilton, pp. 25, 32 & 33.

NINTH GENERATION

- v. Robert.
- vi. Marshall, b. 4/6/ 1935; m. 11/6/1959 (& div.) Carolyn Blake. Three children.
- vii. Beverly, m. Frank Burcham. Five ch.
- viii. Marilyn, m. Alan Johnson. Three ch.
- ix. Noreen, b. 10/31/1944; m. Larry Dutch. One son.
- x. Althea, m. & div. David Bouchard. One son.
- xi. Robert L., b. 1/1940; m. Patricia Smith. 3 ch.

240. Otis Jackson Roberts, Jr. (Otis[8], Otis[7], Amos[6], George[5], Jonathan[4], George[3], John[2], George[1]), son of Otis Jackson and Marcia Alice (Jackson) Roberts, was born in Dexter, Maine, February 14, 1914. He married Glennys Flewelling at Silver Mills, Dexter, August 31, 1935. Glennys is the daughter of Thomas and Effie Flewelling and was born in Skowhegan, Maine, January 13, 1917. The following children were born in Dexter.* Children:

283.
- i. Otis Jackson III, b. 5/4/1939.
- ii. Patricia Effie, b. 11/18/1941; m. Phillip White, 8/5/1958. 3 ch.
- iii. Linda Jane, b. 1/27/1951; m. Richard Farrar. 2 ch.

241. Omar Warren Roberts (Otis[8], Otis[7], Amos[6], George[5], Jonathan[4], George[3], John[2], George[1]), son of Otis Jackson and Marcia Alice (Jackson) Roberts, was born in Dexter, Maine, July 6, 1921. He was a W. W. II vet and apparently still alive in 1987. He married Julia Mae Atwater, the daughter of Edgar Atwater, February 8, 1947 in Dexter. She was born in Dexter, May 26, 1921. The following children were born in Dexter.⁺ Children:

- i. Barbara Jean, b. 2/3/1948; m. Anthony Welch, 6/22/1968. 4 children.

---

* Hilton, pp. 44 & 46.
⁺ Hilton, pp. 46-7.

ii. Omar Warren, Jr., b. 2/6/1950; m. Belinda Randall, 10/21/1978.

242. **Wayne Seavey Roberts** (Winfield[8], Otis[7], Amos[6], George[5], Jonathan[4], George[3], John[2], George[1]), son of Winfield Twombly and Esther Mabel (Seavey) Roberts, was born in Dexter, Maine, July 20, 1923, and died November 23, 1969, at New Haven, Connecticut. He married firstly Jeanne Towle Davis, February 9, 1946, at Hopkinton, New Hampshire. Wayne and Jeanne had one child, Kathy. They were divorced, and Wayne married, secondly, Eunice Ernestine Engelharte in New Haven, Connecticut, December 19, 1959. Wayne and Eunice adopted a daughter, Kimberly Angelia, who was born February 4, 1962. Wayne was a sergeant in the Engineers Corp. and served thirty-four months in the European and Pacific theaters during World War II.* Children:

i. Kathy.

ii. Kimberly Angelia.

243. **John Roderick Roberts** (Roderick[8], Charles[7], Jonathan[6], Seth[5], Jonathan[4], George[3], John[2], George[1]), son of Roderick Garfield and Myrtle (Harris) Roberts, was born in Omaha, Nebraska, November 30, 1906, and died in Forest Grove, Oregon, February 24, 1969.

He married Pauline Esabel Eresch, May 22, 1934, in Seattle, Washington. The daughter of Theodore and Anna (Anderson) Eresh, Pauline was born in Leavenworth, Washington, January 6, 1908, and died in Forest Grove, January 30, 1971.

John was a professor of biology at Pacific University in Forest Grove for over twenty-seven years He was a graduate of the University of Washington, with a B.S., M.S. and, in 1932, a PhD. In addition to his duties as department chairman, John coached the golf team and ran the time clock for the basketball team. He was active in a number of civic organizations, from the Lions Club to the Volunteer Fire Department, where he was assistant chief. Pauline practiced as a registered nurse prior to becoming a full-time

---

* Hilton, p. 46.

NINTH GENERATION

homemaker.* Children:

    i. Helen Ann, b. 3/12/1937, Seattle, WN; m. Dale BeVier. They lived for many years in Canandaigua, New York, where Dale practiced optometry, and where their four children were born. They moved to the South to pursue a career in the entertainment field, and also developed real estate. Helen went back to school and completed a degree in horticulture and in 1993 was working as head gardener at Longwood Gardens, in PA. Dale had a position there in the security department.

    Children(BeVier):

    (1) Edward Ambrose, an aviation engineer, b. 8/23/1957; m. Gail Lorraine Jenkins, 6/23/1979; living in Fairhope, AL in 1993. Children(BeVier): Andre Brooks(b. 9/15/1986) & Corey Anne (b. 12/3/1989).

    (2) Deborah Anne, a human resources director, b. 12/16/1958, m. Randal Allen DeMay, 9/29/1990; living in Williamson, NY in 1993.

    (3) Douglas Andre, an aircraft mechanic, b. 10/3/1961; m. RaNae Marie Bartholomew, 5/9/1987; living in Broken Arrow, OK in 1993.

    (4) Craig Andrew, a counselor and Clemson Univ. grad., b. 7/4/1968; m. Ellinor Catharine Preston, 8/8/1992; living in Erwin, NC in 1993.

284.   ii. John William, b. 2/22/1941, Moscow, ID.

285.   iii. Tim Arden, b. 1/5/1947, Forest Grove, OR.

---

*Family records of John William Roberts.

244. William Arthur Roberts (Roderick[8], Charles[7], Jonathan[6], Seth[5], Jonathan[4], George[3], John[2], George[1]), son of Roderick Garfield and Myrtle (Harris) Roberts, was born in Denver, Colorado, November 24, 1922. He married Juliana R. ("Judy") Otto. "Bill" Roberts served as an officer in the U.S. Army in World War II. He graduated from the University of Washington, B.A. and L.L.B. and practices law in Seattle, Washington.[*] Children:

    i. John William. An artist living near Seattle in 1993. Children: Teague Kathleen, b. 4/24/1977, Tristan Adeline, b. 5/27/1978, and Brock William, b. 3/14/1982.

    ii. Janis Marie, m. Reed D. Parsley, 11/5/1976. Twins - Bart Roberts Parsley and Chase Clayton Parsley, b. 1/21/1981. Live in Seattle.

    iii. Sally Jean, unm. in 1993. An artist and interior designer in Seattle.

245. Irving R. Roberts (Frederick[8], Willis[7], Eliphalet[6], Eliphalet[5], Eliphalet[4], George[3], John[2], George[1]), son of Frederick Ransom and Caroline (Slack) Roberts, was born in Strafford, Vermont, February 12, 1891, and died in Bethel, Vermont, April 4, 1958. He married Grace Pinion, daughter of John and Harriet (Phillips) Pinion. Grace was born in Rutland, Vermont, April 17, 1893.[+] Children:

    i. Mildred, b. 1/17/1918(?); m.(1) Franklin Dickey, div., (2) Clyde Campbell, 2/28/1955. One child.

    ii. Marjorie Esther, b. 4/27/1919; m. Everett Ellis, 9/29/1937. 4 children.

246. Linwood Belknap Roberts (Frederick[8], Willis[7], Eliphalet[6], Eliphalet[5], Eliphalet[4], George[3], John[2], George[1]), son of Frederick Ransom and Caroline (Slack) Roberts, was born in Royalton, Vermont, October 11, 1895. He married Lena Ellen

---

[*] Family records of the author.
[+] Roberts, Blanche J., p. 548.

NINTH GENERATION

Blood, the daughter of Fred F. and Ellen (Jaquith) Blood, September 25, 1927. Lena was born in Oklahoma.* Child:

    i. Janet Lucia, b. 6/2/1930.

247. Stanley L. Roberts (Frederick^8, Willis^7, Eliphalet^6, Eliphalet^5, Eliphalet^4, George^3, John^2, George^1), son of Frederick Ransom and Caroline (Slack) Roberts, was born in Royalton, Vermont, October 14, 1902 (or 1903?). He married in South Royalton, May 29, 1924, Doris I. Greene, who was born in St. Albans, Vermont.+ Children:

286.	i.	Carleton Wayne, b. 3/3/1929.
287.	ii.	Conrad Craig, b. 4/5/1934.

248. Baxter Walter Roberts (Calvin^8, Lucian^7, Eliphalet^6, Eliphalet^5, Eliphalet^4, George^3, John^2, George^1), son of Calvin Blanchard and Amanda (Blanchard) Roberts, was born in Vermont, November 2, 1877, and died in Wilder, Vermont, June 24, 1961. He married Blanche Lydia Judd, the daughter of Arthur Luman and Jennie Adelia (Kendall) Judd, November 28, 1908. Blanche was born August 20, 1885, and died July 27, 1973. She compiled most of the data on the Vermont branch of this family. The children below were born in Sharon, Vermont.# Children:

	i.	Evelyn Florence, b. 10/3/1908; m. Robert I. Gilman, 6/23/1929. Two children.
288.	ii.	Elihu Luman, b. 12/8/1910.
	iii.	Marion Blanche, b. 4/13/1915; m. Chester H. Dodge, 9/30/1934. Five children.
289.	iv.	Ralph Calvin, b. 1/31/1918.
290.	v.	Philip John, b. 5/10/1921.
	vi.	Margery Janet, b. 3/5/1923; m. Reynold B. Juul, 2/1/1946. Four children.

---

* Roberts, Blanche J., p. 556.
+ Roberts, Blanche J., p. 564.
# Roberts, Blanche J., p. 530.

291. vii. Richard Baxter, b. 3/27/1927.

249. Edward Baxter Roberts (John^8, Lucian^7, Eliphalet^6, Eliphalet^5, Eliphalet^4, George^3, John^2, George^1), son of John and Daisy (Sargent) Roberts, was born in Sharon, Vermont, October 30, 1893, and died there June 6, 1941, and is buried in the Pine Tree Cemetery. He married Marion Elizabeth Patten, the daughter of C. Edward and Lizzie (Honey) Patten.* Children:

    i. Jacqueline Marie, b. 7/23/1923; m. Walter McNallan, 12/5/1945, in Texas.

    ii. Janet Alice, b. 6/10/1925; m. (1) Howard T. Brown, 5/15/1946, div., (2) William Murphy, 7/19/1950. Two children.

    iii. Phyllis Marion, b. 2/6/1928; m. Harlan M. Deos, 11/17/1946. Two children.

250. Clessant Charles Roberts (Charles^8, Lucian^7, Eliphalet^6, Eliphalet^5, Eliphalet^4, George^3, John^2, George^1), son of Charles and Viola (Penn) Roberts, was born in Hartford, Vermont, May 1, 1905. He married Bernice A. Hadlock, September 25, 1928, in Hudson, New York. The children below were born in Brattleboro, Vermont.⁺ Children:

    i. Beverly Ann, b. 9/7/1935; m. Robert G. Warwick, 5/25/1957(?). One child.

    ii. Brenda Carolee, b. 6/17/1943.

251. Glenn Edward Roberts (Charles^8, Lucian^7, Eliphalet^6, Eliphalet^5, Eliphalet^4, George^3, John^2, George^1), son of Charles and Viola (Penn) Roberts, was born in Norwich, Vermont, March 3, 1908. He married, firstly, Leona Etta Williams, November 18, 1924, and secondly, Helen Carleton, February 28, 1938.# Children:

    i. Joyce Blanche, b. 8/26/1926; m. Donald W. Carruth, 9/29/1946. Two children. Lived in NJ

---

    ^ Roberts, Blanche J., p. 538.
    ⁺ Roberts, Blanche J., p. 534.
    # Roberts, Blanche J., p. 544.

NINTH GENERATION

  ii. Glenn Edward Jr., b. 3/17/1940.

  iii. Viola Harriet, b. 9/22/1941.

  iv. Louise Hellen, b. 9/22/1941; m. William Mattison, Newport, NH.

252. Earl Foster Roberts (Charles^8, Lucian^7, Eliphalet^6, Eliphalet^5, Eliphalet^4, George^3, John^2, George^1), son of Charles and Viola (Penn) Roberts, was born in Hartford, Vermont, May 1, 1910. He married Pearl M. Rivers, October 7, 1933, in Hudson, New York. The following children were born in Brattleboro, Vermont.*
Children:

  i. Betty Marie, b. 6/4/1934; m. (1) Richard Anderson, 11/22/1952, (2) Alden Jackson, 7/24/1955. Two children.

  ii. Robert Foster, b. 3/12/1945.

253. Edwin Gilbert Roberts (Albertus^8, Daniel^7, Amphias^6, Daniel^5, Eliphalet^4, George^3, John^2, George^1), son of Albertus Royal and Alice (Gilbert) Roberts, was born in Pomfret, Vermont, January 9, 1912, and died in North Thetford, Vermont, December 31, 1959, and is buried in the Hewittville Cemetery. He married Stella May Warren, the daughter of Laban and Lillian (Kimball) Warren, December 15, 1934. Stella was born in 1914.⁺ Children:

  i. Barbara Ann, b. 3/23/1936.

  ii. Daniel West, b. 4/17/1937; m. Verna M. Clark, 11/25/1961.

  iii. Florence May, b. 9/25/1938.

  iv. Dorothy A., b. 1941; m. Francis G. Strout, 8/27/1960.

292. v. Raymond Gilbert, b. 1/21/1945.

---

* Roberts, Blanche J., p. 537.
⁺ Roberts, Blanche J., p. 538.

DESCENDANTS OF GEORGE & MARY ROBERTS

  vi. Leola Stella (twin), b. 9/12/1952.

  vii. Lilla Louise (twin), b. 9/12/1952.

254. Richard Lester Roberts (Carl^8, Frank^7, Orlando^6, Moses^5, Eliphalet^4, George^3, John^2, George^1), son of Carl Jackson and Agnes Harriet (Thresher) Roberts, was born in Hancock, Vermont, June 8, 1911. He died November 15, 1963, at Fayston, Vermont, and is buried in Huntington, Vermont. Richard married Eva Estelle Gorton, March 18, 1933, at Starksboro, Vermont. She is the daughter of Ernest Oliver and Emma Stella (Tillotson) Gorton. Eva was born June 22, 1917 in Huntington, Vermont, and lives at the present time in Shelburne, Vermont. After Richard died, Eva married, firstly, Harry Everett Zimmerman in 1965, and, secondly, Eugene Ladue, in 1986.* Children:

	i.	Beauzetta "Bobbi" Ernestine, b. 7/2/1933; m. 6/2/1951, Roderick Bryant. They live in South Burlington, VT.
293.	ii.	David Calvin, b. 7/30/1939.

---

 * Bryant and Verret notes.

TENTH GENERATION

255. Furber S. Roberts (Wellington[9], James[8], Jonathan[7], Josiah[6], Samuel[5], Jonathan[4], George[3], John[2], George[1]), son of Wellington J. and Addie (May) Roberts, was born August 26, 1920, in Maine. He married Florence -----. This family lived in the Panama Canal Zone.[*] Children:

    i. a child.

    ii. Stephanie.

256. John Dimon Roberts (Lawrence[9], James[8], Jonathan[7], Josiah[6], Samuel[5], Jonathan[4], George[3], John[2], George[1]), son of Lawrence James and Olive M. (McCarty) Roberts, was born in Belfast, Maine, December 15, 1920, and died April 28, 1984, in South Portland, Maine. He married Marilyn Babbidge, who was born in Islesboro, Maine, May 1, 1925.[+] Child:

    i. Janice, b. 7/10/1940, Rockland, ME; m. (1) William Latham, (2) Kenneth Lowell, 10/12/1981, (3) Frank McDonald, 1992. Two children.

257. Ralph L. Roberts (Lawrence[9], James[8], Jonathan[7], Josiah[6], Samuel[5], Jonathan[4], George[3], John[2], George[1]), son of Lawrence J. and Olive M. (McCarty) Roberts, was born in Islesboro, Maine, June 11, 1924. He married Nellie Williams, who was born in Islesboro, November 8, 1924. This family retired to Florida City, Florida.[#] Children:

    i. Judith Elaine, b. 2/5/1948, Belfast, ME; m. Richard Plogger; lived in Berkley, MA. 2 Ch.

294.   ii. Russell Stephen, b. 5/28/1949.

295.   iii. Michael Stephen, b. 2/23/1955.

258. Allen H. Roberts (Lawrence[9], James[8], Jonathan[7], Josiah[6], Samuel[5], Jonathan[4], George[3], John[2], George[1]), son of Lawrence J. and Olive M. (McCarty) Roberts, was born in Islesboro, Maine, May 6, 1927. He married, firstly, Marie Combs, secondly, Patricia Wood, and, thirdly, Grace Morrill, in July of 1981. The following

---

[*] Cafferty, p. 190.
[+] Cafferty, p. 191.
[#] Cafferty, pp. 192-3.

children are by Patricia, who was born January 17, 1930, and died January 8, 1980.* Children:

    i. James, b. 10/27/1958, Portland, ME; m. Debra Morse, 8/1/1982.

    ii. Gregory, b. 9/4/1960, Portland, ME.

259. Arthur Neil Roberts (Arthur^9, James^8, Jonathan^7, Josiah^6, Samuel^5, Jonathan^4, George^3, John^2, George^1), son of Arthur B. and Hazel (Bridges) Roberts, was born in Rockland, Maine, July 14, 1919. He married, firstly, Carrie Small (the mother of the first two children below) and, secondly, May 10, 1952, Judith L. Gordon (the mother of the remainder). This family lives in Belfast, Maine.* Children:

296.	i.	James Arthur, b. 9/11/1944.
	ii.	John Kenneth, b. 8/15/1946; m. Kathy Stockmen 11/1968.
	iii.	Rose Mary, b. 1/30/1953.
	iv.	Andrea Maria, b. 3/20/1955.
297.	v.	Neil Leroy, b. 3/14/1957.
	vi.	Rita Ann, b. 7/13/1961; m. Michael Harvey, 9/16/1978. 2 children.
	vii.	Vernon Abram, b. 7/26/1967.

260. Dennis Roberts (Luther^9, Cyrus^8, Jonathan^7, Josiah^6, Samuel^5, Jonathan^4, George^3, John^2, George^1), son of Luther Earl and Georgia (Small) Roberts, was born in Belfast, Maine, February 23, 1920, and died in Swanville, Maine, June 7, 1982. He married Evelyn Clements, who was born in Belfast, December 3, 1912, and died in 1992.# Children:

---

  * Cafferty, p. 193.
  * Cafferty, pp. 194-5.
  # Cafferty, pp. 196-8.

TENTH GENERATION

298. i. Dennis Earl, b. 3/28/1942.
299. ii. Loren E., b. 1/24/1944.
       iii. Joyce, b. 8/29/1945; m. & div. 8/15/1975, Leslie Tibbetts. Lived in Swanville, ME. One child.

261. Everett Ervin Roberts (Luther^9, Cyrus^8, Jonathan^7, Josiah^6, Samuel^5, Jonathan^4, George^3, John^2, George^1), son of Luther Earl and Georgia (Small) Roberts, was born in Maine, January 13, 1922, and died in Bangor, Maine, September 9, 1983, and is buried in Grove Cemetery in Belfast, Maine. He married, firstly, Windna William, and, secondly, Arlene -----. The child below was by Windna.* Child:

   i. Shirley Ann, b. 10/15/1942, Belfast, ME; m. 6/18/1960, Robert Cushman. Five children.

262. Roger Lloyd Roberts (Frank^9, Frank^8, Jonathan^7, Josiah^6, Samuel^5, Jonathan^4, George^3, John^2, George^1), son of Frank Herbert and Jeanette (Patterson) Roberts, was born in Maine, January 27, 1936. He married Judie Campbell. They live in Belfast, Maine.$^+$ Child:

   i. Scott Elliot, b. 8/3/1961, in VA.

263. Norman Roberts (Frank^9, Frank^8, Jonathan^7, Josiah^6, Samuel^5, Jonathan^4, George^3, John^2, George^1), son of Frank Herbert and Jeanette (Patterson) Roberts, was born in Maine, April 2, 1947. He married Sandra Howes. They live in Searsmont, Maine.$^\#$ Child:

   i. Beth Ann, b. 2/24/1973, Camden, ME.

264. Reginold Roberts (Stanley^9, Leslie^8, Levi^7, Josiah^6, Samuel^5, Jonathan^4, George^3, John^2, George^1), son of Stanley and Nillie (Fuller) Roberts, was born in Maine, July 5, 1942. He married, firstly, Donna Gum. Reginold and a second wife were living in Wilmington, Massachusetts, about 1990.** Child:

---

* Cafferty, p. 198.
$^+$ Cafferty, p. 201.
$^\#$ Cafferty, p. 202.
** Ervin Roberts notes.

DESCENDANTS OF GEORGE & MARY ROBERTS

    i. Burton.

265. Garry Roberts (Robert^9, Leslie^8, Levi^7, Josiah^6, Samuel^5, Jonathan^4, George^3, John^2, George^1), son of Robert and Ellen (Duley) Roberts, was born in Maine, June 6, 1947. He and his wife Barbara were living in Belfast, Maine, about 1990.* Children:

    i. Leslie.

    ii. Lisa.

266. Robert Roberts (Robert^9, Leslie^8, Levi^7, Josiah^6, Samuel^5, Jonathan^4, George^3, John^2, George^1), son of Robert and Ellen (Duley) Roberts, was born in Maine, February 12, 1950. He married April Dudley, who was born November 12, 1951. This family was living in Belfast, Maine, about 1990.$^+$ Children:

    i. Cameron, b. 2/2/1973.

    ii. Aneke, b. 4/16/1976.

267. Ernest James Roberts (Ervin^9, Ernest^8, Levi^7, Josiah^6, Samuel^5, Jonathan^4, George^3, John^2, George^1), son of Ervin and Viola (Crosby) Roberts, was born in Maine, June 26, 1958. He married October 1, 1980, Gina Porcaro, who was born April 9, 1960. This family was living in Gorham, Maine, about 1990.$^\#$ Children:

    i. Rhiannon, b. 4/5/1982.

    ii. Kevin, b. 3/5/1984.

268. Randall Frank Roberts (Raymond^9, Raymond^8, Alpheus^7, Watson^6, Samuel^5, Jonathan^4, George^3, John^2, George^1), son of Raymond Sylvester and Shirley Avis (Lowe) Roberts, was born in Bangor, Maine, September 4, 1949. He married Diane Chase of Unity, Maine. She was born March 22, 1946 in Brooks, Maine, where they now reside (c. 1990).** Children:

---

* Ervin Roberts notes.
$^+$ Ervin Roberts notes.
$^\#$ Ervin Roberts notes.
** Hilton, pp. 9-10.

TENTH GENERATION

 i. Jenney Beth, b. 8/7/1973.

 ii. Joshua Chase, b. 11/2/1974.

 iii. Jessica Rae, b. 7/2/1976.

269. Frank Stanwood Roberts Jr.(Frank^9, Frank^8, Nathan^7, Amos^6, George^5, Jonathan^4, George^3, John^2, George^1), son of Frank Stanwood and Clare (Ridley) Roberts, was born in Columbus, Georgia, March 1, 1922. He married Charmaine Smith in Tampa, Florida, January 28, 1950.* Children:

 i. Debrah Ann, b. 2/24/1951, Atlanta; m. Jeffrey S. Walachiks, 6/17/1972. One daughter.

 ii. Clare Ridley, b. 1/9/1957, Atlanta.

270. Sewell Wilbur Roberts (George^9, George^8, George^7, Amos^6, George^5, Jonathan^4, George^3, John^2, George^1), son of George Brinton and Jennie (Kirkpatrick) Roberts, was born October 25, 1904 and died in Bangor, Maine, March 27, 1971. He married Emily Violette Saucier in 1930. She was born in Canada and died in October of 1966.⁺ Child:

 i. Patricia, b. Boston; m. Ronald Springer, 1960. 2 ch.

271. Dwane Bartlett Roberts (Wilbur^9, George^8, George^7, Amos^6, George^5, Jonathan^4, George^3, John^2, George^1), son of Wilbur Prescott and Charlotte (Bartlett) Roberts, was born October 9, 1919. He married Mary Everett.# Children:

 i. Mary Elizabeth, b. 9/15/1944.

 ii. Martha Jean.

 iii. Elaine Ann, b. 12/27/1956.

272. Forest Rupert Roberts Jr.(Forest^9, George^8, George^7, Amos^6, George^5, Jonathan^4, George^3, John^2, George^1), son of Forest Rupert and Beatrice (Gilbert) Roberts, was born November 14,

---

 * Hilton, p. 14.
 ⁺ Hilton, p. 22.
 # Hilton, p. 18.

1940. He married Hazel Keene, the daughter of Henry and Madelyn (Higginbopha) Keene, in Concord, New Hampshire, July 8, 1963. Hazel, also known as Penny, was born August 27, 1946.* Child:

    i. Julie Ann, b. 5/21/1969, Bar Harbor, ME.

273. **Lewellyn Thomas Roberts** (George[9], Frederick[8], George[7], Amos[6], George[5], Jonathan[4], George[3], John[2], George[1]), son of George Frederick and Lillian E. (Thomas) Roberts, was born October 21, 1906 and died November 4, 1951. He married Alphena St. Pierre.[+] Children:

    i. Lewellyn Lloyd. No children.

    ii. James Richard. Five children.

    iii. Faye Raye. Four children.

    iv. Carol, unm.

274. **Glen W. Roberts** (George[9], Frederick[8], George[7], Amos[6], George[5], Jonathan[4], George[3], John[2], George[1]), son of George Frederick and Lillian E. (Thomas) Roberts, was born in Fort Kent, Maine, February 22, 1916. He married Pearl Rita Clark, January 12, 1939. She was born in Presque Isle, Maine, August 11, 1917.[#] Children:

300.   i. Spencer Clark, b. 8/8/1939.

    ii. Glenda Chance, b. 5/6/1945, Presque Isle; m. Colby Grant, 6/15/1974. Three adopted children.

275. **Frederick Parkhurst Roberts** (George[9], Frederick[8], George[7], Amos[6], George[5], Jonathan[4], George[3], John[2], George[1]), son of George Frederick and Lillian E. (Thomas) Roberts, was born in Fort Kent, Maine, August 23, 1920. He married Patricia Shaw, July, 1953, in Presque Isle, Maine. She was born in Eagle Lake, Maine, September, 1931. All of the following children were born

---

   * Hilton, p. 18.
   + Hilton, p. 19.
   # Hilton, p. 19.

TENTH GENERATION

in Presque Isle.* Children:

    i. Michael Earle, b. 2/6/1954.

    ii. Lillie Ann, b. 1/8/1955.

    iii. Leslie Sue, b. 12/7/1958.

    iv. Lisa Marie, b. 1/10/1962.

    v. Elizabeth Jo, b. 6/27/1963.

    vi. John Frederick, b. 3/16/1965.

276. Kenneth Pinkham Roberts (Earle^9, Frederick^8, George^7, Amos^6, George^5, Jonathan^4, George^3, John^2, George^1), son of Earle Henry and Ella Augusta (Pinkham) Roberts, was born July 14, ?? He married Wilma Richards, September 1, 1944.⁺ Children:

    i. Sandra Ann, b. 10/21/1945.

    ii. Susan Louise, b. 6/21/1951.

    iii. Sharon K., b. 2/10/1955.

277. David Mark Roberts (Earle^9, Frederick^8, George^7, Amos^6, George^5, Jonathan^4, George^3, John^2, George^1), son of Earle Henry and Ella Augusta (Pinkham) Roberts, was born May 7, 1923. He married Cecile L. Peletier in August of 1946.# Children:

    i. Lynn M., b. 6/18/1947.

    ii. Diane, b. 10/19/1949.

278. Herbert A. Roberts (Stanley^9, William^8, Amos^7, Amos^6, George^5, Jonathan^4, George^3, John^2, George^1), son of Stanley W. and Etta (Eldridge) Roberts, was born in Newport, Maine, September 9, 1900, and died in Concord, New Hampshire, September 8, 1970. He married firstly Vera M. Albee, who was born August 24, 1898 and died March 14, 1931, and secondly, Susie Stanley, October 13,

---

    * Hilton, p. 20.
    ⁺ Hilton, p. 21.
    # Hilton, p. 21.

DESCENDANTS OF GEORGE & MARY ROBERTS

1933. The following children are by the second marriage.[*] Children:

 i. Mervin Stanley, b. 7/7/1936, m. 8/1960 -----.

 ii. Ann Marie, b. 9/3/1937, Newfane, N.Y.

 iii. Mary Jane, b. 10/10/1945, Milo, Me.

279. Ernest A. Roberts (Stanley^9, William^8, Amos^7, Amos^6, George^5, Jonathan^4, George^3, John^2, George^1), son of Stanley W. and Etta (Eldridge) Roberts, was born in Dover-Foxcroft, Maine, January 16, 1914, and died in Waterville, Maine, October 13, 1977. He married Velma Wheeler, June 1, 1935. She was born in Fairfield, Maine, February 3, 1913.[+] Child:

 i. Marilyn Jean, b. 12/4/1937; m. Warren B. Moulton, 10/7/1956. One son.

280. Arthur Edwin Roberts (Menza^9, William^8, Amos^7, Amos^6, George^5, Jonathan^4, George^3, John^2, George^1), son of Menza Alfred and Harriett (Sheehan) Roberts, was born in Salem, Massachusetts, October 28, 1917. He married Virginia Alice Dautrich, in Winsted, Connecticut, December 31, 1941. The last six children shown below were born in Winsted.[#] Children:

 i. Arthur Edward, b. 6/25/1945, Paris, Texas.

 ii. Neil Alfred, b. 7/21/1947.

 iii. Barbara Alice, b. 6/21/1949.

 iv. Mark Phillip, b. 5/29/1951.

 v. David Theodore, b. 8/21/1954.

 vi. Ann Frances, b. 10/14/1957.

 vii. Glenn Thomas, b. 5/14/1960.

281. Victor Colby Roberts (Timothy^9, Adrian^8, Amos^7,

---

[*] Hilton, p. 26.
[+] Hilton, p. 27.
[#] Hilton, p. 29.

TENTH GENERATION

Amos⁶, George⁵, Jonathan⁴, George³, John², George¹), son of Timothy Victor and Abbie Clara (Colby) Roberts, was born in Skowhegan, Maine, February 15, 1912. He married Grace Gertrude Grant, October 9, 1932. They live in Skowhegan.* Children:

    i. Grace Gertrude, b. 6/7/1933; m. & div. twice.

    ii. Vicki Patricia, b. 1/8/1940, Skowhegan; m. (2) James Sayre, 6/3/1966. Live in Zanesville, OH. Four children.

282. Adrian Everett Roberts (Timothy⁹, Adrian⁸, Amos⁷, Amos⁶, George⁵, Jonathan⁴, George³, John², George¹), son of Timothy Victor and Abbie Clara (Colby) Roberts, was born in Skowhegan, Maine, March 26, 1913. He married Glema Daggett, June 17, 1933. They live in Skowhegan.⁺ Child:

    i. Jo Anne, b. 7/25/1934, Skowhegan; m. Arthur E. Hill, 8/14/1954. Two children.

283. Otis Jackson Roberts III (Otis⁹, Otis⁸, Otis⁷, Amos⁶, George⁵, Jonathan⁴, George³, John², George¹), son of Otis Jackson Jr. and Glennys (Flewelling) Roberts, was born in Dexter, Maine, May 4, 1939. He married Alice Jane Bailey at the Methodist Church in Dexter, June 22, 1963. Alice is the daughter of Harold and Arlene Lander Bailey and was born in Cambridge, Massachusetts, August 19, 1941.# Children:

    i. Dawn Marie, b. 11/14/1963, Idaho Falls, ID.

    ii. Jeffrey Allen, b. 11/24/1966, Ludlow, MA.

284. John William Roberts (John⁹, Roderick⁸, Charles⁷, Jonathan⁶, Seth⁵, Jonathan⁴, George³, John², George¹), son of John Roderick and Pauline (Eresch) Roberts, was born in Moscow, Idaho, February 22, 1941, and now (1993) lives in Austin, Texas. John married Kathleen Cummins, the daughter of Robert L. and Clara Cummins, in Phoenix, Arizona, May 21, 1966. After five years of teaching high school physics and mathematics in various locations,

---

  * Hilton, p. 31.
  ⁺ Hilton, p. 32.
  # Hilton, p. 46.

from Yakima, Washington, to Guam (Mariana Islands), John changed professions. His work in the field of computers took the family from Yakima to Phoenix to Long Island, New York, to Tucson, Arizona, where they lived for twelve years, before relocating to Austin. While in Tucson Kathleen completed a law degree at the University of Arizona and became a practicing attorney.* Children:

> i. Brad Arden, b. 3/30/1967, Guam; m. 10/13/1991, Anne Marie Burgoyne. He graduated from the University of Pa., worked as a management consultant in Boston, and was completing his M.B.A. at Harvard Univ. in 1993.
>
> ii. Rebecca Ann, b. 6/20/1970, Phoenix, AZ; graduated from Rice Univ.

285. Tim Arden Roberts (John^9, Roderick^8, Charles^7, Jonathan^6, Seth^5, Jonathan^4, George^3, John^2, George^1), son of John Roderick and Pauline (Eresch) Roberts was born in Forest Grove, Oregon, January 5, 1947. He married Margaret Jane Unger of Hillsboro, Oregon, July 13, 1968. Tim graduated with a B.A. in Biology from Portland State University in 1969 and earned his D.M.D. degree at the University of Oregon School of Dentistry in 1973. He served in the U.S. Air Force in Japan, from 1973 to 1976. Tim and Margaret now (1993) live in McMinnville, Oregon, where Tim practices dentistry.⁺ Children:

> i. Jennifer Lynn, b. 3/3/1971, Portland, OR; m. Brian Maselli, June 19, 1993. A 1993 graduate of Westmont College. Live in McMinnville.
>
> ii. Amy Michelle, b. 4/17/1973, Portland. Attends Whitworth College.
>
> iii. Sara Jane, b. 2/7/1977, McMinnville. A student.

---

* Family records John William Roberts.
⁺ Family records of Tim Roberts and the author.

TENTH GENERATION

iv. Eric Mathew (adopted), b. 7/22/1979, San Antonio, TX. A student.

286. Carleton Wayne Roberts (Stanley^9, Frederick^8, Willis^7, Eliphalet^6, Eliphalet^5, Eliphalet^4, George^3, John^2, George^1), son of Stanley L. and Doris I. (Greene) Roberts, was born in Royalton, Vermont, March 3, 1929. He married Ruby Hazel Campbell. This family lived in Skaneateles, New York.* Children:

i. John Wesley, b. 2/10/1955.

ii. Anna Karen, b. 6/20/1958.

287. Conrad Craig Roberts (Stanley^9, Frederick^8, Willis^7, Eliphalet^6, Eliphalet^5, Eliphalet^4, George^3, John^2, George^1), son of Stanley L. and Doris I. (Greene) Roberts, was born in Royalton, Vermont, April 5, 1934. He married ----- ----- in England. This family lived in Bedford, Massachusetts.⁺ Children:

i. Dale.

ii. Cheryl.

288. Elihu Luman Roberts (Baxter^9, Calvin^8, Lucian^7, Eliphalet^6, Eliphalet^5, Eliphalet^4, George^3, John^2, George^1), son of Baxter W. and Blanche (Judd) Roberts, was born in Sharon, Vermont, December 8, 1910. He married Ester (Saarela) Nelson, the daughter of Johan Aukust Saarela and Selma Johanna Hendrickson, November 10, 1934, in New York City. Ester died in New York, and is buried in Pine Hill Cemetery in Sharon. Ester's daughter Dorothy Grace Nelson was legally adopted by Elihu.# Children:

i. Peter Judd, b. 11/7/1950.

289. Ralph Calvin Roberts (Baxter^9, Calvin^8, Lucian^7, Eliphalet^6, Eliphalet^5, Eliphalet^4, George^3, John^2, George^1), son of Baxter W. and Blanche (Judd) Roberts, was born in Sharon, Vermont, January 31, 1918. He married Lillian Bates, July 16,

---

* Roberts, Blanche J., p. 531.
⁺ Roberts, Blanche J., p. 564.
Roberts, Blanche J., p. 539.

1945, in Woodstock, New York. Lillian, who was born in Woodstock May 12, 1920, is the daughter of Fred and Eugenia (Atwood) Bates.* Child:

    i. Ann Lydia, b. 3/13/1947; m. -----Dame.

290. Philip John Roberts (Baxter^9, Calvin^8, Lucian^7, Eliphalet^6, Eliphalet^5, Eliphalet^4, George^3, John^2, George^1), son of Baxter W. and Blanche (Judd) Roberts, was born in Vermont, May 10, 1921. He married Dorothy Drake, the daughter of Charles and Florence (Plummer) Drake, January 2, 1941. Dorothy was born in West Lebanon, New Hampshire, April 16, 1920. This family lived in West Lebanon, where the following children were born.⁺ Children:

    i. Judith Elizabeth, b. 9/3/1941; m. Forrest R. Alger, 6/12/1964. One child.

    ii. Philip John, b. 11/17/1945.

    iii. Kenneth E., b. 9/26/1950.

291. Richard Baxter Roberts (Baxter^9, Calvin^8, Lucian^7, Eliphalet^6, Eliphalet^5, Eliphalet^4, George^3, John^2, George^1), son of Baxter W. and Blanche (Judd) Roberts, was born in Hanover, New Hampshire, March 27, 1927. He married, firstly, Dora Norris, the daughter of Roy and Leah (Bourette) Norris, July 1, 1944, in Fitchburg, Massachusetts. Dora was born in Massachusetts, October 21, 1928. Richard married, secondly, Judith Strout, the daughter of Carl and Carmen (Kemp) Strout, in Keene, New Hampshire, July 1, 1957. Judith was born in Webster, Massachusetts, May 9, 1934.# Children:

    i. Gloria Jean, b. 10/29/1944, Leominster, MA.

    ii. Richard Ralph, b. 10/14/1945, Leominster, MA.

    iii. David Gary, b. 5/11/1947, Leominster, MA.

---

  * Roberts, Blanche J., p. 532.
  ⁺ Roberts, Blanche J., p. 562.
  # Roberts, Blanche J., p. 563.

TENTH GENERATION

    iv.   June Lydia, b. 12/25/1957, Bellows Falls, VT.

    v.   Daniel Richard, b. 2/8/1959, Lebanon, NH.

    vi.   Amelia Rose, b. 7/1/1960, Lebanon, NH.

    vii.   Samuel Baxter, b. 8/8/1962, Lebanon, NH.

    viii.   Beth, b. 10/2/1965.

    ix.   Jennifer, b. 5/15/1967.

292. Raymond Gilbert Roberts (Edwin^9, Albertus^8, Daniel^7, Amphias^6, Daniel^5, Eliphalet^4, George^3, John^2, George^1), son of Edwin Gilbert and Stella (Warren) Roberts, was born in Vermont, January 21, 1945. He married Irene Kate Benjamin, the daughter of George C. and Adele (Rainville) Benjamin, September 5, 1964, in North Thetford, Vermont. Irene was born July 23, 1945.* Child:

    i.   Gail Marie, b. 6/18/1967.

293. David Calvin Roberts (Richard^9, Carl^8, Frank^7, Orlando^6, Moses^5, Eliphalet^4, George^3, John^2, George^1), son of Richard Lester and Eva Estelle (Gorton) Roberts, was born in Burlington, Vermont, July 30, 1939. He married Jane Louise Verret, who was born September 2, 1942, in Burlington, Vermont, the daughter of Omer Francis and Marie Alice (Brigham) Verret. David and Jane live in Burlington, where he works as a sales co-ordinator and she as a produce clerk.⁺ Children:

301.   i.   Robert Francis, b. 3/2/1962.

    ii.   Sarah Anne, b. 3/11/1963; m. 8/3/1985, Mark Adrian Jennings. Live in Hartford, VT.

    iii.   Neil Edward (twin), b. 11/4/1964. Lives in Fairfax, VT.

    iv.   Nora Louise (twin), b. 11/4/1964. Lives in Burlington.

---

* Roberts, Blanche J., p. 562.
⁺ Bryant and Verret notes.

- v. Sharon Marie (twin), b. 1/24/1969. Lives in St.Paul, MN.
- vi. Karen Eva (twin), b. 1/24/1969. Lives in Burlington.
- vii. David Daniel, b. 12/7/1974. Lives in Burlington.

ELEVENTH GENERATION

294. Russell Stephen Roberts (Ralph[10], Lawrence[9], James[8], Jonathan[7], Josiah[6], Samuel[5], Jonathan[4], George[3], John[2], George[1]), son of Ralph L. and Nellie (Williams) Roberts, was born in Portland, Maine, May 28, 1949. He married Deborah Judd, who was born in Bardstow, Kentucky. This family lived in Jacksonville, Florida.* Child:

    i. Darlene Michelle, b. 1/1/1974, Hamilton, Bermuda.

295. Michael Stephen Roberts (Ralph[10], Lawrence[9], James[8], Jonathan[7], Josiah[6], Samuel[5], Jonathan[4], George[3], John[2], George[1]), son of Ralph L. and Nellie (Williams) Roberts, was born in Bourne, Massachusetts, February 23, 1955. He married Janet Mills, who was born in Parkersburg, West Virginia, August 28, 1957. This family lived in Columbus, Ohio.+ Children:

    i. Sadie Ann, b. 4/3/1981, Ft. Campbell, KY.

    ii. Dallas Warren, b. 6/28/1982, Columbus, OH.

296. James Arthur Roberts (Arthur[10], Arthur[9], James[8], Jonathan[7], Josiah[6], Samuel[5], Jonathan[4], George[3], John[2], George[1]), son of Arthur Neil and Carrie (Small) Roberts, was born in Belfast, Maine, September 11, 1944. He married October 17, 1964, Linda N. Ward, who was born August 24, 1946.# Child:

302.   i. James Arthur, Jr., b. 3/30/1965.

297. Neil Leroy Roberts (Arthur[10], Arthur[9], James[8], Jonathan[7], Josiah[6], Samuel[5], Jonathan[4], George[3], John[2], George[1]), son of Arthur Neil and Judith (Gordon) Roberts, was born in Maine, March 14, 1957. He married March 10, 1985, in Belfast, Maine, Kelly Flannagan, who was born in Apple Valley, Minnesota. The following children were born in Belfast.** Children:

    i. Adam Lee, b. 4/2/1985.

    ii. Chelsea Lynn, b. 7/26/1986.

---

  * Cafferty, p. 193.
  + Cafferty, pp. 192-3.
  # Cafferty, p. 194.
 ** Cafferty, pp. 194-5.

iii. Brandon Neil, b. 11/7/1988.

298. Dennis Earl Roberts (Dennis[10], Luther[9], Cyrus[8], Jonathan[7], Josiah[6], Samuel[5], Jonathan[4], George[3], John[2], George[1]), son of Dennis and Evelyn (Clements) Roberts, was born in Belfast, Maine, March 28, 1942. He married Nancy Lee Knowlton, who was born in Belfast, November 2, 1940.* Children:

    i. Cheryl Lynn, b. 3/27/1960; m. Douglas J. Libby. Two children.

    ii. Tamie Lee, b. 5/3/1962; m. William B. Dusoe. Two children.

    iii. Steven, b. 8/19/1966.

303.   iv. Dennis Earl, Jr., b. 9/1/1970.

299. Loren E. Roberts (Dennis[10], Luther[9], Cyrus[8], Jonathan[7], Josiah[6], Samuel[5], Jonathan[4], George[3], John[2], George[1]), son of Dennis and Evelyn (Clements) Roberts, was born in Belfast, Maine, January 24, 1944. He married Glenda Grealy, September 24, 1960. They live in Swanville, Maine. The following children were born in Belfast.⁺ Children:

304.   i. Loren Everett, b. 12/20/1960.

    ii. Tamice Dee, b. 4/22/1962; m. Michael H. Warren. Two children.

305.   iii. Frederick Dennis, b. 2/25/1964.

    iv. Jeffrey George, b. 7/23/1967.

300. Spencer Clark Roberts (Glen[10], George[9], Frederick[8], George[7], Amos[6], George[5], Jonathan[4], George[3], John[2], George[1]), son of Glen W. and Pearl Rita (Clark) Roberts, was born in Presque Isle, Maine, August 8, 1939. He married Darlene Skinner, in Canada, in March of 1964. The following children were born in

---

  * Cafferty, p. 196.
  ⁺ Cafferty, p. 197.

ELEVENTH GENERATION

Presque Isle.* Children:
- i. Mark Spencer, b. 9/23/1964.
- ii. Todd Matthew, b. 2/15/1966.
- iii. Terri Marie, b. 3/10/1970.
- iv. Julie Anne, b. 7/7/1971.

301. Robert Francis Roberts (David[10], Richard[9], Carl[8], Frank[7], Orlando[6], Moses[5], Eliphalet[4], George[3], John[2], George[1]), son of David Calvin and Jane Louise (Verret) Roberts, was born in Burlington, Vermont, March 2, 1962. He married Elizabeth Jane Lihatsh, May 27, 1984. She was born in Springfield, Vermont. Robert and Elizabeth live in State College, Pennsylvania, where Robert is a professor.⁺ Children:
- i. Nicholas David, b. 4/13/1987, St. Paul, MN.
- ii. Anastasia Marie, b. 6/12/1989, St. Paul, MN.
- iii. Natalie Elisabeth, b. 6/20/1992, State College, PA.

---

* Hilton, p. 19.
⁺ Bryant and Verret notes.

TWELFTH GENERATION

302. James Arthur Roberts Jr.(James[11], Arthur[10], Arthur[9], James[8], Jonathan[7], Josiah[6], Samuel[5], Jonathan[4], George[3], John[2], George[1]), son of James Arthur and Linda N. (Ward) Roberts, was born in Belfast, Maine, March 30, 1965. He married Paula Marie Harron, May 27, 1985. She was born May 27, 1964.* Child:

    i. Joshua Alden, b. 2/24/1988, Belfast, ME.

303. Dennis Earl Roberts Jr. (Dennis[11], Dennis[10], Luther[9], Cyrus[8], Jonathan[7], Josiah[6], Samuel[5], Jonathan[4], George[3], John[2], George[1]), son of Dennis Earl and Nancy Lee (Knowlton) Roberts, was born in Maine, September 1, 1970. He married Sherry Gibbs, who was born in Brooks, Maine.⁺ Child:

    i. Derrick Earl, b. 1/15/1989, Belfast, ME.

304. Loren Everett Roberts (Loren[11], Dennis[10], Luther[9], Cyrus[8], Jonathan[7], Josiah[6], Samuel[5], Jonathan[4], George[3], John[2], George[1]), son of Loren E. and Glenda (Grealy) Roberts, was born in Belfast, Maine, December 3, 1960. He married Cheryl Jackson, October 7, 1978. She was born July 16, 1963.# Children:

    i. Matasha Joy, b. 4/22/1979, Rockland, ME.; d. 6/15/1981.

    ii. Amanda Ruth, b. 2/5/1983, Belfast, ME.

    iii. Ashley Lynn, b. 10/17/1986, Belfast, ME.

305. Frederick Dennis Roberts (Loren[11], Dennis[10], Luther[9], Cyrus[8], Jonathan[7], Josiah[6], Samuel[5], Jonathan[4], George[3], John[2], George[1]), son of Loren E. and Glenda (Grealy) Roberts, was born in Belfast, Maine, February 24 (or 25?), 1964. He married Debbie Foss. They live in Lewiston, Maine.** Children:

    i. Jennifer Lynn, b. 7/13/1987.

    ii. Ryan Frederick, b. 5/8/1990, Waterville, ME.

---

* Cafferty, p. 194.
⁺ Cafferty, p. 197.
Cafferty, p. 197.
** Cafferty, p. 197.

BIBILIOGRAPHY

As can be seen from the footnotes, this work has relied on a large number of works by prior Roberts researchers and local historians. Only the most important of these are mentioned here.

Quint. In the 1850's Alonzo H. Quint, a local antiquarian of Dover, prepared a short article on the genealogy of the first two or three generations of the descendants of Thomas and Rebecca Roberts. This was published in the *New England Historical and Genealogical Register* (January 1854, pp. 63-4).

Scales. From about 1890 to about 1920, the Dover Historical Society and a local historian, John Scales, published at least three volumes of early Dover town records, sketches of local families, and vital records. The Thomas Roberts family features prominently in these works. (*Historical Memoranda Concerning Persons and Places in Old Dover. . .*, *Collections of the Dover, N.H. Historical Society*, and *History of Dover. . .*) These have all have been reissued by Heritage Books in recent years.

Noyes, Libby and Davis. In the 1920's and 1930's Noyes, Libby and Davis published various installments of their *Genealogical Dictionary of Maine and New Hampshire*, which covers the first two or three generations of virtually all of the early families of those two states. The section on the Robertses is not extensive, but it is safe to say that the present book could not have been written without reliance on this landmark of early American genealogy.

Hardon. In the early 1900's Henry W. Hardon began an ambitious compilation of all of the descendants of Thomas and Rebecca Roberts. His book never made it to publication, but the type-written rough draft, in six volumes, compiled shortly before his death in 1934, is on file at the New Hampshire Historical Society library in Concord, New Hampshire. It has been microfilmed and is available through the L.D.S. Family History Center network (Films 15,533 and 15,534). Hardon had done a lot of careful research into early deed and probate records. The first three or four generations of the Hardon manuscript have been thoroughly cross-checked to other sources where possible. The manuscript itself is far from publication readiness, its cross-referencing and numbering are incomplete and inaccurate, there are many typographical errors, and its organization of later generations is very poor. Despite the flaws it is an invaluable source for Roberts research for New Hampshire and Maine. It also has a good deal of data on various unconnected Roberts lines.

While the family of Thomas and Rebecca Roberts of Dover has been dealt with in some detail by prior genealogists, nothing has ever been published on the early descendants of the family of George and Mary Roberts of Exeter. By the time local historians got around to compiling genealogies of the early families of the Exeter vicinity (in the late 1800's), there were virtually no Roberts-surnamed descendants left in that part of New Hampshire. The vast majority of them were in Maine and Vermont by that time.

Grant. In the 1890's Amorena (Roberts) Grant published a very attractive book, replete with photographs of many Robertses of the early 1800's, *The Roberts Family Genealogy*. This book covers the Robertses who pioneered Buckfield and Brooks, Maine, specifically the descendants of Joseph (No. 12) and Hannah (Young) Roberts. The book was based on first-hand interviews and some records of Buckfield from the 1780's and on, so it doesn't go back into the first three generations. The book is not well organized and is very hard to find. The L.D.S. library in Salt Lake City has the copy that I consulted.

Hilton. A compilation of the known descendants of Jonathan (No. 13) and Elizabeth (Webb) Roberts has been admirably presented by Elizabeth Hilton in the *Roberts Family History*, most recently updated about 1980. Unfortunately, the Hilton book, which is in the form of a mimeographed report, has not circulated outside of a small group of descendants who meet once at year in Maine.

Blanche J. Roberts. For Vermont Blanche (Judd) Roberts' *Vital Records of Strafford, Vermont*, collected in the mid-1900's and published by the local D.A.R. in 1984-5, is a very important source. There are some errors to be found, however, especially in Mrs. Roberts' attempts to connect the Vermont branch of the Robertses to their New Hampshire antecedents. This work is also very hard to find. The L.D.S. library in Salt Lake City has a copy, but it does not seem to have been microfilmed for general circulation to other Family History Center libraries.

For New Hampshire genealogical research in general the

definitive work is *New Hampshire Genealogical Research Guide* by Laird C. Towle, Ph.D., and Ann N. Brown (Bowie, MD: Heritage Books, 1983.). A very good fairly recent general history of New Hampshire and Maine is *The Eastern Frontier: The Settlement of Northern New England, 1610-1763* by Charles E. Clark (Hanover, NH & London: University Press of New England, 1970, 1983.) Critical to an understanding of the early decades of colonial New Hampshire, especially the political background and troubles with the Indians and the Mason heirs, is Jeremy Belknap's *History of New Hampshire*, which has gone through three revisions/editions, since its original publication in 1784. The best is one edited with numerous genealogically-inspired footnotes, by John Farmer in 1831. This edition has recently been reprinted by Heritage Books, Inc.

Stephen Roberts (p. 98)

Joel Roberts (p. 63)

Flora Belle (Roberts) Richardson (p. 141)

Almira Roberts (p. 98)   Anna A. (Roberts) Meader (p.98)
Source: Wilson

Thomas Roberts(p.96)   Elizabeth (Roberts) Roberts(p.96)

Susan L. Roberts (p.175)   Elwood Roberts (p.176)

Emma M. Roberts (p.176)   Clarence C. Roberts (p.176)
Source: Messer

Hiram R. Roberts (p. 130) James A. Roberts (p. 174)
Source: Hurd   Source: Little

Harriet (Roberts) Elliot (p. 269)

Jacob Roberts (p. 267)   Gilman Roberts (p. 268)
                         Source: Grant

Mary (Roberts) Fogg (p. 253)

John Roberts (p. 271)

William P. Roberts (p. 268)

Ellen C. Roberts (p. 268)
Source: Grant

Joseph Roberts (p. 270)   Winslow Roberts (p. 274)

Hamlin M. Roberts (p. 299) Leslie M. Roberts (p. 298)

Ahira Roberts(p. 303) Amorena (Roberts) Grant(p.300)
Source: Grant

Huldah J. Roberts (p. 268)   Alfred J. Roberts (p. 272)

Nathan H. Roberts (p. 274)   Rufus Roberts (p. 275)
Source: Grant

Milton M. Roberts (p. 297)   Isaac P. Roberts (p. 298)

Barnabus M. Roberts (p. 300) Porteus B. Roberts (p.302)

Francis A. Roberts (p. 327) Floyd J. Roberts (p.333)
Source: Grant

Sylvanus I. Roberts (p. 277)   Eli Roberts (p. 283)

Charles L. Roberts (p. 301) Albert A. Roberts (p. 309)
Source: Grant

Thomas A. Roberts (p. 309)   Freeman M. Roberts (p. 329)

Cassius C. Roberts (p. 328) Charles A. Roberts (p. 331)
Source: Grant

Parepa R. Roberts(p.329)   Paulina(Roberts) Lawler(p.329)

Lloyd A. Roberts (p. 333)   Albert Roberts (p. 332)
Source: Grant

Charles E. Roberts(p.319)   Charles A. Roberts(p.348)

Theresa Avis Roberts (p. 320)
Source: Jacobsen

Roderick G. Roberts & Myrtle (Harris) Roberts (p.346)

Jane (Roberts) Durham &   Andrew B. Jacobsen & Myrtle
John W. Durham III(p.347)   (Roberts) Jacobsen(p.347)
                                               Source: Jacobsen

John R. Roberts (p. 368)

William A. Roberts (p. 370)

Roderick A. Jacobsen (p. 348)

Linda M. (Jacobsen) Loomis (p. 348)
Source: Jacobsen

Author's family: Hilary M., Deborah W., Thomas A. and Sara F. Jacobsen (p. 348)

INDEX

ABBOT, Chloe 300 Isaac 300
  Phebe Susan 300
ABBOTT, Nellie M 152
ABORN, Eliza 269
ACKERMAN, Patience Comfort
  163
ADAMS, Abijah 111 Angie 366
  Earl 341 Edna 186 Helen 341
  John M 186 Lucy 111 Mary
  111
ALBEE, Vera M 381
ALEXANDER, Ida 289
ALGER, Forrest R 386 Judith 386
  Julia Ann 320
ALLARD, Love 123
ALLEN, Archie 211 Eleanor 170
  Eliza Jane 211 Elizabeth Holt
  211 Joshua 49 Margaret 261
  Rebecca 276 Sidney A 276
ALLENDER, Alonzo F 159 Ellen
  159
AMBROSE, Sarah 167
AMES, Charles E 200 Emma 336
  Jane C 200 Rose 200
ANDERSON, Anna 368 Betty 373
  Emelyn Karen 207 Emily 207
  Matthew 207 Richard 242 373
  Susannah 242
ANDRE, Major 76 77
ANDREWS, Martha J 163
ANGEL, Julia 291

ANNE, Queen Of England 223
ARMSTRONG, Daniel N 202
  Mary Louise 202 Matilda M
  202
ARNOLD, Ann Eliza 137 Dina
  137 James 137
ARTHUR, 320
ASHE, Katherine 344 Rudolph 344
ATKINSON, David 88 Phebe 88
ATTWOOD, Frank C 354 Olive E
  T 354 Sarah M 354
ATWATER, Edgar 367 Julia Mae
  367
ATWOOD, Eugenia 386 Louisa
  140
AUDSLEY, Mary A 365
AUSTIN, Ann 55 Anne 29 Cynthia
  312 Elijah 40 Faustena 200
  Hannah 40 Lilla V 334 Martha
  98 Mary A 312 Nathaniel 40
  Sarah 40 Winslow 312
AVERY, Caroline M 259 Charles
  290 Elizabeth 290
AXLING, Emily 207
AYER, George Washington 88
  Julia 88 Priscilla 88
AYERS, A E 275 Juliette 275
AYLWARD, Elizabeth 219
BABB, Clinton R 147 Elizabeth
  147
BABBIDGE, Marilyn 375

BABCOCK, Esther 204
BACHELDER, Susan 268
BADGER, Cynthia 304 Harriet 291
    Laura Marinda 291 292 Virsel
    291
BAGLEY, Lillie Ann 199 Mary
    199 Orlando J 199
BAICH, Mary 62
BAILEY, Alice Jane 383 Arlene L
    383 Gilbert H 284 Harold 383
    Lydia Salmon 286 Nancy 284
    Samuel L 286
BAKER, Charles 48 Love 123
    Mary 143 Mary Ann 143 Sarah
    48 Thomas 143
BALDWIN, Jennie 332
BALL, Caroline 277 F 277
BALLARD, Nora 160 Royal O 160
BALLOU, Almira 269 John 269
    Mary 111 Maturin M 111
BANGS, Maria 274 Mehitable 35
BANKS, Mary Jane 123
BANNISTER, Arthur 213 Roberta
    213
BANNON, Ethel 196 James H 196
BARKER, Edith 305 Rebecca 67
    Wilbur 305 William P 67
BARNES, Cynthia 194 Duane 194
    Hinda 194
BARROW, David W 320 Myra
    320
BARROWS, Adeline 322 Herman
    322 Huldah 268 Joseph H 268
BARRY, Emma 336 Perley 336
BARSTOW, Robert 284 Sarah W
    284
BARTHOLOMEW, Ranae Marie
    369
BARTLESS, Zenas W 81
BARTLETT, Charlotte 362 Leono-
    ra 81 Nathaniel 362 Ruth 362
BASHAW, Leona 366

BATES, Eugenia 386 Fred 386
    Lillian 385
BEACHAM, Ann Eliza 166 John C
    166 Olive 166
BEAN, Eliza 112 Ella 211 Evelyn
    203 Hannah 63 James 63 Joe
    322 Sarah 322
BEAR, Carrie 301 John E 301
BECK, Sarah 61
BECKWITH, Addison 317 Sadie
    317
BEDELL, Ellen 130
BEEDE, Anna 98 Eliza 64 Hannah
    F 95 John 64 Jonathan 98
    Miriam 96 Moses 96 Olive 263
    Sarah 98
BELKNAP, Ellen 350
BELL, Arthur 302 Calvin H 92
    Emma C 206 Fanny 302
    Frances 92 Gertrude 206 Wil-
    liam L 206
BELLOWS, Grace 213
BENJAMIN, Adele 387 George C
    387 Harriet 324 Irene Kate 387
BENNETT, Althea 367 Beverly
    367 Carl 366 Carolyn 367
    Ceolia 141 Charles H 141
    David 366 Everett 366 James J
    328 Leona 366 Margaret 328
    Marilyn 367 Marshall 367 Mary
    137 Noreen 367 Norris W 346
    Oscar 366 Parepa 329 Patricia
    367 Robert 367 Robert L 367
    Thelma 346 Virene 366 Wil-
    liam I 329
BENTON, Francese 261 Henry
    Willard 261
BERKELEY, Ellen 160
BERRY, Abigail 212 Bernard 365
    Bertha Jane 198 Elizabeth A
    166 Elsie 365 Grace 166
    Hannah 166 Herbert F 162 Ida

BERRY (Continued)
Dorry 198 John M 114 Leah
114 Lena 162 Lovell 198
Lovell W 166 Mary 201 Melissa A 198 Ray N 201
BETZER, Alfred J 165 Maude 165
BEVIER, Andre B 369 Corey A
369 Craig A 369 Dale 369
Deborah A 369 Douglas A 369
Edward A 369 Ellinor 369 Gail
369 Helen 369 Ranae 369
BICKFORD, Abigail 43 Charles E
198 Cora I 198 Ellen J 100 106
Jonathan 43 Lillian Albertha
198 Mary 94 Rebecca 168 Sally
251
BILLINGS, Frances 186
BISHOP, Christiana 282 Ellen 185
Jonathan 282 Julia 145
BLACKSTONE, Hollis 273 Sarah
273
BLAISDELL, Enoch 101 Esther
101 Mary 101
BLAKE, Carolyn 367 Charles F 94
Harriet 261 Henry S 261 Joanna
81 Sarah 225 Susan 94 William
T 81
BLAKELEY, Ella 196 Johnson
196
BLANCHARD, Amanda 352 Anna
258 Electa Mehitable 321 Isaac
352 Lounetta F 191 Mary Diana
191 Melvin B 191 Nathaniel
258
BLESSIN, Bessie 171 Otto J 171
BLOOD, Ellen 371 Fred F 371
Lena Ellen 371
BLOODSWORTH, Lucy 343
BLOUIN, Ethel M 158
BODGE, Avis Jane 285 Sarah 285
Stephen T 285
BOEHM, Ernest 341 Ruth 341

BOLTZEN, Margaret 357
BONNEY, Faithful 281
BOODY, Ann Mary 305 Clarendon
272 Dora 272 Edward 272 Rose
272
BOOTH, Mary Elvira 288
BORLAND, Edith 343 Hugh K
343
BOSWORTH, Calla 345 Harry 345
BOTSFORD, Emily Wilbor 128
Josiah L 128 Lucy Anne 128
BOUCHARD, Althea 367 David
367
BOURETTE, Leah 386
BOWDOIN, Hannah 144
BOWEN, Levi 253 Lovina 253
BOWLES, Sarah 60
BOYLE, James 92 Sarah 92
BOYNTON, Daniel F 85 Lydia 85
Molly 249
BRADBURY, Albert C 147 Caroline 147
BRADEEN, Charles 342 Marguerite 342
BRADLEY, Jonathan 231
BRADWAY, Doris 206 Frank 206
Josephine 206
BRAGG, Freedom 351 George H
351
BRANT, Clark T 197 Elizabeth
197 Ellen 197
BREWSTER, Lucy Anne 128
BRIDGES, Adeline 345 Hazel 358
BRIGGS, Alonzo 156 Hattie 334
Lovina 236 Lydia 156 Nathan
236
BRIGHAM, Marie Alice 387
BRILEY, Josie 308
BROCK, Elizabeth 104 James L
104 Judith 52 118 Simeon 52
BROWN, Amos 255 Eliza 256
Elizabeth 71 Hannah 65 Harriet

BROWN (Continued)
    352 Harriet N 292 Howard T
    372 Janet 372 John 237 338
    Marcia 190 Margaret 86 Mary
    237 255 Phebe 338 Sarah 255
BRUCE, Martha 353
BRYANT, Bobbi 374 Christiana
    282 Harriet 163 Phelina T 291
    Roderick 374 William 282
BUCHANAN, Andrew 125 Lydia
    125
BUNKER, Eliza Ann 120 Lydia
    250 Sabrina 173
BURCHAM, Beverly 367 Frank
    367
BURCHARD, Prudence 164
BURGESS, Clara 314 Evora 203
    Lila Lizette 203 Vernon 203
BURGOIN, General 244
BURGOYNE, Anne Marie 384
BURKE, Mary Jane 135
BURLEY, Laura E 266
BURNHAM, James W 216 Josephine 274 Lydia A 216 Mary
    Langley 216 Mehitable 49
    Nathaniel 49 Susanna 49
BURNS, Ruth 342 Skip 342
BURRILL, Amorena 330 Bela 330
    Mary 256
BURWELL, Grace 275
BUTLER, Charles 76 Hannah 144
    Hannah Ann 144 Lydia 199
    Margaret F B 182 Nancy 76
    Sarah 76 Thomas 144
BUTTERWORTH, Ellen 160
    Joseph 160
BUZZELL, 39 Aaron 264 Deborah
    113 Dorothy 136 John 39 Lydia
    216 Sarah 39
CADY, Julia 290 Leonard D 290
CAFFERTY, Audrey 341 Edward
    H 341

CALEF, Eva 163 Everett L 163
    Frank 116 Grace 116
CAMPBELL, Clyde 370 Hugh R
    209 Judie 377 Mildred 370
    Ruby Hazel 385 Sarah 209
CANEDY, Emily 189 Randolph G
    189
CANNEY, Ann 98 Anna 133
    Benjamin 55 Elizabeth 133
    John 98 133 Love 98 Sarah 27
    55 Susanna 97
CARD, Estelle 306
CARGILL, Ethelyn H 122
CARLE, Christiana 282 Henry J
    282
CARLETON, Edward 266 Elizabeth 266 Helen 372
CARLSON, Olga K 336
CARNEY, Agnes 291 David J 291
CARPENTER, Eunice 324
CARR, Bradbury 264 C C 319
    Catherine 103 Elizabeth 48
    John 48 Mehitable 264 Moses
    N 103 Polly 264 Sarah 48 264
CARRUTH, Donald W 372 Joyce
    372
CARTER, Carlie 324 Frank E 324
    Julia 322 William F 322
CARVER, Eunice E 184 Isaphena
    335 James 184 Mary 184
CASWELL, Sally 247 Walter 247
CATE, Cora 192
CATER, Isaac S 136 Mary 136
CATES, Elizabeth 252 John 252
CATON, Frank L 205 Louise 205
CHADBOURNE, Alice 309 William C 309
CHALMERS, Angeline 195 Winifred R 195
CHAMBERLAIN, David T P 175
    Idella 175
CHAMBERLIN, Electa 321

CHAMBERLIN (Continued)
Olin 321
CHAMBERS, Florence 333
CHANDLER, Mercy 117 R M 292 Sarah 292
CHARLES I, King Of England 4
CHARLES II, King Of England 25
CHASE, Abbie 273 Alice 296 Diane 378 Flora 148 George 256 Hannah 256 Madison 251 Mary 57 272 Michael 272 273 Nancy 251 251 Paul 243 Sarah 243 Simeon B 296 William 57
CHENERY, David L 146 Evelyn 146
CHENEY, Ada 215 Edith 215 Evelyn 330 Herbert 215
CHESLEY, John 157 Phebe Ella 157 Rosetta M 95
CHICK, Myra M 162
CHRISTMAN, Ethel 349
CHURCH, Charles E 288 Deborah 32 Fanny 288 John 32 Sarah 32
CHURCHILL, Caroline 158 Ezra 51 Hannah 270 Lester L 158 Mary 51
CILLEY, Catherine 280 George 312 Ida 312 Mary 283 Nancy 271 Sarah 255
CILLY, Emerson 269 Florilla 269
CLAPP, Faustena 200 Frank 200 Mildred Austin 200
CLARK, Alexander 326 Almira 260 326 Anna Belle 165 Bradbury 165 Carleton H 364 Effie 291 George E 149 Harriet 292 Hattie Almira 326 Joseph S 291 Lyman 292 Mabel 149 Mary 165 Mary N 292 Pearl Rita 380 Robertson A 260 Ruth 364 Shirley 359 Susan 86 Verna M 373

CLARKSON, Helen 160 Martha J 160 Thomas 160
CLEAVER, Mabel 178
CLEMENT, Abiah 251 Elmira 251 Sarah 86
CLEMENTS, Evelyn 376 Job 51 Mary 51 Romilia A 306
CLIFFORD, Elizabeth 279 Joseph T 279 Julia 279 Margaret A 279 Mary 279 Thomas J 279
CLOGSTON, Eunice 245 John 245
CLOUGH, Mary 261 William D 261
CLOUTMAN, Caroline E 115
COBB, Joel A 118 Martha 118 Sarah 266
COGSWELL, Frederic 119 Hannah Rogers 119 Judith Frances Upham 119 Mary Adeline 119
COIT, Lewis D 321 Mary 321
COKER, Charles G F 172 Elizabeth 172
COLBATH, Mehitable 49
COLBY, Abbie Clara 366 Angie 366 Della 324 Ethel M 158 Frank 324 George B 366
COLCORD, Paulina E 328
COLD, Antoinette 202
COLDBATH, Cynthia 168 George 168 Mary 168
COLE, Nellie 209
COLLINS, Ella 211 Mary 169 Sadie 211 Samuel 211
COLVILLE, Addie 276 Frank 276
COMBS, Marie 375
COMSTOCK, Albert P 290 Helen 290
CONANT, Abigail A 108 Paulina 107
CONNOR, Charles E 215 Edith F 215 Florence 215

CONOVER, Daniel P 272 Lenora 272
CONVERSE, Elizabeth 214
COOK, Anna 71 Cordelia 260 Julia Ann 56 Leonard 260 Wentworth 49
COOKSON, Ada 190
COOLIDGE, Lucy 111
COOMBS, Sarah 281
COPP, Ellen Melissa 94 Hazel 357 Ralph 357
CORBETT, Arvilla M 210 Bertha Maude 210 David T 210
CORSON, Charles 73 Elizabeth 73
COSTELLO, Siobhan 348
COULTHURST, Helen 341 John 341
COUNTER, Harriet O 293
CRAM, Agnes 340
CRANE, Carrie M 310
CRISP, Hannah 80 Morris 80
CRITCHETT, Mary 227 Thomas 227
CROCKETT, Elizabeth 47 Martha 83 Richard 47 William C 83
CROSBY, Leola Mae 366 Viola 360
CROSS, Sarah 76 Susan 199 William M 199
CROSSMAN, Amos H 326 Lutheria 325 Polly B 326
CRUSEY, John 245 Margaret 245
CULLIS, Mary 143
CULVER, Ann 296 Chandler 296 Henry A 296 Mary 296 Newell 264
CUMMINGS, Abigail E 313 Abigail L 186 Florence Mabel 186 Horace L 186 Jonathan 313 Olive Melissa 313
CUMMINS, Clara 383 Kathleen 383 Robert L 383

CURRIER, Daniel 49 Harley J 350 Mary 49
CURRY, Abigail 186
CURTIS, Charity 91 Edna 178 Floyd 178 Jane 91 Janice 359 Robert 359
CUSHING, 33
CUSHMAN, Robert 377 Shirley 377
DAGGETT, Allen 271 Glema 383 Julia 271
DAM, Ada Annet 185 Joseph S 185 Mary J 185
DAME, Adeline 175 Albert W 175 Ann 386 Daniel W 111 Elizabeth 73 Joseph 73 74 Lydia 74 Mary 111
DAMON, Sarah 177
DANIELS, Alice Souther 186 Charles E 186 Frances M 186 Mary Ann 164 Nathaniel 164 Sarah Elizabeth 164
DARBY, Alfred 352 Kate 352
DAUTRICH, Viginia Alice 382
DAVIS, 39 Anna 336 Ashel 260 Belle Frances 204 Benjamin 32 Caroline 272 Catherine 260 Charles 282 Charles E 336 Charlotte 93 113 Cora 218 Elizabeth 39 Ella 157 Emelda 318 Esther 204 Hannah 103 Jeanne Towle 368 Joseph 272 Lois 166 Lucy A 141 Mary 93 249 Miriam 32 Molly 249 Nancy 260 Paine 204 Phebe 91 Prudence 282 Ralph E 157 Samuel 91 103 Susan 141 Susana 237 Walter 141 William 249
DAY, Eliza Jane 93 Eva 345
DEACON, Abigail 51 Daniel Crocker 51

DEAN, Agnes 354 Emily 305
DEANE, Mary 103
DEARBORN, Dorothy 94
DEBS, Eugene V 347
DEERING, Elizabeth 150
DELAND, Daniel 68 Sarah 68
DELFENDAHL, Clarence 149 Harriet 149
DEMAY, Deborah 369 Randal A 369
DEMERS, Marie Madeleine 29
DENNETT, Alice Augusta 188 Minerva 188 Simon 188
DENSMORE, Arthur W 352 Bertha 352
DEOS, Harlan M 372 Phyllis 372
DEVOLL, David 344 Hattie 344 Olive B 344
DEXTER, Susan 141
DIANA, Princess Of Wales 257
DICKENSON, Eleanor 171 L Porter 171
DICKEY, Franklin 370 Grace 342 Mildred 370 Nina 342 Walter 342
DIKE, David K 261 Edith 190 George P 190 Lucinda 261
DINGEE, Harriet A 312
DINGER, Harriet A 312
DINSMORE, Prudence 282 Sylvanus 282
DIXON, Achsa Stanton 158 Caroline 158 Edith G 159 Frank 206 Frederick 158 Marguerite Ione 206 Violet 206
DOBLE, Lydia 276
DODGE, Charles H 172 Chester H 371 Marion 371 Ruth 172
DOE, Lydia 276
DOLLOFF, Frances 340 Robert 340
DOLLY, Pamelia 181

DONAGHY, Lizzie 324
DOUGLAS, Harry 212 Julia 305 Lottie M 212 Madeline 212
DOUW, Mary 203
DOW, Abigail 260 Asa 260 Jonathan 40 Keziah 40
DOWNES, Abigail 26 Thomas 26
DOWNING, Eliza 105 William 105
DOWNS, Aaron 105 Abigail 74 Elizabeth 105 Frederick G 64 Hannah 48 James W 74 Mary 154 Reuben 48 Ruth 64
DOYLE, Josephine 217
DRAKE, Charles 386 Dorothy 386 Florence 386 Nancy 251
DRESSER, Martha 174 Mary A 174 Richard 174
DREW, Andietta 65 David L 65 Elizabeth 35 John 35 Sarah 35
DUDLEY, Annie 189 April 378 Charles S 189 Isabel 189
DUFFANY, John 326 Lutheria 326
DUKETT, Florence 355
DULEY, Ellen 359
DUNHAM, Ebenezer 263 Elizabeth 263 Eunice 295
DURGIN, Mary Ann 303
DURHAM, David 347 Jane 347 410 John W 410 John Wyatt 347 Ruth 347
DUSOE, Tamie 390 William B 390
DUTCH, Larry 367 Noreen 367
DYER, Caleb F 365 Hannah 103 Marian 365
EASTMAN, Abigail 61 Hannah 159 Lydia 297
EASTON, Harvey 171 Maria Ortentia 171 Sarah 171
EATON, Abigail Morrill 197 Isabelle 194 Jane 191 Mary E 191 Nancy 145 Sally 255

EATON (Continued)
  Samuel S 191 Silvenus 255
  Thomas 197
EDGERLY, Clarissa Harlowe 114
  Josiah 113 114 Louise 318 Mary
  113 114 256 Priscilla 113 Rufus
  256 Sarah 113
EDMUNDS, Edith May 325
EDSON, Letty 352 Mary Ellen 166
  Wilfred 352
EDWARDS, Ruth 277
ELDRIDGE, Etta E 364
ELIOT, Dorothy Alice 357
ELKINS, John 99 Mary 99
ELLIOT, Caroline 269 Drusilla
  184 George W 269 Harriet 269
  401 Israel 269
ELLIS, Everett 370 Lottie 212
  Manly 304 Marjorie 370 Mary
  304
EMERSON, Albert E 118 Charles
  S D 189 Clarissa 155 Ella 330
  Frank W 194 Hannah 134
  Harriet L 149 Isabelle W 194
  Jane 194 John 155 Oscar R 330
  Sarah J 155 Sidney 189 Susan
  118 Winnefred 108 188
EMERY, Frances 32 James 32
  Margaret 32
EMMONS, Abigail S 183 Christiana 183 Daniel H 183 Elizabeth
  108 Grace 336 Ralph 336
ENDERSON, Bertha 178
ENGELHARTE, Eunice Ernestine
  368
ENGLISH, Lydia 259
ERESCH, Anna 368 Pauline
  Esabel 368 Theodore 368
ESTES, Benjamin 70 Caleb 42
  Dorothy 70 Gertrude 324 Mary
  41 Mary E 127 Sarah 42 Willis
  324

EVANS, 39 Abram 191 Anne 99
  Benjamin 122 Bessie Winnifred
  191 Dudley 168 Elizabeth 39
  Emma 329 George 99 Josephine E 191 Lydia 122 Mary 99
  258 Mary E 168 Rebecca 168
  Rosillah 204 Stephen 54
  Thomas 99
EVERETT, Mary 379 Sarah 171
EVESLAGE, Bernard 339 Waneta
  339
FALL, Elizabeth 53 108 John 53
  Lydia 53 Mary Jane 147 Nancy
  72 150 Oceana Fitzgerald 204
  Otis 204 Phoebe 147 Rhoda
  108 Rosillah 204 Stephen 108
FALLOWS, Alice Ann 178 Mary
  178 Matthew 178
FARNHAM, Carolyn 283
FARNUM, Mary F 282 Mary J 105
FARRAR, Linda 367 Myrtle Estelle 345 Richard 367
FARROW, Bethia 241
FASSETT, Adoniram H 317
  Lametta 317
FELCH, Martha 191
FELKER, Ellen Deborah 345
FELTON, Amos 245 Elsie 245
FENNER, Lena Maria 341
FERGUSON, Charles H 120 Mary
  120
FERNALD, Alice 115 Auguste 87
  Deborah 112 158 Edwin 87
  Elizabeth 112 118 Eva Gertrude
  319 Judith 118 Mary E 155
  Tristram 118 William 112
FERRIS, Cora B 268 Mary L 203
  Mary Vanrensselaer 203 Morris
  P 203
FIELD, Elizabeth 31 Emma 217
  Luther 217 Mabel 217 Sarah 26
  35 Zachariah 26

FIFIELD, Elizabeth 64 John 64
FILES, Adeline 275 Eleanor 270 Joseph 270
FISH, Mary 184 Ruby 184 Seth H 184
FITTS, Clarissa 155
FITZ, Herman 126 Mary 126
FLANDERS, Ellen 301 Eloise Annie 190 Franklin P 301 Marcia A 190 Samuel B 190
FLANNAGAN, Kelly 389
FLEMING, George 335 Isaphena 335 Sierra Nevada 335
FLETCHER, Daniel 257
FLEWELLING, Effie 367 Enoch 344 Ethel 344 Glennys 367 Thomas 367
FLOYD, Elizabeth 76 Fred 339 Marguerite 339
FOBES, Anna 257 Arza 243 Benjamin 242 257 Bethia 242 257 Jonah 257 Judith 242 Miriam 257 Rebekah 243 Zadock 242
FOGG, Calvin 253 Catherine 279 Esther 256 Frederick 344 George 256 279 Katherin 344 Lydia 279 Mary 253 402
FOLSOM, Alice 289 Israel 222 223 John 135 Mary 222 Nathaniel 222 Susan 135 Susan F 135
FOOTE, Emily 212
FOOTMAN, Francis 43 Hannah 43 Susan 139
FORD, Betty 336 Lucy 315
FOSS, Abigail 78 Caroline Celesta 135 Debbie 393 Elizabeth 78 Hannah 38 Harriet L 154 John 135 Joshua 78 Lydia 135 Mary 154 William 154
FOSTER, Arthur J 211 Clark 184

FOSTER (Continued)
Estella 211 Eunice 184 Glenn E 326 Mary 326 Winifred 211
FOUNTAINE, Albert 353 Celia 353
FOX, Alvira 261 350 Charles 261 Daniel 71 Elizabeth 259 Gershom 259 Lucille 340 Margaret 261 Mary 71 Neal 340
FRADD, Faustena 201 John E 201
FRATARILLA, George 339 Irish 339
FREDERICK, Hannah 303 Sylvester 303
FREDETTE, Mary 326 Mina 326
FRENCH, Deborah 114 James M 326 Stella 326
FRISBEE, Martha 160
FROST, Dorothy 136 Lucy 124 Lydia Buzzell 136 Nathaniel 136 Sarah 121
FRYE, Sarah 156
FULLER, Nillie 359
FURBER, Mary 50 Nehemiah 50 Sarah 50
FURBUSH, Daniel 36 Dorothy 36 Mary 36
FURLONG, Franklin G 87 Mary 87
GAGE, Abibail B 169 Caroline 94 Dorothy 94 Elizabeth 31 Frederick 94 Gerry R 169 Hannah 62 Ida Florence 169 John 31 39 Maria A 94 Mary 39 62 Mary Rounds 177 Moses 62 94 177 Sarah 177
GAMAGE, Nancy 199
GAMMON, Anna 257 Lois 284 Stephen W 284
GARBORINO, Frank J 344 Ida 344
GARDNER, George 269 Nancy E

GARDNER (Continued)
  273 Tabitha 269
GARFIELD, 320
GARLAND, Abigail 45 Daniel 36
  Ebenezer 45 Elizabeth 78
  Rebecca 45 Richard 78 Sarah
  36
GARTON, Hilda Ruth 200
GARVIN, Elizabeth 67 James 67
  John 78 Rebecca 78 Samuel 90
  Sarah 67 Susanna 90
GATCHELL, George 340 Lucille
  340
GEORGE, Peggy 288 289
GERRISH, Bertha 182 Elizabeth
  108 Ellen 159 Forrest E 159
  Jane 182 John E 182
GERRY, Katherine 164
GIBBS, Sherry 393
GIBSON, Eleanor 170 Lois 124
  Margaret Jane 170 Robert 124
  William N 170
GIFFORD, Geo G 309 Mary 309
GILBERT, Agnes 354 Alice M 354
  Beatrice 363 Edwin A 354
  Henry R 363 Mattie 314 Nellie
  M 363
GILE, Lucy 188
GILES, Daniel 230 Lydia 230
GILMAN, Evelyn 371 Jane 182
  Octavia 167 Oliver J M 167
  Robert I 371 Sarah 54
GILSON, Hannah 264
GLANDERS, Anna Amelia 205
GLIDDEN, Ida 216
GLINES, Adeline 153
GOFFE, John 235 241
GOLDEN, Mary 291
GOLDSMITH, Hubbard 80 Joanna
  80
GOODALE, Frances 112 Roany
  351

GOODWIN, Abigail 30 Daniel 30
  Elizabeth 104 Frank 157
  Hannah 116 Jeremiah 104
  Joanna 59 Martha 66 Mary 104
  Sarah 157
GOOLD, Alan O 181 Alice 181
GORDON, 238 Abigail 229 Elizabeth 229 243 Judith L 376
  Lydia 259 Thomas 229
GORGES, Fernando 2
GORTON, Emma S 374 Ernest O
  374 Eva Estelle 374
GOSS, Margaret 235
GOULD, Abigail 149 Caroline 325
  Claribel 338 Ella Rose 179
  Emily 149 James 149 Lucy 179
  Mary 325 346 Robert 338
  Sheldon B 179 Waltz C 325
GOULET, Helen 295
GOVE, Abigail 138
GRACE, Lois 196
GRAHAM, Caroline 179 Ralph
  179
GRANT, 17 Amorena 300 403
  Colby 380 Glenda 380 Grace
  Gertrude 383 Lemuel C 300
  Lucy 342
GRAVES, Ellen 185 Inza 185
  Osgood 185
GRAY, Iola G 214
GREALY, Glenda 390
GREENE, Doris I 371 Ellen 157
  Moses H 157
GREENLAW, Ada 314
GREENLEAF, Ann 188 Charles 87
  George W 188 Gertrude May
  188 Mary 87
GREENVALL, Alexander M 318
  Hazel 318
GREENWAY, Mary 202
GRIFFIN, Ella 310 Florence 340
  Lonnie 340 Nancy 89

GRIFFITH, David 60 Sarah 60
GRIMES, Rachel S 196
GRUBB, Charles 357 Margaret 357
GUM, Donna 377
GUPTILL, Georgeanna 275 John A 77 Robert 77 Ruth 77 Susan 77
GURLEY, Grace 307
GUSHEE, Daisy 339 Freeman 339
HADLEY, Emily R 351 Roany 351 Thomas D 351
HADLOCK, Bernice A 372
HAGER, Eula 318 Frank A 318
HAGGERT, Gilbert W 332 Ruth 332
HAIGIS, Virginia 201
HAINES, John W 316 Mary 316
HALE, George 66 Lyman L 193 Martha 66 Mercy 121 Samuel S 121 Sarah 193
HALEY, Rosanna 149
HALL, Abigail 26 86 Amelia 174 Annie 334 Clarissa 132 Elizabeth 65 Enoch 334 Hatevil 251 Jerusha 166 Joanna 132 John 26 274 Julia Ann 320 Lounetta 191 Marcia 274 Margaret 251 Mary 270 Miriam 282 Philip 132 Ruth 90 251 Samuel 270 Sarah 65 86 252 Shadrach 252 Silas 86 William 65
HAM, Betty 48 Charles E 155 Edgar J 116 Elizabeth 38 41 48 John 38 48 130 Joseph W 87 Lena 155 Lydia 31 Martha 116 Mary 36 Mercy 130 Ruth 130 Samuel 31 Sarah 87
HAMILTON, Daniel 252 Esther 252 Mary 57 Millet 57
HAMLIN, Esther 251 256 Joseph 251
HAMMOND, Howard D 303

HAMMOND (Continued) Huldah 303 Joseph 121 Mary 64 Sarah 121 William 64
HAMMONS, Joseph 73 Susan 73
HANCOCK, Dolly 236 Jeff 236
HANSCOM, Annie 159 Hannah 56 John 56
HANSON, Abigail 43 Achsa 98 Alice 48 Ann 55 Anna 55 David 48 Eliza 95 Elizabeth 55 97 Hannah 55 56 Helen 196 John B 97 John T 95 Jonathan 48 Joseph 98 Lois 56 Mary 48 57 104 Maul 55 Moses 104 Patience 92 Silas 43 Thomas 55 56 Verna 306 Willis C 196
HAPGOOD, Alice 322 Arthur S 322
HARDING, Emeline 146 Mary 152
HARDON, 17
HARDY, Eleanor 171 Henry W 171
HARFORD, June 359
HARLAN, Katherine T 328
HARRIMAN, Asa 126 Asa M 126 Chastine 126 David L 116 Elizabeth 229 Hannah 116 Lydia 126 Rachel M 116
HARRIS, Clara 346 Elsy 261 John W 346 Louise 153 Myrtle 346 410 Simon B 261
HARRON, Paula Marie 393
HART, Hattie Adel 344 Mary 50
HARTE, John Mrs 222
HARTFORD, Melissa 198
HARVEY, Clara 314 John 314 Mary Elizabeth 307 Michael 376 Rachel Ella 315 Rita 376
HARWOOD, Augusta 271 Reuben 271
HASKELL, Mary 277
HASTY, Paulina 107

HATCH, Clara 154 Doris 358
  Emma Rebecca 183 George A
  154 Israel 183 Leonard B 89
  Mary 89 Rebecca F 183
  Wyman 358
HAVENER, Clarinda 253
HAWKINS, Gertrude 322 John
  250 Lovey 250 Lydia 250
  Richard 1 Rush 322 Sophronia
  251
HAWKS, Benjamin 66 Ruth 66
HAYES, Abigail 183 Asa Brewster
  122 Austin J J 183 David 81
  Deborah 114 Elizabeth 72 Etta
  195 Ezra 116 Hannah 82 Icha-
  bod 114 Inez 160 Joseph 81
  Leah 114 Lillian 196 Lucy 161
  Marcia 81 Mary 72 81 Mehita-
  ble 122 Rachel 116 Seth W 196
  Solomon 82 Susan Ann 116
  Susanna 49 Tamsen Mehitable
  122 Walter E 195 Wentworth
  49 72 William T 160
HAYFORD, Estella 211
HAYMAN, Lillian 151 Stuart R
  151
HEARD, Benjamin 23 Dorothy 87
  Eliza Ellen 166 Elizabeth 23
  Hannah 87 95 166 James 30
  Jesse 166 Joshua 64 Lucy 64
  Margaret 41 Mary 30 41 56
  Nathaniel 41 Phebe 56 Thomas
  56 87
HEDRICK, Lawrence J 363 Verna
  363
HEINRICH, Annie 198
HEMINGWAY, Mary 150
HEMMENWAY, Jonathan 109
  Martha 109 Sarah 109 Sarah B
  109
HENDERSON, Abigail 163 Clara
  172 Hannah 137 Howard 27

HENDERSON (Continued)
  John H 137 Lydia 84 Maria 85
  Sarah 27 Thomas 84 Wilbur A
  172
HENDRICKSON, Selma J 385
HENRY, David 350 Edith May
  325 Jennie 350
HERD, Cynthia 290 Joseph B 290
HERSHOM, Benjamin 71 Dorcas
  71 Elizabeth 71
HESLIN, Alice 213 John 213
  Martha Moore 213
HEWITT, Amanda 184 Asa 184
  Cora Jane 184
HICKOKE, Elizabeth 284
HICKS, Cora Jane 177 Philip 177
  Sarah 177
HIGGINBOPHA, Madelyn 380
HIGGINS, Annie 112 177 Emma
  206 Noah G 112
HILL, Abigail 107 Annie L 159
  Arthur E 383 Charles 107
  Cyrus 245 Elizabeth J 150 Elsie
  245 Eula 318 Fred S 318 Isaac
  39 Isaiah 150 Jo Anne 383
  Linnie E 127 Lydia 39 Lyman
  H 159 Mabel Rosina 159 Maria
  109 Martha 107 Viola Jane 150
HILLAM, Nellie Moon 363
HILLIARD, Hannah 237
HILLMAN, Eva 345
HILLS, Hannah 156
HILTON, 3 17 22 Andrew 128
  Edward 2 21 Eliza Ann 128
  Eliza Jane 128 William 2
HINES, Emily 161 Rufus 161
HITCHCOCK, Margaret 32
HOAGLAND, Clara 346
HOBBS, Laura 120 Mercy 89
  Priscilla 88 Sarah 67 Susan 78
  Wentworth B 120
HODGDON, Eliza 100 Olive 126

HODSDON, Elizabeth 58 John 58
HOEYE, Mathilda 188
HOFFMAN, Abby 313 Frank 317
 Frederick 313 May 308 Sadie
 317
HOGAN, Frank 305 Maud 305
HOIT, Mary 235
HOLBROOK, Thomas 257
HOLLAND, Emily S 204 John 204
 Lelia Jameson 204
HOLMES, Lucy 315
HOLT, Caroline 111
HONEY, Lizzie 372
HOOVER, Alice Maud 201 John
 M 201 Mary 201
HOPLEY, Elizabeth 29 Robert 29
HORN, Abigail 176 Barzillai 176
 Daniel 49 Elizabeth 61 119
 Eunice 104 George 105 Huldah
 66 James 102 James H 66 John
 61 104 Lucy 176 Martha 102
 Mary 61 Noah 115 Pamela 105
 Paul 119 Rachel 136 Rebecca
 110 Rebecca Pinkham 115
 Relief 49 Rhoda 118 Sarah 115
HOUGH, Andrew J 95 Mary 95
HOUSTON, Jennie 311
HOWARD, Asa 81 Daisy 339
 Edith 159 Eleanor 189 Eliza-
 beth 81 Joseph 80 Joseph L 189
 Sarah 322 Walter B 159 Wil-
 liam 322
HOWE, Adeline 134 135 Celia 353
 Ellen 266 Freeman P 134 135
 George 266 Horace P 266
 Putney L 353
HOWES, Sandra 377
HOWLAND, Benjamin 266
 Dorcas 266 Lydia Cole 266
HUBBARD, Delia 291 Elizabeth
 31 132 George 291 Henry A
 132 Judith 322 Nelson 322

HUBBARD (Continued)
 Philip 31 Sarah 291
HUFF, Calla 345 Herbert 345
HUGGINS, Elizabeth 295
HUGHES, Agnes 155 Elizabeth 53
 Frederick 155 Margaret 155
HUME, Sarah 171
HUNT, Cynthia 289 322 Elizabeth
 290 Judith 244 Moses 244
HUNTOON, Clara 115 Clarence
 115
HUNTRESS, Eunice 149 James K
 149 Tyra Ann 149
HURD, Eliza Ellen 166
HUSSEY, Benjamin 173 Chester L
 318 Eliza 175 Eula 318 Leon-
 ard 318 Louise Achsa 318
 Lydia Maria 173 Sabrina 173
 Sarah H 318
HUTCHINS, Charles 324 Jenny
 324 Joanna 90 Judith 77
HUXFORD, Miriam 269 Renselaer
 269
HUZZY, Mary F 327
HYDE, Ellen 116 Violet 206
HYSLER, Evelyn A 127
ILLSLEY, Lucinda 264
INGRAHAM, Eunice 324 Jer 324
 Laura 324
INGRAM, James 283 Rebekah 283
INMAN, Arthur E 318 Kate 318
IRELAND, Abigail 297 Corydon G
 297 Edward 365 Hazel 365
IRISH, Elizabeth 241 Elvira 274
 Miriam 254 Stephen 274
 Thomas 241
JACKMAN, Augusta 168 William
 H 168
JACKSON, Adeline 345 Alden 373
 Betty 373 Charles 345 Cheryl
 393 Harriet 271 James 85
 Marcia Alice 345 Mariah 281

JACKSON (Continued)
Mary 85 Myrtilla A 123 Susan 135 William N 281
JACOBSEN, Amy 348 Andrew B 347 410 Deborah 348 Deborah W 412 Gillian 348 Heidi 348 Hilary M 348 412 Linda M 348 411 Myrtle 347 410 Rick 348 Roderick A 348 411 Samantha 348 Sara F 348 412 Siobhan 348 Thomas A 348 412 Vanessa 348
JACQUES, John J 269 Miriam 269
JAMES, David 62 Frances 21 John H 154 Patty 62 Rosetta 154
JAMES I, King Of England 2 4 22
JAMES II, King Of England 25
JAMISEN, Eleanor 365 Howard A 365
JAQUITH, Ellen 371
JELLISON, Jane 280 Mary E 314
JENKINS, Abby 267 Albert 304 Elijah 56 Elizabeth 56 Gail Lorraine 369 Grace 342 Hattie 304
JENKS, Lillian M 326
JENNINGS, Mark A 387 Sarah 387
JOHNSON, Alan 367 Captain 240 Elizabeth 112 Louisa 259 Lydia 231 Marilyn 367 Philip 235 241 Samuel 230 231
JONES, Abigail 32 74 105 Betsey 260 Cynthia 290 David 73 E G 290 Edward F 115 Elizabeth 30 31 53 73 172 Ellen 273 Emily 115 Emma L 176 Ephraim 260 George 97 221 222 Gertrude 140 Harry T 204 James 71 James I 140 James W 273 Jeremiah 73 John 176 John Paul 11 Joseph 73 74 Joseph B 105

JONES (Continued)
Lavinia 260 Lydia 74 112 Lydia A M 113 Martha 71 Mary 73 112 221 Mary J 176 Mehitable 74 Nancy 283 Rosillah 204 Sarah Amelia 171 Stephen 31 Susanna 97 Tamsen 73 William 53 171
JORDAN, Hannah 240 James 240 Juliette 189
JOSE, Mary 35
JUDD, Arthur L 371 Blanche Lydia 371 Deborah 389 Jennie 371
JUDKINS, Benjamin 230 Lydia 230 Susanna 230 249
JUUL, Margery 371 Reynold B 371
KAISER, Margaret 153
KEBKER, Ruth 347
KEENE, Hazel 380 Henry 380 Madelyn 380
KEEP, Hannah 264
KEISTER, Josephine 125
KELLY, Abigail 237 Samuel 237
KEMP, Carmen 386
KENDALL, Clarissa 323 Jennie Adelia 371 Jotham 323 Martha 280 Olive Josephine 323
KENDRICK, Frank W H 149 Mabel 149
KENNISTON, Alexander 231 Elizabeth 231 Judith 231
KENT, Clara 210
KERR, Nettie 201
KESSLER, Sadie 308
KIMBALL, Amos 262 Charles 261 Eleanor Cooper 134 Ellen Augusta 159 Ephraim 134 Gertrude 190 Hannah 134 159 261 John 71 Lillian 373 Minerva 188 Moses L 159 Nancy Day

KIMBALL (Continued)
209 Roland G 190 Sarah 71 262
KINASTON, Anna 233 Joseph E
  233
KING, Amelia Gertrude 215 Harriet Jane 353 Prudence 253
  Samuel 253
KINNEY, Noble 126 Sarah 126
KINSLEY, Prudence 253 Samuel
  253
KIRKPATRICK, Jennie 362
KITTRIDGE, Samuel B 286 Susie
  286
KLEINE, Meta 348
KNAPP, Lavinia Solendia 140
KNIGHT, Betsey 243 Elizabeth 38
  Eunice 149 Going 243 John 38
  Joseph 55 Lydia 38 55 270 297
  Mary 89 168 Nathaniel 270
  Sarah 270 Sarah Ann 156 157
KNOWLES, Frank 272 Lenora 272
KNOWLTON, Nancy Lee 390
KNOX, Azuba 105 Bethiah 258
  Charles G 258 Charles O 216
  Danville D 258 Edward 105
  Elizabeth 258 Gladys P 216
  Horatio 168 Ida 216 Mary 168
  Miriam 258
KOWER, Duane 318 Jessie 318
KURSULA, Jos 366 Virene 366
L'OISEAU, Charles 99 Olive 99
LABELLE, Alice May 194 Stella
  325
LABONTE, Agnes 134
LACKEY, Verna M 325
LADD, Drusilla 184 Edmund P
  146 Eva May 184 Harriet 352
  Harriet Arabella 352 Mary 146
  Nathaniel 184 Orrin B 352
LADUE, Eugene 374 Eva 374
LAMBIE, Kenneth G 339 Laura
  339

LAMOS, Abigail 40 62 Deliverance 63 Hannah 62 83 Keziah
  40 Nathaniel 40 62
LAMPHERE, Harriet 291
LAMPKIN, Nancy 349
LANCASTER, Jane Billington 282
LANE, Mary Ann 312
LANGDON, Catherine Whipple 91
  Sarah 91 Woodbury 91
LANGHAM, Mary Sophia 274
LANGLEY, Elizabeth 65 92
  Ephraim 82 Sarah 82 Susan 82
LANGMAID, Priscilla 234
LARRABEE, Mary Olivia 333
LASKEY, Alice Caverly 170 Jonas
  S 170 Sarah 170
LATHAM, Abigail 259 320 321
  Eunice M 296 Janice 375 William 375
LAWLER, James J 329 Paulina
  329 408
LAWRENCE, Ada 214 Arthur J
  302 Blanche 302 Rebecca 183
LAYMAN, Isaac 274 Mary 274
LAYNE, Elizabeth I 158
LEACH, Sophia E 294
LEATHERS, Ann 268 Eleanor 269
  Elmira 316 Enoch 283 George
  W 282 Lois Arseneth 283 Mary
  283 Prudence 282
LEAVITT, Abigail 238 Eunice 237
  John 238 Mary 265 Polly 265
  Sarah 238
LEE, 328
LEEMAN, Kermit 339 Waneta 339
LEIGHTON, Abigail 66 Emily 65
  George 65 Joanna 26 Mary 26
  30 83 Silas 66 Thomas 26
LEONARD, Josephine 206
LEWIS, Alfred W 145 Bessie 145
  Homer P 155 Katherine 155
LIBBEY, James 53

LIBBY, Ann Maria 146 Anna 71
  Belle 311 Cheryl 390 Douglas J
  390 Ebenezer 146 Emeline 146
  Ethel 344 Lester 344 Louise
  273 Otis 273 Samuel 71 Vena
  363
LIGHTBODY, Grace 213
LIHATSH, Elizabeth Jane 391
LINCOLN, Bertha 184 Jerusha 161
LING, Amanda 143 Lorenzo D 143
LINSCOTT, Ella Jane 342
LIPPENCOTT, Jane 300
LISSEN, Nicholas 225
LISTON, Nora 266
LITCH, Jane 161 Jerusha 161 John
  161
LITTLE, Arthur 364 Julia 364
LITTLEFIELD, Addie 172 Elizabeth 172 Hugh 341 Margaret
  341 Thomas B 172
LITTLEPAGE, Ruth 207
LOCK, Agnes 134
LOCKE, Abigail 78
LOGAN, Ruey 364
LONG, Lyman W 88 Mary 88
LOOMIS, Brenda B 348 Linda 348
  411 Scott 348
LORD, Charity 91 Eliza 175 Eliza
  A 134 Elizabeth 91 Hannah 144
  Isaac 175 John 91 Lyman W 88
  Martha 37 Nathan 37 Sabrina
  174 Sarah 37 42 88
LOUGEE, Abigail J 212 Florence
  Isabelle 212 Wilbur S 212
LOVEJOY, Joseph C 259 Mary
  259
LOVERING, Hannah 239 Jane 72
  117
LOWD, Abigail 106 Hannah 71
  146 Mary B 146 Wentworth 71
  106 146
LOWE, Gilbert I 145 Hannah 145

LOWE (Continued)
  Shirley Avis 360
LOWELL, Janice 375 Kenneth 375
  Sarah A 295
LOWRY, C Y 365 Clara 269
  David 269 Elsie 365
LUCE, Alpha 325 Emma 325 Mary
  325
LULL, Clarissa 288 Lora 288
  Samuel 288
LUND, Ada E 190 Gertrude Estella
  190 James B 190
LUNT, Grace Marion 361
LUSK, Sarah Angeline 331
LYNCH, Cynthia 120 Melville A
  120
MACDONALD, Frederick 215
  Helen Leva 215 Margaret 215
MACE, Bertha 184
MACKAY, Doris Bailey 212
  Emily 212 Robert S J 212
MACPHERSON, Agnus J 214
  Annie 214 Sally 213
MAGOON, Alexander 225 Elizabeth 225 Sarah 225
MAIN, Mary 72
MALEHAM, Elizabeth Ann Copp
  136 Joseph 136 Rachel 136
MANN, Alexander 110 Sarah 110
MANNING, Florence 354 Sherman B 354
MANTER, Amorena 268 Ellen 268
  Ezra 268
MARCH, Bertha 350
MARDEN, Emily 68 Faustina 330
  Jane 287 Joseph 287 Marcialine
  287 Sarah 287 Truman R 287
MARQUARDT, Libbie 171
MARR, Lydia 279
MARRIAM, Abby 277
MARSH, Ann 227 Henry 227
  Laura 261 Reubin 261

MARSHALL, Delia 162 Elizabeth M 130
MARSTON, Adelbert C 201 Ann 168 Anna 23 Augusta Catherine 168 Elijah 168 Florence 201 Jonathan 237 Mary 237 Nettie 201 Sarah 177 William 23
MARTIN, Cecile 209 Dorothy 357 Ida 292 Nellie 209 Nelson E 292 Pascoe 209
MARTYN, Hester 23 John 23
MASELLI, Brian 384 Jennifer 384
MASON, 6 Arabella 137 Elizabeth 31 Esther 52 Harry 137 John 2 3 25 52 221 Olive 52 Robert 27
MATCHES, Elaine 361
MATSON, Ellen 197
MATTISON, Louise 373 William 373
MAXFIELD, Hannah 263
MAXWELL, Daphne 278 Ferdinand A 278
MAY, David 264 Hannah 264
MAYNARD, Cora 275 Wesley J 275
MAYO, Annie Louise 177 Annie Lovell 177
MCCARTY, Olive M 357
MCDONALD, Cassandra 312 Frank 375 Janice 375
MCDUFFEE, Jonathan 83 Mary 83
MCFARLAND, Andrew P 210 Clara 210 Mary A 315 Mary Ellen 210
MCHAMY, Jane 278 Jules 278
MCINTIRE, Sarah 118 Walter S 118
MCKAY, Mary 118 William C 118
MCKENNEY, Henry 70 Polly 70
MCKENZIE, Josephine 125 Thomas 351 Vivian 351
MCKINLEY, Isabella M 332

MCKINLEY (Continued) William 332
MCLAUGHLIN, Adeline 279 Christine Marie 345 Harry 346
MCLEOD, Mary Jane 297
MCNALLAN, Jaqueline 372 Walter 372
MCPHEE, Margaret 215
MEAD, Ada 214 Eunice 237 Joseph 249 Mary 249 Polly 249 Sumner R 214 William 237
MEADER, Ann 98 Anna 98 399 Benjamin 92 Hannah 92 Hannan 96 John 98 Patience 92
MELVILLE, Dawn 360
MERCIER, Amy 319 Oliver J 319
MERRILL, Abigail 266 Charles T 110 Emma 110 Nathan 241 Sarah 155 291
MERRITT, Belinda T 135
MERROW, Clarissa 104 Ezekiel 104
MESERVE, Charles Y 93 Elizabeth 93 Jane 40
MESSER, Evora 203
METCALF, Caroline P 301
MICHAELS, Hiram 310 Ruth 310
MILLER, Alvah 290 Cynthia 290 Deborah 33 Florence 215 Louisa 66 Phebe 268 Sarah 44 Sophia Ann 289 Thomas 33 44 Webster 66 William P 268
MILLETT, Lydia 47 Thomas 47
MILLS, Andrew 351 Helena 139 Janet 389 Nellie 351
MINGO, Arthur 342 Ruth 342
MINOR, George A 216 Shirley 216
MITCHELL, Abigail 184 Clarissa 143 Emman 308 Hannah 144 John H 144 Jonathan 241
MOORE, Alice 213 Eliza 195

MORAN, Matilda 307
MOREY, Mary 259 Roswell 259
MORGAN, Mary 105
MORRILL, Grace 375 Harriet B 138 Robert 35 Sarah 35 281
MORRIS, Celeste Cummings 152 Charles R 152 Mary 325 Mary A 152 Mattie 331 Nettie 332
MORRISON, Eliza 86 William K 86
MORSE, Debra 376 Orimel 259
MORTENSON, Ella 341 Gunnar 341
MORTIMER, George 317 Sadie 317
MORTON, Abigail 173 Albert H 173 Cynthia 173
MOSES, Eliot L 169 Harriet 169
MOSHER, Robin 360 Scott 360
MOULTON, Dorcas 66 Herschel 200 Huldah 267 Jonathan 66 Marilyn 382 Mary E 200 Sarah Naomi 200 Warren B 382
MUNSON, Mellissa A 305
MURCH, Helen Augusta 136
MURPHY, Charles M 95 Eliza 95 Janet 372 William 372
MUZZEY, Louisa 259
MYRICK, Beezaleel 267 Huldah 267
NASH, Isabelle Jordan 189 Joseph 80 Juliette 189 Mary 80 Orrin G 189
NASON, Durrell 149 Hannah Melissa 149 Joanna 132 Rosanna 149 Sarah A 174
NAUGLER, Louise 188
NAYLOR, Deborah 123
NEAL, 276 Annie 138 Elizabeth 40 Frederick W 138 James 40 Lydia 40
NELSON, Alexander 124 Dorothy

NELSON (Continued)
G 385 Ester 385 Jane 124 Jessie 364 Roland A 364
NICHOLS, Elizabeth 53 Fanny 287 Marietta 171
NICKERSON, Desire 75 Didamia 75 Elisha 75 Lydia 161 Mary 267
NOBLE, Lydia 85
NOCK, Sarah 76
NORRIS, Anna 290 Clara Augusta 186 Clarissa A 186 Dora 386 Estella 146 Everett J 186 Leah 386 Mary 222 Nicholas 222 P G 290 Roy 386
NORTON, Amanda 184 Bathsheba 58 Clarissa 186 Oliver W 58
NOYES, James B 196 Martha 125 Mary 103 Mary E 196 Osgood 103 Sybil 196
NUGENT, Della 324 Elmer 324
NUTE, Alice 115 Eva E 191 Jeremy O 191 Jotham 100 Martha E 191 Sarah 100 Sophia 100
NUTTER, Abigail 25 Abner J 104 Anne 25 Ella A 121 Hannah 104 Hatevil 25 Margaret 153 Matthias 153 Sarah 153
OLESON, Edith Manila 207 Geolena 207 Mentz 207
ORANGE, William Of 25
ORDWAY, Fannie 324 Harvey B 324
ORNE, Helen 152
OSGOOD, Jane 108
OTIS, Evelyn 146 John F 146
OTTO, Juliana R 370
PACKARD, Alnett 262 Oscar A R 262
PAGE, Clyde 337 Edith M 338 Elizabeth 96 Estelle 282

PAGE (Continued)
Josephine 191 Moses 269
Nathan C 96 Sarah 269 Thelma 337
PAINE, Julia 291
PALMER, Angeline 264 Eliza 162
Ellen N 160 Jonathan 48 Mary 48 Molly 48 Sarah Rebecca 160 William 160
PAQUIN, Bessie 325 Fred 325
PARKER, Amasa J 92 Caroline 92 Harriet 92 Nellie C 154 Robert 92
PARRIS, Virgil 240
PARSHLEY, Augusta 315
PARSLEY, Bart R 370 Chase C 370 Janis 370 Reed D 370
PARSONS, Abbie 314 Abigail A 184 Edith M 184 Emery 184 Mary E 299
PATRIDGE, Hannah M 313 Pattie 313
PATTEN, C Edward 372 Lizzie 372 Marion Elizabeth 372
PATTERSON, Jeanette 359
PAUL, Eliza Ann 128
PAYNE, Charles H 192 Earla 192 Geneva 192 Lucille 340 Paul 340
PEABODY, Andrew 92 Andrew P 92 Caroline 92 Catherine 92 Dean 187 Marjorie 187
PEARL, Susan 154
PEARLEY, Christiana 317
PEASE, Daniel 166 Jerusha 166 Jerusha A 121 Lucy A 166 Nancy 280
PEASLEE, Abigail 138 Elijah 138 Mary Hannah 138 Miriam 96
PEASLEY, Lucy 179
PEAVEY, Addie 337 Hannah 119
PELETIER, Cecile L 381

PENDERGAST, Nancy 82 Timothy 82
PENN, Fred 353 Harriet J 353 Viola Stella 353
PENNEY, Mabel 335
PERCIVAL, Lena 259
PERKINS, Abigail 35 42 148 Barbara 346 George L 159 John F 148 Julia 116 Juliette W 65 Mary 159 Nathaniel 35 Otis K 116 Rose 271 Stanley A 271
PERRY, Barney 309 Charles 92 Marianna 92 Nancy Ellen 309
PETERS, Frances 112 John A 112
PHELPS, Agnes 355 Alice 355 Edwina 151 Leonard 355 Louis B 355 Viola 305
PHILBRICK, Anna 23 James 23
PHILLIPS, Harriet 370 Mary 105
PHILPOT, Benjamin 51 John 37 Olive 51 Rachel 59 Sarah 37 59
PICKERING, Ann 168 Caleb 79 Elizabeth 79 Mary 121
PIERCE, Albert 343 Charles 157 Dedie 157 Elizabeth 119 Hannah J 156 Joan 343 June 155 Marion Annie 343 Waldo T 156
PIKE, Elizabeth 54 Fanny 144 James 54 Robert S 144 Sarah 54 243
PILLSBURY, Daniel 197 Edna G 197 Elizabeth 197
PILSBURY, Frederick J 150 Martha 150
PINEO, Amelia 174 David 174 Minerva 174
PINION, Grace 370 Harriet 370 John 370
PINKHAM, Aaron 95 Almira 63 Asa 364 Catherine C 172 Cora E 192 Cora Ethel 192 Elizabeth

PINKHAM (Continued)
60 Ella 364 Ella Augusta 364
Elsie 133 George F 192 Hannah
95 John 60 Phebe 60
PINNEY, Charles 326 Lutheria 326
PLACE, Abigail 163 Clarissa 67
Jonathan 67 97 163 Joshua 50
Lydia 97 Mary Esther 163
Mehitable 50 Sarah 97
PLAYSE, Alice 185 Linn F 185
PLOGGER, Judith 375 Richard 375
PLUMER, Daniel 44 Deborah 44
PLUMMER, Benjamin 74 Caroline
Hayes 141 Emily 125 Florence
386 Hannah W 77 John W 125
Lydia 79 Pamela 141 Sarah 74
William 141
POLAND, Ashbel 289 Experience 289 Juliana 289
PORCARO, Gina 378
PORTER, Eliza 195 James 195 Lily 195
POTTLE, Frederick A 282 Hannah 282
POTTS, Joanna 27 Thomas 27
POWELL, Abigail 45
POWERS, Ethel 343 Sarah 80 125
PRATT, Martha 125
PRAY, Anna 47 Dorothy 36
Ebenezer 77 Elizabeth 77
Eunice 70 Joshua 42 Sarah 42
PRECKETT, Mary Ann 302
PRESCOTT, Bethia 245 Nathan 245
PRESTON, Bertha Emily 350
Ellinor Catharine 369 Mary 178
259 Mehitable 264
PRIEST, Elizabeth 279
PROCTOR, Mary 165
PULLEN, Rebecca 317
PURSELL, Mary 185

PUTNAM, Amelia 274 Mary A M 285
QUIMBY, Abigail E 313 Eva 321 Franklin B 321
QUINT, Elizabeth 56 Hannah 70
Joseph 70 Levi 89 Lydia 57
Mary 56 Olive 89 Samuel 57
RAINVILLE, Adele 387
RAMSDELL, Hannah Jane 316
RAMSEY, Beza 105 Hannah 105
RAND, Cornelia 274 Esther B 306
Hannah 95 Joan 343
RANDALL, Belinda 368 Judith 51
RANKIN, Anna 64 James 64
RAWLINGS, Abigail 42
RAY, Jennette 274
RAYNER, Mary Jane 135
RECORD, Kittendean Ayers 317
Margaret Ayers 317 Remember 277
REED, Abigail 109 Elizabeth 231
Elwin A 137 Emma 137 Franklin O 109 Mary 109
REEVES, Ann 76
REMICK, Mary 104
RENAUD, Rosa 358 Vincent F 358
RENFREW, Lois 85 Matthew 85
Robert 85 Sarah 85
RENNIE, Mary 338
REYNOLDS, Dorothy Dodge 297
Hannah 269 Samuel 269
RHINELANDER, Philip H 214 Virginia 214
RHODES, Charlotte 125 Martha 125 Oliver 125
RICH, Caroline Barker 111 Carrie
310 Emeline 300 Frances 112
Hamlin 310 Hosea 112 Joseph
299 300 Mary Ann 299 300
Richard 22 23 Sarah 22 23
RICHARDS, Chester 339 Irish 339

RICHARDS (Continued)
   Maxine 339 Ralph 339 Wilma
   381
RICHARDSON, Amy 353 Augusta
   321 Aurora 322 Cynthia 322
   Flora 141 399 Fred 353 Marcus
   321 Mary 276 Mary Ann 353
   Metcalf 141 Sarah B 322
RICKER, Aaron 147 Anna 51
   Caroline Celesta 135 David 85
   Deborah 33 Dorcas 71 Enoch
   52 Esther 52 Ezekiel 101
   Joanna 101 Joshua A 135 Lydia
   85 Mary 76 Mehitable 105
   Nathaniel 51 Oliver 76 Ophelia
   192 Phineas 33 Phoebe 147
   Safronia Porter 147
RIDLEY, Clare 362 Frank 146
   Sarah 146
RIEF, Leslie G 216 Marjorie 216
RILEY, Ernestine 340 George 340
RIVE, Amanda 352
RIVERS, Pearl M 373
ROBERTS, Aahalo 61 Aaron 32
   41-43 52 57 62 76 77 89 93 95
   117 137 Aaron H 89 129 Aaron
   J 94 Aaron Milton 162 Abbie
   282 284 314 342 366 Abbie D
   273 Abbie F 304 Abbie France-
   lia 292 Abby 267 277 Abby A
   278 Abby Isabel 313 Abiah 251
   Abigail 25 26 30-32 35 39 40
   42 43 45 50 51 55 61-63 66 71
   74 Abigail 80 83 86 88 94 108
   114 173 176 183 197 229 233
   237 254 259 Abigail 260 266
   294 304 320 321 Abigail C 106
   Abigail Corson 74 Abigail
   Ellen 96 Abigail Ellura 158
   Abigail H 109 Abigail Hill 107
   148 Abigail Knight 270 Abigail
   Peaslee 138 Abigail Sara 297

ROBERTS (Continued)
   Abigail W 105 Achsa 158
   Achsa R 98 Ada 185 214 314
   Ada F 313 Adaline M 266
   Adam Lee 389 Addie 172 337
   357 Addie D 276 Addie Ellen
   176 Addison 276 Addison J 267
   Adelaide 141 Adelaide S 272
   Adelia 338 Adeline 135 140
   153 275 279 Adeline A 134
   Adeline Amanda 175 Adeline
   Loella 322 Adeline Naomi 164
   Adrian 317 344 Adrian Everett
   366 383 Adrian Greenleaf 258
   286 Agnes 118 134 155 291
   340 354 355 Agnes Elizabeth
   177 Ahira 268 303 403 Ahira A
   303 Alanson 256 Alba 263 294
   Alba James 289 324 Albert 15
   117 303 332 333 408 Albert A
   406 Albert Augustus 16 277
   309 Albert D 295 Albert
   Dudley 316 Albert E 139 Albert
   F 109 152 Albert G 303 Alberta
   327 Alberta Maria 309 Albertus
   Royal 323 354 Albion Woodman 309 Alcesta Clarissa 288
   Alden E 261 Alexander 33 45
   67 101 141 142 226 230 231
   238 249 Alfred 15 265 270 273
   297 304 Alfred J 253 272 273
   280 404 Alfred M 365 Alfreda
   L 304 Alice 48 64 70 115 151
   170 178 186 188 194 201 289
   305 322 344 354 383 Alice B
   256 Alice Harriet 355 Alice
   Julia 185 Alice Kendall 152
   Alice M 312 Alice Maria 296
   Alice Marie 213 Alice Maud
   193 Alice May 275 Alice
   McLellan 181 Alice Melvina
   284 Alice P 177 339 Alice

ROBERTS (Continued)
Prudence 309 Allen 123 168 281 Allen H 358 375 Allen Hamlin 299 327 Allen J 295 Alma 130 133 Alma Lucretia 174 Almeda 316 Almira 63 98 139 269 326 399 Almira Maria 260 Almond B 278 312 Alnett 262 Alonzo 62 94 95 108 124 136 149 150 263 277 310 Alonzo F 130 Alonzo Joseph Martin 193 Alonzo Palmer 161 Alonzo S 262 321 350 Alphena 380 Alpheus 281 315 Alta 163 Alton 330 Alvah Edgar 184 Alvira 261 350 Amanda 143 337 352 Amanda M 143 Amanda Ruth 393 Amarina 280 Amasa 65 Amelia 215 262 274 Amelia M 174 Amelia Rose 387 Amorena 300 403 Amorena Deborah Theresa 268 Amorena Gertrude 330 Amos 72 107 112 148 187 239 255 281 317 Amos B 16 281 316 Amos Gilman 283 Amos K 98 140 Amos M 154 Amos Main 73 111 Amos P 264 Amplias 259 288 Amy 319 Amy Michelle 384 Amy S 353 Anastasia Marie 391 Andietta L 65 Andrea Maria 376 Andrew 60 61 Andrew J 85 262 Andrew Jackson 263 281 295 Andrew L 100 107 Andrew Rose 144 Andrew Torr 95 137 Aneke 378 Angeline 284 Angeline Anstus 195 Angeline Clarissa 264 Ann 76 99 137 141 146 166 167 226 227 251 268 305 Ann C 304 Ann Elizabeth 137 Ann Frances 382 Ann Genette 285 Ann Henry

ROBERTS (Continued)
Langdon 92 Ann Lydia 386 Ann Marie 382 Ann O 296 Anna 23 36 44 47-49 51 55 64 71 72 82 106 108 134 140 158 165 205 233 235 256 258 270 302 330 Anna A 98 399 Anna Dorothy 87 Anna Karen 385 Anna May 336 Anna Mira 290 Anna W 74 75 Anne 29 360 384 Anne Maria 99 Annie 177 189 308 334 Annie Alberta 138 Annie Charlotte 112 Annie Lucretia 343 Annie Maria 167 Ansel Amplias 288 Anstis H 124 April 378 Arabella 181 Arabella Lizzie 137 Arlene 377 Arlene Ruth 346 Arline 339 Arrington 274 Art 348 349 Arthur 140 189 290 Arthur B 337 358 Arthur Campbell 332 Arthur Edward 382 Arthur Edwin 365 382 Arthur Everett 147 186 Arthur Horace 352 Arthur J 114 Arthur L 344 Arthur Leon 150 188 189 Arthur Neil 358 376 Arthur Webster 135 Arthur Wellington 329 Asa 79 Asa J 294 Ashley Lynn 393 Atlee Fitzhugh 343 Audrey Ernestine 341 Augusta 168 281 315 Augusta Ann 271 Augusta M 321 Auguste Phebe 87 Augustus 303 333 Augustus A 322 Augustus Harland 322 353 Aurelia 276 330 Avis 285 Azariah Beede 263 Azuba 105 Barbara 198 219 346 378 Barbara Alice 382 Barbara Ann 364 373 Barbara Jean 367 Barnabas Myrick 268 300 Barnabus M 405 Barnabus

ROBERTS (Continued)
Myrick 15 Bathsheba 58 Baxter Walter 352 371 Beard 155 Beard Page 110 154 Beatrice 363 Beatrice Marietta 307 Beauzetta Ernestine 374 Belinda 135 368 Belle 204 311 Benjamin 11 15 29-31 36 37 41 42 47 51 53 75 78 89 104 119 128 143 144 163 226 227 231 234 235 238 251 253 258 265 271 284 Benjamin Brown 256 Benjamin Dudley 107 149 Benjamin Edward 181 209 Benjamin Franklin 265 Benjamin T 16 Benjamin Tappan 143 Benjamin Thompson 80 Benjie Stuart 323 Bernice 372 Bert 306 Bertha 178 182 184 198 210 350 Bertha Amanda 352 Bertha Annabel 193 Bertha Mabel 165 Bertha Myra 330 Bertha Palmer 331 Berthua Lillian 184 Bessie 191 Bessie A 311 Bessie Ella 171 Bessie Maud 145 325 Beth 387 Beth Ann 377 Bethia 242 245 Bethiah 258 Betsey 242 246 250 289 Betsey A 288 Betsey Ann 289 Betsey Hayes 111 Betsy 38 Betty 48 54 336 Betty Marie 373 Beulah May 198 Beverly Ann 372 Bill 370 Billy 346 Bion 109 Blake 294 Blanche 215 330 371 Blanche Lenore 302 Bobbi 374 Brad Arden 384 Bradford 100 107 Brandon Neil 390 Brenda Carolee 372 Brock William 370 Burton 378 Burton West 293 Caleb 78 118 Calla 345 Calvin 251 265 Calvin Blanchard 321 352 Cameron

ROBERTS (Continued)
378 Campbell Myrick 303 331 Carl 355 Carl Freeman 211 Carl Jackson 170 201 326 354 Carl Noyes 196 216 Carleton Lewis 212 Carleton Wayne 371 385 Carlie Josephine 324 Carlyle Berry 198 Carol 380 Caroline 111 115 135 141 142 151 259 269 272 277 301 325 350 Caroline C 94 Caroline Eustis 92 Caroline Josephine 175 Caroline M 140 Caroline May 111 Caroline Rebecca 158 Caroline Waldron 179 Caroline Whipple 92 Caroline Whitney 147 Carolyn 283 Carrie 310 376 Carrie Gertrude 334 Carrie Isabel 310 Carrie Louise 301 Cassandra 312 Cassius C 407 Cassius Clay 15 16 299 328 Cassius Harlan 329 Cassius Philip 329 Catharine 280 Catherine 47 91 103 172 260 279 322 Catherine W 92 Cecile 190 209 381 Celeste 152 Celia Ann 364 Celia Laura 353 Celia Maud 334 Cementhe 310 Ceolia Josephine 141 Charity 91 Charles 71 100 106 121 129 141 176 191 205 253 263 307 320 322 353 Charles A 274 306 407 409 Charles Aaron 137 176 Charles Addison 301 331 Charles Alfred 273 Charles Alonzo 188 Charles Andrew 124 169 Charles Arthur 198 320 334 348 Charles Bartlett 113 Charles Burnham 216 Charles Carroll 102 Charles Clarence 96 134 175 Charles Connor 215 Charles D 316 342

ROBERTS (Continued)
Charles E 409 Charles Edson 199 217 Charles Edwin 121 140 148 178 187 286 319 346 Charles Ellery Fordyce 106 146 Charles Francis 153 Charles Frank 261 Charles Frederick 158 190 Charles Gilman 309 Charles H 271 305 Charles Harris 347 Charles Henry 93 Charles Hill 107 147 187 Charles Justin 15 297 327 Charles L 406 Charles Linneus 268 301 Charles O 154 Charles P 154 Charles Samuel 123 169 Charles Shepherd 206 Charles Sumner 301 330 Charles W 84 Charles Watson 336 Charles Wellington 302 331 Charles Wentworth 16 112 155 156 Charles Wesley 114 115 Charles White 97 139 Charles William 152 189 Charlotte 93 111-113 125 156 254 362 Charlotte Ella 287 Charlotte G 84 Charmaine 379 Chastine H 126 Chelsea Lynn 389 Cheryl 385 393 Cheryl Lynn 390 Chester Allen 334 Chester Merrill 260 289 Christiana 281 317 Christiana A B 282 Christine 345 Claire E 335 Clara 186 195 196 269 314 Clara A 127 154 Clara Bell 168 Clara Elizabeth 167 Clara Helen 115 172 Clare 362 Clare Ridley 379 Clarence 178 338 346 Clarence C 176 400 Clarence H 151 Clarence Herman 137 177 Claribel 338 Clarinda 253 Clarissa 67 71 96 104 114 122 131 143 144 261 Clarissa Tracy

ROBERTS (Continued)
264 Clarkson B 267 Claude 339 359 Clayton Hartley 193 213 214 219 Cleaver 178 Clementine 277 Clessant Charles 353 372 Clifford 66 346 Clifton Wood 193 Clive Malcolm 205 Clyde 211 Clyde Harold 184 210 Clyde Samuel 195 Clyde Thomas 202 Conrad Craig 371 385 Coolidge Sutton 155 189 Cora 177 184 192 268 275 Cora Belle 331 Cora Luella 173 Cordelia 130 260 Cornelia 274 Curtis Barrett 321 351 Cynthia 168 304 312 Cynthia Allen 120 Cynthia Eliza 290 Cynthia Sophia 290 Cyrus 254 277 Cyrus H 278 314 337 Cyrus P 97 Daisy 339 352 353 Dale 385 Dallas Warren 389 Dana 360 Daniel 37 43 51 53 55 62 78 79 85 124 125 246 249 254 262 263 277 283 Daniel Azro 263 295 Daniel Carr 264 296 Daniel Edwards 277 310 Daniel Richard 387 Daniel W 97 140 Daniel West 16 245 259 288 320 321 323 354 373 Daniel William 95 138 Daphne 278 Darius Witt 260 290 Darlene 390 Darlene Michelle 389 David 42 60 61 65 79 92 93 96 117 133 175 236 David Ballard 155 David Calvin 374 387 David Daniel 388 David Emmons 210 David Ezra 316 David Gary 386 David Lloyd 188 David Mark 364 381 David S 112 156 285 David Sands 57 86 134 174 205 217 David Theodore 382 Davis Ballard

ROBERTS (Continued)
111 Dawn 360 Dawn Marie 383 Debbie 393 Deborah 32 33 44 51 52 69 90 112 389 Debra 376 Debrah Ann 379 Dedie 157 Deidamia 75 Deidamia Anne 117 Delancy Amos 161 192 Delia 162 291 Delia L 334 Deliverance 235 Della 355 Della Frances 324 Delora J 310 Delphina H 271 Dennis 148 358 376 Dennis Earl 377 390 393 Derrick Earl 393 Dexter 278 311 Diane 361 378 381 Dianna E 310 Didamia 75 Dimon 72 109 110 Dimon A 107 Dimon Eugene 153 Dodd Edward 215 Dolly 235 236 Donna 377 Dora 272 307 386 Dora Etta 128 Dorcas 66 Doris 206 212 358 371 Doris Albertine 310 Dorothy 67 70 87 192 197 297 357 386 Dorothy A 373 Dorothy Caryl 357 Dorothy Deborah 173 Dorothy Douw 204 Douglas Mitchell 212 Dudley 67 Dudley Avery 263 294 Dwane Bartlett 362 379 Dwight 293 Earl 308 346 Earl Foster 353 373 Earle Frank 182 Earle Henry 343 364 Earle Melvin 334 Eaton 294 Eben 265 Ebenezer 31 33 40 41 44 45 59 61 65 67 130 Ed 205 Eddie 272 Edgar F 289 Edgar Frank 342 361 Edgar Stanwood 160 Edgar Wentworth 146 183 Edith 152 159 178 184 202 207 215 325 338 Edith Adelaide 166 172 Edith Caswell 190 Edith E 365 Edith Gertrude 305 Edith Lola 343 Edith Louise

ROBERTS (Continued)
177 Edith Valma 159 Edmund 11 42 60 92 101 134 293 311 Edmund H 60 91 Edna 178 192 197 Edna H 365 Edna Hazel 337 Edna M 306 335 Edna May 186 Edna Thayer 165 Edson 148 187 Edward 67 153 273 311 Edward Baxter 353 372 Edward Cheney 331 Edward E 99 Edward Everett 135 176 Edward Freeman 330 Edward H 131 Edward Junius 300 329 Edward Nathaniel 335 Edward P 100 Edward W 275 Edwin 128 178 269 305 Edwin Abbott 333 Edwin Ashley 342 361 Edwin Gilbert 354 373 Edwin Jonathan 120 164 Edwin Lindly 139 Edwin Orrin 326 Edwin Pease 166 Edwina 151 Effie 291 Elaine 361 Elaine Ann 379 Eldon Woodbury 331 Eleanor 134 171 269 270 Eleanor Marian 365 Eleanor Viola 189 Electa 321 Eli 257 279 283 406 Elias 76 Elias Thomas 183 209 Elihu Luman 371 385 Elihu Warren 352 Elijah 57 Elinor Elizabeth 195 Eliphalet 11 233 239 241 243 244 248 258 259 287 Elisa J 294 Elisabeth 293 294 Elithea 284 Eliza 64 86 91 100 105 112 120 128 134 153 166 269 291 296 Eliza Ann 84 Eliza Eleanor 175 Eliza Ellen 167 175 Eliza Jane 93 Eliza Plummer 127 Eliza T 95 Elizabeth 23 29-32 35 38-40 42-44 47 48 50 53-56 58 60 61 63-65 67 68 71-73 75-79 81 83 89 91- 93 96 104 105 118 119 130-133

ROBERTS (Continued)
136 151 158 163 166 167 175 197 200 211 214 225-227 233 241-244 250 252 255 259 260 263 283 284 295 298 338 391 400 Elizabeth Abigail 290 Elizabeth Ann 100 107 Elizabeth Aville 132 Elizabeth B 105 Elizabeth C 205 Elizabeth Cates 270 297 Elizabeth Clarice 139 Elizabeth Fall 79 Elizabeth Gertrude 172 Elizabeth J 106 108 132 Elizabeth Jane 96 Elizabeth Jo 381 Elizabeth L 104 Elizabeth March 93 Elizabeth Mary 150 Elizabeth Meder 97 Elizabeth Moses 266 Elizabeth Rounds 147 Elizabeth T 108 Elizabeth U 124 Elizabeth Webb 258 Ella 121 134 164 179 196 199 217 276 310 364 Ella Agnes 157 Ella Dorothy 341 Ella I 111 Ella Mabel 330 Ella Mae 340 Ella Octavia 217 Ella S 82 122 Ellen 94 100 106 116 159 160 273 279 359 Ellen A 275 Ellen Augusta 159 Ellen C 402 Ellen Cecilia 268 301 Ellen E 130 Ellen Frances 139 Ellen Georgianna 157 Ellen Lois 301 Ellen P 265 266 Elmer G 306 Elmer Linwood 185 Elmer Nathan 316 Elmira 251 316 Elmira Haskell 106 Elmira Jane 163 Elnora 140 Eloise 190 Eloise Lucille 213 Elsa 245 Elsie 133 188 194 245 351 Elsie Ella 351 Elsie Louise 189 Elsie M 365 Elsie O 259 Elsy 261 Elvira 98 274 Elwood 176 400 Emelda 318 Emeline 80 287 300 Emeline Hardy 145

ROBERTS (Continued)
Emelyn 207 Emerson 254 Emery J 314 Emily 65 68 108 125 128 149 280 299 305 328 351 379 Emily Ann Gates 115 Emily Esther 268 Emily Janice 189 Emily Spinney 161 Emma 160 176 183 188 308 315 325 329 336 Emma F 306 Emma Francis 118 Emma Hay 308 Emma J 130 Emma Lelia 218 Emma Louise 110 Emma Lucelia 301 Emma M 400 Emma Mabel 176 Emma Norris 187 Emma Sophia 136 Emma Zanette 137 Emmet Livingston 332 Enoch 252 269 Ephraim 38 44 55 60 64 65 81 82 92 117 Ephraim K 134 Eric Mathew 385 Ernest A 365 382 Ernest Arthur 195 215 Ernest Bell 207 Ernest Carroll 293 Ernest Everett 164 Ernest James 360 378 Ernest Linwood 160 192 Ernest Raymond 162 Ernest Tucker 315 340 Ernest Upham 120 164 Ernestine 340 Ervin 340 360 Estella 146 Estelle 282 306 Ester 385 Esther 52 85 101 251 252 256 283 306 345 346 358 Esther Burnham 217 Esther E 296 Esther Emma 205 Esther Myrtle 335 Ethel 158 343 344 349 Ethel Gertrude 196 Ethel May 148 Ethelyn 122 Etta 364 Etta Elizabeth 195 Etta Eugenia 336 Eugene 336 Eugene Charles 166 198 Eugene Roswell 313 335 Eula Rose 318 Eunice 53 63 70 75 104 184 185 237 245 249 295 296 310 368 Eunice Elma 99 Eunice V

ROBERTS (Continued)
97 Eva 184 191 319 345 374
Eva Alger 321 Eva Annette 163
Eva Elizabeth 344 Eva Lucy
138 Eva May 185 Evelyn 127
203 218 330 376 Evelyn Florence 371 Evelyn Frances 341
Evelyn Harding 146 Evelyn V
298 Everard 338 Everett 314
345 366 Everett Anson 161 192
Everett Ervin 359 377 Everett F
154 Everett Lee 192 Everett
Lemuel 120 165 Everett W 272
305 Everyn 338 Evie E 327
Ezekiel 64 71 99 100 106 234
245 Ezekiel L 100 Ezra 15 50
75 236 255 269 279 281 281
282 303 316 Ezra Kellogg 143
Faithful 281 Fannie May 324
Fanny 144 288 Fanny A 288
Fanny Fern 302 Faustena
Austin 201 Faustina 330 Faye
Raye 380 Fern Meta 349 Fidelia 276 Flora Bella 141 Flora
Belle 399 Flora M 148 Florence
186 187 201 212 333 337 340
355 375 Florence Agnes 354
Florence Arvella 210 Florence
May 211 373 Florilla Decker
269 Floyd J 405 Floyd John 333
Folsom 293 Forest Rupert 343
363 379 Forrest K 306 335
Frances 21 32 340 Frances
Amy 355 Frances Augusta 95
Frances Earline 192 Frances
Elizabeth 112 Frances Lear 92
Francese Almira 261 Francis 35
36 48 72 103 117 328 365
Francis A 84 405 Francis Alton
299 327 Francis H 296 Francis
Jane 62 Francis R 324 Francis
Rufus 289 Francis Wayland 131

ROBERTS (Continued)
173 Frank 15 144 182 185 301-
303 306 326 Frank Augustus
332 Frank Ernest 206 Frank
Gilman 334 Frank H 276 308
314 337 Frank Henry 158 190
Frank Herbert 146 184 338 359
Frank Jonathan 163 Frank M
127 Frank Orlando 291 325
Frank Samuel 211 Frank
Stanwood 342 362 379 Frank
W 315 342 Frank William 170
Franklin 103 174 Franklin B 16
321 351 Franklin George 164
Franklin Kimball 16 133 173
Franklin W 100 Franklin White
107 Fred 140 Fred Barnabas
331 Fred D 185 Fred E 315
Fred G 324 Fred Herbert 159
191 Fred Howard 124 Fred
Leslie 276 308 Fred Morton
173 202 Fred Paine 205 218
Fred Richard 168 Frederick
Belknap 135 Frederick D 100
Frederick Dennis 390 393
Frederick E 321 Frederick L
315 338 Frederick M 127
Frederick Mead 214 Frederick
Parkhurst 316 343 364 380
Frederick Ransom 321 350
Freedom 351 Freeman 330
Freeman Edwin 334 Freeman
M 407 Freeman Myrick 16 300
329 Freeman Otis 303 333
Furber S 357 375 Gail Marie
387 Gardner Brewster 171 201
Garry 360 378 Geneva 192
George 6-9 11 12 16 17 35 42
45 47 54 61 66 69 70 77 86 96
101 103 125 127 136 138 141
144 179 198 205 221-223 226
231-233 238 239 242 245 246

ROBERTS (Continued)
255 256 260 261 265 281 282
George A 100 147 George
Alvin 63 George Atwood 304
334 George B 16 George B M
281 316 George Bean 310
George Belknap 15 93 135
George Bradbury 165 197
George Brinton 316 342 343
362 George Clinton 181 209
George Copson 47 69 George E
113 George Edward 169 283
George Edwin 113 156 157
George Eugene 326 George F
197 George Fillmore 199 216
217 George Franklin 120 164
George Frederick 343 363
George H 141 George Hall 132
George Henry 16 108 144 150
159 181 182 George Herbert
140 George K 63 84 95 George
L 190 212 George Litch 162
194 George Merton 363 George
Roland 162 George Royal 183
210 George S 314 388 George
Seacord 331 George Seward 79
120 George Thomas 102 142
George W 67 95 101 142 293
George Washington 105 251
266 George Wells 289 323
George William 142 178 179
Georgeanna 275 Georgia 299
312 358 Georgia Anna 301
Georgie Etta 313 Gertrude 162
188 190 195 206 323 Gertrude
Helena 140 Gertrude Lurline
Estelle 190 Gertrude M 151
Gertrude R 324 Gertrude S 322
Gideon 61 Gilbert Jeremiah 140
Gilbert M 287 Giles 9 Gilman
252 268 270 279 299 304 312
401 Gina 378 Gladys 216

ROBERTS (Continued)
Gladys G 337 Gladys May 308
Glema 383 Glen Edward 326
Glen W 363 380 Glenda 390
Glenda Chance 380 Glenn 354
Glenn Arthur 323 353 Glenn
Edward 353 372 373 Glenn
Thomas 382 Glennys 367
Gloria Jean 386 Goodwife 225
Gordon Leroy 210 Grace 182
213 275 307 331 361 370 375
383 Grace Anna 165 Grace
Darling 116 Grace E 336 Grace
Genevieve 166 Grace Gertrude
383 Grace May 174 Granville C
66 Gregory 376 Gussie 363
Guy 184 292 Guy Hall 274 307
Gwendolyn 213 Hall 91 131
171 202 Hallie 333 Hamlin 300
Hamlin M 403 Hamlin Myrick
267 299 301 Hannah 36 38 40
43 44 48 52 56 60-65 68 70 71
77 80 83 87 92 95 96 103 104
122 133 144-146 149 234 239
240 245-247 252 254 261 263
264 269 270 276 289 313 316
343 Hannah Augusta 95
Hannah Catherine 303 Hannah
E 84 Hannah J 139 Hannah
Jane 282 Hannah L 82 Hannah
Maria 137 297 Hannah P 256
Hannah Quint 104 Hannah S 82
Hannah Smith 105 Hanson 56
84 93 134 Harold 194 Harold
Arthur 211 Harold Clifton 195
215 Harold E 345 Harold J 183
Harold Kirkwood 159 Harriet
122 127 130 138 149 154 161
163 269 271 293 298 312 324
352 365 401 Harriet Augusta
132 Harriet Christiana 210
Harriet E 289 Harriet Edna 366

ROBERTS (Continued)
Harriet Ella 149 Harriet Langdon 92 Harriet Louella 261 Harriet M 293 Harriet May 168 324 Harriet Norma 169 Harrison 354 Harrison F 134 176 Harry 311 Harry Arthur 166 198 Harry Carleton 187 Harry Edgar 320 349 Harry Edwin 164 197 Harry Fletcher 196 215 Harry W 334 Harvey Easton 171 201 Hatevil 26 27 30 37 38 51 52 77 Hattie 326 334 344 Hattie A 291 Hattie C 304 Hattie E 292 Hattie May 334 Hazel 317 318 357 358 380 Hazel Dell 335 Hazel Viola 308 Hazel W 365 Heard 42 67 Heleaa Belle 335 Helen 136 160 190 215 295 311 357 362 372 Helen A 132 Helen Ann 369 Helen Charlotte 169 Helen F 122 Helen Hayes 196 Helen Louise 341 Helen Melissa 288 Helen P 290 Helen Walcott 152 Helen Waldron 173 Helena 139 Henrietta 352 Henry 197 205 261 294 314 Henry Ambrose 168 Henry Benjamin 163 196 Henry Burns 114 Henry C 337 Henry Clay 134 Henry Edson 216 Henry G 337 Henry H 148 Henry Harrison 288 322 Henry Kirkwood 115 159 Henry L 113 304 Henry Laurens 113 157 Henry M 273 Henry Sands 175 204 Hepsibah 104 Herbert 157 358 Herbert A 365 381 Herbert Arthur 162 194 Herbert E 178 207 Herbert Elwyn 298 Herbert F 304 334 Herbert Howard 147 186 Herman 188 Herman C 163

ROBERTS (Continued)
195 Herman Ellery 150 187 Herman Winfield 115 160 Hester 23 Hezekiah 73 Hezekiah Wentworth 111 Hilda 200 Hinda 194 Hiram 78 117 131 Hiram Hall 172 Hiram Norton 89 Hiram R 53 401 Hiram Rollins 15 90 130 Holland Sands 218 Holley 361 Horace 107 147 148 279 Horace Herbert 163 196 Horatio Gates 113 157 Horatio Walter 337 Hovey L 334 Howard 332 Howard Augustus 309 Howard Emerson 149 Howard Franklin 194 Howard Leroy 308 Howard Millet 85 95 124 Hugh Wellington 125 Hulda 280 284 Huldah 66 267 Huldah J 404 Huldah Jane 268 Huldah Margaret 303 Iantha 276 Ichabod 11 41 59 91 132 Ida 169 198 289 Ida Anne 158 Ida Charlotte 170 Ida Florence 149 312 Ida Luella 295 Ida Mary 216 Ida May 292 344 Idella E 204 Idella May 175 Inez 308 Inez Annie 160 Inza 185 Iola 214 Ira 93 135 Irene 387 Irene Janette 216 Irish 339 Irving R 351 370 Irving Rowe 217 Isaac 32 42 80 90 92 129 133 252 266 Isaac H 16 126 Isaac P 405 Isaac Pennington 267 298 Isabel 176 273 331 Isabella 332 Isabelle 189 Isac 293 Israel N 100 Ivory 72 150 Ivy Alice 159 J Clifford 140 Jackson 125 169 170 Jacob 148 239 252 267 269 300 304 401 Jacob Francis 147 185 Jacob Waterhouse 107 147

ROBERTS (Continued)
Jacob Wellington 267 299
James 11 39 44 45 55 56 59 62
63 66-68 70 71 73 78 81 83 86
95 98 104 109 110 118 126 148
235 242 251 252 256 258 284
376 James A 117 401 James
Albert 285 James Alton 275
James Arnold 177 206 James
Arthur 15 16 133 174 376 389
393 James Benton 153 James
Cutts 110 153 James Depeyster
204 James Ezekiel 145 182
James Franklin 265 James H 64
90 100 129 130 133 296 James
Howard 149 James Louis 182
James Lull 260 288 James
Madison 74 James Morton 203
James Pike 82 James Porter 195
James Richard 380 James
Rollins 38 41 58 James S 314
336 James Stanton 158 James
Thompson 283 James W 99
James Wakefield 15 72 107 148
James Woodbury 154 Jane 40
59 72 91 108 117 124 129 161
191 194 200 279 280 282 283
287 300 314 347 387 410 Jane
A 278 Jane Amelia 287 Jane
Pierce 156 Janet 207 389 Janet
Alice 372 Janet Carol 206 Janet
Lucia 371 Janice 375 Janice
Marie 359 Janis Marie 370
Jaqueine 359 Jaqueline Marie
372 Jay 15 272 333 Jeanette
359 Jeanne 368 Jedediah 47 70
93 104 134 Jeffrey Allen 383
Jeffrey George 390 Jennette
274 Jennette Adele 332 Jenney
Beth 379 Jennie 311 332 350
362 Jennie E 321 Jennie M 352
Jennifer 387 Jennifer Lynn 384

ROBERTS (Continued)
393 Jenny Lind 324 Jeremiah
15 41 59 63 74 91 95 96 114
130 132 Jeremiah Bartlett 115
Jerusha 121 260 Jesse 63 98
Jesse Nina 193 Jessica Rae 379
Jessie 307 Jessie L 298 Jessie
Louise 318 Jessie Mae 364
Jessie Maria 335 Jo Anne 383
Joan Elizabeth 206 Joanna 27
33 38 44 48 51 53 54 59 60 69
80 81 90 101 311 Joanna W 81
Job 59 Joel 63 399 Johanna 169
John 6 8 11 21-23 25-27 29 31
32 35 36 38-41 43-45 48-50 53
56 58 59 61 65 68 70 72-74 81
82 84 85 90 91 93 97 103 108
111-113 123 125 126 196 222
223 225 226 229-231 235-237
239 241 246 249 251 253 254
259 262-264 271 285 293 306
322 352 368 384 402 John A
148 John B 86 John Carr 48
John Charles Fremont 145 183
John Clendenin 86 127 John
Comley 112 John Davis 93 136
John Dimon 358 375 John
Edgar 286 319 John F 123 John
Franklin 113 169 John Frederick 381 John G 77 John H 16
109 151 John Ham 131 John
Harrison 115 158 John Harry
172 202 John Herbert 122 John
Hilton 128 170 John Homan
125 John Hyde 206 John I 314
John Jones 116 John Kenneth
188 376 John L 295 John Lord
263 John Love 74 115 John
Meader 97 John Meder 139
John Nelson 274 307 John P 16
277 John Philip Bartlett 158
John Pike 167 199 John Place

ROBERTS (Continued)
163 195 John R 411 John
Roderick 347 368 John S 16
154 John Sawyer 249 John
Smith 168 200 John Stillings
110 John W 88 133 John
Wesley 121 385 John Weston
110 153 John William 369 370
383 John Yeaton 81 122 Jonas
134 Jonathan 11 53 78 79 83
226 227 233 235 236 239-242
246 253 255-258 262 278 282
283 285 Jonathan Bradley 231
235 Jonathan D 280 313 Jonathan Dame 73 112 Jonathan Ely
119 Jonathan M 16 Jonathan
Martin 263 295 Joseph 6 7 11
23 26 29-31 38 39 40 47 49 53-59 69 73 82-85 89 108 113 117
122 161 221 230 233 237 239-243 248 249 251-253 256 270
276 292 297 403 Joseph A 280
Joseph Arthur 114 Joseph
Augustus 113 157 Joseph B 130
Joseph Banks 174 203 Joseph
Clarence 172 202 Joseph D 75
117 Joseph Dennett 72 107
Joseph Doe 15 131 172 Joseph
Hall 16 87 Joseph J 112 156
157 Joseph Johnson 261 291
Joseph March 82 Joseph Martin
161 193 Joseph Warren 88
Josephine 125 274 Joshua 11 12
30 38 45 47 53 54 58 68 79 80
81 101 102 119 121 230 237
250 Joshua Alden 393 Joshua
Chase 379 Joshua F 119 Joshua
Thomas 67 Josiah 42 255 280
Josiah W 278 311 Josie 308
Josie Stclair 175 Jotham 253
276 Joyce 377 Joyce Blanche
372 Juanita Pearl 362 Judah

ROBERTS (Continued)
233 Judie 377 Judith 51 52 76
77 119 231 232 239 242 244
376 386 Judith Elaine 375
Judith Elizabeth 386 Judith M
322 Judy 370 Julia 143 145 279
290 291 297 305 320 335 367
Julia A 116 129 279 Julia
Almeda 271 Julia Ann 56 88
322 364 380 Julia Ann Maria
115 Julia Priscilla 88 Julia True
106 Juliana 289 370 Julie 317
Julie Anne 391 Juliette 65 275
Julius 325 Julius D 291 325
June 155 359 June Lydia 387
Junius Everett 330 Justin 267
297 Justin Everett 298 Karen
Eva 388 Kate 327 352 Kate
Emelda 318 Katherine 155 164
290 328 344 Kathleen 383 384
Kathleen Ruth 214 Kathy 368
376 Katie 327 Keith Everett
198 Kelly 389 Kenneth 182
Kenneth E 386 Kenneth Frederick 182 Kenneth Pinkham 364
381 Kevin 378 Keziah 40 57
Kimberly Angelia 368 Kittendean 317 Kittie 317 Kyle Bevan
219 L F 62 Lametta Eva 317
Larkin 260 290 Laura 125 266
273 291 292 324 Laura Alzina
261 Laura Anna 313 Laura F
129 Laura Frances Cogswell
120 Laura M 339 Laurel 199
Laurel Tobias 166 198 Laurens
15 278 Lavinia 117 140 260
Lawrence Bailey 197 Lawrence
James 337 357 Leah 114 210
Leah Helen 114 Leavitt 238
250 Leavitt Sylvester 16 266
Lee 307 Lee Wesley 210 Leila J
271 Lelia 204 327 Lena 259

ROBERTS (Continued)
341 341 370 371 Lena M 155
Lena Mabel 162 Lena May 341
Lenora Avilda 272 Leo Francis
365 Leola 366 Leola Stella 374
Leon Chester 185 212 Leona
372 Leonora 81 Leota 326 361
Leslie 339 378 Leslie Burton
315 339 Leslie Edson 217
Leslie Freeman 185 211 Leslie
M 290 403 Leslie Manter 298
Leslie Perry 308 Leslie Sue 381
Letty Ruby 352 Levi 15 96 238
251 280 314 315 340 Levi F 75
116 Levi M N 100 Levi True
146 Lewellyn Lloyd 380
Lewellyn Thomas 363 380
Lewis 99 151 Lewis E 312
Libbie R 171 Lila 150 203 Lilla
334 Lilla Louise 374 Lillian
193 196 198 305 308 326 363
385 386 Lillian Estelle 173
Lillian Isabelle 199 Lillian
Louise 151 Lillian Marie 308
Lillie 199 Lillie Ann 381 Lillie
Martha 130 Lily 195 Lincoln
Hamlin 303 332 Linda 389
Linda Jane 367 Linneus A 313
Linnie 127 Linnie May 176
Linwood Belknap 351 370 Lisa
378 Lisa Marie 381 Lizzie 265
324 Lizzie E 306 Llewellyn 303
Lloyd 16 278 310 Lloyd A 408
Lloyd Albert 333 Lloyd Garri-
son 214 Lois 56 57 85 124 129
283 284 Lora 288 Lora Jose-
phine 181 Loren E 377 390
Loren Everett 390 393 Lorenzo
D 134 Loring 276 Loring John
183 210 Loring True 106 145
Lorraine 346 Lottie 311 Lottie
Adelia 329 Louis Eugene 152

ROBERTS (Continued)
Louisa 66 68 129 140 151 259
264 Louise 202 318 Louise C
273 Louise Davis 205 Louise
Hellen 373 Love 11 30 35 36
47 48 70 71 97 98 105 123 146
Lovey 250 Lovina 236 253
Lovisa 299 304 Lovy 236
Lucian 260 287 321 Lucille 340
Lucina 264 Lucinda 245 261
264 Lucullus 278 311 Lucy 124
126 138 141 148 166 264 315
323 338 342 343 354 Lucy
Adams 155 Lucy E 87 Lucy
Ellen 312 Lucy Isabelle 166
Lucy M 64 Luella 158 Luke
108 150 Luke Hemmenway 109
152 Luther Earl 337 358 Luther
Hayes 159 Luther Hilton 170
Lutheria 325 326 Lydia 27 30
31 37-40 45 47 52 55-57 66 67
79 81 84 85 89 93 112 113 126
136 142 154 156 161 162 173
230 231 254 255 259 266 270
276 286 297 303 Lydia Augusta
175 Lydia E 139 Lydia Ellen
156 157 Lydia Emily 101 Lydia
G 66 Lydia M 74 Lydia Maria
125 Lydia S 122 Lynn M 381
Mabel 140 159 178 182 217
245 335 Mabel Frances 152
Mabel Huntress 149 Madeline
212 Mae Bethia 333 Malcolm
Mackay 212 Mansir Hamilton
287 322 Manter A 15 Manter
Alverado 273 Manter Wellington 302 Maranda 327 Marcella
295 Marcia 81 345 350 Marcia
Ann 132 274 Marcialine Rosetta 287 Margaret 50 86 153 170
182 236 245 251 269 279 309
328 341 357 384 Margaret

ROBERTS (Continued)
  Anne 357 Margaret Livingston
  Dresser 204 Margery Janet 371
  Marguerite 206 339 342 Maria
  85 94 109 171 274 275 309
  Maria A 124 Mariah B 281
  Mariam 262 Marian 153 209
  340 366 Marian A 365 Marian
  Alice 311 Marianna Langdon
  92 Marie 362 375 Marie
  Madeleine 29 Marietta 171 312
  Mariette Jane 145 Marilyn 375
  Marilyn Jean 382 Marion 182
  200 343 372 Marion Beatrice
  354 Marion Blanche 371
  Marion Emerson 189 Marjorie
  187 Marjorie Esther 370 Marjorie Lucille 216 Marjory 254
  Mark 54 80 Mark L 116 Mark
  Phillip 382 Mark Spencer 391
  Marsters 277 Martha 58 66 67
  71 98 105 107 109 117 125 133
  163 174 202 213 Martha Ann
  102 116 Martha Brown 151
  Martha Emily 150 Martha Etta
  149 Martha H 106 Martha J 280
  Martha Jane 118 Martha Jean
  379 Martha T 83 Martin Luther
  159 Mary 12 17 26 27 29-31 33
  35 36 38-41 44 47-51 53-57 60
  62 67 69-71 75 78 83 87 89 91
  93 94 99 101 103-105 119 121
  123 124 126 127 133 135 137
  138 143 145-147 150 151 155
  163 166 168 177 191 196 202
  203 210 216 221-223 226 227
  235 237 241 249 250 253 255
  256 258 259 265 267 270 274
  276 277 279 280 282 285-288
  291-293 297 299 302 303 307
  309 310 312 314-316 326 327
  331 333 338 340 346 353 365

ROBERTS (Continued)
  379 402 Mary A 87 103 129
  293 352 Mary Abby 96 Mary
  Adaline 80 Mary Adeline 118
  120 140 260 321 Mary Angeline 321 Mary Ann 62 103 106
  111 126 136 138 156 256 272
  Mary Ann Adams 111 Mary
  Ann E 261 Mary Ann Gray 127
  Mary Anne 111 155 Mary B G
  94 Mary Bertha 159 Mary
  Blanche 331 Mary Brown 256
  Mary C 85 Mary Caroline 104
  144 Mary Charlotte 109 151
  Mary E 85 88 154 Mary E P
  112 Mary Egeton 168 Mary
  Eliza 99 Mary Elizabeth 137
  138 152 284 379 Mary Ella 88
  111 Mary Ellen 95 117 136 183
  302 Mary Emeline 146 Mary
  Emily 102 Mary F 314 Mary
  Frances 203 275 Mary G 75
  Mary H 89 306 Mary Hall 87
  Mary Hemmenway 110 Mary
  Hoover 201 Mary Horn 93
  Mary J 79 Mary Jackson 88
  Mary Jane 76 81 100 107 121
  283 286 382 Mary Josephine
  217 Mary L 64 Mary Lillian
  199 326 Mary M 291 292 304
  Mary Main 73 Mary Pervilla
  264 Mary R 296 Mary Ruth 310
  Matasha Joy 393 Mathew 117
  Mathilda 188 Matilda 307
  Mattie 314 331 Maud 305
  Maude Adelaide 165 Maurice E
  337 358 Maxine 339 363 May
  308 May Elizabeth 127
  Mayhew Tristram 162 Mehita-
  ble 35 50 74 77 105 Melissa
  Marcia 288 Mellissa 305
  Melvin Albert 109 Melvin C

ROBERTS (Continued)
297 Melvin W 304 334 Melvina
193 Melzar 327 Menza Alfred
344 365 Mercedes Alexander
307 Mercy 58 75 81 89 110 117
140 273 284 Mercy Adeline
121 Mercy Hall 132 Merton
Ellingwood 185 211 Merton
Elmer 343 363 Merton Urban
192 Mervin Stanley 382 Meta
348 349 Michael Earle 381
Michael Stephen 375 389
Mildred 200 370 Mildred
Elizabeth 179 Mildred Francis
205 Mildred Helen 195 Mildred
Jane 218 Mildred Sarah 174
Millard Knox 216 Millet
Wentworth 105 144 Millicent
152 Milton 80 270 298 Milton
Lincoln 332 Milton M 267 297
298 405 Milton S 132 Mina 326
Minerva 174 Minnie Edson 187
Miriam 32 254 257 258 269
282 323 Molly 48 59 69 83
Morris Ferris 204 Moses 32 36
37 41 43 44 48-52 58 62-64 70
76 83 89 97 100 119 132 173
245 260 Moses N 100 Myra
162 Myra Florence 320 Myron
C 288 Myrtie Jane 326 Myrtilla
123 Myrtle 151 178 345 346
347 410 Myrtle Grace 347
Nahum 72 108 Nahum Frank
153 Nancy 71 76 82 89 114 133
209 251 258 265 271 273 279
280 283 309 390 Nancy C 72
150 251 Nancy E 100 286
Nancy Ellen 284 Nancy Maria
285 Natalie Elisabeth 391
Nathan 11 38 52 53 77 253 282
Nathan Alfred 297 Nathan
Charles 176 205 Nathan F 281

ROBERTS (Continued)
315 Nathan H 404 Nathan Hall
253 274 Nathan Lewis 146 185
Nathaniel 27 31 32 42 60 83
123 Nathaniel Brown 235
Nathaniel Burnham 74 114
Nathaniel Frank 136 Nathaniel
Knight 270 Neil Alfred 382
Neil Edward 387 Neil Leo 355
Neil Leroy 376 389 Nellie 152
154 306 324 375 Nellie Annette
351 Nellie Blanche 197 Nellie
R 137 Nelson 299 Nelson C
321 350 Nettie 125 142 155
332 Nicholas David 391 Nicholas Hanson 56 57 63 83 87
Nillie 359 Nina 342 Nina Belle
343 Noah 101 246 247 264
Noah Horn 115 158 Nora 266
Nora Clarkson 160 Nora Louise
387 Nora May 325 Norma 340
Norman 359 377 Norman
Dennett 188 Oceana 204 Octavia Heard 167 Odin 194 214
Olga 336 Olive 38 51 52 89 126
129 133 262 263 313 323 333
350 354 357 Olive Ann 99
Olive Carolyn 217 Olive G 335
Olive Naomi 250 Oliver 124
129 Oliver Ayer 16 88 128
Oliver Brewster 128 Oliver
Frank 169 200 Oliver Heard 57
88 Oliver L 84 123 Olivette J
142 Olney T 99 Omar Warren
345 367 368 Orena 269 Orilla
288 Orimel 259 Orin Winfield
167 Orlando 276 Orlando
Hartwell 261 291 292 Orlin 291
Ormond 202 Orpheus 16 278
310 Orrin 123 Orrin Nason 265
Orsino 16 126 Orville 281
Orville Leslie 329 Oscar 15

ROBERTS (Continued)
Oscar E 274 306 Otis Jackson 15 318 345 367 383 Otis Oakes 16 239 282 318 Owen 294 Owen Swain 110 154 Pamela 105 Parepa R 408 Parepa Rose 329 Patience 163 281 Patricia 375 376 379 380 Patricia Effie 367 Pattie 313 Patty 62 Paul 11 32 52 71 75 76 106 Paul Billings 186 212 Paul Henley 179 207 Paul Ramon 194 Paula 360 393 Paulina 107 328 408 Paulina E 329 Pauline 368 Pauline Alice 209 Pearl 373 380 Peavey 56 Penny 380 Perley James 196 Perrin 289 325 Persis 264 Peter 48 71 150 Peter Judd 385 Peter Stillings 107 148 Phebe 33 56 91 157 250 251 300 338 Phebe Ann 88 Phebe E 314 Phebe Young 268 Phelina 291 Philander 109 151 Philip John 371 386 Phillip John 386 Phyllis Marion 372 Polly 70 71 103 247 249 250 264 265 Porter Alonzo 150 188 Porter D 94 Porter Sands 108 Porteus B 405 Porteus Beezaleel 268 302 Porteus Henry 331 Preston Fremont 137 177 Preston Trask 217 Priscilla 70 113 201 234 Priscilla Arabella 114 Procinda 134 Prudence 253 276 Prudence G 282 Rachel 59 60 116 130 143 196 315 Ralph 147 301 Ralph Benjamin 209 Ralph Calvin 371 385 Ralph Clifford 343 Ralph L 358 375 Ralph Newell 164 Ralph Vernon 355 Randall Frank 361 378 Ray Daniel 326 Raymond 153 346

ROBERTS (Continued)
Raymond Gilbert 373 387 Raymond Renworth 315 341 Raymond Sylvester 315 341 342 360 361 Rebecca 12 17 21 45 67 74 86 115 276 282 317 Rebecca Ann 384 Rebecca Eloise 208 Rebecca Forst 50 Rebecca Hobbs 78 Rebecca Horn 110 Rebekah 243 Rebekah Abigail 283 Reginald Thomas 210 Reginold 359 377 Relief 49 Remember 277 Reuben 59 72 76 90 117 161 Reuben Davis 104 143 Rex Nute 191 213 Rhiannon 378 Rhoda 47 75 80 108 118 Richard 69 82 122 123 168 346 374 Richard Baxter 372 386 Richard Henry 336 Richard Lester 355 374 Richard Lovell 192 Richard Ralph 386 Richard Sewall Woodbury 168 200 Richard Smith 72 Rita 361 Rita Ann 376 Rita Elizabeth 182 Robert 9 68 339 359 360 378 Robert Foster 373 Robert Francis 387 391 Robert Whitehouse 193 213 Roberta 213 Robin 360 Rod 347 Roderick G 410 Roderick Garfield 320 346 Rodney Bradford 218 Rodney Gould 207 Rodney McKay 179 207 208 Roger Ernest 341 360 Roger Lloyd 359 377 Roland Edward 172 Rollins 172 Romilia 306 Ronello F 145 Rosa 336 Rosa A 358 Rosabelle 322 Rosanna 284 286 Roscoe Benjamin 284 Roscoe W 284 Rose 344 Rose Alba 272 Rose Ina 271 Rose Mary 376 Rosella

ROBERTS (Continued)
318 Rosemary 207 Rosetta 95
154 Rosillah 204 Roxalana 264
Roy Ralph 333 Royal 259 288
Royal E 321 Ruby 385 Ruby
Pearl 184 Ruey 364 Rufus 15
253 275 404 Rufus K 119
Rufus T 127 Russell Stephen
375 389 Ruth 52 64 66 69 77
129 130 165 172 203 207 253
277 332 362 Ruth Bradway 206
Ruth Cummings 186 Ruth
Elinor 215 Ruth Elma 99 Ruth
Frances 217 Ruth Havenner 342
Ruth Mae 364 Ruth May 172
Ruth Muriel 333 Ruth Olive
341 Ruth Retta 194 Ruth Tibbetts 64 Ruth Willard 310 Ryan
Frederick 393 Sabina 323 Sabra
66 99 Sabra 106 Sabrina 174
Sadie 211 214 308 317 Sadie
Ann 389 Sadie Bell 135 Safronia 147 Sally 80 213 214 247
249 250 255 280 294 Sally Jean
370 Sally P 251 Samuel 30 31
37-39 41 42 51 52 59 69 76 82
133 163 227 233 234 237 242
254 255 262 278 279 293
Samuel B 62 Samuel Baxter
387 Samuel E 119 162 Samuel
Gilman 15 303 332 Samuel H
81 84 Samuel K 59 Samuel
Sleeper 236 Samuel Woodbury
123 167 200 Sanborn 251
Sander 238 Sanders 251 Sandra
361 377 Sandra Ann 381 Sara
Jane 384 Sarah 22 23 26 27 33
35-40 43 44 48 50-52 54 55 58-
62 65 67-69 71 72 74 76 78 80
81 85 89 92 97 98 101 104 105
109 110 113 115 117 121 123
125 126 129 130 133 155-157

ROBERTS (Continued)
160 164 171 174 181 193 200
209 233 236 238 240 243 244
249 250 252 256 261 262 264
266 269 272 281 284 287 294
295 314 322 331 Sarah A 280
Sarah Abigail 245 Sarah Angeline 260 320 Sarah Ann Maria
116 Sarah Anne 387 Sarah B 82
Sarah Barstow 285 Sarah E 88
100 116 136 154 Sarah Elizabeth 118 120 262 Sarah Ellen
146 Sarah Estella 291 Sarah
Frances 169 273 Sarah Hall 87
Sarah Helen 193 Sarah J D 262
Sarah Josephine 322 Sarah L
129 278 Sarah Mabel 209 Sarah
Merrill 292 Sarah Olivia 109
Sarah Pottle 93 Sarah Torr 95
124 Scott Elliot 377 Selwyn
Prentice 298 Seth 16 242 243
255-258 279 Sewall Trevett 123
166 Sewell E 82 Sewell Edson
122 167 199 Sewell Wilbur 362
379 Sharon 271 305 361 Sharon
K 381 Sharon Marie 388
Shepherd McGregor 177 205
206 Sherman 302 Sherman
Foster 211 Sherry 393 Shirley
359 360 Shirley Ann 377 Shirley Lillian 216 Sidney 315
Sierra 335 Silas 43 61 Silas S
132 Simeon 282 Simeon Brock
118 162 Simon 11 53 77 78 118
Smith S 293 Sophia 76 100 289
290 294 Sophia Davis 93
Sophia E 294 Sophronia 251
267 Spencer Clark 380 390
Stanley 339 359 Stanley J 305
Stanley L 351 371 Stanley W
344 364 Stella 325 373 Stella
Sarah 326 Stephanie 375

ROBERTS (Continued)
Stephen 31 40-42 44 56-59 62 63 83 85 86 88-91 96 98 125 126 131 138 171 245 261 292 326 350 399 Stephen Herbert 128 170 Stephen N 85 Stephen William 15 124 Steven 390 Sumner Mead 214 Susan 69 77 78 82 93 101 116 135 152 154 199 268 278 279 Susan A 94 Susan Amanda 139 Susan Ellen 118 Susan H 73 Susan Jane 131 Susan L 400 Susan Lamb 96 175 Susan Louise 381 Susan M 86 Susan Maria 321 Susan P 126 Susan Rosetta 250 Smith 183 Susan V 293 Susana 237 Susanna 49 50 59 60 86 90 110 195 255 Susanna Canney 97 Susannah 75 242 249 Susie 286 381 Sylvanus 278 Sylvanus I 406 Sylvanus Irish 254 277 Sylvia 218 Sylvira 283 T Henry 150 Tabitha 11 252 256 269 284 Tamice Dee 390 Tamie Lee 390 Tamsen 43 73 122 Teague Kathleen 370 Temperance 69 Temple 57 86 Terri Marie 391 Thelma Pearl 346 Thelma Ruby 337 Theresa 319 320 Theresa Avis 320 409 Thomas 1-3 6-9 12 17 21-23 25-27 29 30 32 36 38 40 44 45 49 50 53 54 56 61-63 66 74 79 80 83-85 93 96 161 175 221 230 234 237 238 251 262 265 293 309 400 Thomas A 407 Thomas Arthur 309 Thomas Elwood 96 139 Thomas Gilmore 125 Thomas H 84 124 Thomas Heard 87 128 Thomas Herbert 116 160 Thomas J 126 Thos Jefferson

ROBERTS (Continued)
270 Thomas Joshua 67 Thomas Loring 15 276 308 Tim Arden 369 384 Timothy 11 30 36 49 50 72 153 Timothy T 253 273 Timothy Victor 344 366 Tobias 12 54 79 81 119 121 165 Tobias Westerly 81 121 Todd Matthew 391 Tomasita Margarita 335 Triphena 280 Tristan Adeline 370 Tristram Fernald 118 Tryphena Burnham 74 Tyra 149 Urbana 278 Vada 335 Velma 382 Vena 363 Vera 381 Verna 306 325 363 373 Vernon Abram 376 Vicki 360 Vicki Patricia 383 Victor B 214 Victor Colby 366 382 Victor Wentworth 194 214 Victoria Elizabeth 298 Viola 150 305 353 360 Viola Harriet 373 Virginia 201 214 382 Vivian Florence 351 Wade Hanson 203 Waldo Preston 193 213 Walter 63 84 99 141 352 Walter Clifford 336 357 Walter Henry 275 307 Walter Hill 147 186 Walter J 130 Walter Jackson 127 Walter Scott 131 171 Walton E 286 Wanda 339 Waneta 339 Warren Norton 267 298 299 Watson 255 272 280 Watson Clifford 16 279 313 Wavey 350 Wayne Seavey 346 368 Wealthy 294 Wellington 280 Wellington J 337 357 Welthia 284 Wendell Fremont 210 Wendell Phillips 146 Wendi 360 Wentworth 73 111 Wentworth Thomas 145 West Daniel 260 262 289 291 292 Wilbur Prescott 343 362 Will 307 Will

ROBERTS (Continued)
C 295 Willard 254 277 Willard Harris 283 William 7 29 35 41 47 57 58 69 79 87 119 120 132 150 169 178 210 244 247 249 254 258 259 262 273 286 294 William A 411 William Aaron 138 177 William Arthur 348 370 William Burchard 165 197 William Davis 250 William E 286 315 338 William Edgar 210 William Edward 162 194 William Estes 95 William Eugene 350 William H 58 163 278 281 William Hall 91 131 173 191 203 William Harrison 106 145 335 William Henry 147 William Henry Harrison 109 151 273 306 William J 88 304 William Jones 75 115 William L 140 178 William Lewis 344 364 William Love 146 184 William Merrit 263 William Otis 317 344 William P 402 William Pinkney 268 William Pitt 158 191 William S 148 William V 127 William Webster 143 181 William Wingate 83 113 157 190 William Winworth 334 Willie Crosby 110 153 Willie M 299 Willie O 306 Willie Sherman 296 Willis 141 Willis Elmer 342 361 Willis G 324 Willis L 260 287 320 Wilma 381 Wilma Emery 184 Wilma Lila 203 Windna 377 Winfield Adams 135 Winfield Scott 175 204 Winfield Twombly 319 345 Winifred 211 Winnefred 108 188 Winnie 184 Winnie L 316 Winona May 325 Winslow 15

ROBERTS (Continued)
253 274 275 403 Wintie 145 Wolcott 331 Woodbury Davis 301 330 Woodbury Langdon 217 Zaccheus 76 Zerah Norton 259 287 323

ROBERTSON, 16

ROBIE, Eunice 249 Harriet 127 Phebe 250 Samuel 249

ROBINSON, Benjamin 273 Cora F 218 Emeleine 80 Evelyb 218 Georgia A 299 Isabel 273 John 80 239 243 248 Marian I 366 Mary 26 Rodney F 218 Sarah 43 Timothy 26

ROBLIN, Mary 201

ROBY, Isabel 189

ROGER, Helen 295

ROGERS, Anna 74 Charles C 159 Daniel 74 Ivy 159 Leota Maud 326 Mabel 182 Mary 287 Sarah 181

ROLLINS, Abigail 42 Elizabeth 41 Jeremiah 41 Lillian 196 Lucinda 196 Mark 57 Mary 40 Samuel H 131 Sarah 57 Solomon 196 Susan 131

ROMA, Elmira 163 James 163

ROOT, John 287 Martha 287 Mary Ann 287

ROSCOE, Emma 217

ROSS, Henry T 179 Mildred 179 Sarah 245 Sewell 245

ROSSITER, Sabina L 323

ROTH, Annie 198 Barbara Ozello 198 John 198

ROTHWELL, Elmer E 351 Elsie 351

ROWE, Ella 217 Fidelia 276 Josephine 217 Leonard 276 Sarah 322 Walter 217 William 322

ROWELL, DARIUS T 287

ROWELL (Continued)
  Emeline 287 Hannah 245
  Hannah 289 John 245 289
RUHBERG, George A 333 Mae 333
RUSSELL, Almeda 316 Clarissa 261 Gertrude A 162
RUTLEDGE, Belinda 209 John 209 Sarah Elizabeth 209 Viola 305
RYE, Etta 336 James T 336
RYERSON, Christiana 281 Howell 255 Luke 281 Sarah 281 Susanna 255
SAARELA, Ester 385 Johan A 385
SAGE, Caroline 179 Ira E 179
SANBORN, Ada 313 Coffin 237 Dora 272 Frank 272 Hannah 237 Isaac G 313 Mary 237 Nathaniel 250 Polly 249 Sally 250 Sarah 250 Susanna 249 Zadock 249
SANDER, Harriet 130
SANDERS, Fanny 287 Samuel 287 Sarah N 287
SARGENT, Adaline 266 Alvora 353 Caleb 266 Daisy 352 Elsie 259 351 Freedom Annette 351 Joseph 259 351 Lucinda 245 Martha 353 Noah 245 Sarah 261
SAUCIER, Emily Violette 379
SAUNDERS, Addison 80 Nathan 104 Sarah 80 104
SAVAGE, Abbie 282 Benjamin 166 Gustavus 282 Lois 166 Mary Ellen 166
SAWYER, Annie 343 Hannah 55 56 Herbert 343 Joseph 82 Mary 126 Moses 243 Nancy 82 Sabina 323 Sarah 243
SAYRE, James 383 Vicki 383

SCAMMON, 222 Richard 221
SCATES, John 154 Lydia J 154 Mary 154
SCHAFER, Elizabeth 205 George L 205
SCHOFIELD, Evelyn 341 John W 341
SCRIBNER, Hannah 247 Joseph 247
SCRUTON, Edith 166 Hervey A 166 Mary 121 Sarah 121 William 121
SEAVEY, Cotton 345 Ellen D 345 Esther Mabel 345 Nancy 323
SEEKING, Adelia 338 David 314 Mary 314
SENGER, Gwendolyn 213 Theodore 213
SEVERANCE, Elbridge G 250 Jacob J 250 Mary 310 Olive 250 Susan 250
SHACKFORD, Eliza 162 Joseph 162 Lydia Jane 162
SHATTUCK, Eliza 291 John 291
SHAW, Jotham 240 Patricia 380 Sarah 240
SHEEHAN, Harriet 365
SHENETT, Anne Elizabeth 360
SHEPARD, Daniel 68 Elizabeth 68 Hannah 68 Henry 325 Lucy M 323 Mary 323 Spalding 323 Verna 325
SHERBURN, Sarah 91
SHINSTROM, Clayton A 173 Helen 173
SHIPTON, Dora L 307
SHOREY, Cora 198
SHUGARS, Jessie 307
SIAS, John E 118 Mary 118
SIBLEY, Edward E 275 Ellen 275
SIDWAY, Amelia 174 Frank S 174
SILSBY, Mercy P 273

SILVER, Susan 350
SIMMONS, Lena 341 William 341
SIMONDS, Roxalana 264 Royal 264
SIMONTON, Christina 69
SINCLAIR, Mariette 145 Nicholas T 145
SKILLINGS, Catherine 47 Deborah 69 Joanna 69 Nathaniel 69 Samuel 47
SKINNER, Darlene 390
SLACK, Annie 167 Caroline Florence 350 Ellen 350 Irving W 167 Jefferson 350
SLATER, James 70 Priscilla 70
SLAVE, Phil 35
SMALL, Carrie 376 Edward A 144 Georgia 358 Howard 80 Joseph P 181 Julia Ann 297 Larrin 314 Lydia 297 Mary 144 Pamelia 181 Phebe 314 Rhoda 80 Richard 297 Sarah Melvina 181
SMART, Samuel S 262 Sarah 262
SMITH, Angeline 264 Charmaine 379 Daniel 132 David 235 Deliverance 235 Eliza C 153 Elizabeth 132 167 227 Elizabeth S 132 Ernest B 194 Esther 205 296 Eugene 153 Ezekiel 227 Hannah 104 261 Helen 357 Jacob 110 Jane 194 John 1 2 167 John H 261 Julia 115 Julia M 74 Lawrence R 205 Linnie E 127 Louise 153 Lucius F 115 Lydia E 142 Margaret 235 Mary 110 Mary Frances 121 Nancy 260 Patricia 367 Rita 361 Sarah 167 Sidney 188 William 357
SNOW, Emma A 160 Mary 103 Samuel 103
SOULE, Lydia 143 Margaret 309

SOUTHARD, Louisa 151
SPAULDING Mary Jane 135
SPEAR, Eunice 99 William 99
SPEARIN, Esther 296 W W 296
SPENCER, Abigail 270 Luther D 270
SPINNEY, Daniel 161 Joanna 51 John 51 Lydia 161 Lydia Ann 161
SPOONER, Dorcas 266 Marie 362
SPRINGER, Patricia 379 Ronald 379
STACEY, Mary 283 William 283
STACKPOLE, Aaron 51 Deborah 51 Eunice 53 Tobias 53
STACY, Lydia 89
STANLEY, Harriet 298 Susie 381
STANTON, Caroline 158
STANWOOD, Abbie Eliza 342 Ella J 342 Nathaniel 342
STAPLES, Cementhe E 310 Daphne 278 Frank G 278 J Wilford 278 Urbana 278
STARBIRD, Emeline 145 Winfield S 145
STEARNS, Elizabeth I 158 Susan 152
STEEL, Eliza Fannie 296 Esther 296 James 296
STEEVES, Edith 365 Stanley 365
STETSON, Melissa 288 Roswell N 288
STEVENS, Elizabeth 54 Eunice 310 Francis Jane 62 Georgiena 363 John 62 Moses 37 54 Sarah 37 78
STEWART, Elizabeth B 158 Ella 134 Elsie 351
STILLINGS, Anna 47 Hannah 87
STIMPSON, Delphina 271 Sarah J 314 Wellington R 271
STOCKMEN, Kathy 376

STODDARD, Ethel 196 Guy H 196 John 289 Juliana 289
STONE, Jane 129 Lois 129
STORER, Frank 146 Sarah 146
STOWELL, Cecile 190 Ellery C 190
STPIERRE, Alphena 380
STRAW, Daniel 48 Joanna 48
STROUT, Carl 386 Carmen 386 Dorothy 373 Francis G 373 Judith 386
STUART, 4
STUBBS, Louis A 338 Lucy 338
STURTEVANT, Elmira 106 Ephraim 106
SULLIVAN, Earla 192 Johanna Elizabeth 169 Mary 169 William 169
SUTHERLAND, Annie E 308
SUTPHEN, Jennie 350 Richard C 350 Robert J 350
SUTTON, Albert 344 Eva 344
SVENSON, Geolena 207
SWAIN, Alice 256 Edith G 159 Mary 121 Micajah 256 Slorim 121
SWAN, Antoinette 202 Arvilla 210 Edith Christine 202 George 202
SWEET, Rosa B 336
SWETT, Amanda E 337 Benjamin 155 Mary E 155
SWIFT, Joseph 323 Miriam 323 Nancy 323
SWINYER, Hattie Alice 354
SYLVESTER, Emma F 315
SYMONDS, Mary 152
TANNER, Luella 158
TASH, Eliza 167 John N 167 Mary 113 114
TATE, Elizabeth 47 Mark 47
TAYLOR, Elizabeth 290 Julius 290 Katherine 290 Mary 241

TAYLOR (Continued) Mathilda 188 Richard 241
TEMPLETON, Herbert A 172 Ruth 172
TERRILL, Elizabeth 319
TETHERLY, Andrew 84 Eliza 84
THAYER, Ella Sophia 164 Prudence S 164 William B 164
THOMAS, Georgiena 363 John 363 Lillian E 363
THOMPSON, 42 Clementine 277 Daniel 105 Hepsibah 104 Mary 200 Mary Jane 277 Olive 105 Sarah 80 Simon 277
THOMSON, David 2
THOREAU, Henry David 257
THORNE, Juanita 362 Ray 362
THRESHER, Agnes Harriet 354 Hattie A 354 Nelson G 354
THURSTON, John 114 Nancy 114
TIBBETTS, Abigail 63 Alice 64 Anna 49 Clara Irene 195 Elizabeth 68 Enoch 49 Ezekiel 64 Grace 182 Hannah 64 John 43 Joyce 377 Leslie 377 Lewis 64 Lois 196 Mary 43 Michael 68 Phebe 60 Philip 63 Ruth 64 Sarah 43 Silas C 196
TILLOTSON, Emma Stella 374
TINGLEY, Dorothy 357 Edward J 357
TIPPETT, Evelyn 298 Frank 298
TITCOMB, Anna 87 Oliver C 87 Sarah 50
TODD, Eva M 345
TOLMAN, Elizabeth 132 Samuel 132
TOMPKINS, Edith 343 Harvey A 343
TORR, Mary 94 124 Sarah 94 Vincent 94
TOTMAN, Iantha 276 John 276

TOWLE, Anna Maria Elizabeth 158 Beulah 198 Deborah 112 158 Gerald E 198 Joel 57 Lois 57 Philip 112 158
TOWNSEND, Nancy A 199 Obediah 199 Susan 199
TOZER, Martha 37
TRACY, Charles 321 Mary 321
TRASK, Ella 82 Ella Sophia 199 Lydia 199 William P 199
TREADWELL, Caroline K 151
TREFETHAN, Albert M 158 Ida 158
TREVETT, Anna 82
TRIPP, Charles 188 Emma Payson 188 Lucy 188
TRUE, John 105 Sarah 105
TUBBS, Frederick E 183 Susan 183
TUCKER, Alice 344 Elizabeth 29 John 29 Mary 259 Payson V 362 Ruth 362 Ursula 29
TUFTS, Lucinda 196
TURNER, Cynthia 194 Lovisa 299 304 Rose 344
TUTTLE, Abigail 169 Ann Mary 141 Ebenezer 33 Hannah 43 James 54 Joanna 54 Mary 38 Mercy 284 Otis 43 Phebe 33
TWEEDIE, Maxine 363 Walter W 363
TWOMBLY, Benjamin G 66 Ira F 93 Lucy 138 Lydia 66 Rosella Morgan 318 Sarah 100 Sophia 93
UNGER, Margaret Jane 384
VADNEY, George E 313 Georgia 313
VALYOU, Della Beatrice 355 Frances 355 Lynn 355
VANDENBURG, Charles H 140 Mary 140
VANDERBECK, Anna 302
VARNEY, 277 Abigail 43 Almira 139 Andrew 139 Anna 44 Deliverance 63 Elihu 175 Elijah 43 Eliza 175 Elizabeth 43 Eunice 63 Isaac 43 John 43 Joshua 44 Rita 182 Roscoe C 182 Sarah 43 Sarah 43 Stephen 63 Susan 139 Tamsen 43 Thomas 43
VERRET, Jane Louise 387 Marie A 387 Omer F 387
VERRILL, Clifford L 360 Wendi 360
VESPER, Lucinda 264
VINAL, Sarah 170
VINE, Elizabeth 319 Theresa 319 William 319
VIRGIN, Mary 106 Mary Jane 145 Nancy 145 Uriah 106 William 145
WAGNER, Nettie A 125
WAITE, Mary 143
WAKEFIELD, Abigail 72
WALACHIKS, Debrah 379 Jeffrey S 379
WALBRIDGE, Levi 350 Marcia 350 Susan 350
WALCOTT, Mary E 152
WALDRON, Anna 36 Cynthia 173 John 36 Mary 36 Nancy 114 Pamela 141
WALKER, Arline 339 Elmer 339 Hannah 276 Harriet 132 Isaphena 335 William S 132
WALLACE, Eunice 295 Marcella N 295 Martin 295
WALLINGFORD, John 38 Mary 38 Sarah 38 Sarah 58
WARBRICK, Susanna 195
WARD, Linda N 389
WARREN, Alice 151 152 Alta 163

WARREN (Continued)
  Ernest R 152 Laban 373 Lillian 373 Maranda W 327 Margaret 41 Mercy 58 Michael H 390 Remember 277 Stella May 373 Susanna 50 Tamice 390 William 50
WARWICK, Beverly 372 Robert G 372
WATERHOUSE, Abigail 149 Arabella 181 Charles 321 Dexter 299 Eban 181 Eugene 278 Jane 278 Mary 299 Sarah 181 Susan 321
WATSON, Alfred F 270 Anna 270 Mary 67 199
WEATHERHEAD, Kate 327
WEAVER, Jaqueine 359 Robert 359
WEBB, Bethia 241 Elizabeth 241 Samuel 241 Sarah 270
WEBSTER, Benjamin 143 Julia Ann 143 Lydia 143 Mary 143 Rachel 143
WEEKES, Addie 176 John E 176
WEEKS, Braddock 57 Elizabeth 295 Hannah Patten 343 Keziah 57 Susan A 268
WEINREB, Deborah 348
WELCH, Anthony 367 Barbara 367 Emily 204 Judith 76
WELLS, Betsey 289 Fanny 288 N C 288 Nicholas C 289 Peggy 288 289
WELTON, Harriet 366 Leo 366
WENTWORTH, Abigail 80 Bartholomew 90 Benjamin 54 Benjamin E 175 Betsey 111 Daniel 111 Deborah 90 123 Dorothy J 67 Ebenezer 33 Elizabeth 53 71 Isaac 138 Joanna 33 53 101 John 77 110

WENTWORTH (Continued)
  John S 80 Joseph C 74 Julia 335 Lillian Ruth 193 Lucy 138 Lydia 175 303 Mark 53 Mary 56 Mercy 110 130 Paul 123 Rebecca 110 Ruth 90 Samuel 33 Sarah 33 52 54 115 123 153 Sybil 196 Timothy 71 Tryphena 74
WEST, Albert J 138 Daniel 243 Elizabeth 243 Eva 138 George 152 Mabel 152 Sarah 105
WETHERBEE, Persis 264
WEYMOUTH, Esther 52
WHEAT, Polly B 326
WHEELER, Abigail 254 Ann 92 John 254 Truman H 92 Velma 382
WHIPPLE, Alice 339 Howard 339
WHIPPS, Belinda 209
WHITE, Almira 269 Christina 69 Patricia 367 Phillip 367 Ruth 69 Sabra 99 100 106 Samuel 99 106 William 69 269
WHITEHOUSE, Benjamin J 192 Edna Josephine 192 Elizabeth 43 Marion 182 Melvina 193 Ophelia J 192 Rachel 43 Sarah Helen 193 Thomas 43
WHITING, Dorothy 197 Francis P 197
WHITMAN, Pearl M 183 Susan 183
WHITNEY, Helen 362 Mason 362
WHITTEN, Lois 129 Mary M 265 Sarah 249
WHITTIER, Alvin M 88 Julia 88 Lois 129
WHITTUM, Blanche 330
WIGGIN, Chandler E 297 Hannah 265 270 Hannah 297 James 270 Kate 265 Nancy C 265

WIGGIN (Continued)
  Winthrop 265
WILBUR, Barbara Louise 219
  Elizabeth A 219 Harold G 219
WILCOX, Henry 322 Rosabelle
  322
WILEY, Esther 358
WILKINSON, Harriet Ann 161
  Isaiah 161 Lucy D 161
WILLARD, Amy 353 Prudence
  253
WILLEY, Hannah 122 Harriet 122
  Lillian 196 Mary 75 Nathaniel
  122 Sarah 81 Sarah E 115
WILLIAM, Windna 377
WILLIAMS, 39 Dina 137 Fern 349
  Frank L 349 Hannah 263
  Herbert A 349 Jessica H 349
  John S 349 Leona Etta 372
  Nancy 349 Nellie 375 Peter A
  349 Sarah 39 285 Stephen A
  349
WILLIS, Hall B 81 Joanna 81
WILLS, Betsey 246 John 246
WILSON, Abigail 304 Marion 354
  Mary 79 Nathaniel 79 Rebecca
  86 Wayne W 354
WING, Mary 286 Pliney B 286
WINGATE, Abigail 39 Deborah
  113 Elizabeth 50 58 Eunice 63
  John 97 Jonathan 63 Joshua 39
  Love 97 Lydia 135 Mary 31
  Samuel 31 50 Sarah 50 Sarah
  Abigail 113 Susanna 97 William 113
WINKLER, Laura Josephine 125
WINSLOW, Ruth 251
WISE, Joanna 80 Samuel 80
WITCOMB, Curtis 292 Hattie 292
WITHAM, Gertrude L 195

WOLCOTT, Freeman 289 Harriet
  289 Julia Adelia 290 Mary 331
WOLFF, Agnes 177 Harold W 177
WOOD, Malcolm 340 Marian 340
  Patricia 375
WOODBURY, Agnes 118 Florence May 337 Francis 340
  Henrietta Sylvia 352 Lillian
  305 Norma 340 Susan 69
WOODHOUSE, James 101 Sarah
  101 Susan 101
WOODMAN, Hannah 276 Jonathan 309 Maria Louisa 309
WOODRUFF, Blanche 215
  Edward 215
WOODSUM, Martha 67
WOODWARD, Moses 60 Sarah 60
WOODWORTH, Lizzie E 265
WORK, Ella 340 Guy 340
WORMWOOD, Charles 77 Judith
  77
WRIGHT, Martha 202 Mary 202
  William 202
WRISLEY, Anna 75 Jewett 75
WYER, Joseph 365 Mary 365
  Mary Ann 365
WYLIE, Eliza 211
YEATON, Lydia 81 Mary 121
YERXA, Gussie 363
YORK, Aurelia Julana 330 Deborah 69 Edna G 197 Joanna 69
  Lydia D 93 Samuel 69
YOUNG, Abigail D 114 Anna 256
  258 Daniel 239 Hannah 239
  252 Henry E 258 John 252
  Mary 27 Olive 166 Thomas 27
ZIMMERMAN, Elmer F 165 Eva
  374 Harry E 374 Ruth 165
ZINCK, Elsie Louise 188 Louise
  188 Nathaniel 188

www.ingramcontent.com/pod-product-compliance
Lightning Source LLC
Chambersburg PA
CBHW070006010526
44117CB00011B/1440